TOM BOWER is an investigative journalist well known for his unauthorised biographies of controversial tycoons and politicians. His subjects include Tiny Rowland, Robert Maxwell, Conrad Black, Bernie Ecclestone, Mohamed Fayed, Geoffrey Robinson, Tony Blair, Gordon Brown, Simon Cowell and Richard Branson. He is also noted for pathfinding books about Nazi war criminals and spies during the Cold War. His 2003 book *Broken Dreams: Vanity, Greed and the Souring of British Football* was the William Hill Sports Book of the Year.

Also by Tom Bower

*Blind Eye to Murder: Britain, America and the Purging of
Nazi Germany – A Pledge Betrayed*

Klaus Barbie: Butcher of Lyon

*The Paperclip Conspiracy: The Battle for the Spoils
and Secrets of Nazi Germany*

Red Web: MI6 and the KGB Master Coup

Maxwell: The Outsider

Tiny Rowland: A Rebel Tycoon

*The Perfect English Spy: Sir Dick White
and the Secret War, 1935–90*

Heroes of World War II

Maxwell: The Final Verdict

*Nazi Gold: The Full Story of the Fifty-Year Swiss–Nazi Conspiracy
to Steal Billions from Europe's Jews and Holocaust Survivors*

Blood Money: The Swiss, the Nazis and the Looted Billions

Fayed: The Unauthorized Biography

Branson

The Paymaster: Geoffrey Robinson, Maxwell and New Labour

Broken Dreams: Vanity, Greed and the Souring of British Football

Gordon Brown: Prime Minister

Conrad and Lady Black: Dancing on the Edge

The Squeeze: Oil, Money and Greed in the Twenty-First Century

No Angel: The Secret Life of Bernie Ecclestone

Sweet Revenge: The Intimate Life of Simon Cowell

Branson: Behind the Mask

Broken Vows: Tony Blair – The Tragedy of Power

TOM BOWER

REBEL KING

THE MAKING OF A MONARCH

WILLIAM
COLLINS

William Collins
An imprint of HarperCollins*Publishers*
1 London Bridge Street
London SE1 9GF
www.WilliamCollinsBooks.com

HarperCollins*Publishers*
Macken House, 39/40 Mayor Street Upper,
Dublin 1, D01 C9W8

First published in Great Britain as *Rebel Prince* by William Collins in 2018
This William Collins paperback edition published in 2022

7

A catalogue record for this book is
available from the British Library

ISBN 978-0-00-829177-8

Printed and bound in the UK using 100%
renewable electricity at CPI Group (UK) Ltd

This book is produced from independently certified FSC™ paper
to ensure responsible forest management.

For more information visit: www.harpercollins.co.uk/green

To Veronica

Contents

	List of Illustrations	ix
	Preface	xi
1	New York, 22 September 1999	1
2	Plots and Counterplots	6
3	The Masters of Spin	30
4	Uneasy Lies the Head	38
5	Mutiny and Machiavellism	53
6	Body and Soul	72
7	The Masterbuilder	83
8	Teasing the Government	99
9	Diana's 'Rock'	108
10	A Family at War	121
11	A Butler's Warnings	141
12	A Struggle for Power	162
13	A New Era Begins	170
14	Shuttlecocks and Skirmishes	183
15	The Queen's Recollection	189
16	A Private Secretary Goes Public	205
17	Money Matters	212
18	Whitewash	223
19	Revenge and Dirty Linen	229
20	Drowning Not Waving	235
21	New Enemies	243
22	For Better or Worse	254
23	Resolute Rebel	261
24	Rules of Conduct	277
25	King Meddle	287
26	The Divine Prophet	296

27   Scrabbling for Cash   306
28   Marking Time   316
29   The Prince's Coup   330

     Acknowledgements   339
     Sources   341
     Index   349

Illustrations

The royal family at Balmoral in 1960. *(Keystone/Stringer/Getty Images)*

Charles's investiture as Prince of Wales at Caernarvon Castle in 1969. *(Central Press/Stringer/Getty Images)*

Charles and Camilla after a polo match in 1975. *(REX/Shutterstock)*

Camilla's marriage to Andrew Parker Bowles. *(Wood/Stringer/Getty Images)*

Andrew Parker Bowles shared a love of polo with Charles. *(Anwar Hussein/Contributor/Getty Images)*

Geoffrey Kent. *(Tim Graham/Contributor/Getty Images)*

Charles and Diana in 1981. *(Anwar Hussein/Contributor/Getty Images)*

The couple's visit to Seoul in 1992. *(Anwar Hussein/Contributor/Getty Images)*

The royal family showing a typically united front in public. *(Jeff Overs/Contributor/Getty Images)*

William, Charles and Harry. *(Will Oliver/Epa/REX/Shutterstock)*

Charles with Sinn Féin leader Gerry Adams. *(Damien Eagers/PA Archive/PA Images)*

Charles and Camilla with Laura and George W. Bush. *(John Stillwell/PA Archive/PA Images)*

Charles's 1997 visit to Hong Kong. *(AFP/Stringer/Getty Images)*

Charles, the passionate countryman, with Michael Fawcett. *(Eddie Boldizsar/REX/Shutterstock)*

Charles fox-hunting. *(Dave Bebber/REX/Shutterstock)*

The proposed National Gallery extension, described by Charles in 1984 as a 'monstrous carbuncle'. *(PA/PA Archive/PA Images)*

Richard Rogers with the queen. *(Matt Dunham/AP/WPA rota/PA Archive/PA Images)*

Charles and Camilla pose for their wedding photo. *(ZZ/NJ/DHT/ROO/REX/Shutterstock)*

The royal family on Buckingham Palace's balcony after Prince William's marriage to Kate Middleton. *(Geoffrey Robinson/Alamy Stock Photo)*

Charles and Michael Fawcett. *(Tim Graham/Contributor/Getty Images)*

Michael Peat. *(Dave Penman/REX/Shutterstock)*

Charles and Mark Bolland. *(Tim Graham/Contributor/Getty Images)*

Fiona Shackleton. *(Joanne Davidson/Silverhub/REX/Shutterstock)*

Paul Burrell and Diana. *(Trinity Mirror/Mirrorpix/Alamy Stock Photo)*

Diana's sister Sarah McCorquodale. *(REX/Shutterstock)*

Detective Chief Superintendent Maxine de Brunner and Detective Sergeant Roger Milburn. *(Scott Barbour/Stringer/Getty Images)*

Marriage to Camilla transformed Charles. *(Chris Jackson/Staff/Getty Images)*

Charles reduced the number of royals who appeared on the balcony at Buckingham Palace. *(Chris J. Ratcliffe/Stringer/Getty Images)*

Tom Shebbeare. *(Nick Razzell/REX/Shutterstock)*

Robin Janvrin. *(PA Archive/PA Images)*

Stephen Lamport. *(Photograph by Robert Simpson, Camera Press London)*

Michael Fawcett. *(Max Mumby/Indigo/Contributor/Getty Images)*

Charles entertaining celebrities at one of his charity events. *(Chris Jackson/Staff/Getty Images)*

Joan Rivers and Robert Higdon. *(Robin Platzer/Contributor/Getty Images)*

Charles with a group of children from an inner-city school. *(WPA Pool/Pool/Getty Images)*

The queen and Don McKinnon. *(Kirsty Wigglesworth/PA Archive/PA Images)*

Malcolm Ross. *(Tim Graham/Contributor/Getty Images)*

Christopher Geidt. *(Max Mumby/Indigo/Contributor/Getty Images)*

Charles at Highgrove. *(John Paul Brooke/REX/Shutterstock)*

Preface

This book is the story of Prince Charles's battle for rehabilitation after Diana's death, and his refusal to obey the public's expectations of a future king. Many books have been written about Charles, but none has fully described the crisis he faced after 1997. For nearly ten years, he was buffeted by scandal. His approval rating fell to the lowest figure for any royal in recent times. His succession to the throne was endangered.

Among the most serious disclosures to undermine public confidence in the prince were those exposed during the unsuccessful prosecution for theft in 2002 of Paul Burrell, Diana's butler and confidant; the simultaneous revelation of disreputable behaviour within Charles's household; and the possibility that he had personally interfered in the judicial process. At the end of that two-year drama, Charles's survival as heir to the throne was on a knife-edge.

Additionally, throughout those years he was repeatedly criticised by the media and politicians for his extravagances. His father denounced him for being a rent-a-royal, yet he continued to sell access to himself – to raise money for his many charities and to indulge in ostentatious luxury. At the same time he provoked a fractious relationship with Tony Blair in his years as prime minister which undermined the prince's constitutional duty to stay impartial. And he blithely disregarded the disdain of many Commonwealth leaders, which wrecked his assumption that he would automatically inherit leadership of the association of fifty-two countries.

During this period of turmoil, one issue dominated Charles's life – the status of Camilla Parker Bowles. Ever since they had resumed their relationship in the mid-1980s, he had stubbornly fought to rescue their reputations. Single-mindedly he confronted all the Establishment forces, including the queen, who was determined to prevent their marriage. His principal ally was Mark Bolland, a young media consultant, who for the first time has revealed in this book the intrigues that he masterminded on behalf of Charles and Camilla, which climaxed in their wedding in April 2005. Thereafter, the scandals in Charles's life diminished, although it would take another six years before the departure of his five most senior advisers signalled the end of the turbulence.

By November 2011, Charles's reputation as a rebel was truly established. Not only had he defied the nation to marry Camilla, but his championship of controversial causes including the environment, architecture, fox-hunting, complementary medicine and education, had aroused fierce opposition – and also praise. 'I have never known a man who had better motives for all the trouble he caused,' comments Thomas Fowler about the eponymous 'Quiet American' in Graham Greene's novel; the same could be said about Charles. Few doubted the sincerity of his campaigns, but many feared that his provocative dissent made him unfit to be king.

He has repeatedly mentioned his devotion to his duty. He believes passionately that he can make Britain a better country and that he can help the disadvantaged. Whatever criticisms may be levelled at him have been mitigated, especially by his admirers, by his commitment to many valuable causes. Many Britons have personal experience of his dedicated visits to schools, hospitals and hospices. Carefully briefed, he talks engagingly to staff, pupils and patients, leaving them all with an enduring memory of his decency.

The contrast for the majority who have not enjoyed a personal encounter is stark. During the many scandals that would have destroyed a lesser man, there has been no evidence that he has suffered a moral struggle. Shame and guilt seem foreign to him. Despite all the eyewitness accounts of his melancholia and self-doubt, Charles has never admitted any wrongdoing. In general terms, he is certainly not misunderstood by the public.

My decision to write about such a familiar character was taken after several months of research. With the exception of Anthony Holden and Jonathan Dimbleby, most of Charles's subsequent biographers recite events, statements and comments in reverential tones. They do him a disservice. In reality, his life has been a gripping political, financial and personal drama. With hindsight, his survival today may seem preordained, but there were long periods when his future was in doubt, especially after Diana's death. That his conflicts have been conducted in the spotlight makes his story even more interesting because so much of what occurred has remained in the shadows. I make no claim to have unearthed every truth, but after interviewing over 120 people, many of whom served the royals for long periods and with great distinction and have not given their accounts before, I believe that this book does reveal many new insights about the future king.

As with many of the other personalities I have investigated, I started this biography with limited knowledge about Charles's life beyond the media reports. Because I have 'lived' with him throughout my life – we are of similar ages – I could not fail to be conscious of his exceptional tribulations, but I was unsure how much my research could reveal. The incentive was the suspicion that Charles, like all powerbrokers, must have deployed guile to conceal his tracks.

In the past, my criteria for choosing a personality to investigate have been his or her use – and misuse – of fame and fortune to influence society. Newspaper owners, billionaire tycoons and successful politicians all want to change our lives, and simultaneously to enhance their own reputations. What has fascinated me in all those I have previously covered is their climb from obscurity up the slippery pole, then their battle to stay on top. Along the way they have crushed rivals and subtly altered their own biographies. Often they have publicly paraded their service to mankind, while in reality pursuing largely self-interested agendas.

Charles of course was born at the top of the pole, and though he has not exactly falsified his life's story, he has concealed many truths. Determined to be a figure of consequence – a long-lasting influence is a sign of greatness – he has used his position since the early 1980s to influence how Britain is governed, and after the mid-1990s employed his powers as a royal to massage the media in order to secure his and Camilla's survival. My quest was to discover how he manipulated those levers of power.

To my surprise, I found that Charles's conduct has created a substantial number of victims, many of whom are saddened over how he acted, both in general and towards them. His loyalty, like his attention span, is limited. Embraced today, a favourite can be cast out tomorrow. Like some feudal lord, he presides at the centre of a court with no place for democracy or dissenting views. Unlike the queen, with her genius in being able to unite the nation, especially in difficult times, Charles divides his countrymen. Clearly he enjoys provoking argument, but only on his terms. He has refused to engage in debate. Advisers know that to say 'No' will simply prompt his search for a replacement who will say 'Yes.' Every decision is his and his alone.

For over thirty years, the Prince of Wales has been prey to his follies. Since 1997 he has resorted to machination and media manipulation to restore his position. Although the large number of British people who previously supported the succession passing directly from the queen to William gradually diminished and then rose again, Charles's rehabilitation is still unfinished business. His popularity, as I write in early 2018, remains disconcertingly low.

As a committed monarchist, I want Charles to become king, to bequeath the throne in a healthy state to his son, whose popularity will protect the institution during his father's short reign. Whether and how that happens depends on Charles's age at the time of his coronation. At the moment, neither Charles nor indeed anyone can predict how the country will react to the queen's death. Will Britain allow him to inherit the throne smoothly, and watch Camilla anointed as queen? Or will the nation resent Charles and his final ascent? He will undoubtedly become king; but the circumstances are in doubt.

The central question posed at this stage of his life is what kind of monarch will Charles make – given that he is the most unpopular heir for generations. Had the queen died a decade ago, his controversial interventions could well have provoked a constitutional crisis. However, over the past seven years he has moderated his speeches in public, and has tried to encourage the belief that his takeover will be much more acceptable than even the most loyal monarchist could have imagined. His efforts have not been wholly convincing. After speaking to so many of those who have lived with and loved the royals, I share their trepidation over whether Charles can become a unifying monarch. At the end of writing this book, I am convinced that he is determined to make his mark on British history, and will not choose an impartial silence during his inevitably short reign. He remains a historian, writer and political activist, and will want to cement Charles III in people's memories for centuries to come. How he might achieve that of course remains a puzzle, but to some extent is answered in what follows.

During my research, I inevitably encountered a large number of different opinions. All are reflected in the book. Readers will not be surprised that many of the quotations are anonymous. Those who still associate with Charles and Camilla – as friends or employees – understandably do not want their relationship endangered. To protect them, I have made a point of disguising many of my sources. However, the reader can be assured that every quotation is accurate and was noted during my interviews. Although the two decades covered in my book can be understood only by referring to aspects of what went before, I have restricted such excursions into the past to what is sufficient to understand the present.

Finally, researching this book has been an unexpected pleasure, not only because I have come to understand so many previously unknown conflicts and hitherto imperfectly reported events, but also because Charles emerges as an exceptional character. Easy to like and easy to dislike, he is the unique product of Britain's genius – a rebel prince, eventually to become a rebel king.

1

New York, 22 September 1999

Her anger was uncontrolled.

'I won't stop it. It's my life and it's the right thing to do.'

From a suite in New York's Carlyle Hotel, Camilla Parker Bowles was laying down the law. Her outburst was directed not only at the Prince of Wales but also at his friend Nicholas Soames, the Conservative MP and grandson of Winston Churchill. At the other end of the line, Charles was three thousand miles away, fretting in his study at Highgrove, his Gloucestershire home. He had just passed on the news that Soames had been protesting about her high-profile visit to America.

'There's too much publicity,' Soames had told Charles. 'It's that bloody man Bolland.'

'Well,' the heir to the throne had replied, 'let's all have a meeting with Mark when he returns and he'll explain everything.'

Thirty-three-year-old Mark Bolland was in theory the prince's assistant private secretary, his job since 1996, but in reality he was far more than that – the orchestrator of how Charles and Camilla appeared to the world. He stood now in the Carlyle suite witnessing their argument. Also present was Michael Fawcett, Charles's trusted servant of over twenty years, again far more than a valet. Both men admired Camilla's scathing dismissal of Charles's pleas. In Bolland's opinion, the London media reports about Camilla's hectic itinerary in Manhattan justified his gamble to defy Buckingham Palace's demand that she remain unseen and instead propel her into the spotlight.

'We have to break eggs to push it,' he had warned Charles before finalising plans for the four-day trip. 'Things don't happen by themselves.' Charles's doubts had been dismissed by Camilla, who was determined to emerge from the shadow of her predecessor's

glorious conquering of America in 1985. The fifty-two-year-old
Camilla was not pulling back. She handed the phone to her media
adviser.

Ever since he was hired, a year before Diana died, Bolland had
enjoyed a good relationship with Charles. His sole purpose, his
employer had stipulated, was to reverse Camilla's image as his privileged, fox-hunting mistress, make her acceptable to the public and
overcome the queen's hostility to their being together. At the outset,
in 1996, there were constant arguments about how Charles's relationship with Camilla would end. Three years on, she smelt success.
'Why can't I meet your mother?' she had asked. More frequently she
would snap, 'You're off to the theatre with friends, so why can't I
come?' Or, 'You're off on Saturday to stay with people who are my
friends too, so I should be with you.' To satisfy her, Bolland's tactics
had hit a new level. 'We were turning up the gas,' he would say,
'because the queen was unmovable.'

'The strategy,' he explained to Charles, 'is to scare the horses a bit.
To move the dial.'

'Go ahead,' Charles agreed.

Back in London, the *Sun* had responded to Bolland's overtures
with the headline 'Camilla Will Take New York by Storm Today',
and had listed the celebrities 'clamouring for invitations to lunch
and dinner'. Further to promote her, Bolland had revealed to the
paper that the revered TV personality Barbara Walters was invited
to one dinner, while Edmond Safra, a billionaire banker, would give
a drinks party and the formidable New York socialite Brooke Astor
would host a lunch – at which film star Michael Douglas would
describe to Camilla the curing of his sex addiction at an Arizona
clinic. In Bolland's currency, Camilla's appearance on the newspaper's front page was a triumph.

Soames had protested about such orchestration. 'Charles,' he
complained, 'is not a political campaign. He is not a political party.'
Bolland's tactics also shocked Robin Janvrin, the queen's private
secretary. The *Sun*'s threat to campaign against the queen, he
protested, was typical of the divisiveness masterminded by Bolland.

Over lunch with the publicist, David Airlie, one of the queen's
most respected advisers, had voiced similar unease. Bolland had
retorted, 'Well, give me the alternative of how we will achieve what
we want.'

'Don't make it too obvious,' was Airlie's advice.

'What's the alternative?' Bolland repeated.

Airlie grimaced but made no suggestions. Employment by the palaces, Bolland understood, brought out the worst in even the best of people.

Accompanied by her loyal assistant Amanda McManus, Camilla had flown to New York on Concorde. Their tickets had been bought by Geoffrey Kent, the financier of Charles's polo team and the founder and owner of Abercrombie & Kent, the millionaires' travel agent. Bolland was waiting at Kennedy airport, having flown ahead to supervise the final preparations. Among those helping him were Peter Brown, a well-connected British PR consultant, and Scott Bessent, a rich financier who worked with George Soros.

As soon as Camilla touched down, Bessent flew her to his home in East Hampton to give her two days to recover from jet lag (even the three hours it took Concorde to cross the Atlantic could upset her). He would provide a helicopter to fly her from there to Manhattan. Robert Higdon, the chief executive of Charles's charity foundation in America, was then meant to introduce the team to Camilla's hosts, but in the aftermath of a tussle among the courtiers he had been abruptly excluded. Languishing in the hotel lobby while Camilla raged at Charles, Higdon nevertheless negotiated for her visit to be hyped in New York's society columns. 'Camilla and Charles knew that I was being beat up by the others,' said Higdon, 'but the Boss and the Blonde kept me because they knew the money I was bringing in.' Charles might not have warmed to him, but he could not do without his money-raising talents.

Over the previous four years Higdon had developed huge affection for Camilla, who, he told a journalist, 'has more self-confidence than anyone I know. Unlike Charles, who is doubtful and whiney, she's so tough. She never questions anything.' That judgement was about to change.

The tension led to disagreement between Charles and his four horsemen Bolland, Kent, Brown and Bessent. Their confidence in the value of publicity had been eroded.

'It wasn't the right time,' concluded Higdon. 'It didn't feel right for Camilla. It was too soon.' She was 'not great' with Americans. Even worse, she was lazy. 'For her to get up in the morning and survive until nightfall is a major effort. It was even hard for her to get out of bed. She tries her best to do nothing during the day.' On the American trip, 'the biggest problem was persuading her to dress up for a big occasion. The effort was overwhelming. Camilla was pissed off by the whole thing. It was horrible, a disaster.'

While Camilla argued on the phone, Peter Brown was fretting in Brooke Astor's luxurious Park Avenue apartment. The guest of honour was already thirty minutes late. 'She's gossiping with you-know-who,' Brown confided to one of the guests, unaware of the true circumstances. But when Camilla did finally arrive, no sign of any argument was visible. That skill offset her limitations, and was adored by Charles.

On public occasions she did her best to shine. Three days before flying to New York she had appeared to enjoy a dinner for fifty guests in the Chelsea home of the Greek shipping and steel magnate Theodore Angelopoulos and his wife Gianna, and a few days earlier she had been jolly at Geoffrey Kent's fifty-sixth birthday party, despite her intense dislike of two of her fellow guests, Hugh and Emilie van Cutsem, both close friends of Charles.

In her unusual world, Camilla was happier when having dinner later that night at Harry's Bar with Andrew Parker Bowles, her former husband, and his new wife. Andrew was one of the few among her associates who aroused no antagonism among the courtiers. Others, she discovered, were less fortunate in the vicious intrigues around the court.

A new plot, allegedly inspired by Galen Weston, a Canadian billionaire, had sought to oust Geoffrey Kent from Charles's inner circle. Weston was irritated that Charles played for Kent's polo team, and that Kent, rather than Weston, was the team captain. Their rivalry had spilled out into a dispute about a joint property development near Palm Beach. Now Weston was seeking to persuade Charles to dump an ally. Venomous spats among courtiers were not unusual for Charles. Despite the generosity shown to him by Kent, a global networker, Charles rarely reciprocated loyalty. 'We don't have close friends,' he had told a member of the polo team. 'The royal family does not allow anyone to become too familiar and be privy to our secrets.'

During a helicopter trip – a moment chosen so the police escort could not overhear – Bolland had spoken to the prince about his benefactor's fate. 'He's been a good and generous friend,' agreed

Charles. 'Tell Stephen not to do anything. I've changed my mind.'
Stephen Lamport, Charles's senior private secretary and Bolland's
superior, was accustomed to cutting off those who had displeased
his master, and readmitting those who were pardoned.

Charles's decisions were often influenced by money, and in recent
years Camilla had adopted the same criterion. The previous month,
she and Charles, her two children and over twenty friends had sailed
around the Aegean on the *Alexander*, the world's third largest
private yacht. They were the guests of Yiannis Latsis, a foul-mouthed
Greek shipping billionaire whose fortune, some gossiped, was based
on black marketeering, collaboration with the Nazis, and bribing
Arabs for a stake in the oil trade. Six weeks later, after her introduction to Edmond and Lily Safra in New York, Camilla discovered that
the billionaire banker also owned a luxury yacht, as well as an eight-
een-acre estate in the south of France, La Leopolda, valued at over
$750 million.

'Is there any chance,' Camilla had asked Higdon, who had made
the introduction, 'that I could stay at Lily Safra's?' An invitation to
visit St James's Palace was duly issued to Safra, and soon afterwards
Michael Fawcett was arranging Camilla's holiday on the estate.

Her current trip to New York was part of Charles's campaign to
win over the British people; but in 1999 that struggle was far from
won.

2

Plots and Counterplots

Charles's campaign to make Camilla accepted had started in 1996, one year before Diana's death, a period that marked a new peak in the public's disgust with the lives in the royal palaces. A succession of scandalous books, tapes and television interviews had reduced the prince's approval rating to less than 10 per cent. Fearful that he would not inherit the crown, and even worse, that he might buckle under the pressure, Camilla had discussed his plight with Hilary Browne-Wilkinson, the solicitor who had managed her divorce from Andrew Parker Bowles. Soon after, Charles and Camilla invited Hilary and her husband, Nicolas 'Nico' Browne-Wilkinson, a senior judge, for dinner at St James's Palace. The third guest was Fiona Shackleton, Charles's divorce lawyer, at that time a decisive influence in his life.

'You must deal with your media image,' Nico Browne-Wilkinson told Charles.

Nico's wife offered a solution. While working at the Press Complaints Commission she had met Mark Bolland, the Commission's twenty-nine-year-old director and in his private life the partner of Guy Black, a Cambridge graduate and political adviser. Bolland, Hilary Browne-Wilkinson said, was charming and well-connected, and had good relations with London's senior media executives. He was also an outsider. Unlike other palace officials, he had been educated at a grammar school in Middlesbrough and had gone neither to Oxbridge nor the army, but had read Chemistry at York University. His understanding of the real world made him an ideal choice to promote Camilla and secure the public's acceptance of her relationship with Charles. Hilary was supported by Fiona Shackleton, who said Bolland should be appointed as soon as Charles's divorce was finalised.

By the end of the evening, Charles and Camilla were half-persuaded. Both Shackleton and Hilary Browne-Wilkinson appeared relieved. Dabbling in that world, with access to the heir to the throne, was a fizzy experience for both lawyers. Charles's reliance on such people signalled his anguish. In 1996 he was searching for scapegoats to blame for a decade of horror. Prone to grasp at any excuse, he agreed with the latest judgement of his inner circle of friends that Richard Aylard, his private secretary, was mainly responsible for his plight.

In their opinion, Aylard's cardinal error had been to encourage Charles two years earlier to open his heart to the journalist Jonathan Dimbleby for a biography and a two-hour television documentary.

Over the previous months Aylard had spent nearly every day and many nights responding to his employer's cries for protection from criticism, sacrificing his own private life and his marriage. To overcome Charles's bouts of depression, he had encouraged him to cooperate with Dimbleby. When the resulting book and film proved a personal disaster, Charles refused to accept any blame for pressing Aylard to arrange the extraordinary access to his secrets.

The Dimbleby project had been born from Charles's anger that he was being treated as a mere ribbon-cutter rather than as the heir to the throne. His status had been devalued among courtiers in Buckingham Palace and some cabinet ministers by his refusal to end his relationship with Camilla. At that time, the very notion that the couple might marry was ridiculed by a country that had lost respect for the man who had betrayed his wife Diana. Unless Camilla was ousted, the critics agreed, Charles could not remain the queen's automatic successor. Inaction might even jeopardise the monarchy itself. The huge majority of the public reflected the homily of Walter Bagehot, Britain's nineteenth-century constitutional expert: 'We have come to regard the monarchy as the head of our morality.' Charles failed that test.

His fate had been dictated by a series of humiliations, not least by Diana's disclosures in Andrew Morton's 1992 book *Diana: Her True Story*. Morton's revelations had broken through the carapace of lies about the royal marriage. Diana had portrayed her estranged husband as an unloving and unfaithful father without a care for anyone except himself. 'It is so very awful,' Charles wrote to Nancy Reagan, the former president's wife; 'very few people would believe it.' Through Dimbleby, Charles wanted to right the balance but also to retaliate, to have his revenge against a wrecker.

First he agreed to the queen's insistence that he and Diana formally separate. The announcement was to be made by John Major, recently re-elected as prime minister.

A strong prime minister would not have tolerated the warfare between Charles and Diana, and would have halted the books and briefings. Instead, Major believed that his duty was to reconcile the two and restore the public's trust. Sympathetic to Diana's side of the case, he did not underestimate his task, particularly after a private flight when Diana had emerged from the plane's lavatory covered in blood. There was no explanation other than that she was psychologically unwell.

Major's intentions were obstructed by Buckingham Palace. Robert Fellowes, the queen's private secretary, gave no clear guidance about the royal family's attitude. Until the circumstances were compelling, Fellowes judged, the queen would remain reluctant to interfere. Her inactivity magnified the ineptitude of her advisers. 'The trouble is that Charles is a Hanoverian,' a senior civil servant observed, 'and now that he's delivered "an heir and a spare" and has done his duty to the nation, he thinks he's entitled to live the way he wants.' In the coded language of the official classes, he added, while Diana Spencer could trace her family's British ancestors back to 1478, the Windsors had been invented only in 1917. Their history became irrelevant when the queen's hand was finally forced by Diana's secret cooperation with Morton and her untruthful denials of that pact to Fellowes.

At Charles's request, Aylard had insisted to Major that when announcing the formal separation he should tell the House of Commons that 'no third party' was involved; and so on 9 December 1992 the lie was formally announced in a speech drafted by a quartet of officials: cabinet secretary Robin Butler, Robert Fellowes, Buckingham Palace's senior spokesman Charles Anson, and Aylard.

To control the narrative, Charles expected Aylard to dictate the 'truth' about the separation, a divorce and the possibility of remarriage by employing the usual convenient formulas: 'There are no plans ...' or 'It is not the intention that ...' Silence and denial were his tactics to become king – a contested succession, as some senior bishops doubted whether an adulterer could lead the Church of England.

Aylard knew that loyalty meant suspending the conventional role of a private secretary. Unlike the queen's supportive working relationship with Fellowes, Charles would not tolerate Aylard discussing whether muddying the facts about his relationship with Camilla was tolerable. To continue as Charles's adviser required acceptance that the heir was infallible, divinely ordained, and that his 'truth' remained unchallenged. That fiction had been instilled in Charles since childhood. Reminded of the fate of Europe's other royal families, he had learned that the House of Windsor's survival depended upon minimising the public's indifference, assuaging its hostility and dispelling any suggestion of insecurity.

To fulfil that ambition, Robin Butler had included in Major's statement a second fiction. Despite their legal separation, Major would tell MPs, there were no constitutional implications; with a formal separation rather than a divorce, on Charles's accession Diana would still be queen. Butler would later concede that his advice was wrong.

Early on the morning of his announcement, the prime minister shuttled between Diana in Kensington Palace and Charles in St James's Palace to seal their final approval. Any satisfaction he may have felt was shredded a few hours later when his statement in the House evoked widespread derision. His suggestion of a monarchy of two separate individuals offended the British reverence for their royal family. Instead of calming the public, the speech raised speculation that Charles might abdicate.

The queen had already responded to the danger: persuaded that she had to reprimand her son, she had forbidden him to move from Kensington Palace into Clarence House, the queen mother's home, after formally separating from Diana. The prospect of Charles entertaining Camilla in a palace shared with his grandmother, then aged ninety-two, was offensive. He had been assigned instead to St James's Palace, a cold, comfortless dwelling.

At which point, his troubles increased. Five weeks later the *Daily Mirror* published the transcript of an eight-minute telephone conversation between Charles and his mistress. Millions around the globe listened as he told Camilla how he yearned to 'live inside your trousers' and be reincarnated as 'God forbid, a Tampax, just my luck

… to be chucked down the lavatory and go on and on forever swirling round the top, never going down'. Charles fled to Sandringham, hoping never to see a newspaper again. He was, however, unable to escape a *Daily Telegraph* report that his approval rating had fallen to 4 per cent. Further crises seemed imminent. He lacked even the authority to demand an investigation into who had targeted him. The obvious suspect was a rogue employee at the government's intercept agency GCHQ who had recycled his work to amateur radio hams.

'You have to be careful which shadows you decide to chase,' Diana told Patrick Jephson, her private secretary, to explain why no proper inquiry had been demanded. Like Charles, she suspected that her police protection officers leaked her and Charles's secrets, especially their adulteries. The police had accumulated considerable influence over the royals, not least after Diana and Princess Anne had affairs with their protection officers. Unethically, other officers had used that information to cultivate lucrative relationships with the media.

Charles stopped talking to journalists in 1993, even during foreign trips. Damaged by the recent revelations, he now repeatedly complained about the lack of safeguards. A senior Downing Street official was summoned to St James's Palace and asked to ban photographers from around Balmoral, the queen's fifty-thousand-acre estate in north-east Scotland. 'There's not much we can do if you go near the public highway,' Charles was told. 'You'll just have to find somewhere on the estate which they can't see, even if it's less attractive.'

That exchange jarred after the news emerged about Charles's negotiations over an authorised film and biography. Jonathan Dimbleby was the younger son of Richard Dimbleby, the hugely respected BBC journalist and the nation's trusted commentator on all state occasions until his death in 1965. That pedigree was ignored beyond St James's Palace. Speaking on behalf of the senior officials in Buckingham Palace, Robert Fellowes had strongly advised Aylard to resist Dimbleby's offer. After Charles made his enthusiasm plain, the queen was advised to intercede. As usual, she replied that Prince Philip should be asked for his opinion; together they decided not to interfere.

Their reluctance stemmed from the breakdown in relations with their son. Charles had publicly blamed his parents, particularly

Philip, for an unloving childhood and being forced into an unhappy marriage. In graphic terms, he saw his father as an emotional gangster. He wanted to appeal through Dimbleby for the public's sympathy. To present Charles's point of view, Dimbleby was given unprecedented access to his private papers, his friends and employees, and extensive interviews with Charles himself.

Controversy, the prince knew, was inevitable. While reading the proofs of Dimbleby's book during a trip on the royal yacht *Britannia*, he regularly shouted his protests to Aylard, who in turn negotiated changes with Dimbleby – who, as he sympathised with Charles's predicament, was usually receptive. But no one ever sought to stop publication. The result was a remarkably intimate but ultimately destructive profile.

Dimbleby presented a portrait of a vulnerable, friendless forty-six-year-old, still bearing the scars of his harsh school years at Gordonstoun. In the journalist's graphic description, Charles never understood close companionship between schoolboys or the mutual reliance that existed among friends. Immune to the social revolution of the sixties, he resented his peers for not appreciating or understanding him.

At Cambridge he remained 'the prince', denying himself any relationship between equals. Nurtured to believe in his superiority, he became intolerant of criticism and refused to accept blame. Speaking to Dimbleby may have provided some therapy to relieve his demons, but by exposing his limited self-confidence he showed himself as self-destructive, thin-skinned and over-eager to find fault with others, especially his parents.

As a young man, Charles had craved a spiritual guide. He found one in Laurens van der Post, the South African explorer, writer and somewhat eccentric philosopher. Employing mystical terms, van der Post offered the young Charles a voyage of self-discovery and a comfortable port by telling him that, despite his possibly limited time as king, he could prove his greatness as Prince of Wales. Inspired by van der Post's lectures about African tribesmen, environmental pollution and the benefits of complementary medicine, Charles developed a ragbag of beliefs linking mysticism, divine powers, geometric measurements, orthodox Christianity and Islam.

Dimbleby's book revealed other impolitic principles. Previously, the public had been unaware that the heir to the throne was not a conventional Anglican. One single sentence threatened centuries of British stability. As monarch, Charles told Dimbleby, he would prefer to be 'defender of faith rather than of The Faith'. The Church of England and constitutional experts alike were disturbed by his doubt about swearing the traditional coronation oath to protect the Protestant settlement of 1701. There were now not one but two religious objections to Charles succeeding.

In Dimbleby's television documentary, the aspiring king pleaded for understanding. 'It's not a holiday, you know,' he said to camera. 'It's all so difficult … I can't describe the horror of seeing your life set in concrete.' Instead of offering himself as a visionary leader, he came across as a picture of harassed weakness. As he rambled on, with a series of eye-rolling expressions, grimaces and scowls, his audience was left perplexed. 'Who are you?' he was asked by a child in the documentary. 'I wish I could remember,' he had replied.

In preparation for the programme, uppermost in the TV producers' thoughts had been 'the Camilla question'. The relationship had never been officially confirmed. After some discussion, Charles believed that a confession would 'clear the decks'. Dimbleby's enquiry about his marriage was straightforward: 'You were, because of your relationship with Camilla Parker Bowles, from the beginning persistently unfaithful to your wife and this caused the breakdown?' Instead of briefly expressing his regret, Charles replied, 'I was faithful until it was clear to me that my marriage had irretrievably broken down.' He then admitted his adultery, denied that he was considering divorce, and insisted he would be king. Royalist newspapers proclaimed that Charles had 'willingly cooperated in [his] own destruction'. The *Sunday Times* headline for its serialisation of Dimbleby's book summarised its central message: 'Charles: My Agony'.

The public was aghast. Soon after publication he made a ceremonial return to Caernarvon, where twenty-five years earlier a global TV audience had watched his investiture as Prince of Wales. Just days after his televised confession, Charles drove through the town's empty streets; local television did not interrupt its coverage of racing from Sandown Park.

In hindsight, Dimbleby's highlighting the facts about Charles's marriage had in one way been a blessing, forcing the pace for his divorce. But while Charles may have settled the score, he had prepared the way for far-reaching repercussions that he could never have anticipated.

The battle with Diana had revealed the woeful mismanagement of the royal family by the queen as well as by Charles's senior advisers. The prince's relationships with his private secretaries had always been fractious. Aylard, appointed in 1992, was his fourth in seven years. Edward Adeane had resigned in 1985 after a row about Charles's uncontrollable love of controversy; John Riddell, a genial businessman who was appointed in 1985, laughed about the chicanery of courtiers and cursed the shambles of Charles's lifestyle. 'Every time I made the office work,' Riddell observed, 'the prince fucks it up again. He comes in, complains that his office is "useless" and people cannot spell and the world is so unfair, and then says, "This is part of the intolerable burden I put up with. This incompetence!"' Such outbursts manifested the prince's intolerance rather than a desire for perfection. After Riddell resigned five years into the job, Charles refused to award him the customary knighthood, an omission later rectified by the queen. 'Charles would be fantastic as a second-hand-car salesman,' Riddell told a colleague. 'He has the right enthusiasm and conviction to sell. Then you remember he's heir to the throne.'

Riddell's successor was Major General Christopher Airy, the former commander of the army's London District. Airy was hired only after being vetted, at Charles's request, by Jimmy Savile. The TV personality, dressed in a silver tracksuit and sporting gold bangles, had met the candidate in Kensington Palace. 'My job,' explained Savile, 'is to persuade you not to take the job. That's what Prince Charles has asked me to do.' Airy was bewildered. How, he wondered, had Savile – posthumously exposed as a serial predatory paedophile – induced the royals to allow him to make unannounced visits to Kensington Palace and be invited to Charles's fortieth birthday party? The prince had even sent Savile a box of Havana cigars – a gift from Fidel Castro – with a note: 'Nobody will ever know what you've done for this country, Jimmy. This is to go some way in thanking you.' On his second interview, Airy was told by Savile that his appointment had been approved – but to expect lengthy waits whenever summoned by Charles.

The prince's misjudgement about Savile coincided with his sympathy towards another sexual offender. He allowed Peter Ball, the Bishop of Lewes and Gloucester, to live in a property in Somerset provided by the Duchy of Cornwall despite the prelate's admission that he had abused boys. The police, documents would later reveal, had cooperated with leaders of the Church of England, particularly George Carey, the Archbishop of Canterbury, to 'prevent a scandal', partly because Ball was 'friendly with Prince Charles'. 'I wish I could do more,' Charles wrote to the paedophile in 1995, angry that Ball had not been re-appointed as bishop. 'I feel so desperately strongly about the monstrous wrongs that have been done to you and the way you've been treated.' Ball would be jailed in 2015.

These shameless relationships were unfamiliar to Airy. Within a year of his appointment, the ceremonial guardsman was reprimanded for suggesting to Charles that a forthcoming and unwelcome visit was 'your duty, sir'.

'Duty is what *you* do!' Charles shouted at him. 'Duty is what I *live* – an intolerable burden.'

Soon after, unaccustomed to his employer's campaigns about poverty and his propensity for flying to hot climates for environmental summits, Airy was summarily fired – knifed, some speculated, by Aylard, his successor. Airy's misery on his dismissal was later rekindled by gratuitously unpleasant comments about him in Jonathan Dimbleby's book. Charles was a bad enemy. He carried grudges. That was the background to his disillusionment with Aylard. The fallout from the Dimbleby project exposed Aylard as hidebound by court procedure and unable to think outside the box. His lack of sympathy for new ideas increased the temptation for Charles to recruit Mark Bolland. He needed a saviour to relieve the agony of the previous fifteen years.

Ever since 1981, when a billion people around the world had watched his marriage to Diana, the battle of the Waleses had aroused global fascination. The accepted story of a selfish and cruel older man betraying a beloved icon was, Charles believed, the product of mismanagement by his advisers, although Charles conceded that even the best spin doctors would have been overwhelmed by the revelations about his private life.

Ken Stronach, a junior valet, had written a book about Charles's affair with Camilla and was suspected of taking photographs of the royal bed; Wendy Berry, a Highgrove housekeeper, claimed to have witnessed not only Charles's trysts with Camilla but Diana's affair with her riding instructor, Major James Hewitt. But in November 1995 both scandals were eclipsed by Diana's television interview on the BBC's *Panorama*. After reciting her rehearsed criticism about the royal family, she admitted her adultery with Hewitt, and voiced her doubts about whether Charles would ever be king. The next moment, she accused Camilla of committing adultery with Charles from the first day of her own marriage, even intimating that her rival had slept with Charles the night before their wedding. Camilla, claimed Diana, was a permanent presence on their return from honeymoon: 'There were three of us in the marriage, so it was a bit crowded.'

Britain was divided about where the guilt lay. The majority, especially women, blamed Charles. They believed the version written by Richard Kay, the *Daily Mail* journalist and Diana's confidant: 'I knew a girl of utter simplicity, even naïvety – frightened, uncertain and delightful company. She needed to be understood. She was not manipulative, but pushed to extremes of misery by the commentators. She just dreamed of being ordinary with a humdrum routine. "They don't know how lucky they are," she said about the millions of anonymous women envious of her looks and lifestyle.'

Visitors to Balmoral described a very different figure. Their accounts portrayed a manipulative woman intent on wrecking relationships, especially her own with Charles and with his mother. Some recalled an occasion when the queen, happily anticipating walking through the fields with her grandsons during an autumn pheasant shoot, was taken aback to be told that Diana had insisted instead that her children go swimming in a local public pool. Those same eyewitnesses blamed Diana for deceiving her staff about her covert cooperation with both the Morton book and the *Panorama* interview. They indicted royal advisers, especially Fellowes and Aylard, for failing to prevent the recurring crises.

Blame also fell on Camilla. Many times, her critics believed, she could have stood back to allow Charles and Diana to reconcile. Instead, she coldly pushed her rival aside. The climax was a confrontation between the two women sometime in 1989, when Diana arrived unexpectedly at a birthday party at Annabel Goldsmith's house in Ham, near Richmond. Charles was with Diana, while both the Parker Bowleses were already there. As the rest of the room fell suddenly silent, Diana challenged Camilla to leave Charles alone. While acknowledging the hurt she was causing, Camilla controlled her fury and commented only about Diana's 'unacceptable behaviour in a private house'. The princess, she said was poorly placed to complain. While Camilla confined herself to a single, conventional relationship, Diana, she had been told by friends, was 'working her way through the Life Guards'. Camilla's intimates blamed the bruising encounter on Diana for creating 'such a public scene'. Others accused Camilla of bitchiness.

Following Diana's *Panorama* interview, the queen and Prince Philip – neither of whom Charles viewed as well-meaning advisers – told him that he could not rebuild his image nor dampen the controversy about the succession until he broke with Camilla. His misery deepened, and under pressure from his mother he agreed that he and Diana should divorce. Racked by self-doubt, he telephoned friends for reassurance, often talking well into the night. He mainly sought consolation in long calls with Fiona Shackleton and Camilla. 'No one else,' he later remarked, 'was willing to lift a finger to help me.' Less than twenty miles from Highgrove, damned as a marriage-wrecker, Camilla hid out in her house. Fuel was poured onto the flames by the Archbishop of Canterbury, who privately let it be known that, while he would crown Charles, he would not crown Camilla.

'What more do I have to do?' Charles tearfully asked Sandy Henney, a media adviser on his staff, and Aylard, her superior. 'What's the solution?' He took the advice on offer, then made his decision: first, he ordered Aylard to announce that he had no intention of remarrying. Second, he followed Henney's suggestion: 'Push the PR to show "business as usual". Project your work, sir.'

One of his first initiatives was to visit a market in Croydon, in south London. After walking through the stalls eating jellied eels, he met locals in a pub. As with his earlier trip to Caernarvon, the media ignored his visit. On the same day, spectators and journalists besieged Diana at a Paris fashion show, and for twenty-four hours she once again dominated the world's headlines. There were times in her years in the limelight when she was the most photographed person in the world.

Charles realised that in media terms it was no contest, and ordered Aylard to send him only cuttings with good news. 'Mama down the road,' he told a visitor, 'reads newspapers; I don't. It would drive me mad.' Instead he listened to Radio 4's *Today* programme while on his exercise bike. Occasionally, enraged by an item, he threw an object at the radio. The set was always being repaired.

The modern world continued to infuriate him. At a conference to promote the Prince's Trust, the umbrella for all his charities, he was introduced to young people using computers, which he disliked. 'Show His Highness how Google works,' one girl was asked. 'Tap in "Prince of Wales".' The first item to appear was about a Prince of Wales bar in Seattle, on America's west coast. Charles did not appreciate the general laughter.

Highgrove was his sanctuary, although even there he was not totally safe. One day Bruce Shand, Camilla's father, paid a visit. The Mayfair wine merchant told the prince that Aylard's announcement that Charles would not marry again had upset both Camilla and himself. 'You can't treat my daughter like this,' he said. 'She's neither fish nor fowl.'

The entire House of Windsor also seemed ranged against him. At Christmas 1996, Charles brooded over his suspicion that his brothers, Edward and Andrew, were plotting his downfall. Andrew, he believed, had been spreading poison about Camilla to the queen and Prince Philip; now, mindful of Diana's prediction on *Panorama* that he would not be king, Charles convinced himself that Diana and Sarah, Andrew's estranged wife, were hatching plans to replace him as heir by announcing that on the queen's death or abdication Andrew would be Regent until William was eighteen, when he would take over. 'Andrew wanted to be me,' Charles later told Bolland. 'I should have let him work with me. Now he's unhelpful.' As for Anne, his sister had aggravated the situation; instead of mediating between her siblings, she had criticised Charles for his adultery. 'She's one to talk,' he said, irritated by her Goody Two-Shoes image. 'Look at her past.' Anne, he declared, had enjoyed an intimate friendship with Andrew Parker Bowles at the same time that Charles was with Camilla.

By the end of the Christmas holiday, Charles had decided to ignore his parents and continue his relationship with Camilla. Once his divorce was finalised, he would no longer suffer the indignity of meeting her only in secret. Succumbing to the public's displeasure was beyond the price of duty. Convinced that the nation's hostility would diminish if her virtues were explained, he telephoned Alan Kilkenny, the public relations consultant who in late 1994 had helped guide Camilla through her divorce, to ask for assistance.

Kilkenny had already been advising Charles to shed his 'uncool', fogeyish image. As usual with such requests, Charles expected Kilkenny to work without payment. The publicist might expect a Cartier clock embossed with Charles's crest, but nothing more. The prince's plan for Camilla's divorce had been discussed at a meeting between himself, Dimbleby (present as a close friend), Camilla and her sister Annabel Elliot, Annabel's husband Simon, Aylard and Kilkenny at the home of Patty and Charlie Palmer-Tomkinson. The Palmer-Tomkinsons lived seventy miles from Highgrove and were close friends, particularly after an incident in Switzerland in 1988, when an avalanche had swept Charles and his skiing party towards a cliff edge. Andrew Parker Bowles was not told about the summit.

The plan backfired when news of the Parker Bowleses' divorce was leaked and private photographs of the family, stolen from their home, were published. Over the following months Kilkenny did his best, but by the middle of 1996 Charles feared that Camilla's cause was being pushed 'the wrong way and too hard'.

Undecided what to do next, he had lost confidence in Aylard and forged an even closer relationship with Fiona Shackleton. Educated at Benenden, the tall, blonde, loquacious lawyer had earned a reputation as one of Britain's best and most expensive divorce specialists. Now she, Hilary and Nico Browne-Wilkinson agreed: the solution was to oust Aylard and to appoint a really first-class public relations consultant.

At the ensuing dinner in St James's Palace, the three lawyers did not limit themselves to discussing Charles's reputation. Hilary Browne-Wilkinson also spoke sympathetically about Camilla's frustration that, while Diana basked in popular esteem, she was cast as the self-seeking adulteress. 'I'm not this awful person,' Camilla complained. 'I just wish someone would do something about it.'

Over the previous fifteen years, she had been forced to reassess her opinion of her rival. At the beginning of Charles's marriage, in 1981, she had called Diana a 'mouse'. But that evening with the Browne-Wilkinsons she spoke about a 'wretched woman' who was creating havoc by refusing to conform to her society's expectations in dignified silence.

Charles felt the same anger. While he spoke to the public about medicine, architecture, education and the environment and was generally ignored, Diana won global adulation by hugging children suffering from Aids, visiting hospices and sponsoring an anti-drugs campaign. 'Clip her wings,' Aylard had told the Foreign Office.

'Good God, the games they play,' was Diana's reaction after an invitation from the British ambassador to Japan for her to visit the country had been cancelled. 'We want to put her in her box,' Aylard openly told Patrick Jephson, Diana's private secretary.

Yet despite all attempts to reduce Diana's glow, her star remained undimmed. And on her own Diana had been remarkably successful in frustrating Charles's efforts to make Camilla acceptable. Repeatedly, she had called amenable journalists to pour scorn on her former husband and his mistress.

Agitated by her slurs, Charles and Camilla finally agreed that Mark Bolland should be appointed as soon as Charles's divorce was finalised. Hilary Browne-Wilkinson intimated that she had secured the support of David English, the legendary editor-in-chief of the Daily Mail group. Bolland's appointment was supported by Shackleton, who spoke out after having secured the approval of Robert Fellowes, not only the queen's private secretary but Charles's former brother-in-law. Prodded by Camilla, Charles agreed; Bolland would serve as his assistant private secretary under Aylard, and would also be Camilla's adviser, friend and provider of the prize gossip she adored.

Entrusting his fate to someone like Bolland was the last throw of the dice for the supreme aristocrat. Charles's big hope was that Bolland possessed the allure and the media contacts – both of which Kilkenny and Aylard had lacked – to mastermind the revolution he needed. Inevitably, his close friend Patty Palmer-Tomkinson wanted to vet the proposed appointment. Invited to the Browne-Wilkinsons' for lunch in the extended kitchen of their terraced house in Islington, north London, Palmer-Tomkinson exposed the social gulf between the prince and his proposed saviour: 'So where do you normally eat dinner?' she asked with genuine bewilderment. Shortly after, Bolland's appointment was formally approved. 'Charles has intro-duced a cuckoo into the nest,' Kilkenny would drily observe. 'His brief is to get rid of Aylard.'

The wheels duly turned. Charles and Diana's divorce was finalised on 28 August 1996. Days later, Bolland was introduced to Charles. 'We need to improve my media image,' said the prince. 'To get me out of this hole.' Reversing the Dimbleby blowback was the priority.

Bolland's attraction for Charles was unsurprising. The prince was animated by new personalities, especially a self-confident, streetwise soothsayer. For his part, Bolland offered loyalty and true friendship, especially to Camilla. She quickly passed on one observation she had learned early about her partner's limitations. 'Never push Charles too hard,' she advised. 'Always remember his terrible childhood, and how he was bullied at school and by his parents.'

Bolland understood his terms of employment, but first he had to assess the people close to the prince. He was struck by the extent to which Charles disliked critical advice and surrounded himself with sycophants. Chief among them was Michael Fawcett, the son of an accountant from Orpington. Officially, Fawcett was Charles's principal valet, but in reality he was his closest aide and most trusted comforter. Known as 'the Fixer' and 'the Enabler', he seemed omnipresent, loading Charles's guns at Sandringham, wrapping his Christmas presents and caring for Camilla. An indispensable perfectionist, he smoothed his master's existence. Unseen by outsiders, he also dominated a mendacious war zone competing against Paul Burrell, his opposite number in Diana's court. Employed initially at Buckingham Palace in 1976, the nominal butler Burrell had next worked for Charles and Diana at Highgrove, and after the separation moved with Diana to Kensington Palace. Ever since, he had become a confidential accomplice in Diana's life, witnessing her extreme moods and secret affairs.

Of the two, Michael Fawcett's position was the more uncertain, because Richard Aylard was plotting his removal. Bolland took a different view. 'Fawcett is a good and decent man,' he concluded after a short time, opting to conceal his antagonism towards Aylard, who he recognised was under threat.

'I know why you're here,' said Sandy Henney, the deputy press officer at St James's Palace, on the day Bolland was formally appointed, 12 May 1996. 'It's to make Camilla Parker Bowles acceptable.' Bolland smiled. He had agreed with Charles that this often unkempt, horsey countrywoman should be transformed into the prince's future wife, dressed by the best couturiers.

The impetus for Charles's instructions to Bolland often followed an agitated telephone conversation with Camilla. 'You know, Mark,' Charles would say, in what became a familiar routine, 'I think people should be told about …' The public should be aware, he complained, of his family's demand that he abandon Camilla. The pressure on him, he continued, was unrelenting. On one occasion he read out a letter from his father urging him not to marry Camilla; Bolland was told to leak its contents, and Richard Kay of the *Daily Mail*, so often the royals' first port of call, was duly briefed. Bolland also briefed the *Daily Telegraph* that after his divorce Charles would remain celibate, and would never see Camilla again.

Disseminating that canard served several purposes. In their eagerness to stay close to Charles, few of his old circle welcomed Camilla's proximity to the throne. Soon after Bolland's appointment, Nicholas Soames, Berkshire landowner Gerald Ward, the Palmer-Tomkinsons and Charles's other close friends visited him at St James's Palace to ask about Charles's relations both with other members of the royal family and with Camilla. The 'three in the marriage' scenario painted by Diana, they said, was not the whole story. There had always been other women in Charles's life, including Eva O'Neill, a statuesque German blonde, and of course the Australian Dale 'Kanga' Tryon, whom he would visit as he drove between London and Gloucestershire (on which occasions Kanga's husband conveniently made himself scarce). Charles, they said, was unlikely to marry Camilla.

Bolland was not yet in a position to judge his employer's intentions. He quickly saw that Camilla, like so many hunting women, was fun and fearless. Her romantic adventures as a teenager were no secret, nor was her unusual relationship with her husband Andrew. The husky captain in the Royal Horse Guards, 'the Blues', was famous for his affairs, and so had been unconcerned about Camilla's first meeting Charles in the early 1970s, before their marriage. In Andrew and Camilla's banter – she was prone to exaggeration – she had laughed about the prince being an emotionally immature boy suitable for a fun fling until, seven years into her relationship with Parker Bowles, she persuaded the captain to propose to her.

Their engagement was presented by Charles, through Jonathan Dimbleby, as the missed opportunity of his life. At the time he was serving as a Royal Navy officer in the Caribbean. Ignoring the reality that Camilla neither loved him nor was interested in marriage other than to Parker Bowles, he lamented not having proposed before his rival. 'The surge of raw feelings,' wrote Dimbleby, 'reduced him to tears of impotence and regret, the more severe because he was lonely and so far from home.' (Twenty-three years later, Camilla's biographer would claim that Charles had written to her one week before her wedding, urging her not to marry – but no letter has been produced.)

From the outset, the Parker Bowles's marriage was unusual. Army officers expected their wives to play their part in regimental life, tolerate regular relocations of home, and maintain appropriate standards in dress and housekeeping. Among her husband's fellow officers, Camilla was known to avoid all that, not least because, as he admitted to his friends, 'she's bone idle'. Andrew Parker Bowles circumnavigated their untidy country home by living in London during the week.

'Camilla was unhappy,' observed a friend, 'because Andrew was always putting her down.' Sensing her disdain for army life, Parker Bowles avoided any permanent relocations abroad, not least because he was conducting successive affairs in London. By 1979, after he had been posted to Rhodesia as the last military liaison officer before independence, Camilla started seeing Charles. Few were shocked. Her family was known for adultery, desertion and divorce, and Parker Bowles made no protest. On the contrary, he preferred a bachelor's life in Rhodesia while his wife enjoyed Wiltshire – and Wales. For Charles, Camilla was a relief after Amanda Knatchbull, Earl Mountbatten's granddaughter, had rejected his proposal of marriage.

At the time, Mrs Parker Bowles was the perfect match for Charles. Sexually experienced, she was content to accommodate herself to his demands and his schedule – polo, shooting, fishing and his royal duties. Most of all, she showed genuine interest in everything he said. Her husband only became aware how far the relationship had progressed when in 1980 he invited his wife to Salisbury, Rhodesia's capital. One week later, she welcomed Charles as the queen's representative at the country's independence ceremonies. While Parker Bowles spent most days in a helicopter in the company of an attractive American woman photographer (and was also beginning an affair with Charlotte Hambro, the married sister of Nicholas Soames), gossip columnists hinted that Camilla was the perfect escort for Charles. Typical of the risqué nature of their social set, Charlotte's husband Richard was the brother of Rupert Hambro, Camilla's first serious boyfriend. Tactful understanding precluded anyone frowning over Andrew's behaviour. 'Always one of the lads, but not a lad himself,' said a fellow officer with a smile. Parker

Bowles, promoted to major, may have resented the suggestion that Charles and Camilla had flown out to Rhodesia together and had isolated themselves in Charles's private quarters on the plane, amid sniggers that they were joining the mile-high club, but generally her affair was acceptable so long as it remained discreet.

Charles broke that rule after all three had returned from Africa and met again at the annual Cirencester Ball. Parker Bowles watched the prince kiss Camilla passionately while dancing with her. 'HRH is very fond of my wife,' he told friends flatly, 'and she appears very fond of him.' Parker Bowles's circle assumed that he was thrilled that Charles was in love with his wife. Their marriage could continue so long as the façade did not jeopardise his good relations with the queen, and especially the queen mother. Invitations from Buckingham Palace for shooting and fishing holidays, and hospitality at Ascot and Cheltenham, were invaluable. Nor was he perturbed when in 1980 Charles bought Highgrove, near Parker Bowles's family home in Gloucestershire. For their part, Charles and Camilla felt no guilt about their affair until February 1981, when he announced his engagement to Diana.

Both Camilla and Andrew Parker Bowles individually invited Diana for lunches. Camilla's much-publicised meeting with Charles's fiancée took place at a well-known London restaurant. By contrast, Andrew's lunch, at the Turf Club, was discreet. Both were diplomatic successes. Thereafter, Charles and Diana stayed for weekends with the Parker Bowleses. On one occasion, in front of others, Andrew told Charles, 'Diana is the girl for you.' Charles had nodded in appreciation, and as a signal of their friendship replied, 'You must tell me if I'm ever pompous.'

Andrew believed that, with the advent of Diana, his wife had decided to break off her relationship with Charles. When invited by mutual friends for dinner, she would ask, 'Are the Waleses coming?' If the answer was yes, she would refuse the invitation. 'It's easier if we don't meet,' she told her husband. Some were suspicious about such protests, especially after Diana's denunciation of Camilla in 1992 and her allegation that Camilla had slept with Charles on the night before their wedding. Somewhat bewildered, Parker Bowles asked his friends whether they recalled that night. All would honestly reply that Camilla returned to the barracks with him from the party at Buckingham Palace. The story had in fact been invented by Stephen Barry, another of Charles's disgruntled junior valets.

By the mid-1980s, the truth had become murky. Charles's relationship with Diana collapsed after the birth of Harry in 1984. Clearly unsuited to his young wife, the prince sought comfort and advice, especially from Camilla. In 1986 Andrew Parker Bowles began a passionate affair with Rosemary Pitman, the wife of a friend and fellow officer. He had finally found true happiness, but, to protect his young children and his army career, he resisted divorce. In parallel, Camilla's relationship with the heir to the throne intensified. 'Charles,' Diana told Richard Kay, 'is obsessed by Camilla's tits, and I haven't got tits as big as Camilla's.'

Although Kay was close to Diana, he was simultaneously forging a good relationship with Mark Bolland, an advantage to Charles when, in August 1996, on the eve of his decree nisi, the *News of the World* published a blurred shot showing Charles and Camilla in a garden in south Wales. The caption complimented Camilla on her appearance, because she was smiling rather than scowling: the implication was obvious. Shortly after, Charles took Camilla to a performance by the Royal Shakespeare Company at Stratford-upon-Avon. Journalists were waiting. The tip-off, Charles assumed, had come from Bolland. By this time, just a few weeks into Bolland's new job, Camilla was speaking about the next steps to him, Hilary Browne-Wilkinson and Fiona Shackleton up to six times a day. Besides gaining favourable mentions in the media, Camilla said, her priority was Richard Aylard's removal.

That, Bolland realised, was not Charles's immediate concern. His employer's dominant need was to unburden himself about his feelings towards his family and about the harm Diana had done to him. His young ex-wife, he complained, was badly educated, without any O- or A-Levels, and lacked self-discipline. Nor, he added, did she have any interest in theatre, poetry, music or opera. He seemed to have forgotten that in fact Diana loved opera and ballet, and played the piano daily. Her evenings at the pop concerts he so scorned were to raise money for charity.

Such inconsistencies were irrelevant to Charles. All he demanded was that none of his derogatory comments about Diana's sanity should be quoted to the public. In the narrative he wanted Bolland to create, Camilla was perfect, while he was suffering the burden of dutifully going through life without the woman he loved. Bolland was unsure. Was Charles's relationship with Camilla really the big love story, as Diana made out? Or had two middle-aged people, at the tail end of their marriages, found each other a convenient staging post? Either way, he was certain that his employer was not ideal husband material, and suspected that he could never live permanently with any woman. Even Michael Fawcett warned him against forcing Camilla onto Charles.

Bolland decided that Fawcett's doubts could be discounted. Jealous of others, the valet wanted to be the only person in Charles's life. The reality about Charles and Camilla's relationship could be heard on the Camillagate tape. Charles's reference to being Camilla's tampon was not just unusual, but was calculated to gain her sympathy. Being treated as a child suited him. 'My role in life is to support you and love you,' she cooed. When Charles told her, 'I need you several times a week,' she replied, 'I need you all the week, all the time.' If the young Diana was the mouse, Camilla was catnip. Charles would always return to Camilla because she gave him what he needed emotionally, and was a skilled mistress. The twist was the layers of deceit on which their relationship had been built: the lies uttered by his staff, those assigned to protect them, and the friends who provided houses for their trysts.

In September 1996, during the prime minister's annual visit to the queen at Balmoral, John Major described the public's deep unease about Charles's campaign to promote Camilla. The heir to the throne, the beleaguered prime minister said, should cool his romance with his old flame.

Unspoken was Major's irritation at Charles's lack of self-discipline when at the same time he was publicly criticising the government's mismanagement of mad cow disease, which was causing havoc for farmers and the rural tourist industry. Charles, Major hinted, always blamed others but never himself. After a decade of scandal, many in Westminster suggested that the monarchy would benefit from a period of silence. But by this time Major was a diminished figure, certain to lose the imminent general election, and he proved too weak to influence his royal hosts.

Shortly after Major left Balmoral, Charles and other members of the family congregated for a meeting of the Way Ahead Group, an informal meeting held once a year between palace officials and the

queen and her children. Under Prince Philip's leadership, the royals
were encouraged to discuss fundamental changes by treating the
monarchy as a business. Invited to observe the royals' discussion
were Fellowes, Aylard and Robin Janvrin, as well as David Ogilvy,
the Earl of Airlie, a close friend of the queen whom she always
trusted to deliver unpalatable truths. Also participating was Michael
Peat, a senior accountant appointed in 1990 to reform Buckingham
Palace's finances.

As the meeting got under way, the queen and Prince Philip
listened to their officials' proposals to reduce the number of royals
living on the civil list's annual budget of £55 million (drawn from
the Crown Estate's £94.6 million profits in 1995); to put some
distance between Charles and embarrassing members of the
extended family; and to consider whether a female child could
become the first in the line of succession. During the discussion,
Charles spoke about modernising the monarchy, but remained
silent about the contrast between the queen's frugal lifestyle and his
own.

Also unmentioned was the uncertainty in Charles's household.
His divorce may have been finalised, but the prospect of his appearing in public with Camilla, let alone marrying her, was inconceivable to those at the meeting. Palace officials spoke only about
rehabilitating the prince as fit to marry and as acceptable to be king-
in-waiting by the time of the queen's Golden Jubilee in 2002.

That timetable was unacceptable to Charles. The first obstacle was
Aylard. 'My job in the beginning,' Bolland recalled, 'was to remove
the antediluvian creatures who fuelled the War of the Waleses. Sour
palace courtiers like Aylard and Fellowes, the grey suits who ordered
royals to disappear.'

In late September Charles triggered the endgame. Bolland and
Stephen Lamport, Aylard's deputy, were on a recce to Kazakhstan
and Ukraine, which Charles was shortly to visit. The two men were
drinking warm gin and tonic in a shabby hotel room in Kiev, in
Ukraine, when Camilla phoned Bolland. Charles, Bolland knew,
was listening in on an extension. Camilla wanted to know whether
Lamport would accept Aylard's job. 'Yes,' answered Lamport, 'but I
can't make it happen.'

Charles summoned Aylard to Lochmore, the Duke of
Westminster's shooting lodge in the north of Scotland. 'I think it is

time for you to go,' he told his loyal servant. Aylard departed in tears. Lamport would replace him, with Bolland as the new deputy private secretary.

On the instructions of Charles and Camilla, Bolland's new task was to persuade the queen and her advisers that the heir to the throne's continuing relationship with Camilla was non-negotiable, and that Charles's primacy among his siblings should be conspicuously revived. 'I won't be trodden down any more,' Charles declared.

Soon after, Diana called Bolland. Despite his position in the enemy camp, she was easily charmed by him, and he responded in kind to her wiles. Working together, both agreed, was so much easier than fighting. The Camilla campaign, Diana said, was disturbing: 'I know that as part of the plan she'll give an interview next week, but if and when she does, I will have to make a statement.'

'There's no plan for an interview,' replied Bolland, aware that Diana's ability to manipulate the media was legendary.

Her suspicion about the Camilla campaign was shared in Buckingham Palace. For the first five months of Bolland's job, Robert Fellowes and Charles Anson, the queen's press secretary, regarded him as benign. While both distrusted the media, they assumed that, given his previous employment at the Press Complaints Commission, Bolland would continue to guard William and Harry's privacy. Their own priority was to protect the monarchy, not least from Charles heaping greater disrepute upon his own family and endangering his succession. But once both realised that the new man did not share their view of Camilla, Fellowes spoke about destabilising Bolland's campaign by hiring a private detective to find evidence that he was gay. The plan was ill-conceived. 'You can just ask him,' Fiona Shackleton told Fellowes, 'and he'll admit it.'

The report to Charles about that conversation inflamed his bitterness towards Buckingham Palace's officials, particularly Fellowes. His ex-brother-in-law, he knew, wanted to end his relationship with Camilla. In retaliation, Charles ordered Bolland to tell Fellowes and Janvrin that the queen 'needed to move with the times'. Unsurprisingly, he was ignored. Of the besieged lovers, Fellowes judged: 'Those two are the most selfish people I have ever met.'

At the end of 1996, a BBC TV programme about the royals and their companions called *The Nation Decides* echoed this view. In a poll of three thousand people, Charles was voted the most hated royal, just above Camilla. The popular dislike was personal. A further telephone poll in January 1997 found that 66 per cent of Britons supported the monarchy, slightly less than in previous years.

Finding a permanent solution to the conundrum of Charles, Diana and Camilla was the elephant in the room at the 9 a.m. daily meetings in Buckingham Palace, where the private secretaries and other advisers to the royal family met over coffee to discuss events and problems. Once mundane matters had been agreed, the officials forlornly considered the War of the Waleses. Charles, Fellowes suspected, was unwilling to surrender or even compromise. His judgement was right: Charles fought to win, regardless of any collateral damage. Like Fellowes, the influence of the other officials at the meeting was limited. All deferred to the queen. She could have summoned Charles and Diana to order both to cease manipulating the media, or asked Robin Janvrin, trusted by Diana as an honest broker, to mediate a ceasefire. Or she could have issued an ultimatum to Charles to choose between the crown and Camilla. Instead, she ignored the problem.

The queen's fence-sitting reflected her doubts about Charles's judgement, and also the erosion of her own self-confidence. Five years earlier, her 'annus horribilis' speech, written by Robert Fellowes, had revealed how vulnerable she was. Suffering from the divorce of three of her four children and having witnessed Windsor Castle engulfed in flames, she told Britons, 'No institution – city, monarchy whatever – should expect to be free from the scrutiny of those who give it their loyalty.' Her honesty had won widespread affection. Nevertheless, as 1997 began, she still felt battered.

'I cannot believe what's happened to me,' she confessed to an adviser after describing the state of her family and her continuing struggle with Charles.

'It's common today,' was the consoling reply.

Philip, her most loyal friend, offered little comfort. He merely encouraged distrust of Charles without making any meaningful suggestions other than to reinforce the queen's anger towards Camilla.

On Charles's behalf, Stephen Lamport was in no position to offer a solution. A cautious man seconded from the Foreign Office, he was regarded as indecisive. Cast as middle-class, Lamport knew that his income, home and perks would be terminated at a moment's

notice if the prince were displeased. 'Stephen,' a courtier explained
to a newly appointed official, 'hasn't got much money, so his job is
important for him.' Every obedient courtier, irretrievably bound by
Charles's temperament and outbursts, would search his employer's
face for signs of that hour's attitude. Charles's rages or frosty blanking could be calculated to assert his supremacy over every official,
or just reflect that moment's volatility. Lamport was employed to
obey if his advice was rejected, not to take responsibility. Loyal to
the monarchy, he agreed to be led by his new deputy; after all,
Bolland was acting on Charles's behalf with Camilla's approval.
Whenever Patrick Jephson complained that Bolland was 'monster-
ing the media', Lamport would reply: 'I can find no evidence.' His
sharpest reproach to Bolland was 'We don't do that sort of thing.'
Both men understood their terms of employment – with Charles,
only unquestioning obedience was acceptable.

3

The Masters of Spin

On 1 May 1997, 'spin' won New Labour's landslide victory. Charles, like every powerbroker, was in awe of the conjurer of those arts, Tony Blair.

The two men had first met at a dinner in 1995 at St James's Palace. Blair was hardly a passionate royalist. Only the previous year, he had advocated a smaller, Scandinavian-type monarchy, curbing the rights of the royal family to engage in public controversy. The queen, he suggested, needed to decide whether the monarchy should 'retreat into isolation and the old hierarchical order, or seek to become more like a normal family'. His ideas, popular in the Labour Party, had been criticised by Charles for seeking to transform the family into something 'more pompous and harder to approach'.

Despite their differences, Charles and Blair soon arranged further meetings. Familiarity had not lessened the prince's cynicism about those in government. Concerned for his two passions, the environment and education, he believed politicians to be dishonest, especially about young people's supposed inability to read and enjoy Shakespeare. 'I don't see why politicians and others should think they have the monopoly of wisdom,' he said. Unintentionally, he aspired to emulate the status which Samuel Johnson had attributed in 1783 to his unconventional predecessor, the future George IV: 'the situation of the Prince of Wales was the happiest of any person's in the kingdom, even beyond that of the Sovereign ... the enjoyment of hope – the high superiority of rank without the anxious cares of government, – and a great degree of power, both from natural influence wisely used, and from the sanguine expectations of those who look forward to the chance of future favour'.

Charles had travelled a long way since his first serious encounter with senior functionaries, in 1970. 'I pointed out,' he wrote after an extended meeting with President Nixon in Washington that year, 'that one must not become controversial too often, otherwise people don't take you seriously.' But he added, 'To be just a presence would be fatal.' He refined that thought after flying with Ted Heath and three former prime ministers to the funeral of Charles de Gaulle later the same year. 'Perhaps the most important lesson,' Dimbleby concluded from his conversations with Charles, 'was that his future would be frustratingly circumscribed unless he chose to make more of his role than precedent strictly required – or observers expected.' Twenty-three years later, Charles told an aide, 'I have always wanted to roll back some of the more ludicrous frontiers of the Sixties in terms of education, architecture, art, music and literature, not to mention agriculture.' In middle age, he felt underused and under-appreciated by successive governments. Instead of ceremonial duties, he wanted to promote British culture and industry.

Tony Blair had no interest in Charles's ambitions. Outside the prince's hearing, he did not conceal his feelings about the royal family. At best, he gave the impression to his senior staff that he would 'wing it' with the royals, while officials at St James's Palace concluded that Blair preferred to keep away from those he did not know or particularly like. Nevertheless, he played the part, and was not immune to being impressed. After his first royal audience, he recounted with awe how the queen was 'clued up on current affairs'.

On his first visit to Balmoral, Blair wore a tweed suit and instructed Cherie, although anti-royalist, to be on her best behaviour. He judged the heir to the throne to be a mix of traditional and radical: both princely and insecure, nervous about the public's reaction towards him and uneasy about informality. He had been spared Charles's pained response to his letter which started 'Dear Prince Charles' and was signed 'Yours ever, Tony.' Lamport called Downing Street to stipulate that in future Charles wanted Blair's letters to start 'Sir' and to end 'Your obedient servant'. The prime minister's private secretary replied that he refused to ask his master to change his style. Blair's ignorance of the required etiquette extended to an invitation from Downing Street for Diana and her sons to spend a day at Chequers. Charles was not informed, which he complained was a breach of protocol.

When on 1 July 1997 Charles met Blair in Hong Kong for the former British colony's handover to China, he put such lapses to one side. Instead, in a journal he wrote soon after, he praised Blair as 'a most enjoyable person to talk to – perhaps partly due to his being younger than me!' The prince found it 'astounding' that the prime minister listened to him, but he was critical of Blair's 'introspection, cynicism and criticism [which] seem to be the order of the day. Clearly he recognised the need to find ways of overcoming the apathy and loss of self-belief, to find a fresh national direction.' As a traditionalist, Charles also disliked New Labour's use of focus groups and reliance on untested advisers: 'They take decisions based on market research or focus groups, or papers produced by political advisers or civil servants, none of whom will ever have experienced what it is they are taking decisions about.' Charles did not consider that the same could be said about him.

He had arrived in Hong Kong in a bad mood, having been forced to fly Club Class in the chartered British Airways plane because government ministers had grabbed all the first-class seats. 'It took me some time to realise,' he wrote in his journal, 'that this was not first class (!) although it puzzled me as to why the seat seemed so uncomfortable. Such is the end of Empire, I sighed to myself.' He added a lament about his family's last use of the royal yacht *Britannia* before it was scrapped. Without those perks and privileges, he feared, his status was diminished.

Blighted by monsoon rain, the ceremony in Hong Kong was dire. In his private journal, headed 'The Handover of Hong Kong or The Great Chinese Takeaway', Charles was scathing about the Chinese leaders, in his view 'appalling old waxworks'. Sympathetic to the Tibetans, he regarded Beijing's rulers as 'corrupt', and ridiculed the People's Liberation Army for an 'awful Soviet-style display' of goose-stepping. Wind generators, he noticed, were employed to enable the Chinese flags to 'flutter enticingly'. Charles appeared unaware that his host, President Jiang Zemin, was the architect of the phenomenal economic growth that had tripled China's average wages in fifteen years and was transforming the country into a global power.

Blair would have sympathised with Charles's mockery. His own meetings with the Communist Party chiefs were disappointing. By contrast with the prime minister's tactful concealment of his true feelings, his pugnacious spokesman Alastair Campbell was unchar-acteristically generous towards Charles during the visit, summing him up as 'a fairly decent bloke, surrounded by a lot of nonsense and people best described as from another age'. Campbell astutely added that there was 'something sad about him. All his life, even on the big issues, he had to make small talk, surrounded by luxury, as here, people fawning on him, and yet somehow obviously unfulfilled,' and with his 'private life a mess'.

Campbell was unaware of the full scope of Charles's arrangements during the visit. The prince never travelled without Michael Fawcett. Dressed as a perfect gentleman in an Anderson & Sheppard suit with a silk handkerchief in the breast pocket, a Turnbull & Asser shirt and a silk tie, Fawcett flattered his employer by adopting his style and mannerisms, fashioning himself as Charles's doppelganger, even furnishing his home with items purchased from the prince's suppliers.

With a love of grandeur and extravagance similar to his master's, he was skilled at satisfying Charles's expectations, and set himself to provide the luxury Charles demanded day and night. Every morning, wherever he travelled, the prince was woken by Fawcett who ran his bath and laid out his clothes – matching suit with shirt, socks, tie, handkerchief and highly-polished shoes – all carefully folded between tissue paper for the journey. Every night Fawcett prepared Charles's bedroom with masterly attention to detail. With familiarity spawned by living close to his employer since 1981, he could anticipate his employer's requests without any order being issued. He would discreetly replenish the royal lavatory paper, clean up vomit, wash the royal boxer shorts by hand (salacious gossips on the *Sun* credited Fawcett with revealing that Charles's underwear had to be specially adapted because he was so well endowed), guarded his liaisons, bowed to his tantrums, tested the royal boiled eggs and always spoke in deferential tones. At each of Charles's homes he supervised every detail, ensuring that the gravel on the drive was raked, the paintings hanging precisely, the cushions properly positioned, the kitchens supplied with organic food from the prince's favourite suppliers, the elaborate flower arrangements refreshed daily, and the dining table covered with the appropriate linen tablecloth, silver cutlery and candlesticks.

Some of those who witnessed Fawcett's outbursts of fury when he spotted an error considered him a thug, but Charles embraced this one servant who, in his eyes, could do no wrong. Most royals have a weakness for a special retainer. The queen's was Angela Kelly, her personal assistant; Queen Victoria's her beloved attendant John Brown. Charles would confess, 'I can manage without just about anyone except Michael.' Operating like a general, Fawcett was given the keys to the front and back doors of Charles's homes – and control over his life.

Shortly before leaving for Hong Kong, Fawcett was told about an important dinner party that would be hosted by his master during the trip. Charles was focusing on his charities, for which he hoped to raise money from American billionaires. 'Show your good side,' said Mark Bolland. Searching for a new fundraiser, the prince asked Geoffrey Kent for a recommendation. Kent had heard about Robert Higdon from Alecko Papamarkou, a Greek banker. At the time Higdon was accompanying Margaret Thatcher on her speaking engagements, having been recruited by Thatcher's son Mark, who knew of the American's successful work for Ronald and Nancy Reagan.

In July 1995, Colin Amory, an architect and sometime adviser to Charles, invited Higdon to meet him and Geoffrey Kent at Claridge's. Higdon arrived with the billionaire American publisher Kip Forbes, who was said to have first met him in a Red Lobster restaurant in Florida. Over a drink, Amory and Kent told Higdon that the Prince of Wales's Foundation in America, which had been created two years earlier, needed a professional fundraiser.

'I have met Charles,' said Higdon, 'when he and Diana came to the White House to meet the Reagans.'

Soon after, Kent asked Higdon as a trial to arrange a dinner with potential donors.

'What's your platform?' asked Higdon.

'The Prince of Wales's interest in architecture,' replied Kent.

'No one's interested in that over here,' said the American bluntly. 'I raised money for the Frick, but for the prince there's nothing to discuss.'

Kent managed to overcome Higdon's objections, and a dinner party was arranged in New York for people who had previously 'written a cheque for Charles'. To Higdon's surprise, 150 people accepted the invitation, including members of the Rockefeller family, and the event was reported in the city newspapers' society columns. 'I raised about £75,000,' said Higdon. 'I was the money whore.'

Delighted by the evening's success, Charles asked Kent to sign up the American for further fundraising. 'I'd need to meet Charles again,' replied Higdon. Before long he was in the prince's office at St James's Palace. 'We chatted as long-lost friends,' said Higdon. With Lamport sitting in, 'I bluntly told Charles what would and wouldn't work.'

Lamport interrupted: 'You cannot speak to His Royal Highness like that.'

'Lamport didn't like me or want me to help,' Higdon concluded, 'but Charles trusted me.'

In January 1997 Charles formally asked Higdon to run his foundation under Kent's chairmanship. Within weeks the new recruit encountered obstruction: 'The gatekeepers wouldn't let me speak to Charles. Fawcett and others were fighting against me. I saw no good.' Eventually he met Charles for a third time, at Birkhall, the queen mother's house on the Balmoral estate. 'You won't get a dime for your architecture,' he told Charles, 'because you've got a bunch of cuckoos in this building wanting a pay cheque.' He blamed Fawcett for taking too much interest in his fundraising, and continued, 'You can be so much more and do much more if you have a global vision.' Charles agreed to his reorganising the foundation.

Shortly after, Lamport telephoned Higdon to tell him, 'We need a fundraising dinner for HRH during the handover in Hong Kong.' The target, he said, was $1 million. Higdon now understood that every foreign trip organised by the British government for Charles would be, whatever else was intended, an attempt to raise money for his charities – 'So I became Mr Cash Cow.' Against the odds, he managed to corral a group of local plutocrats.

To set the table for the dinner, Fawcett had brought a full set of eighteenth-century china and glasses to Hong Kong, which would replace the governor's nineteenth-century equivalents. He had also brought a set of special bells used by Charles to summon his staff. After arranging the table decorations, Fawcett turned to the seating plan. The potentially largest donors would be closest to the prince. To ensure that everything went smoothly during the dinner, Fawcett stood behind Charles, protecting him from careless hands spilling wine or food, and waiting, as ever, for the royal click of the finger should his boss need something – the china cup filled with his special tea, an orchestra at short notice, or even, thinking ahead to another event, a private plane. Based on such knowledge and trust,

Fawcett was Charles's Rasputin, empowered to outflank everyone. For that reason, the queen had no time for him. At a dinner in Holyrood, she cringed when his name was mentioned. Fawcett appeared unenthusiastic about Higdon's role. Any competitor for Charles's attention aroused his antagonism, even those who were helpful. 'I was the new enemy,' Higdon recalled after he had successfully met his $1 million target.

One group that Fawcett ignored was politicians, and among the Blairite luminaries to whom Charles was naturally attracted was Peter Mandelson, a principal architect of New Labour's electoral success. Known as 'the Prince of Darkness', Mandelson sought an introduction to Charles with the help of Carla Powell, the wife of Margaret Thatcher's foreign affairs adviser Charles Powell. Powell had invited Camilla to a dinner at which Mandelson made a pitch for a relationship with Charles.

Camilla's favourable report back sealed the ambition of Labour's spin maestro. He was invited to lunch at Highgrove the month after the Hong Kong trip. Charles's ostensible reason was to urge him to discourage Labour's proposed ban on fox-hunting. Pleased that their guest seemed sympathetic, Camilla treated Mandelson as an ally. Recalling election night, she told him that she had worn a red dress at dinner with friends, telling them, 'I'm dressing for the future.' Now the conversation drifted to the problems caused to the government by the recent messy divorce of the foreign secretary Robin Cook. After listening to Mandelson's uncharitable judgement of his beleaguered opponent, Charles mentioned his prime concern. What, he asked, did ministers think about him, the Prince of Wales? In a reassuring manner, Mandelson replied that they saw him as hardworking and civilised, with a deep social conscience. He then grasped the nettle: 'Some people have gained the impression you feel sorry for yourself, that you're rather glum and dispirited. This has a dampening effect on how you are regarded.'

Charles reeled. But Mandelson had not finished, and turned to the prince's relationship with Camilla: 'You will need to be patient. Let things find their own level and not force the pace.'

Again Charles looked stunned. After Mandelson had left, he beseeched Camilla, 'Is that true? Is that true?'

'I don't think any of us can cope with you asking that question over and over again for the next month,' she replied.

'Well, then,' said Charles, 'how about for just the next twenty minutes?'

Humour was often the saving grace between them. Camilla was Charles's rock, and nothing would deter him from hosting a grand party to celebrate her fiftieth birthday in July 1997. The news aroused Diana's bile and Robert Fellowes's fury. According to reports from Buckingham Palace, Fellowes intended to ask the queen not to allow the event. That news encouraged Charles to order Fawcett to plan a spectacular celebration. While he would not remarry, the prince told his former brother-in-law, he would not abandon Camilla. On the contrary, he wanted the world to appreciate her as much as he did. He reported back to Camilla that Fellowes had surrendered.

The birthday party was successful, but the obstacles to progress were confirmed by a BBC poll after a TV show, *You Decide*. Sixty thousand viewers voted that Charles should not be crowned if he married Camilla. Few voted in his favour.

Undeterred, Charles wanted a final reckoning with Diana. In the war of books, he contemplated cooperating with Penny Junor, a well-known journalist sympathetic to his cause and familiar with some of Camilla's Wiltshire set. Junor's book would focus on presenting Camilla in a favourable light, but would also disparage Diana and portray Charles as the victim of a sick wife. To protect himself from the kind of recriminations that had followed Jonathan Dimbleby's book, Charles decided that any cooperation with Junor should be channelled through Bolland.

He also agreed with Bolland's idea that Camilla should host a fundraiser on 13 September for the National Osteoporosis Society (Camilla's mother had suffered and died painfully from the condition). This would be the beginning of a five-year campaign to transform her from adulteress into a suitable wife for the heir to the throne – and future queen. Invitations were sent to 1,500 people, including pop stars and other celebrities. Everything seemed set.

In his wildest dreams, Charles could not have anticipated that a car crash in Paris would destroy his plan and place Camilla 'in deep freeze'. As Robert Higdon summed up, 'Suddenly, I discovered that I was working for the most hated man in the world.'

4

Uneasy Lies the Head

At 6 a.m. on Sunday, 31 August 1997, Higdon, calling from America, reached an acquaintance at Balmoral, where the royal family was staying.

'What shall we do?' he asked.

'Nothing,' came the reply. 'Our worries are over.'

Elsewhere in the castle, Charles was chanting, 'They're all going to blame me, aren't they? The world's going to go completely mad.'

In the hours after Diana's death, her former husband was paralysed by guilt. One of the queen's courtiers would say that even his sons were critical of him for what had happened. Others would point to those same advisers and the royal family itself for encouraging the marriage, and then allowing it to veer out of control. No one had imagined that after a decade of crisis the royals' plight could get so much worse.

Over the following days, the reports about Charles's reactions were contradictory. His critics among the queen's courtiers in Scotland recounted that he dithered about going to Paris until the queen said, 'I think you should get out there.' Others recalled that he insisted, against the queen's wishes, on flying to France to bring back the body, until the monarch was silenced by Robin Janvrin's question, 'Would you rather, Ma'am, that she came back in a Harrods van?' The majority of the media, relying on Bolland, who was at Balmoral, reported that Charles had taken control. They either concealed or were ignorant of his reluctance to fly to Paris. As the media's only 'eyewitness' source, 'Bolland could spin what he liked,' one journalist griped.

There was no precedent for managing the death of a global icon who was no longer a member of the royal family but was nevertheless the mother of the future heir to the throne. The same courtiers who had mismanaged the announcement of Charles and Diana's separation in 1992 struggled to decide whether the flag over Buckingham Palace should, contrary to tradition, be flown at half-mast for Diana's death, and whether she should be buried privately or after a state funeral in Westminster Abbey.

That Sunday morning, none of those involved – Robert Fellowes, Robin Janvrin, Charles Anson and Stephen Lamport – could judge if Diana's death was a tipping point for the monarchy. While the public's perception of Diana could not be ignored, the four officials focused on protecting the queen. Any misstep would have embarrassed the monarchy, and perhaps even jeopardised it.

By the time Charles had accompanied Diana's body back to London, the four advisers still underestimated the scale of the public's distress. The prime minister's description of Diana in his TV address as 'the people's princess', compared with the queen's seclusion in Balmoral, increased the nation's dissatisfaction. As the outrage grew, the queen's advisers searched forlornly for solutions. Unexpectedly, they found themselves relying on Tony Blair.

The prime minister had placed himself in an awkward position, as over the previous months he had built a rapport with Diana. Blair's delusion about a special relationship, born of his desire to politicise the princess as New Labour, had irritated Charles, but he enjoyed receiving telephone calls during which she would comment on a photograph or one of his statements: according to him, they showed that 'she had a complete sense of what we were trying to achieve'. Sympathetic to her challenge to the Windsors' traditionalism, Blair was unconcerned that Diana gave the queen, as he wrote in his memoirs, 'good cause to be worried'. Yet, in the days after Diana's death, he and his Downing Street aides helped the family and their advisers overcome unfortunate obstacles.

Advised by Robert Fellowes, the queen did not adjust her principles. The monarchy, she knew, although buffeted by challenges, would survive if she focused on reaching the agreed destination, namely a funeral that satisfied the nation. By contrast, Charles's inner circle was conflicted. Just when the public longed for him to lead by example, he was indecisive. 'Why do you have to make everything a matter of principle?' Fellowes had once exclaimed to a man who even in mourning considered the world was being unfair to him. To Charles, Fellowes and his family were especially intolerable. Fellowes's wife, Jane Spencer, was Diana's older sister. Diana's eldest sister, Sarah McCorquodale, had been widely reported as Charles's official girlfriend in the late 1970s, but her time as his accepted companion was terminated after an indiscreet remark she made to a journalist. The combination of those old antagonisms and Charles's torrid relationship with Diana complicated Blair's discussions with the queen and Fellowes.

It did not help that the prime minister did not fully understand the conflicts within the royal family. Speaking with limited deference, he saw his duty as 'to protect the monarchy' from the public's rage. The courtiers' initial gratitude turned into suspicion. Blair did not understand that governments do not own the monarchy. Thirteen years later, he admitted that he had presumptuously lectured the queen: 'I talked less sensitively than I should have about the need to learn lessons.'

Despite the heated emotions, a state funeral was belatedly agreed for 6 September, bringing the immediate frenzy to an end. The first-class post across the country was held back for an hour to await the issuing of two thousand invitations to the grand event. When the deadline was missed, the nation's entire fleet of Post Office vans was commandeered for their special delivery.

On the eve of the funeral, as thousands of grieving spectators bedded down along the route and outside the Abbey, the only unresolved detail was whether Charles and his sons would walk behind Diana's coffin on its one-hour-and-forty-seven-minute journey from St James's Palace. During an earlier discussion with Blair's aides, Prince Philip, speaking on the phone from Balmoral, had exploded about the spin doctors' insensitivity: 'Fuck off. We are talking about two boys who have lost their mother.' The question was finally resolved over the family dinner on the night before the funeral. To break the deadlock, Philip said to his grandsons, 'Well, if you don't go, I won't.' The boys decided to walk behind the coffin with their grandfather, their father, and Diana's brother Charles, the ninth Earl Spencer.

While the Windsors debated, Charles Spencer visited the Abbey to rehearse the words he would deliver from the pulpit the next day. He had written an outspoken rebuke to the royal family, but after spotting a lurking palace official he decided to remain silent. His idea that Tony Blair rather than Prince Charles should read the lesson had been rejected, which made him only the more determined. At the funeral the following morning, his accusations against an astonished royal family divided the nation. Some were outraged at Spencer's impudence, while others praised his courage. The art historian Roy Strong, taking his cue from the public's loud applause which could be heard inside the Abbey, wrote that the people 'want a monarchy but they want it human and compassionate. The present cast suddenly looked past its sell-by date.'

Spencer's feelings of enmity towards Charles continued during Diana's interment at Althorp, the Spencer family home, at the end of the day. Afterwards, according to Paul Burrell, the earl's speech was being replayed on television in the room where the prince was offered tea. As the ex-brothers-in-law talked together, Charles volunteered that while Spencer had inherited his title as a young man, he himself had already had to wait decades before becoming king. When details of the conversation appeared in the press, Spencer was accused of leaking the exchange, and Burrell of fabrication because there was allegedly no television in the room.

By the following morning, Spencer's denunciation of the Windsors was overshadowed by the testimony of those who recalled that Diana had accepted Harrods owner Mohamed Fayed's invitation to holiday in France only after her brother, citing potential media intrusion, had withdrawn his agreement that she and her children could spend the summer on the Althorp estate. The desperate mother, according to her admirers, had been abandoned by both her families.

Charles was more melancholic than ever. His popularity rating was stuck at 4 per cent. Critics mocked him without appreciating his insight into the truth. He was receiving, he complained, no credit for carrying the intolerable burden of duty to serve the irredeemably 'awful' monarchy, and feared the public's reaction when he finally emerged from his seclusion at Highgrove. Determined to believe that life without guilt was possible, he decided that his task was to resurrect himself and his lineage. Buoyed by the solid support he always received from the queen mother, he would never renounce the crown. While the queen offered continuity, dignity and traditional values, his fate depended on somehow using Diana's death as a catalyst to overcome his unpopularity.

Disliking Blair's announcement that the royal family intended to 'change and modernise', conjuring up visions of a Scandinavian bicycling monarch, Charles was seeking a formula for reinvention without abandoning the trappings and advantages of royalty. During discussions at Highgrove, he asked his staff, 'How can we get the public to understand what we do? We need to be more accessible. But we must still keep our distance, and must not be like the public.' In reply, Tom Shebbeare, the chief executive of the Prince's Trust, suggested that Charles should speak publicly about Diana. Charles frowned. He shared his family's anger that his ex-wife was being mythologised despite being, in his words, 'a nutter'.

Dignity demanded that the battle of the Waleses should be buried. Other than uttering praise of Diana, Charles would remain silent. Simultaneously, any activity that risked him being portrayed as the 'playboy prince' was to end, and the campaign to have Camilla made more acceptable suspended. 'Emphasise service, one's duties and contribution,' Charles told his staff. The media should be directed towards his various initiatives to do good for the country. 'And please keep pushing them,' he ordered. In parallel, Stephen Lamport was told to ask Peter Mandelson and Anji Hunter, the prime minister's adviser in Downing Street, to arrange for Blair to make speeches in praise of Charles.

'Nothing happens by chance,' Mark Bolland concurred. 'Everything has to be engineered.'

Mandelson duly briefed Jon Snow, the Channel 4 news presenter, that it was Charles's initiative to fly the flags at half-mast, and that only after he had argued his case with the queen and Robert Fellowes was Charles allowed to organise 'a full royal funeral at Westminster'. The resulting impression, said a satisfied Bolland after Snow's 'exclusive' broadcast, was 'Charles at the helm'. As requested, Tony Blair added his blessing during a television interview, stating that despite the Church's disquiet about his divorce, Charles would not only be king, but also the supreme governor of the Anglican Church.

'The world is run by some very nasty, powerful people,' Charles had written to Jonathan Dimbleby. 'Enemies of mine,' he warned, would become Dimbleby's enemies. He had also consoled Camilla about the consequences of their relationship: 'You suffer all these indignities and tortures and calumnies.'

Two broadcasts alone could not halt the opprobrium that was threatening Charles. On a personal level, one salvation was the spiritualism of the poet Kathleen Raine, who had been introduced to Charles by Laurens van der Post. Listening to the prince's laments about his isolation under siege and his forlorn search for meaning, this unusual woman, who lived an unorthodox life in London and was forty years his senior, offered comfort over cups of tea in her Chelsea house. 'She was always there for me because above all she understood what I was about,' Charles explained, voicing his attachment to much older people, 'and that was a profound comfort in an age of growing misunderstanding and almost deliberate ignorance.'

Raine urged Charles to disregard his critics: 'Dear, dear Prince, don't give that riff-raff an inch of ground, not a hair's breadth; stand firm on the holy ground of the heart. The only way to deal with the evil forces of their world is from a higher level, not to meet them on their own.'

Raine's spiritualism, based upon what she called 'prayer in action', the worship of the sacred nature of all life, art and wisdom, buttressed Charles's sense of superiority. In his vision of himself as the protagonist in his own tragedy, and freed from any sense of shame, Charles adopted a formula for survival taught at the Temenos Academy, a charity of which Raine was one of the founders, that divided faith into metaphysics, mysticism and visionary imagination. Casting himself as the exceptional hero, Charles later explained his bravery in a eulogy he delivered at Raine's memorial service: 'I had put my head above the parapet and, yet again, the shells and bullets had been exploding all around me ... The world seemed to be periodically madder and the powers of darkness – as Kathleen described them – closed in. She did her utmost to reawaken an Albion sunk in deadly sleep.' Feeding his self-indulgence, Raine wrote: 'How my heart rejoices that you have mounted that chariot. The chariot of fire between two armies. This is the great battle and where would you, our prince, rather be than in that chariot?' Most sane fifty-year-old men would have ridiculed Raine's inflated rhetoric, but Charles inhaled her words like oxygen.

To survive in the real world, he needed to ignore the risks and make himself visible. Four weeks after Diana's death, he agreed with some trepidation to visit a Salvation Army centre in Manchester. He arrived with a speech drafted by Downing Street's best spin masters, including Peter Mandelson, but then set it aside. Instead, he spoke with unscripted passion to a group of curious spectators. Repeatedly telling them how 'enormously grateful and touched both the boys and myself have been', he was at his best. The media coverage described a loving father of two adored sons speaking from the heart about their grief and grateful for the public's support.

This sympathetic press coverage persuaded Charles to take the thirteen-year-old Harry – who was on safari in Botswana with Geoffrey Kent to alleviate his misery – on a trip to South Africa arranged months earlier by the Foreign Office to meet Nelson Mandela.

'Speak to the media and be friendly,' Mark Bolland advised Charles.

He also told Robert Higdon, 'He wants to raise money while he's there.'

'You're mad,' replied Higdon, 'but I'll try.'

Higdon approached Mary Oppenheimer, scion of the diamond-mining family, to host a dinner for thirty people, including a number of South Africa's billionaires, prepared to contribute to Charles's Global Foundation. 'It was always about money,' recalled Higdon, who was delighted by the event's success and by Charles's praise. Some years later, he revised his opinion: 'The atmosphere to extract donations from the guests was very awkward.'

Media coverage of Diana's son happily meeting South Africa's hero, who had also invited the Spice Girls, liberated Charles. On the return flight to Britain, he offered journalists his new manifesto: 'Tradition is a living thing but to be so it has to be made contemporary in each generation. That is always the great challenge.' A few days later, a South African friend of Charles's wrote reporting Mandela's admiration of him. 'How wonderful,' he replied. 'Why do foreigners praise me but my countrymen never share that feeling?'

He believed that Peter Mandelson could provide the solution. Their relationship had strengthened in the weeks after Diana's death. Reflecting on Mandelson's recent defeat in elections to the Labour Party's National Executive Committee, Charles commiserated: 'It only goes to show, I suppose, what a ghastly, cut-throat business politics is. The throwing of knives into other people's backs seems to be a pretty prevalent blood sport and it is not a pretty sight. But then, you would perhaps expect the representative of an "outmoded" hereditary organisation to make such an observation.' He added that he wrote as 'a person who, despite the inevitable outer carapace which has to be worn to confront the world, nevertheless has a rather vulnerable and sensitive inner core'.

Mandelson was an obvious guest for one of Charles's 'culture weekends' at Sandringham that autumn. Others invited (the guest lists for many of these weekends were orchestrated by the philanthropist Drue Heinz) included Tate director Nicholas Serota, novelist Angela Huth, barrister Ann Mallalieu, Leo Rothschild and Stephen Fry. Clever, funny and endlessly flattering, Fry had an erudite wit that delighted Charles. 'No one complains on his deathbed,' Fry told the guests, '"Oh God, I wish I had spent more time in the office."'

'You'll need black tie and white tie, clothes for walking,' one guest was advised. Asked about attending church on Sunday, the official replied, 'There's no obligation to go, but if you don't you'll be ignored during the following lunch.'

All of this was in the spirit of the royal family. Sandringham formality had been inherited by the queen from her father and grandparents – even on Christmas Day she expected perfect behaviour from her grandchildren. Charles's literary weekends were no different. Although he had not engaged with intellectuals during his time as a student at Cambridge, he enjoyed their company. 'Of course, I know very little about this,' he would say in a self-deprecating manner after mentioning paintings he had bought by little-known artists. His guests would depart on the Monday morning with a sense of privilege and memories of a remarkable performance by their host.

Charles had remained silent about Camilla's absence. She was, he knew, suffering under the strain. 'She's a wreck,' he told a friend, and half-joked to Bolland that in the past he would have been sent into exile and Camilla committed to a dungeon. All he wanted, he told those whom he regularly telephoned, now including Mandelson, was the chance to go out in public with the woman he loved.

By Christmas, the worst was over. The trip to South Africa had placated some critics. In one poll, 61 per cent of those who responded said they were satisfied with Charles, compared to 46 per cent before Diana's death and that 4 per cent immediately after. The dissatisfaction rate had fallen from 42 to 29 per cent. These figures restored some sense of Charles being master of his destiny. His advisers spoke about rebuilding his reputation after a doomed decade. In the new era, he anticipated that an open relationship with Camilla would be possible, despite other polls that showed about 90 per cent of Britons still opposed their marriage.

One obstacle was Robert Fellowes. In a court corroded by inertia, he and the queen were struggling to estimate the damage caused by the ten-year crisis. Neither Charles nor Camilla saw any possibility of a normal life together unless the queen approved, and that was impossible until Fellowes was no longer there to advise her.

Charles's machine went into action. The poison was planted in the *Mail on Sunday*. On 2 November 1997 the newspaper published an attack under the headline 'Another Royal Farce ... Carry On Sir Robert'. The article, by Peter Dobbie, a regular columnist, accused Fellowes of being prejudiced against Charles for wanting to live with Camilla. Worse, he was accused of being 'a joke' who 'evokes loathing' for having been 'one of the prime instruments in the destruction of the monarchy's public esteem'. Fellowes was singled out for blame for the 'public perception of uncaring, dysfunctional senior Royals' after Diana's death. Dobbie ended with the knife-twist: 'By staying on he can only perpetuate his views of outdated incompetence born of arrogant indifference.'

'Robert's been stuffed by Bolland' was the word around Downing Street. Naturally, Fellowes was furious. His friends in Buckingham Palace blamed Charles for wanting to destroy any courtier who opposed his demands. To save himself, the prince had infected the royal palaces with jealousy, vulgar extravagance and deceit.

Fellowes saw no obvious solution. One immediate remedy would be to surrender to the media attack. His departure could be seen as justifiable. The queen needed a new, candid friend to whom she could unburden herself and be advised how to satisfy her headstrong son. In the inevitable negotiations between the palaces, Fellowes was not ideally placed to suggest sacrifices. He and the queen agreed that after seven years' service he should move on; the transition should start for Robin Janvrin, his deputy and a former Foreign Office diplomat, to succeed him.

For his part, Janvrin was immersed in plans for the queen's Golden Jubilee in 2002, which he hoped would restore the monarchy's reputation after a decade of disaster. Securing the queen's approval for the celebration was an uphill battle – the public, she said, were unenthusiastic about the monarchy. But persistent pressure gradually wore down her reluctance. However, retaining her trust depended on months of serenity. There could be no more scandals.

Charles's fate partly depended on the celebrations restoring the romance of the monarchy. Although he himself was not obviously imaginative, Janvrin shrewdly understood how to draw on other people's ideas to make an impact. Among the spinoffs of the Jubilee, he believed, would be a challenge to those courtiers who ignored the public's loss of trust in the 'unworthy' royals. Too many members of the royal family were living off the civil list, receiving police protection and revelling in the free use of private planes, royal trains, boats and castles. Family ties and relationships were bedevilling attempts to persuade these 'unworthy' royals to draw the line voluntarily. Too many of them had too much to lose, especially some of the young royals who demanded privilege and pomp while simultaneously making sham pleas to be treated like everyone else.

A by-product of the Jubilee would be to curb the legacy of the imperial era. More profoundly, here was the opportunity to signal the transition from a belief in the queen's divine right to rule, as affirmed at her coronation in 1953, to Charles's wish for a multi-denominational, inter-faith coronation. Although that was constitutionally impossible, negotiations for a compromise would open discussions about whether Charles's heirs could marry Catholics, and whether a first-born female child could succeed as queen.

Overcoming the obstacles to a constitutional debate depended upon neutralising the queen's dislike of change. 'Well, my father told me this ...' she would still regularly say. Wedded to George VI's influence and with the queen mother urging the most reactionary decisions during her daily telephone calls to her daughter, the queen was shaped by Edwardian precedents. Rigidly conservative, she refused to allow even moving any furniture in Balmoral from the place assigned by Queen Victoria. Charles, she feared, would change everything, not least out of pique. 'My son,' she once complained to a nobleman, 'resents me because I taught him the alphabet.'

On many matters she would defer to her husband, who was well aware of the problems they all faced. 'Throughout history,' Philip told an adviser, 'there's been a difficult relationship between monarch and heir. It's not a job but a predicament.' He wanted his children to follow his way of doing things, but knew that Charles would not forgive his father's apparent 'sins' – including his ordering Charles, as a child, to wear corduroy trousers to a birthday party, the only one present to do so. Even as a middle-aged man, Charles still felt the legacy of that trivial humiliation. He also lacked his mother's genius for concealing what she truly felt and separating her personal values from those of the nation. He would never be able to emulate her landmark speech at a lunch in Whitehall to celebrate her golden wedding anniversary in November 1997, when she had volunteered that the monarchy's existence rested on popular approval – adding, to applause, that she herself was willing to change after listening to the public.

Charles disliked those sentiments. He preferred to confront anyone he disliked, regardless of the fallout. Unlike his mother, he failed to provide a sense of solidarity or stability. He did not stand as a symbol of the country and its heritage, or personify an idea. Not astute enough to create illusions when needed, or to float above the rancour, he was content to pose a threat.

Negotiating peace with the unpredictable heir was complicated by the appointment to head the queen's household of Lord Camoys, a banker from an old Roman Catholic family, as the lord chamberlain. To Charles, Camoys represented the old guard, with its antediluvian understanding of the monarchy. His dislike was exacerbated by Camilla's complaint that Camoys had once accused the Parker Bowles children of cheating in a school race.

Since the 1980s, Charles had sabotaged every attempt by the queen's advisers to coordinate their two courts. To him, Buckingham Palace was not a homogeneous organisation. In his opinion, little had changed since he was born. Within the immutable layers of rank, right down to the servants who laboured in the basement of the palace, there was unyielding respect for the queen and fear of her displeasure, but also an understanding that individual power depended on every courtier's relationship with his or her immediate superior, the high value of intimate information, and ultimately access to the queen. Charles's disdain for that culture was magnified by his dislike of Fellowes, Janvrin and now Camoys.

Janvrin's hope that he could fashion a new relationship with St James's Palace rested on Stephen Lamport's skill in persuading Charles to resist his instincts and stabilise his relationship with Buckingham Palace. But that depended on Charles's whims. Giving honest advice to a man who would explode when contradicted was no easy task, especially as the prince once confessed, 'My problem is that I believe the last person I spoke to.'

Unlike the queen, Charles frowned on people with different ideas from his own. While her lack of dogmatism encouraged free discussion, he was closed to alien thoughts. Every day his public and private life threw up difficulties, and every day Lamport tried to tone down Charles's opinions, especially about the environment, education and fox-hunting – although after their lunch at Highgrove, Peter Mandelson had told journalists that any private member's attempt to introduce legislation banning hunting would not be supported by the government.

In their daily meetings, Lamport tried to measure Charles's intentions in comparison with the precedents established by his predecessors over the previous two hundred years. He then gave advice, but he could not always gauge Charles's reaction. To reach the ideal decision on almost any matter required him to follow a convoluted and uncomfortable route. If his advice were rejected, Lamport suffered in isolated silence: 'I blame the vipers' nest in Charles's private office,' observed an official in Buckingham Palace about the tortuous process. There were layers of hierarchy, with everyone attempting to climb the greasy pole. Whatever was said, one never knew how far it might go, 'who could be trusted and how it would be twisted'. Buckingham Palace and St James's Palace suffered from identical manipulative tussles.

Uncertain about the best course, in the summer of 1998 Janvrin and Fellowes invited Alastair Campbell for lunch. Charles's stubborn grudge, they confided, was a tough, long-term problem made worse by their distrust of Bolland. True to his conviction that 'spin' was the answer to most difficulties, Campbell urged the two to 'get a grip' and embrace a new generation by appointing Simon Lewis, a Blairite public relations expert. On Campbell's recommendation, Janvrin immediately hired Lewis as Buckingham Palace's new spokesman. Unlike his predecessors, Lewis was told to bridge the gap between the monarch and the people – or, at least, to break the mould.

Adopting the Blairite tactic of targeted messages, Janvrin believed, would modernise the brand and help define the monarch's renewed contract to serve the country. Inevitably, some courtiers were puzzled that he was putting so much faith in a New Labour market-ing man with no experience of the royal family. Janvrin replied that Lewis and Camoys would repair the monarchy's vulnerability. As the first anniversary of Diana's death approached, he feared renewed damage from the tabloids.

Lewis, as a newcomer, struggled to understand the tension between the palaces. Hearing critical comments in Buckingham Palace about Charles's weaknesses, the contamination caused by Camilla, and how Bolland was promoting the prince at the expense of other members of the family, bore little resemblance to Westminster's wars. Lewis's proposals to start lobby briefings, issue statements, send an annual report on the queen's behalf to twenty million homes, and harness Buckingham Palace to Cool Britannia (New Labour's gospel to revolutionise Britain) bewildered Janvrin's critics. He replied that changing the culture was essential to prepare for a modern monarchy.

Charles disagreed. Conjuring an air of change was merely colour-ful spin, in his opinion, and ignored the House of Windsor's instinct for self-preservation. Ever since the Saxe-Coburgs had reinvented themselves as the Windsors in 1917 to avoid the fate of the Tsar of Russia, the Kaisers of Germany and Austria and the downfall of other minor European monarchs, the queen had separated herself from Britain's aristocracy. Unimpressed by titles, the royal family was aware of the country's hereditary families only if they were genuine friends or were criticised by the media. The natural order, with the monarch at the head of a pyramid supported by the landed nobility, had vanished.

The gentry's loss of power was of no interest to St James's Palace. After a decade of gossip and misbehaviour, Charles's household yearned for a period free of notoriety. His officials' expectations were frustrated by the prince's feudal exercise of power, a different kind of misbehaviour.

Some long-term employees who had been granted a home were obliged to receive a visit from Charles as a reminder of their place in the scheme of things; others were invited for dinner, or to a garden party at Highgrove. Lesser mortals received gifts. The prince dispensed presents, graded by his opinion of their importance, to paid and unpaid employees: whisky glasses engraved with his motif, or designer salt and pepper grinders. A typed letter signed by

Charles was welcome, but the greatest trophy was a handwritten message in black ink. The universal fear was his expression of displeasure, signalled by the absence of a 'please' or 'thank you'. Finely calibrated blanking – like a Mafia don's kiss of death – was an overt threat to the courtier's job, income, school fees and self-respect. After dismissal, there was nothing. Being cut off without even a much-prized Christmas card to acknowledge the relationship was 'so hurtful', repeated all the casualties. Charles had made himself clear that they were no longer useful. Loyalty was always a one-way street.

Preferring to live at Highgrove to enjoy his garden and to be near Camilla, Charles summoned people to drive the two hours from London for even the briefest meeting, and would regularly keep them waiting. Yet few refused. The outstanding garden, more than thirty-five years in the making, had been designed by a succession of experts. Molly Salisbury, Rosemary Verey, Miriam Rothschild, Julian and Isabel Bannerman, one after another, were enlisted to fill the landscape with trees, hedges, wildflowers, fountains, rare breeds of farm animals and architectural features, all blended into a romantic safe haven. In return, the heir to the throne offered conditional gratitude. Professional gardeners were divided about the extent of Charles's own contribution.

Roy Strong was summoned to advise on the cultivation of hedges. He spent days with his own gardener perfecting his ideas. At the end, he submitted his employee's bill for £1,000 – and was never asked to return, or even thanked. Strong had personally inscribed a copy of his book on gardening to Charles, but it was left in a waiting room rather than included in the prince's library. 'He's shocked by the sight of an invoice,' Strong noted. 'So he likes people who don't charge for their services.' Inevitably, none of those advisers was individually thanked after Charles received the Victoria Medal of Honour from the Royal Horticultural Society, presented by the queen for his services to gardening, in 2009.

'Grace and favour' took on a new meaning. To make up a floragim (a book of paintings of Highgrove's flowers), Charles recruited over twenty artists to paint two or three flowers each, for free. Similarly, he approached Jonathan Heale, a woodcut artist, for some of his work, which he expected to be donated as a gift. One of the few artists known to have rebuffed similar demands was Lucian

Freud. Would Freud swap one of his oils – which sold for millions of pounds – for one of Charles's watercolours? 'I don't want one of your rotten paintings,' Freud replied.

Strong, despite the rebuffs, narrated a BBC TV documentary about Highgrove. He intended to report that Charles had followed fashion by asking Molly Salisbury to build a 'potager' – a vegetable garden, but his draft commentary was returned from Charles's office with the rebuke, 'His Royal Highness never follows fashion.' Strong removed the comment. Charles, clearly, stood 'above fashion and is always right'. Thereafter, Strong stepped back: 'I stayed on the edge with Charles. It was less dangerous.'

In the same spirit, in 1998 Charles called Tim Bell, Margaret Thatcher's media adviser, to ask whether he could borrow Elizabeth Buchanan, employed by Bell to develop relationships with Conservative politicians and bankers, for three days a week. 'You can't turn down a royal summons,' said Bell, knowing that Charles would not pay Buchanan's salary. Buchanan went to work at the royal home.

Charles had chosen an utterly devoted woman. 'Elizabeth curt-sied lower than anyone thought possible,' one household member noticed, 'and then for longer than necessary. She worked all the hours God gave and then some God hadn't thought about.' Dubbed 'the virgin queen' by her fellow staff, she understood the ritual, the pattern and the access Charles expected. He would sit for hours, and sometimes for a whole day, dressed in eccentric clothes in an armour stone garden surrounded by trees and wildflowers, while Buchanan, 'blinded by devotion', pandered to his requirements. On occasions when Charles, in the midst of a meal, took exception to the conversation – especially criticism of his opinions – and stormed out, she was summoned by Michael Fawcett to smooth things over with the guests and to placate the prince. When Charles, near the end of a seemingly pleasant dinner, abruptly headed to his study to spend hours handwriting letters late into the night, it was Buchanan who made excuses to his guests. Tim Bell was unsurprised when she became a full-time employee. Her salary did not reflect her new position as an assistant private secretary, but the media man quietly bridged the gap.

5

Mutiny and Machiavellism

In mid-1998, Mark Bolland and Fiona Shackleton were lunching at the Ivy restaurant off St Martin's Lane when both their mobile phones rang. The Highgrove switchboard connected the prince. 'I've got a terrible problem,' said Charles. 'I've had a delegation of the staff led by Bernie and Tony and they say that everyone will resign unless Michael Fawcett goes.'

The mutiny among Charles's staff at Highgrove had been brewing for weeks. Fawcett had been imposing unreasonable demands, especially on five of the staff serving under him: a valet, two sub-valets, an equerry's assistant and a chauffeur. The result was a revolt by a group of people noted for exaggerating the smallest inconveniences out of all proportion. However, on this occasion Fawcett's behaviour would seem to have been insufferable. Fearful of losing all his employees, Charles had instantly surrendered to the delegation and agreed that Fawcett should resign, despite his seventeen years' service. Then, immediately regretting his decision, he had telephoned Bolland and Shackleton. Both were joyful at the news. Later that afternoon, on Stephen Lamport's orders, Bolland drove to Highgrove. 'Make sure he's fired,' were Lamport's parting words. In unison, the prince's closest advisers 'went into overdrive to make sure Fawcett left before Charles changed his mind'. The thirty-five-year-old, they agreed, was a hated bully. Regardless of Fawcett's usefulness, no one could understand why Charles had chosen to live alongside such a seemingly unpleasant man.

Bolland entered the prince's study to be 'greeted by the sight of Charles and Fawcett crying together'. Amid their tears, Charles told Fawcett that he would have to go, but that provision would be made for him to continue working for him privately. An announcement was made that Fawcett's departure was 'entirely amicable'.

Commentators, misled by spokesmen, mistakenly reported that Fawcett was the casualty of a 'war' within St James's Palace between the old guard and the modernisers.

The backlash began soon after. Led by Patty Palmer-Tomkinson, Charles's friends urged him to recall Fawcett.

'Poor Michael,' said Palmer-Tomkinson.

'It's not my fault,' replied Charles. 'They made me do it.'

The following Friday, Charles and Camilla were invited to Chatsworth by Debo, the Duchess of Devonshire. Debo, at seventy-eight the youngest of the Mitford sisters, was a favourite of Charles. Amusing and resourceful, she was independent-minded and the most practical of duchesses, having rescued the family estate at Chatsworth with her marketing zeal. During his marriage to Diana, Charles and Camilla had often been welcomed by Debo to stay while they discreetly hunted with the Meynell in Derbyshire. Less discreetly, she revealed to a confidential source that Charles and Camilla slept in the same bed on these visits, and that Charles was submissive to Camilla. 'That's why the relationship works,' she had said, smiling, hinting at a deeper meaning to Charles's expressions of adoration in the Camillagate tape.

The next day, while Charles and Camilla were out hunting, Debo summoned Bolland and Lamport to drive up immediately from London. Within minutes of their arrival, she reprimanded them: 'You're making Charles unhappy about Fawcett. This must stop.' Charles, it became obvious, had been easily persuaded by his hostess that Fawcett was too important to lose, especially as Camilla remained so indebted to him.

During the months after her separation from her husband, Camilla had lived in comparative impoverishment. Receiving £20,000 a year in alimony, she could barely afford to run her Wiltshire home. Without Fawcett's help, Debo reminded Bolland and Lamport, Camilla's life would have been 'seriously unpleasant'. Thanks to him, food had been sent from Highgrove, her laundry was returned pristine, and Andy Crichton, a former police protection officer, had been made available to act as her driver. Moreover, Fawcett was a great survivor. Ten years earlier, John Riddell had arranged his dismissal, only to discover that Charles had reneged on their agreement. The same would happen now. Fawcett, Debo made clear, was non-negotiable. As one of Charles's senior staff was to observe, 'The man who puts the death mask on the king will be Fawcett.' However, neither man was persuaded to reverse his dismissal.

On their return from hunting, Charles and Camilla were frosty towards the two private secretaries, whom they inexplicably blamed for Fawcett's plight. One solution, they nevertheless speculated, would be for him to be employed by Robert Kime, the prince's favourite interior decorator. Kime was invited to Highgrove for dinner the following Saturday.

Around the table a week later sat Charles, Kime, Lamport and Bolland. Kime advised that Fawcett be employed as a private contractor, as Charles had suggested originally, but after listening to Bolland and Lamport discuss the valet's fate, Charles expressed his fears. For the past week he had lived through the horror of life without Fawcett. No doubt the valet had crossed the line by bullying the staff, but he was more important than any friend. He also posed an enduring threat, as at any time he could succumb to the temptation to sell his story to the media.

Kime was concluding that Fawcett was not going anywhere when there was a commotion. Arriving late, Camilla had entered Highgrove through the kitchen, where several employees were milling about. Dressed as the woman in charge rather than in her usual country clothes, she told them, 'I hear you're being beastly to Michael and I'm angry with all of you.' Her direct language, Roy Strong later said, brought 'the common touch to the household which Charles lacked'. After extracting grovelling apologies, she headed for the dining room, where Kime was pleading Fawcett's case. Finally, at 2 a.m., it was agreed that he would stay, and that some of the members of staff who had complained about his bullying would be fired.

During the previous week, Camilla's assistant Amanda McManus had shifted her attitude. On Monday she had told Robert Higdon, 'I hate Michael. He's not honest and he's a liar. He should go,' but by Thursday she was willing 'to go through hell to help Camilla on Fawcett's behalf'. Survival, she evidently realised, depended upon unquestioning sycophancy.

The crisis had been a failure of management. Unlike conventional executives, Lamport could not tell Charles to his face that his loyalty to Fawcett was unwise. Such outspokenness would guarantee his dismissal. Quietly, he implemented the royal wishes. Fawcett's authority was restored, and indeed magnified. Outsiders seeking an appointment with Charles increasingly approached Fawcett in the hope that he would deign to be helpful.

The contrast between Charles's management of his personal kingdom and his mother's concern for the realm was captured soon afterwards at a meeting of the Way Ahead Group in Buckingham Palace's cinema.

As he stood chatting with Simon Lewis, Lord Camoys and Michael Peat, Robin Janvrin felt particularly proud of his creation of the group back in 1993. The four officials who had taken over the queen's private office presented themselves as the new generation. In the past, Richard Aylard had simply kept the show on the road, while Robert Fellowes had been the firefighter. Now Janvrin, jokingly dubbed 'the angry young man' by David Airlie, stood before the royals under a metaphorical banner that read 'We must have change.' In his opinion, his opponents offered the 'doctrine of unripe time'. Gathering the key members of the royal family together, he suggested, could resolve their differences, and would help them plan the monarchy's response to the tabloids' intention to scratch open the raw scars once again as the first anniversary of Diana's death approached.

The queen, Philip and their four children arrived, kissing each other warmly without betraying any tensions. Despite their rivalries, the family ostensibly remained friends. Janvrin's tripwire was Charles. The heir's natural stubbornness, he hoped, would melt away in the face of his unemotional presentation of the advantages of reform.

In anticipation of the meeting, Lewis had sent the queen a report based on a Mori opinion poll. Commissioned by Janvrin, it had been opposed by Michael Peat as a waste of money. Its conclusions were the basis of Lewis's one-hour presentation, complete with slideshow.

The six royals understood the sharp difference between the public's attitude towards the monarchy and towards other British institutions. Each of the four nations and each age group had differing attitudes towards the family. To rebuild its popularity, Lewis advised, over the coming months they should take up a dual focus: on Scotland, and on forging a relationship with Britain's youth.

The queen agreed. Janvrin proposed to lighten the tone of her official tours. Meetings with the uniformed county lord lieutenants would be reduced, and instead she would visit schools, a pub, take a ride in a London taxi, sign a Manchester United football, walk past a McDonald's and meet some of the homeless and unemployed. The queen agreed again. To placate Anne's anger that Charles was occupying too much of the spotlight, Janvrin proposed that the princess should be given special status in Scotland. The queen's continuing approval encouraged the Blairite modernisers.

The next item was the Jubilee, four years in the future. 'What will we do?' asked Philip, starting a family discussion. The unity crumbled. Charles wanted to reduce the numbers of the family appearing on the Buckingham Palace balcony and the number of teenage royals entitled to police protection. His particular targets were Andrew's two daughters, Beatrice and Eugenie. Then he mentioned in a critical tone the commercial activities of his two brothers. 'Enough has been done,' interrupted Philip. He urged the queen to protect tradition. Amid that discord, the meeting ended.

Nervous that the Mori poll's findings would provide negative headlines, Janvrin forbade Lamport to show the results to Bolland. Regardless, Charles ensured that some critical figures were leaked to the *Sunday Times*, partly because he disliked the idea of the Way Ahead Group and the meetings, and partly because he wanted to assert his primacy over his siblings. 'I'm the Prince of Wales and they're not,' he said. To reassert his status still further, he opposed Janvrin's plan to improve cooperation between himself and his mother by merging the two palaces' press offices and appointing Lewis at their head. He ridiculed the idea of a New Labour spin master overseeing 'The New Monarchy' and prying into his plans, not least because he was becoming disenchanted with the government.

That disenchantment would soon become public knowledge. In June 1998, Charles declared war on Labour's support for genetically modified crops. In an interview with the *Daily Telegraph*, he warned that scientists were straying into 'realms that belong to God, and God alone', and questioned whether man had the right to 'experiment with and commercialise the building blocks of life'. Genetic food engineering to produce long-life tomatoes, pest-resistant crops and soya beans with added protein would, he asserted, create a man-made disaster and deprive the public of organic foods.

Consumers should consider the profits made by the manufacturers of the pesticide DDT and asbestos – both once hailed as scientific wonders but eventually proven to have potentially fatal side-effects – as an omen for GM crops.

Forewarned about the prince's attack, Blair told Alastair Campbell, 'We're going to have running troubles with Charles because on many issues he's more traditional than the queen.' In the hope of securing an armistice, the two drove to Highgrove in the September sunshine. By then, Blair's acerbic spokesman had become hostile towards Charles. The begrudging agreement by Highgrove's staff that Campbell could use the swimming pool – which he found 'a bit manky and with too many leaves floating around' – did little to improve his temper. The visit, he declared, was 'a journey back so far back in time it felt extra-planetary'.

After his swim, Campbell was offered lunch in the staff canteen. Inside the house, Blair was sharing a meal with his host, who for over fifteen years had championed a number of unfashionable causes, a category which until recently had included environmental protection. Ignoring Tory ministers' mockery, he had warned about the failure to combat acid rain, protested against farmers burning straw, demanded a ban on CFC gases to protect the ozone layer, forecast 'the problems and dangers of possibly catastrophic climate changes through air pollution', warned about plastic bags and bottles polluting the seas, and lamented the mass extinction of species as a result of the loss of tropical forests. All his campaigns, Charles believed, had been dismissed by lethargic politicians and ignorant officials. Almost without exception, they had ignored the threats to mankind. The latest of that breed, he suspected, was Tony Blair.

Dealing with the royal family was difficult for any politician. To have a direct conversation with someone with unusual preoccupations was inevitably uphill, but a dialogue with Charles was especially perilous. The various self-deprecating cartoons of the prince in the guest lavatory did not signal democracy in the household, but rather the owner's vanity. Blair understandably wanted to know in advance where any discussion would end. There was no answer. His caution proved justified when four weeks later a newspaper published an account of their meeting. Blaming the 'national disgrace' of using unproven technology for ruining farmers in 'an arms race against Nature', Charles publicly urged Britons to boycott

GM crops – or, as environmental campaigners described them, 'Frankenstein foods'.

The indiscretion surprised Blair. Not only did Charles explicitly oppose government policy, but, as Mark Bolland witnessed, 'he didn't care' about a public disagreement. Far from upholding traditional royal impartiality, Charles thought only about his 'duty', discounted the government's problems and ignored the danger of his overt prejudice. Blair asked Peter Mandelson to caution the prince, and in a telephone call from New York, Mandelson, who believed that Charles's views 'were anti-scientific and irresponsible in the light of food shortages in the developing world', told the prince that his remarks were 'unhelpful'. He congratulated himself that his royal hearer did 'tone down his public interventions on the subject', but his success was temporary.

Charles now switched his attention to Camilla. The discretion about their relationship, he decided, had to end. Camilla wanted to be seen with Charles at the theatre, go on holiday with him openly, and establish a bond with his sons; but a relationship akin to marriage could be considered only after the public had accepted her. Her principal opponents remained the queen and the queen mother. Neither would allow her to be in the same room with them, yet both welcomed her ex-husband to receptions, race meetings and house parties. To show their affection for him, a palace official had lobbied that he should be promoted from colonel to brigadier, and appointed director of the Royal Army Veterinary Corps. Both suggestions were approved. In protest, the army's senior vet resigned, a rare exception to the universal enchantment with the new brigadier.

Charles could not understand the queen's sympathy for Diana and her antagonism towards Camilla. After all, Diana's theatrics in the media had damaged the family, while Camilla had remained utterly discreet. Why, he asked, could his mother not approve of a traditional Englishwoman who loved the countryside and horses? Camilla's case had been raised by the Earl of Carnarvon, the queen's racehorse trainer and close friend. His efforts as a go-between having proved unsuccessful, he switched to the queen's side. Princess Margaret had also tried on Charles's behalf, but her sister had replied that she wanted neither to meet nor to talk about Camilla. Few understood the reason for her disapproval: the queen was nervous that the character exposed in the Camillagate tapes was that of a shrewd mistress. 'Oh darling, I love you,' Camilla had gushed. The much less savvy Diana never made such over-the-top declarations. Carried away by a gust of tenderness towards himself, Charles complained that neither Diana nor his mother ever sympathised with his needs.

Exasperated by what he termed an intolerable situation, and egged on by Princess Margaret, he approached his mother late one night while he was staying at Balmoral and asked that she soften her antagonism so he could live openly with Camilla. He assumed that the queen, who rarely interfered or directly forbade anything, even the Dimbleby project, would not object.

But on that evening she had had several Martinis, and to Charles's surprise she replied forcefully: she would not condone his adultery, nor forgive Camilla for not leaving Charles alone to allow his marriage to recover. She vented her anger that he had lied about his relationship with what she called 'that wicked woman', and added, 'I want nothing to do with her.' Met with a further hostile silence, Charles fled the room. In his fragile state, her phrase – 'that wicked woman' – was unforgettable. Tearfully, he telephoned Camilla. She in turn sought consolation from Bolland, who later received a call from Charles with a verbatim report of his conversation with his mother. Shortly after the confrontation, an opinion poll found that 88 per cent of Britons opposed their marriage.

Not everything was bad news. Good fortune had pushed disagreeable characters to one side. 'Kanga' Tryon, Charles's Australian former girlfriend, had died suddenly after a period of declining health, so removing one potential source of mischief; and Charles Spencer, Diana's brother and an outspoken critic of Charles, had damaged his own reputation with an acrimonious divorce.

With two irritants removed, Charles decided to defy the queen and take a small but critical step towards Camilla's acceptance. On 12 June 1998 he introduced Camilla to William at St James's Palace. On the eve of his sixteenth birthday, his son assumed that the twenty-minute meeting would remain private, but in what turned out to be a genuine mistake Camilla's assistant leaked it. In the tabloid storm that followed, Camilla found herself implicated in Diana's death. To fight back, she and Bolland arranged that Stuart Higgins, a former editor of the *Sun*, would write a flattering article in the *Sunday Times*. At the recent Way Ahead Group meeting, Higgins wrote, the royal family had agreed as a priority to normalise Camilla's position in the royal household. That was inaccurate: she had not even been mentioned during that summer's meeting. But the distortion, approved by Charles, chimed with his campaign during the weeks before his fiftieth birthday. In Downing Street no one was fooled. Alex Allan, the prime minister's private secretary, had written about the obstacles that faced Charles and Camilla, and concluded that nuptials were unlikely.

Disregarding the resentment towards them, Charles, Camilla and Bolland met at Highgrove to construct another campaign. The first hurdle was to demythologise Diana by radically changing her image and portraying her as a manipulative hysteric. The vehicle was to be Penny Junor's book. The author's plan had changed since Diana's death. Instead of focusing on Camilla, Junor intended to shatter the image of the late Princess of Wales as the put-upon innocent and to cast Charles as a helpless victim, with neither parents nor friends to provide support. The publication of *Charles: Victim or Villain?* was timed to coincide with his birthday in November. Enriched by dramatic disclosures, the book described Diana as 'sick, irrational, unreasonable and miserable' on account of her bulimia, and therefore an unbalanced and unfaithful woman who compelled Charles to return to his true love. '[Charles] had to put up with years of tantrums and abuse,' wrote Junor. He 'cut his friends out of his life at Diana's insistence, and even gave away the dog he loved in an effort to make Diana happy'.

Junor questioned Diana's sanity by quoting a diagnosis of borderline personality disorder, arrived at by scouring the internet, for an explanation of her behaviour. Charles supported the diagnosis: 'We must get this out,' he said. In a further attempt to damage Diana's reputation, Junor wrote that the princess had been the first to commit adultery. In a series of revelations, the book described Diana bombarding Oliver Hoare, a married art dealer with whom she was having an affair, with anonymous telephone calls. Diana had denied the relationship, even though it had lasted some months, but accurately blamed a mischievous schoolboy for the nuisance calls. The book also unmasked her affair in 1986 with Barry Mannakee, one of her police protection officers, as well as confirming her long *amour fou* with James Hewitt.

Junor's book shocked Diana's loyalists, who were outraged by the complicity of Charles's staff. Throughout his life, Charles had never been able to give and take. Thinking only about himself, he resented suggestions of equality with his wife. Diana's supporters recalled his jealousy of her popularity during their first visit to Australia in 1983. Junor, they noted, had omitted from her book the argument between Charles and Diana on their plane after it landed at Alice Springs about who should go down the steps first (Charles won). Later that day, the roaring welcome that the children in the crowds gave to Diana had infuriated the prince. 'I should have had two wives and just walked in the middle,' he said grumpily to an aide.

At first, Diana had not grasped her husband's feelings of resentment, and when she did, she fuelled them. At a music college during their second visit to Australia in 1988, Charles scraped a bow over a cello, whereupon Diana glided across to a piano to play perfectly a favourite piece by Grieg. To the media's bemusement, Charles looked crestfallen. She had stolen his show. While she glowed as the global icon, he was the middle-aged man typically photographed on a Scottish estate, dressed in tweeds, resting against a shepherd's crook.

To combat that image, Junor described incidents that appeared to be fuelled by Charles's desire for revenge. The book mentioned the speculation about Diana's death threats to Camilla in telephone calls, and her attempted suicide while pregnant with William. However, she omitted any description of Diana's misery during her honeymoon on *Britannia* after she heard Charles talking on the phone with Camilla, conversations also overheard by the ship's crew. Nor was there any mention of Diana's acts of vindictiveness: that Charles had entered their suite on the yacht to find her in tears cutting up a watercolour he had just completed (a version of that episode would be included in Junor's admiring biography of Camilla in 2017). The book had only minimal sympathy for the neglected twenty-year-old bride. Undoubtedly, Diana had fabricated and exaggerated Charles's drift towards adultery, but equally Junor did not reveal the complete truth about his relations with Camilla. In 1973, while waiting for Andrew Parker Bowles's proposal, Camilla had many admirers but only two other serious boyfriends. Andrew, she knew, was not passionately in love with her, but he was charming, good-looking and well-connected. As a close friend would say, he was a thirty-three-year-old officer who needed to marry. Camilla was the best of the bunch as a potential wife, fun and good with people, yet he expected his bachelor life to go on as before.

One week before their wedding, Charles had telephoned Camilla from his Royal Navy ship. Sounding desperately lonely, he asked whether she was sure about marrying, but did not propose himself. After ending the call, Camilla immediately repeated the conversation to her fiancé. They both laughed, knowing that Charles felt isolated and depressed as a result of his sister Anne's marriage to Mark Phillips.

In hindsight, even Andrew Parker Bowles would realise that he could never have been loyal to Camilla. Despite his Catholicism and his intention to be a good husband, he started his adulteries earlier than he had anticipated. Not long after their wedding, Camilla discovered her husband's affairs. She was upset but resigned. Her feelings for Charles changed only after Andrew abandoned her during long foreign trips. Even then, she was not genuinely in love with Charles. Many friends were convinced that she continued to love Andrew, but was flattered by the prince's attentions.

The much-trumpeted newspaper serialisation of Junor's book was accompanied by a statement from Charles's office that he had 'not authorized, solicited or approved' it. Junor would confidently contradict that assertion, and offered details of the help she had received, with Charles's authority, from his staff.

For his part, Mark Bolland denied providing any material critical of Diana, but Robin Janvrin did not believe him. In his opinion, Bolland's fingerprints were all over the book, which marked a sharp escalation of the campaign to make Charles's relationship with Camilla acceptable to the British public. As another Buckingham Palace official sniped, Charles reigned over 'an old-fashioned court filled with a sack-full of snakes'. In the midst of the Junor headlines, ITV reported that Charles would be 'privately delighted' if the queen abdicated. Shortly after, following an unrecorded hour-long conversation with the prince, Gavin Hewitt reported on the BBC that Charles was frustrated by Buckingham Palace's withholding of power. Janvrin was incandescent. Not only were the tabloids using Junor's book to reignite stories about Charles's adultery, but simultaneously his birthday party at Highgrove for 350 people was spawning headlines about the queen's 'snub' – her rejection of his invitation because of Camilla's presence. Further to enhance his client's reputation, Bolland circulated a comment from Mario Testino, Diana's favourite photographer, who when asked whether Camilla should be queen, replied, 'Definitely. Have you met her? She's a great person. If you meet her, you want to hang out with her.'

In Janvrin's opinion, Bolland's operation was out of control. Charles contacted his mother from Bulgaria to protest his innocence about the abdication report. His denial was suspicious to those around the queen who knew of his impatience to be king, while Bolland's declaration of innocence was discounted. The tabloid headline-writers were ecstatic.

Janvrin's anger reflected the queen's bewilderment. The monarchy, her advisers believed, did not need spin like Downing Street. During a visit to St James's Palace, Janvrin told Stephen Lamport that there was no reason for Charles to campaign so energetically to promote Camilla. Bolland was acting as a free agent rather than as part of the team, and by standing between the tabloids and the royals he risked getting 'run over' for his misjudgement.

Lamport could have honestly pleaded ignorance. He was unable to manage Bolland, who with the two principal plotters excluded him from their discussions. To keep face, he volunteered that, whenever relevant, Janvrin would be kept informed about Charles's plans, and that his opinion would be taken into account. He added that Bolland might not be a desirable presence, but he was effective, and said that Charles would like to introduce Janvrin to Camilla, who by chance was in the building. 'Certainly not,' replied Janvrin – any meeting would need the queen's permission. With that, he walked out of the palace. Charles was furious.

In an effort to calm the storm, David Airlie took Bolland for lunch at White's, his club in St James's. The older man counselled that things were done in a certain way, and that Her Majesty would be grateful if he could stick to the rules. In his defence, Bolland contended that Stuart Higgins, acting as an adviser to ITV, had distorted a conversation between them. 'Stuart screwed me up,' he said, and refused to speak to the former journalist again. 'But it was a tricky week,' he admitted.

Reports of the lunch at White's reached Camilla. She feared that her agent was 'moving to the dark side' and taking orders from Buckingham Palace. Bolland rushed to reassure her, and in turn

Charles, who on reflection decided there was no alternative but to treat Janvrin as an ally. Bolland was dispatched to tell the courtier about a weekend party Charles was hosting at Sandringham. Among the guests would be Jacob Rothschild, Peter Mandelson and Susan Hussey, a trusted friend and lady-in-waiting to the queen. Under pressure from Camilla, Charles agreed that she should also be invited. The tabloids would undoubtedly highlight her presence in the queen's home despite the monarch's disapproval. To Bolland's relief, instead of protesting, Janvrin consulted the queen, who agreed that as it was a private party, she did not need to be involved.

Janvrin also averted another argument, this time about Michael Fawcett. Charles had insisted that Fawcett supervise the preparations for his official birthday party at Buckingham Palace. The queen, who still disliked Fawcett, objected, but Janvrin persuaded her that he 'must be kept onside' because of his importance to Charles.

Shortly after this, the plotters delivered their coup: a major birthday party for Charles, this time at Highgrove, with Camilla on public display. She was duly photographed arriving at the party looking regal, having prepared herself for the event with a week's cruise on Yiannis Latsis's yacht in the Aegean. Charles presented himself as a man who had found peace with the woman he loved. The event was arranged by Emilie van Cutsem, a socially ambitious Dutchwoman, the wife of an old friend of Charles from his Cambridge days. Having cared for William and Harry during the worst years of the prince's marriage, she was distrusted by Camilla, but that undercurrent went unnoticed during the riotous celebration. However, what was not so easy to overlook were the absentees: of the royal family only Princess Margaret turned up. None of Charles's three siblings accepted his invitation.

His close friends were divided. Some supported him for 'pushing at the right pace'. Others, mindful of their relations with the queen and fearful of losing invitations to Sandringham and Balmoral, spoke loudly about the advantage of caution. This group included Nicholas Soames; Emilie van Cutsem's husband Hugh; Charles Lansdowne, owner of Bowood House in Wiltshire near Ray Mill, Camilla's home; Piers von Westenholz, an antique dealer; and Charles and Patty Palmer-Tomkinson. One malicious critic told of Patty's panic during a motorway journey. Charles had telephoned to say he was unsure whether he could be present at her daughter Santa's wedding. Patty pleaded, and finally Charles and Camilla agreed to come, but arrived separately. In the background hovered Annabel Elliot, Camilla's sister. The Elliots protected Camilla from Soames and the Palmer-Tomkinsons. Their vigilance, sniped some, stemmed from their fear of losing influence. Everyone seemed to have mixed motives, but few forgot Diana's carping about the 'brown-nosers' around Charles, whom she called 'oilers'.

Two nights later there was yet another birthday party, this time at Hampton Court. Camilla was there too. Early the next morning, Charles left for Sheffield to meet a group of disadvantaged young people. Such visits not only placated his critics but also reflected his genuine interest in the young. The following evening, nearly a thousand guests, including Margaret Thatcher and Tony Blair, arrived for Charles's official birthday party at Buckingham Palace. Camilla was not among them.

'Everyone here,' said the queen, turning to her son during her speech, 'has benefited from the breadth of your interests and from your vision, compassion and leadership.' Listening alongside Blair was Peter Mandelson. Both must have appreciated Charles's political talent in his endearing reply to 'Mummy', concealing his true feelings about the absence of his mistress.

Six weeks later Mandelson, newly appointed as minister for trade and industry, was forced to resign after failing to reveal a loan from Geoffrey Robinson, a Treasury minister, to help buy his house while Robinson was under formal investigation by his own department. As Mandelson sat tearfully in his ministerial office listening on the telephone to Blair's fatal reprimand, Alastair Campbell, who was in the room with him, noticed a Christmas card from Charles occupying pride of place on his desk. Campbell dismissed the prince as an interfering, privileged fool, but Mandelson defended him, grateful for Bolland's reassurance that his relationship with Charles would be unaffected by the scandal. Charles could not afford to cast aside a valuable if tainted supporter just as he was heading for another showdown with the media.

Thanks to Bolland's introductions, the prince had established personal relations with several newspaper editors. After receiving invitations to the birthday party at Hampton Court, they published positive articles to 'build him up' and prove that the Camilla campaign had not been harmed by the queen's boycott. Just two days after the party, several papers published photographs of Camilla on horseback, with her approval.

The next task was to begin repairing the damage caused by Penny Junor's wholesale damnation of Diana, an assault Charles half-regretted. Although Junor had written that he remained in love with Diana and prayed for her every night, his denial of any involvement with the book had not convinced anyone. In mitigation, he pleaded that his reputation would be restored by the publication of his personal documents long after his death. When that did little to silence the criticism, he was persuaded to release copies of his handwritten letters to 'a close relative' to the *Daily Mirror*. Apparently composed during their fractious journey around Australia in 1983, the letters professed his love for Diana. He especially admired 'her wonderful way of dealing with people. Her quick wit stands her in excellent stead, particularly when silly people ask what she has done with William or why hasn't she brought him etc.' He went on, 'Diana has done wonderfully throughout this gruelling exercise and has won everyone's heart – including some of the most hard-bitten Aussie "knockers".' He added, 'I do sometimes worry so much about what I have landed her in at such an impressionable age. The intensity of interest must be terrifying for her.'

In another letter, written a year later, when the couple's marriage was already under severe strain, Diana had confessed to the same 'relative': 'I can't stand being away from him.' She wrote that Charles's early return from a fishing trip was a 'wonderful surprise', and in yet another letter described a 'marvellous' time at Balmoral. Since that contradicted the recollection of her friends, who recalled her permanent misery in Scotland, some suspected that an unseen hand had fabricated all the letters as a way to promote Charles.

On the following day the *Mirror* published more excerpts from letters apparently written to the same 'close relative' by Charles in 1988 and 1989, three years after the marriage's collapse. The prince admitted to depression and insecurity because his public work had little impact and his arguments were ignored. 'Sometimes I am terrified by the expectations people have of me and of the immense responsibility thrust on me,' he confided. 'I sometimes feel that I am going to let people down, however hard I try … I sometimes wonder why we rush about so much or why I, in particular, feel I have to solve all the nation's problems single-handed? It must be a basic weakness of character which advancing age may cure!' That was Charles's genuine voice. The doubts about the authenticity of the early letters arose only after Mark Bolland confessed honest ignorance about the identity of the 'close relative' who released them to James Whitaker, the *Mirror*'s royal correspondent. Whitaker, loyal to Charles, added a flourish about the lonely prince's virtues: 'Listening to Charles talking about his lack of self-esteem, one could easily cry for him … The important thing to understand about this tortured, complex man is that he does feel he has the cares of the world on his shoulders. He tries so hard to deliver, to do his duty as he thinks is right.'

The letters' publication gave Charles confidence to use the media more aggressively. 'Let's risk the biscuit,' he told Bolland after several newspapers published photographs of his visit with Camilla to a London theatre. The positive comments encouraged him once again to confront his mother over their relationship, only this time in public.

In the weeks after his birthday, they had not spoken. The atmosphere at Sandringham over Christmas must have been frosty. Now he wanted to stage a spectacular event to establish Camilla as his permanent partner. He needed a photograph that was neither snatched nor contrived. The ideal moment would occur on 29 January 1999, seventeen months after Diana's death, when Annabel Elliot celebrated her fiftieth birthday at the Ritz hotel in Piccadilly.

'The prince must come,' she wailed. 'It would be terrible if he didn't.'

'Let's lance the boil,' agreed Bolland, arguing that snatched photographs by the paparazzi were poor-quality and rewarded only the photographer. In what Bolland regarded as Charles's 'cunning and tough' directives, it was agreed to transform the couple's exit from the hotel into a historic milestone.

A tip to a *Daily Mail* diarist revealed Charles's ruse. 'Will they arrive or leave together?' the diarist was prompted to ask in his column. Bolland then telephoned Arthur Edwards, the *Sun*'s royal photographer, to draw attention to the item. From there, reaction snowballed. The first of over two hundred photographers and TV crews staked out their positions opposite the Ritz three days before the event. They were allowed to block the pavement and the street to record a romance that according to legend had started twenty-seven years earlier. The royal command overrode any official opposition from the police or Westminster council. On the night, anxious newspaper editors delayed printing their main editions while journalists called Bolland – dining with the editor of the *Sunday Times* in a City restaurant – for reassurance that the 'historic' appearance would indeed happen.

Just before midnight, Charles and Camilla stepped from the hotel's entrance amid a thunderclap of flashing lights, and posed briefly before getting into a car. Dressed in a sombre suit, the prince looked serious while Camilla appeared radiant. The results exceeded Charles's expectations. Across the world, the photographs were interpreted even more positively than he had planned. 'At Last' blared the *Mirror*. 'Meet the Mistress' was the *Sun*'s less fawning headline. There was unanimity about the fallacy of previous predictions. Over the past decade, so many clever people had forecast that the next stage would never happen: first, few believed that Charles and Diana would separate, then that they would divorce. Next, they discounted an enduring public relationship between Charles and Camilla. Now, relying on Buckingham Palace's spokesman, the same soothsayers dismissed the idea of Charles marrying Camilla, and ridiculed the notion of Camilla eventually becoming queen. The queen remained silent, actively supported by the queen mother during their regular conversations. Charles was stubborn. He had pushed recognition one step further, but he did not underestimate the continuing obstacles before he could finally override his mother's wishes. The media would be his weapon.

That same media which for years he had cursed for being intrusive, and for cynically disbelieving his denials of adultery, had now become his ally. Rather than revile their misrepresentations, he encouraged Mark Bolland to welcome more editors to St James's Palace and to drip-feed stories: about Camilla wearing a brooch from him as a token of love; about the smiles towards the couple during further visits to the theatre; and, to please the *Sun*, a visit to the Soho gay pub that had been nail-bombed by a neo-Nazi fanatic.

Just before flying to New York in 1999 to promote Camilla, Bolland met the senior editors of Rupert Murdoch's tabloid newspapers at Wapping, News Corporation's London headquarters. Both the *Sun* and the *News of the World* continued to reflect their readers' love for Diana and their dislike of Charles and Camilla. Winning over working-class women – who made up many of the newspapers' readers – was a priority. Bolland's hosts were Les Hinton, the corporation's chief executive, and Rebekah Wade, an editorial director at the *Sun*. Both distrusted the royals' spokesmen. Too often their journalists had approached the palaces' media officials for a comment about a murky revelation only to be rebutted with an outright lie. All that, Bolland promised, would change. He would speak the truth, not least because he needed the Murdoch press's support against the queen. 'We were turning up the gas,' he would later say, 'because the queen was unmovable.'

Nine months after the New York trip, in early June 2000, Bolland returned to Wapping for lunch with Rebekah Wade, who by then had been introduced to Charles and Camilla. Using Wade as an ally posed no difficulty for Bolland, but the alliance led to a standoff between Wade and the normally unflappable Robin Janvrin, who was surprised when she asked, 'When is Her Majesty going to give the green light for Charles and Camilla to marry?'

'Public opinion is against it,' he replied.

'Well,' said Wade, 'we would have to go against the queen, because our readers are for Camilla. The queen should think again.' She added, 'We might move to support an abdication and let Charles take over.'

Days later, the headline on the *Sun*'s front page blared 'Marry Her, Sir'. Inside the same edition was a prominent report, with photographs of Charles, dressed in military uniform, taking the salute in France for seven hundred Dunkirk veterans on the sixtieth anniversary of their evacuation. 'This is very much the Dunkirk spirit,' he told them. That weekend was a victory for Charles, Camilla and Bolland; they were starting to dictate the agenda.

In Buckingham Palace, the normally even-handed Janvrin was shocked. The *Sun*'s threat to campaign against the queen was typical of the divisiveness masterminded by Bolland. Ever since he had been hired, the battle between the palaces had turned into a public brawl.

In June 1999, a poll had shown that 57 per cent of the British public supported a marriage between Charles and Camilla, up from 30 per cent two years earlier. More relaxed than previously, Charles now entered receptions looking confident – but also, Roy Strong observed, unfashionably 'Hanoverian' and often surrounded by courtiers chosen apparently because they were shorter than him. Tony Blair also noticed Charles's new self-confidence. Anji Hunter, his special assistant, was sent to ask Bolland if Charles was intent on marrying Camilla. Officially, Hunter was instructed not to interfere, but privately she told Blair about Charles's resolve.

To neutralise the Earl of Carnarvon's support for the queen's opposition to his remarriage, Charles recruited Angus Ogilvy, the brother-in-law of Lord Airlie, to negotiate on his behalf. Ogilvy was married to Princess Alexandra, a trusted cousin of the queen. Briefed by Charles, he relayed to the queen that her son would not compromise or surrender. This was not the rebellion of a petulant prince, but reflected a man unafraid, even delighted, to challenge authority.

6

Body and Soul

Charles wanted the monarchy to champion unfashionable causes. His most potent weapon to promote his status was his charities, about twenty organisations engaged in a diverse range of activities helping tens of thousands of people and many valuable causes every year. Charles had decided that only being forthright would guarantee an impact, and his charities gave him a powerful platform. Stoking controversy risked his being accused of breaking constitutional expectations of political impartiality, but the brave savoured risks. Ever since the Prince's Trust had been created in 1976, an initiative of pure altruism, financing his charities had become a preoccupation. However, Charles and his officials did not anticipate the financial problems that would accumulate.

Charles's insatiable appetite for money for his charities attracted Manuel Colonques, the founder of Porcelanosa, a Spanish tile manufacturer. Colonques had successfully promoted his company across the world by paying celebrities including Kevin Costner and George Clooney to endorse Porcelanosa's expanding empire. One by-product of his philosophy – 'The more you give, the more you receive' was his motto – was regular features in ¡Hola!, the Spanish Hello! magazine.

Always searching for new superstars, Pedro Pseudo, a Porcelanosa director, had hit on Charles in the mid-1990s. In his efforts to meet the prince he approached Chrysanthi Lemos, the wife of a Greek ship-owner and a fundraiser for the Philharmonia Orchestra in London. Lemos had no difficulty persuading Pseudo to give money to the orchestra; in return he would receive an invitation to its concert at Highgrove. Included among the audience were Luciano Pavarotti, Richard Branson, Donatella Versace and other celebrities. Lemos told Charles about Colonques's enthusiasm for Charles's charities, and after the concert Charles took the Spaniard and his party on a tour of his garden. 'After that meeting,' Lemos recalled, 'Fawcett took over. I wasn't needed any more.' With Fawcett as intermediary, Charles hosted a party in 1998 at St James's Palace to celebrate Porcelanosa's twenty-fifth anniversary, and another to thank the company for a donation to the Prince's Foundation. The pattern of selling access to himself funded Charles's principal achievement. But this success had also bred embarrassing controversies.

In 1976 Charles's office had telephoned the television journalist Jon Snow, interested in replicating Snow's small charity for disadvantaged youths. 'I want to make a difference,' the prince explained. Together they invented the name 'the Prince's Trust', with an initial fund of £7,471, Charles's pay-off from the Royal Navy. Thereafter, fundraising by Tom Shebbeare, the trust's chief executive, was uncomplicated. When Charles and Diana patronised a London pop concert, the charity received £1 million. With a minimum of red tape, the trust's administrators were empowered to write out cheques for disadvantaged young people, to finance travel for an interview, or set up a business, even to remove tattoos. As its funds increased, the Prince's Trust became noted for taking unusual risks. 'If I don't do it,' Charles said purposely, 'it won't exist.'

Encouraged by public acclaim, he next supported Stephen O'Brien, the founder of Business in the Community, a new charity for galvanising entrepreneurs to invest in deprived areas. 'What really worries me is that we're going to end up as a fourth-rate country,' Charles wrote in 1984. Business leaders were invited to meet him in city slums and support their renewal. 'I have no political agenda,' he wrote, describing his ambition to put the 'Great' back into Great Britain. Presenting himself as a social crusader determined to help Britons to live in a civilised environment, Charles sought the financial support of powerbrokers wherever he could find them.

By 1996, besides the Prince's Trust, Charles had created charities for education, the environment, architecture, complementary medicine, animals, the sick, the poor and rural communities. But he was careless about their governance. He gave the impression that the trustees of each charity – with its own niche focus, independent board, trustees and funds – acted free of his interference, since by law he was denied any role in their management. The reality was different. The Charity Commission complained that Charles was playing an unauthorised role in the running of the charities. The solution was to appoint new chairmen.

Finance presented a more pressing problem. Charles was an excellent fundraiser, and all the charities relied on him, competing for his appearances at receptions and dinners. Each charity chairman would assure each corporate chief executive that Charles would be present at a reception and would meet the charity's beneficiaries. Charles encouraged such promises without considering the impossibility of fulfilling all of them, or the folly of repeatedly targeting the same donors. 'He can pursue different projects simultaneously,' observed one adviser, 'but in parallel rather than together.'

Even after a donation and an event had been agreed, those making the plans would encounter 'the nightmare of Charles's bureaucracy', complained the long-serving director of one of the charities. His officials, either former civil servants or military officers, invoked his authority to block arrangements. 'They were always negative that he should not do things,' complained one charity executive, 'but they hadn't seen the real world, and got it wrong.'

In a pattern that repeated itself over the next twenty-five years, Charles's good intentions were often derailed. Because he spread himself so thinly, some of his charities failed to raise sufficient funds, while the Prince's Trust, which employed three hundred staff in a splendid Nash house opposite Regent's Park, spent an excessive amount on administration.

Unspoken at his charities' meetings was the fact that Charles's work had been tarnished by duplication. For example, in 1987 he had launched Inner City Aid, a self-help project founded in partnership with the architect Rod Hackney. On the same day he had also founded the Prince's Youth and Business Trust. Both charities targeted the same disadvantaged groups.

During those meetings, Charles would frequently say, 'I have always thought it would be a jolly good idea if we could do something to help …' Speaking in third-person messages rather than giving a clear directive, he watched as his audience – Shebbeare, his successive private secretaries, and Julia Cleverdon, an imaginative, energetic but occasionally chaotic campaigner renowned as a 'whirlwind of activity', recorded his wishes on A4 notepads. Sycophancy prevented anyone from challenging Charles to ask, 'I wonder, sir, if that's a good idea?' They knew how sensitive the prince was to confrontation. The rare contradiction would be followed by a communal sharp intake of breath, then stony silence. Palace etiquette forbade any hint of rebuke. Cleverdon would wave aside questions about shaky finances with cryptic advice such as that to Peter Davis, her deputy: 'Beware of tidy graveyards.'

Like Cleverdon, Shebbeare was both enthusiastic and deferential, but when faced with the necessity of giving unwelcome advice, he too preferred to stay silent. The most either would say was, 'Yes, sir, but …' before tailing off. Power did not want to hear the truth. 'It was difficult to say "No,"' Shebbeare admitted to a friend, 'because the automatic punishment was that he would find someone else to say "Yes."'

Persuading Charles to reverse a poor decision was best done by putting on an elaborate act. First, one had to be the last person to talk to him on a chosen subject, by remaining in the room after others had left. Then, graciously thanking His Royal Highness for the opportunity of a private moment, the adviser would preface his presentation with an offer to interpret His Royal Highness's wishes with a wholly unthreatening offer of help: 'Sir, might we just do the same by just a slightly different route?' Such manoeuvres protected Charles from many mistakes.

One of the casualties of this system was Jeremy White, a successful British businessman based in Los Angeles who had been recruited in 1993 to manage the Prince's Youth and Business Trust. Among the reasons he accepted the job was Charles's successful negotiation with David Young, one of Margaret Thatcher's favourite ministers, that the government would match all the money raised by Charles. With ample funds, the trust helped forty thousand young people to start micro-businesses. But this achievement, White discovered, was not admired by Shebbeare or Cleverdon. To impress the prince, both appeared to White to enjoy stamping on his fingers rather than cooperating to protect his success. The climax of the warfare arose in 1997, after the auction of a Lotus car, donated by the manufacturer, to help raise money for the trust. Lotus formally complained to Charles that White had failed to attend the event. 'I would have been there if Shebbeare had told me about it,' commented White, who immediately resigned and went on to earn his own fortune as a businessman. 'He was from the commercial world,' sniffed Shebbeare to an aide, 'and didn't get on with people.'

White's departure did not trouble Charles. He believed that his saviour was to be Tony Blair, the new prime minister, who decided that Labour's broad programme to help the disadvantaged was in synch with Charles's ambitions. This meant that Shebbeare could attract more funds from the government.

For Charles to carve out a unique position in British public life would require more than just leading a large grouping of charities. He felt impelled to be noticed, admired, and considered relevant. His targets were vested interests: architecture, education and medicine. Over the years he had crafted a singular philosophy about the world, and his place at its apex, to justify his rebellion against modern society. His charities would provide a platform and justification for his campaigns.

He started with medicine. Few professions were more entrenched. The first hint of his coming campaign had been his 1982 address to the annual conference of the British Medical Association. To celebrate his election as the BMA's new president, he used the invitation to criticise the profession's rejection of alternative or complementary therapies.

Ever since he had been introduced to homeopathy by his grandmother and by Laurens van der Post, Charles had preached the virtues of unconventional treatments. Taking mixtures of plants, herbs and minerals, he believed, stimulated the body's self-healing mechanism to treat serious illnesses. He also advocated acupuncture, chiropractic therapy and spine manipulation. Releasing the body's vital forces, blocked by misaligned vertebrae, he was certain, was a verified therapy. Consistent with his belief in the power of God acting through the Divine Spirit, he was convinced that a sick person's 'inner awareness' could enable them to 'will' their recovery 'in relation to the cosmos'. A patient confident about 'holism' should welcome the simultaneous treatment of their illness and their spirit. Charles dismissed any doubts by referring to van der Post's enthusiasm for the Swiss psychoanalyst Carl Jung, whose work on the 'collective unconscious', which unites mankind through a common vital force, advocated the power of such forms of healing.

Charles urged his audience at the conference to embrace alternative medicine, as 'practised by folk healers who are guided by traditional wisdom'. For a thirty-four-year-old with a mediocre degree in history to preach the power of spiritualism, based on a jumble of ideas inherited from van der Post, Jung and the sixteenth-century Swiss healer and alchemist Paracelsus, and then to denounce, to an audience of doctors, the science that produced the drugs that had eradicated polio and tuberculosis, was as frightening as it was brazen – especially to a profession that was still struggling to cure heart disease, cancer and other fatal conditions.

His audience's polite applause was welcome after the derision being heaped upon him every week for his eccentric beliefs in ITV's satirical *Spitting Image*, and he would later admit that he had expected to be misunderstood and criticised by his audience. But the doctors were tolerant. They listened patiently as he lamented that it was his fate to 'accept it is God's will that the unorthodox individual is doomed to years of frustration, ridicule and failure in order to act out his role in the scheme of things, until his day arrives and mankind is ready to receive his message'.

Convinced of the ancestral wisdom of tribal societies, Charles idolised the pre-modern world. For him, the rationality of science was abhorrent. Believing in the hereditary principle, he invoked God's power to appoint him as the spokesman for people's unspoken concerns. 'I have come to realise,' he said, 'that my entire life so far has been motivated by a desire to heal – to heal the dismembered landscape and the poisoned soil; the cruelly shattered townscape where harmony has been replaced by cacophony; to heal the divisions between intuitive and rational thought, between mind, body and soul so that the temples of our humanity can once again be lit by a sacred flame.'

Such thoughts were unusual for an heir to the throne. Some would criticise Charles for his pretensions of intellect, others for being a fantasist. To illustrate his so-called 'crankiness', they repeated gossip about Charles's interest in a book about aliens recommended by Charlie Palmer-Tomkinson.

In hindsight, the doctors' response to Charles's speech was generous. Recognising his insecurity and pride, they paid lip service to his spiritual values. In a deferential gesture, Sir James Watt, the president of the Royal Society of Medicine, organised a series of eight seminars and a working party within the BMA to examine complementary medicine. Charles himself attended three meetings at the

Royal Society, but was impatient with anyone advocating exclusive reliance on conventional medicine. 'Science,' he had told the doctors, 'has tried to assume a monopoly – or rather a tyranny – over our understanding of the world around us ... We are only now beginning to understand the disastrous results.' His hostility towards drugs reflected his anger about doctors' separation of the soul from the body. A healthy body, he told his audience, depended on treating soul and mind as one. His listeners were bewildered by his belief in the ability of the 'soul' to cure cancer. 'Alternative medicine,' one doctor would retort, 'should remain the luxury of the well-to-do hypochondriac.' The BMA issued a report concluding that complementary medicine was worthless, but it still approved further discussion.

Undeterred by his limited progress, Charles continued to argue that natural foods, proper education, sport and a healthier lifestyle, rather than drugs and hospital treatment, were the cures for illness. He visited the Bristol Centre, an 'alternative' drug-free cancer clinic established in 1981, and regularly championed environmental policies. He converted the Duchy of Cornwall's farms to produce only organic food. Seemingly unaware of his apparent fickleness, he repeated the attacks against the doubters that he had first voiced in his BMA speech in 1982: 'I have often thought that one of the least attractive traits of various professional bodies and institutions is the deeply ingrained suspicion and outright hostility which they can exhibit towards anything unorthodox or unconventional.'

With the tenacity of a proselytiser, in 1987 Charles began a campaign to make complementary medicine mainstream. The Maurice Laing Foundation was persuaded to donate £1.5 million for the first British university department devoted to the subject at Exeter University. Supported by Charles's regular visits, in 1993 the university appointed Edzard Ernst, a forty-five-year-old medical doctor, to become the country's first professor of complementary medicine. Ernst appeared an ideal choice. As the director of rehabilitation medicine at the Vienna Medical School, he had led a department of 120 in a two-thousand-bed hospital, and like many German doctors had routinely prescribed complementary medicines. During his ten-year contract at Exeter, he was tasked to 'develop research into the techniques and effectiveness of the various branches of complementary medicine and to encourage the assimilation of appropriate complementary medicine techniques into orthodox medicine'. He anticipated bringing his skills as a scientist, university professor and clinical practitioner to subject complementary medicine to its first-ever evaluation based on impartial scientific trials. To test its credibility, additional staff would be funded by grants from government and private institutions.

Charles was optimistic that Ernst's work would encourage British doctors to integrate complementary medicine into the NHS's conventional treatments. But he failed to anticipate the German doctor's refusal to judge all complementary medicines uniformly. Among more than four hundred alternative therapies and food supplements, Ernst sharply distinguished between herbs, acupuncture, osteopathy, aromatherapy, oils, diets and homeopathy.

Charles's particular interest was homeopathy. True believers prescribed highly diluted doses of natural substances to treat bee stings, snakebites and mushroom poisoning, as well as more serious illnesses. By producing the same symptoms, they argued, the body would automatically stimulate its natural defences. Until 1993, tests of homeopathy had produced results ranging between encouraging, inconclusive, and having no effect whatever. In extreme cases, patients who relied exclusively on complementary medicine had died. Charles dismissed such findings as unreliable, and expected Ernst to confirm his own beliefs.

To supplement Ernst's efforts, in 1993 Charles asked his friend Hugh van Cutsem and Ian Marks, a Cadbury's philanthropist, to recruit Simon Mills, a herbal practitioner, to establish what became the Foundation for Integrated Health, which he expected to prove that mainstream medicine and complementary therapies could work together. The finance would be provided by Bach Barcapel, a charity funded by a manufacturer of complementary medicines. Mills accepted the position, but progress was slow, and four years later a dissatisfied Charles commissioned a working party to examine the obstacles. Called 'Integrated Healthcare', the subsequent report suggested ways to provide the public with information about and access to both types of medical care, and how to increase research, training and regulation of unorthodox treatments. To implement the recommendations, Marks appointed Michael Fox, the chief executive of an NHS trust, as the first director of a new foundation that would be financed by Charles. The appointment was strange, given that Fox was not convinced of the benefits of complementary medicine.

Fox met Charles six times a year to describe his progress. By 1998 he had barely started to overcome the medical profession's resistance to the introduction of complementary medicine into the NHS. The prince, once again, was not pleased – as Mark Bolland explained to Fox, he was 'not used to opposition'. Then, in 1998, Charles was confronted by an unexpected challenge.

After five years of research, Edzard Ernst changed his opinion. Applying scientific methods, he and his team of academics had become disillusioned. Too many arguments in defence of alternative medicine represented a flight from reason into the absurd. Manufacturers of homeopathic remedies were attempting to persuade patients that worthless but expensive coloured water was beneficial. Ernst rejected such chicanery. Placebos which generated a 'false positive result' with no medical effect, he decided, were not harmless. Sick people were dying as a result of relying on pseudo-science (including acupuncture and chiropractic) rather than receiving conventional treatment.

The country's only professor of complementary medicine was not only arguing against his own specialty, but was critical of Charles for being 'unwilling to distinguish between real health care and blatant quackery'. Ernst even criticised Exeter University's BSc degree in complementary medicine as 'a course in claptrap taught by uncritical believers to brainwash youngsters with mystical nonsense'. In his opinion, the supporters of complementary medicine, especially the fourteen thousand people registered with the Federation of Spiritual Healers, were unqualified preachers who resisted independent scientific research, especially that by medically trained academics.

To bridge the chasm between Charles and the medical profession, James Watt persuaded Lord Winston, a pioneer of *in vitro* fertilisation, that the House of Lords Science and Technology Committee should take up the subject of complementary medicine. Simon Mills, the peers agreed after a series of meetings, would write the committee's report. To Mills's relief, by the end of their hearings the peers recognised complementary medicine's popularity, acknowledged some benefits, and accepted that some practitioners were

Portraits of the royal family at Balmoral in 1960 and the investiture of Charles as Prince of Wales at Caernarvon Castle in 1969 reinforced the impression of the royal family's rock-solid happiness. Few could have guessed at Charles's complaint that the queen and Prince Philip were bad parents.

The iconic image of Charles meeting Camilla after a polo match in 1975 has been misused to suggest a frustrated love affair. In truth, Camilla wanted in 1973 to marry Andrew Parker Bowles, the army officer she always loved.

Charming and popular, Andrew Parker Bowles (above, third from left) shared a love of polo with Charles, himself a brave player, whose own team was financed and captained by Geoffrey Kent (below, left), who would become chairman of the Prince's American Foundation.

Few could have imagined in 1981 that the fairytale romance between Charles and Diana would end in the public humiliation of the couple's visit to Seoul in 1992, amid bitter recriminations which would eventually slash Charles's approval ratings to just 4 per cent.

Despite the queen suffering embarrassment from her family's serial indiscretions, adulteries and divorces, she and Charles always managed to appear calm and content in public. Above, in 2001 outside Clarence House.

In private, Charles never concealed his dislike of Sinn Féin leader Gerry Adams (above, left); of President George W. Bush, because of his anti-environmental opinions; and of the Chinese leaders whom during his visit to Hong Kong in 1997 he described as 'old waxworks' – but in public he disguised his disdain for most politicians.

As a passionate countryman, Charles lobbied hard to deter the Labour government's ban on fox-hunting. An excellent shot, supported by his valet Michael Fawcett (above, right), Charles was determined to protect countryside traditions from metropolitan critics. Here in 1990 (above) and 1999 (right).

Launching his role as a meddler in 1984, Charles damned the proposed extension of the National Gallery (shown in this architect's model) as a 'monstrous carbuncle', and thereafter waged a campaign against modern architects like Richard Rogers (below, left) for, as he saw it, wrecking the soul and style of Britain's cities. Their battle climaxed with Charles's defeat of Rogers over the Chelsea Barracks redevelopment in 2009.

reputable. However, pummelled by the searing scientific criticism directed at the new sciences by the biologist Lewis Wolpert – 'That guy took the air out of our lungs!' admitted Mills – the peers were sceptical about the value of most unorthodox therapies. The public, as Mills was forced to admit in his final report, was unprotected against the majority of untrained, unregulated and 'incompetent' practitioners, and many remedies lacked high-quality research. The peers' conclusions were accepted by the government, ignored by the media and, as Mills decided, dismissed by complementary medicine practitioners as 'rather too balanced for some tastes'. Charles conceded that after sixteen years he had made only pitiful progress against the most vested of interests – the medical profession. His foundation, he admitted in despair, had also failed. 'It's become a talking shop for like-minded people,' Mills confirmed, 'and not getting off the ground.'

Charles did seize on one of the peers' recommendations: cooperation between conventional doctors and complementary medicine practitioners within the NHS should be improved. Pressured by him, the Department of Health agreed to give £18.5 million to the Royal London Homeopathic Hospital, and urged more access for the sick to the new sciences as part of the 'integrated medicine' promoted by Charles's foundation. Encouraged by that success, the prince supported the introduction of a postgraduate course in the subject at Exeter, to attract more GPs to the faith. The pioneers included Michael Dixon, a Devon GP who dispensed complementary medicine and was active in the NHS Alliance.

Not surprisingly, Exeter's medical school had sided with Charles against Ernst. Dixon now negotiated with Professor John Tooke, the Dean of the Peninsula Medical School at Exeter, to launch 'Pathway in Integrated Health', a course to encourage doctors to use complementary medicine.

By 2002, Charles's irritation at Edzard Ernst's criticism hit a new peak. Every study by Ernst's department had denounced homeopathy as worthless. Ernst also opposed Charles's foundation's initiative to recruit GPs. 'The information the foundation puts out,' he wrote, 'is dangerous and misleading. It's an attempt to brainwash GPs and patients.' That criticism was a good reason not to consult Ernst about the medical school's new degree. Dixon's official reason was bland: 'The course was for generalists and practitioners –

doctors and nurses. Ernst was not a clinician but a researcher. He was angry not to be consulted because he was used to Vienna's hierarchical system, but it's different in Britain.'

The prince felt vindicated, and looked around for a new target. He settled on the 'barbarians' ruining Britain's landscape and cities.

The Masterbuilder

Towards the end of 1999, Charles's disenchantment with Tony Blair increased. Much of New Labour's promise of a fresh beginning – Blair's pledge to be 'whiter than white, purer than pure' – had quickly become tainted. The exposure of Downing Street's sleazy relationship with Bernie Ecclestone, the owner of Formula One motor racing, Alastair Campbell's devotion to deceptive 'spin', the dispiriting arguments about school standards, and the plans for a vacuous dome in Greenwich to celebrate the millennium, all aggravated his mistrust. Charles blamed government ministers for evasion, especially about the environment. In turn, they felt that his expectations were often unrealistic. But honest debate was difficult with a dynast unwilling to listen to other points of view.

A fierce exchange with John Drummond, the arts administrator and BBC music controller, after a concert at the Bath Festival was an exception. The Bartók and Schoenberg he had just heard, Charles complained, was 'like scraping a nail over a blackboard'.

'Your taste in music,' Drummond replied after a pause, 'is as execrable as is your taste in art and architecture.' Charles, he knew, enjoyed the more traditional music of Hubert Parry, composer of 'Jerusalem'.

As their argument rolled on, the lord lieutenant of Somerset, who had accompanied Charles to the concert, became disturbed. 'You must stop this,' he urged Charles's courtiers. 'Interpose your body between them.'

'I'm enjoying this,' said Charles, laughing. 'I like John. No one's honest with me like that.'

Another who did not shrink from giving his opinion to power was Richard Rogers, the prominent British architect who in 2017 was to criticise the prince severely in his autobiography, *A Place for*

All People. For years he had openly called Charles ignorant, privileged and feudal. His candour was not appreciated by its target, not least because in 1999 Rogers appeared to have registered a major victory over him. Not only had he designed the Lloyd's insurance building, an edifice of glass, exterior metal pipes and lopsided steel, in the middle of the neoclassical City of London, but also the gigantic white fibreglass Millennium Dome, looming over the Thames at Greenwich.

For sixteen years, the two men had fought about the virtues and vices of modernist and traditional architecture. Rogers denounced Charles's self-appointment as the people's representative against modern architects as symbolic of anachronistic privilege. For his part, Charles was unyielding in his judgement of a man he regarded as a hypocritical champagne socialist. During the early years of Blair's government, their battle was unequal. As an admirer of New Labour, Rogers had won the prime minister's support for 'Urban Vision', his scheme to improve the quality of city life without regarding old buildings as untouchable. In 1998 John Prescott, the deputy prime minister, who was responsible for the environment, adopted Rogers's scheme as government policy.

In 2000, soon after Ken Livingstone's election as London's mayor, Rogers was appointed his architectural adviser. Livingstone was paying Rogers £130,000 a year, even though the mayor's office would also be considering the architect's applications for planning permission in central London. Both shrugged aside any potential conflict of interest. Some of Rogers's recommendations might have attracted Charles's support, but architect and prince found any common ground distasteful. Charles wanted to protect London's ancient skyline, especially the distant views of St Paul's Cathedral; Rogers preached enthusiasm, endorsed by the mayor, for skyscraper office blocks.

The campaign to protect Britain's heritage had started in the 1950s. Conservationists were appalled by the post-war modernists' crusade to build a utopian society as part of a political and cultural class war. Besides building on the rubble that was the Luftwaffe's legacy, the unsentimental modernists were demolishing rundown rows of Victorian terraces to erect tower blocks, and creating new towns on rural sites. The conservationists were in perpetual retreat. Their protests against 'barbarism', 'New Brutalism' and neo-industrialisation had only just prevented the demolition of St Pancras station, the Tate's portico and all of Whitehall's Victorian buildings, including Scotland Yard.

Characterised by some as a 'sod you' architect, and at fifty-one already in his pomp, Rogers scorned non-believers like Charles because, as one observer noted, the prince 'lamented the diminution of his royal power in the world and was distressed by the historical processes set in motion by the industrial revolution. His dreams of traditionally designed cities are dreams of a world where people forever know their place and the "divine order" would be resurrected.'

Curiously, Prescott, an Old Labour tub-thumper, appreciated Charles's campaign for people to live in attractive, socially mixed communities and not in 'hideous little boxes'. With other ministers, he agreed to meet the prince in the Cabinet Office for a twenty-minute slideshow followed by a speech in which Charles urged them to preserve listed buildings rather than sell them. Thereafter, Prescott would go to Charles's receptions and listen to criticism of his own schemes to bulldoze swathes of restored Victorian houses across northern England. The deputy prime minister accepted that the modernists' unqualified derision of the traditionalists was no longer a vote-winner. Most Britons had been converted to the charm of restored Victorian buildings, condemned by the modernists decades earlier as eyesores. Charles could claim some credit for that change.

By 1984, aged thirty-six, Charles had decided that change only happened as a result of provocation. Keen to assert influence, even control, over events, the role of subversive crusader appealed to him. By then he was weary of his private secretary Edward Adeane, whose cautious advice was that he should remain a silent constitutional heir. Instead he would abandon the sidelines and become a heroic troublemaker. He set himself 'to roll back some of the more ludicrous frontiers of the 1960s' – including those championed by the arch-priests of modern architecture.

To traditionalists like Charles, Richard Rogers and his fellow social engineers ignored the wishes of communities and aggravated the problems they sought to cure. In retaliation, the prince commissioned Léon Krier, a classical architect born in Luxembourg, to build Poundbury, a new town of 2,500 houses on land owned by the Duchy of Cornwall near Dorchester in Dorset. Poundbury was intended to showcase all the traditional designs and values espoused by Charles. Krier's attraction was not only his sympathy with such ideas, but that, as a former modernist, he was a convert from an ideology he now condemned as 'utter nonsense. The [modernists'] conception of life was sordid.'

In Charles's opinion, modern civilisation had become dependent on unsustainable technology, consumerism, economic growth and globalisation, and had disrupted Nature and the 'organic order'. While critics condemned the tower blocks conceived by modernist architects as ugly and uninhabitable, Charles interpreted their brutalism as a threat to the ancient mysticism that bound mankind. He described modern architecture in opaque language: 'The prerequisite of the health of each of the Earth's vital support systems', he wrote, was 'an interconnected, harmonic system which could be geometrically measured'. Over centuries, that system protected the world and the natural, divine order of life. Modernist architecture disturbed 'spiritual harmony' and led to human misery.

At his happiest playing polo or holding a paintbrush, Charles imagined himself as a scholarly, sensitive Lionheart. To illustrate the power of geometry to restore the natural order, in 2010 he would publish *Harmony: A New Way of Looking at Our World*, in which he would spell out, over three hundred pages, his core principles.

To gather material for his campaign, he had recruited two like-minded experts, Jules Lubbock, an architect, and Christopher Booker, a journalist and campaigning conservationist to whom he had been introduced by Laurens van der Post. Both were delighted to help. Their arrival in Kensington Palace coincided with an invitation to Charles to attend the 150th anniversary celebration of the Royal Institute of British Architects (RIBA) at Hampton Court. The prince was to make a speech, present a prize to an outstanding architect, and enjoy a dinner hosted by Michael Manser, RIBA's president. For over twenty years, RIBA had supported industrialised building techniques, and praised modernists' projects such as the history faculty at Cambridge University, designed by James Stirling, regarded as one of Britain's greatest architects. In 1984, sixteen years after it was completed, the university damned the building as ugly and intolerable to occupy during the summer because it overheated. For Charles and his two advisers, many of RIBA's members, including Stirling, epitomised the vandals they detested.

The modernists' latest outrage, Charles believed, would be Peter Ahrends's proposed extension of the National Gallery in Trafalgar Square. Westminster council was about to approve the plans, distinguished by a round tower built of concrete, steel and glass stuck onto the front of the building. For traditionalists, the tower defiled the majestic Regency and Edwardian façades around the historic square. In Charles's opinion the gallery would be transformed to resemble 'a kind of municipal fire station'. As he considered his strategy, he assumed that some of his audience would have supported the proposed demolition in the 1970s of large parts of Soho and Covent Garden (halted at the last moment by Geoffrey Rippon, a nonchalant Tory minister for the environment who made his decision while watching cricket at Lord's), and had not opposed a similarly 'modern' plan to impose a network of motorways on inner London.

Charles knew that cautious comments to RIBA's members would dilute the impact he sought. The palace of Hampton Court was an appropriate venue for privilege to address the privileged. Like him, none of the architects present lived in soulless, stained tower blocks marooned in barren landscapes, but for the most part in period houses in leafy Chelsea or Hampstead – none more so than Rogers, who occupied two Georgian terraced houses knocked together in Chelsea. He had gutted the interior to increase the height of the living spaces, but had kept the original façades, which by default appeared to bear out Charles's argument.

As the prince stood to begin his speech on the evening of 20 May 1984, no one anticipated what Michael Manser – the one person in the audience who had been briefed about the speech in advance – called 'a secret bombshell'. It was a warm, cloudless night – 'a velvet atmosphere', thought the developer Peter Palumbo, one of Charles's unsuspecting targets.

Charles opened with an attack on a proposed nineteen-storey office block designed by the world-famous architect Mies van der Rohe. The tower, clad in amber glass and bronze, would be built by Palumbo at One Poultry, adjacent to the neoclassical Bank of England and Mansion House, and would dominate the heart of the City. Charles of course opposed the Mammonist tower. 'It would be a tragedy,' he told his audience, 'if the character and skyline of our capital were to be further ruined and St Paul's dwarfed by yet another giant glass stump better suited to downtown Chicago than the City of London.' Palumbo was mortified. He had not been forewarned of the royal attack, which would have damaging financial consequences. Charles was a polo teammate whom he regarded as a friend.

The mood in the room chilled as Charles moved on, comparing pre-war London to Venice and criticising the destruction of English cities that followed the Luftwaffe's bombing. He then turned to Ahrends's design for the National Gallery. The proposed extension, he told his audience, would be like 'a monstrous carbuncle on the face of a much-loved and elegant friend'.

Outrage spread through the hall. The end of Charles's speech was met by stilted applause. Ahrends was reeling. 'The prince's remarks,' he said, 'were offensive, reactionary and ill-considered. He seems to be looking backwards rather than forwards.' Others agreed that Charles was rude to have used the celebration for such an attack. If a guest of honour at a dinner in Kensington Palace had denounced the monarchy, he would have been just as appalled.

'Why did you say that?' Palumbo asked him at the dinner afterwards.

'I just thought I'd stir things up a bit,' replied Charles with obvious pleasure, clearly untroubled by the damage he had inflicted on Palumbo and Ahrends.

'A Peterhouse fogey,' thought Palumbo, a reference to the Cambridge college, notorious for breeding right-wing codgers with an unusual sense of humanity. Trinity, Charles's own college and the home of Newton, Byron and Wittgenstein, had obviously failed to make an impression on him. Fogey or not, the royal guest had crossed the Rubicon. Naturally he could not prove that he was right, but he was pleased to have seized his chance to make an agonised complaint, a prophecy and a plea.

In the aftermath, architects were divided. Some declared that they wanted no part in desecrating historic cities. Rogers, however, happily adopted the mantle as defender of modernism. Although he was not responsible for the design of the National Gallery's extension, he denounced Charles as a philistine for confusing the concrete monstrosities erected by villainous councillors with the technological magnificence championed by architects including Norman Foster, Michael Hopkins, David Chipperfield and himself, the designer of the ultra-modern Pompidou Centre in Paris. But that was precisely Charles's complaint. In his opinion, the Pompidou Centre disturbed the beauty of the surrounding nineteenth-century buildings. The extremes could not agree.

When James Stirling was asked for his reactions to Charles's speech, he replied after a pause, 'God save the queen.' He had reason to be fearful. Charles's opposition to the van der Rohe tower and the Ahrends extension delivered knockout blows: both schemes were abandoned. Palumbo's final, reduced design would be expensively challenged, with Charles's support, all the way up to the House of Lords. The developer would eventually secure permission to build a comparatively small 'stump', designed by James Stirling.

Overnight, Charles became the common man's hero and won influence over key projects. New ammunition was handed to those campaigning for planners to consider how communities wanted to live. Those who complained 'I don't like that modern buildings' discovered that architects were no longer totally deaf to other opinions. While modernists disparaged as pastiche Charles's belief that new buildings should include neoclassical features like columns, spires and porticos, the public increasingly admired his championship of traditional design.

Shortly after his speech, Charles made his first visit to Italy. Over the previous twenty years, his travels across Britain and the old Commonwealth had isolated him from European culture. In 1985, as he toured the region around Rome, he had his first sight of Italy's cultural heritage. Like Richard Rogers he was inspired by the country's seventeenth- and eighteenth-century Baroque and Rococo architecture, and overwhelmed by the combination of light, stone buildings and lifestyle. Impressed by Italy's preservation of ancient towns and their communities, he felt the controversy he had ignited at RIBA's dinner was all the more justified, and started to search for new opportunities.

Charles had personally witnessed more destitution across Britain than most of Labour's well-off supporters. Since its beginnings in 1976, the Prince's Trust had helped thousands of young people from deprived backgrounds to start a new life. Believing that he should 'do' as well as speak, Charles launched two charities to help disadvantaged youth: Inner City Aid and the Prince's Youth Business Trust. Confiding in his main helper, Rod Hackney, a pioneer of community architecture, Charles revealed his concern about British society. Without authority, Hackney repeated their conversation to the *Manchester Evening News* in October 1985. The headline was electrifying: 'Prince Charles: My Fears For the Future'. According to Hackney, Charles was dismayed that by the time he became king, Britain could be divided into a have and have-not nation plagued by no-go areas. Those views precisely mirrored the Labour Party's complaint about the Conservative government that was then in power.

Infuriated with Charles's dabbling in politics, prime minister Margaret Thatcher demanded an explanation from the palace. None was forthcoming. In retaliation, she rejected Charles's invitations to engage in his causes. While Hackney was quietly dropped from Charles's court for his indiscretion, his former boss, seemingly unconcerned by the political storm, set about orchestrating a new debate, encouraged by newspapers that for the first time appointed specialist architectural correspondents. However, the image of a rebel delighted by the controversy he had created was deceptive.

Beyond public view, Charles was racked by self-doubt. Confused by the unexpected realisation that if you wag a finger in politics it might get bitten, he was shaken by the negative reactions he had attracted. 'They want to destroy me, or get rid of me,' he wrote to a friend. He then went on to say on radio, 'There is no need for me to do all this, you know. If they'd rather I did nothing, I'll go off somewhere else.' Protesting that his master was 'misunderstood', a sympathetic courtier explained, 'By exposing himself, he prevents a consistent opinion about himself.' Pertinently, James Boswell quotes Samuel Johnson on 1 November 1784 reflecting an appropriate insight into Charles: 'Nothing deserves more compassion than wrong conduct with good meaning; than loss or obloquy suffered by one who, as he is conscious only of good intentions, wonders why he loses that kindness which he wishes to preserve; and not knowing his own fault, if, as may sometimes happen, nobody will tell him, goes on to offend by his endeavours to please.'

All the excuses could not disguise Charles's relentless search for public glory. In 1987, three years after the 'carbuncle' speech, in a speech at the Mansion House, he again confronted 'the architectural mafia'. His theme was the proposed redevelopment of Paternoster Square, close to St Paul's. One of the competing designs, by Arup

Associates, he said, 'seemed to put St Paul's in a prison camp and surrounding it with this spiky roofline', while those by Norman Foster and James Stirling would create a windswept urban square in the midst of bland concrete buildings, a sad feature of many British cities. Again, he illustrated his argument with a headline-grabbing phrase: 'You have to give this much to the Luftwaffe. When it knocked down our buildings, it didn't replace them with anything more offensive than rubble.'

The uproar was once again led by Richard Rogers, who had been a peripheral candidate in the competition. The battle lines were set: the privileged prince who advocated neoclassical designs in brick and stone to complement Wren's cathedral, up against Rogers, the buccaneering son of Italian immigrants. To some, the prince's and the architect's modi operandi were strikingly similar. At his Chelsea house, Rogers had acquired the nickname 'the Godfather', alternately threatening and charming his enemies: 'You must kiss his ring.' The atmosphere at St James's and Highgrove was not dissimilar. While Charles disdainfully observed that the focus of Britain's millennium celebrations would be Rogers's fibreglass dome, the architect could not have imagined that the prince was waiting for a new opportunity to strike him down.

Emboldened by supporters, Charles threw more pebbles in the pond. His first hit the National Theatre, on London's South Bank, which he described as 'a clever way of building a nuclear power station in the middle of London without anyone objecting'. The building, he said, was 'more like a bunker than a palace [which] followed the fashion for concrete … to cheer up the concrete gulag of an arts complex'.

Next, he described the reading room of the new British Library in St Pancras as 'like the assembly hall of an academy for secret police', unlike the 'beautiful' reading room in the British Museum which it replaced. Sir Colin St John Wilson, the library's architect, was devastated. Charles, he complained, used tactics 'based on ridicule and abuse. You cannot put the clock back. The Nazis tried and look what happened.' St John Wilson was also embarrassed that his original scheme had required the partial demolition of historic Bloomsbury. Fifteen years later, those who had advocated the destruction of old city centres were condemned as vandals. His final scheme would be completed many years late and over-budget.

Charles then lambasted the City of London's planners, who had allowed its 'soul' to be conquered by 'the hovering hordes of concrete giants'. Noticeably, neither Norman Foster nor David Chipperfield was explicitly named as a villain. Unlike Rogers, they had no wish to enter the ring against Charles, although like most architects they were united in their mockery of the prince after a BBC film about the development of Canary Wharf in London's docklands, in which Charles was shown pointing at Cesar Pelli's fifty-storey office block and asking, 'But why does it need to be quite so high?' 'With all due respect, sir,' replied Roy Strong, the curator of the Victoria and Albert Museum, who was standing beside him, 'if that argument had pertained in the Middle Ages, we would not have got the spire of Salisbury Cathedral.' He did not get a reply.

To consolidate his campaign against the modernists, in 1991 Charles organised a summer school for architects at Villa Lante, a sixteenth-century house in Italy. The following year, he established a permanent headquarters for 'The Prince of Wales Institute of Architecture' in Regent's Park, partly financed at his request by the ruling family of Saudi Arabia and other Arab sheikhs, and the Sultan of Brunei.

Charles's ideals for the course were further proof that there was no common ground with Richard Rogers. In a circular to prospective sponsors, he emphasised the principles of 'the architecture of the Heart'. In puzzling, mystical language, he explained that the core of his belief was 'a Divine Source which is the Ultimate Truth as passed down by our predecessors. That Truth can be expressed by means of numbers – i.e. through geometrical principles and that, if followed correctly, these principles can be expressed with infinite variety to produce Beauty. Beauty, in turn, issues from the fact that its manifestation is a reflection of the order of the Cosmos.' Man, continued Charles, is 'a microcosm of this macro-cosmos and that in order to reflect the inherent harmony of the Universe in this Earthly Dimension we need to follow the basic Geometrical principles in this building process'. Such was his blueprint for an educational institution.

The prince further instructed his first director, 'I want the Institute to teach its students reverence – reverence for the landscape and the soil; for the human spirit which is a reflection in some small measure of the Divine.' His aim was for architects to allow 'the correspondence of the natural world with the idea of God; the expression of God within the human spirit; and the potential for architecture to give physical form to those sublime relationships'. Buildings should represent civilisation, hope and 'human feeling'. Followers of his thoughts were confused. Was Charles simply dreamily idealistic, or was he expressing fears about capitalism and suspicions of technology? Regardless of any judgement, what followed characterised his usual approach.

The institute's attraction was the surprisingly generous budget. Each student cost over £40,000 to educate, including free trips to New York and Italy for short architectural courses. 'Charles threw money at his students,' noted David Porter, a university teacher of architecture. 'Six times more for every undergraduate than the state sector.' Despite the largesse, fewer than thirty people enrolled each year, and the results were described as 'inept, crude and lifeless' by Adrian Gale, another respected professor of architecture. Gale derided the course – which had not been endorsed by RIBA: 'The students were being used as Charles's cannon fodder to promote traditional architecture. They didn't like that. They just wanted a career. It was a token folly.'

From the outset, the institute's management was weakened by personality clashes. Charles was criticised for expecting too much from the directors and expressing no gratitude for their efforts. As two of his charities for young people had collapsed under poor management, wasting £14 million, Charles was accused of using his status to establish the institute without sufficient attention to detail or to finance.

Among the casualties was Jules Lubbock. After struggling to solve the institute's lack of organisation, he travelled by train to Highgrove to ask Charles for payment, and explained to him that he relied on his income to live. An irritated Charles left the room. Shortly after, a private secretary came to tell Lubbock that the interview was over and he should leave. Like so many in the crew who sailed with Charles, Lubbock found he had a limited life on board. The price for any perceived heresy was to be discarded, usually as quickly as possible. And asking for money was definitely a big mistake. His friends would later say that no car was provided to take the now former adviser back to the railway station, a scenario he disputed.

The pattern was to be repeated in 1997, the year of the monarchy's crisis. Hilary Browne-Wilkinson, the new chairman of the Institute of Architecture, was asked by Charles to find a new director, the fifth in six years. The incumbent, Richard Hodges, was an archaeologist without any relevant teaching experience, and his appointment was deemed to have been an error. Browne-Wilkinson, originally appointed to resolve the institute's embarrassing legal problems, recommended Adrian Gale, a friend of her husband, as Hodges's successor. Although a modernist and a pupil of Mies van der Rohe, an idol of post-war architects, Gale felt after his introduction to Charles that they got on well. 'He was excited,' he recalled. 'I caught him in the raw. I could help him build better houses.'

Gale arrived with Adrian Porter, another modernist, to improve the institute's teaching. At the time there were fewer than twenty students. Browne-Wilkinson's mission, recalled Porter, was 'to make Charles less fogeyish and more modern'. As usual, the prince was enthused by new faces, but he doubted that Gale approved of Poundbury. Mark Bolland, in overall charge, was also suspicious of a professor wearing a black shirt. 'Are you a modernist or traditionalist?' he asked. Porter replied, 'That's cheeky. The world doesn't divide neatly that way.'

Even more wary of Gale and Porter was David Lunts, an urban planner recruited in 1996 to manage Charles's Urban Villages Group, yet another new charity, to pioneer the regeneration of towns. But at the outset, neither wanted to challenge Browne-Wilkinson's judgement. The following year, Lunts and Bolland had to confront the institute's annual £2.5 million deficit.

'It's a basket case,' Bolland told Charles.

'I must subsidise it,' came the reply. 'I'll sell my paintings to support it.'

'You can't do that,' said Bolland, laughing. 'You're the next king of England. We must rationalise and make it sensible.' He astutely did not mention that Charles's paintings sold for barely £2,000.

Much to Charles's distress, the first target for cuts was *Perspectives*, a magazine he had created in 1994. Its purpose was to restore the 'spiritual sense ... to the evolution of a new architecture', inspired by 'temporary technology' and traditional buildings. The magazine was deep in debt, which was disallowed by the charity laws. Giles Worsley, the respected editor, was tormented by Charles's constantly changing opinions. As the magazine wilted, Worsley's influence waned and he complained of being 'compromised and ultimately silenced' by Charles. *Perspectives* finally closed in 1998.

The magazine's fate coincided with the prince's decision that the institute should no longer focus exclusively on architecture. With a new name – 'The Prince's Foundation for Architecture and the Urban Environment' – Gale suggested that the Palladian buildings in Regent's Park were inappropriate headquarters. 'We need to move to proper London,' he told Charles, 'not remain in a happy part of the world.'

With a friend, he found an abandoned fur warehouse in Shoreditch, a rundown area in east London. Over lunch at Highgrove, Charles excitedly agreed to find a donor to buy and restore the building – the budget was £4.6 million. He discussed how the new student courses would teach the 'design of habitation without pastiche' and 'the journey from public places into the privacy of a home'. The move to Shoreditch, he agreed, would rebrand the school. Rather than posing as an opposition group, the new institute would be recognised as mainstream by the educational establishment. To finalise that ambition, Gale returned to St James's Palace. The prince entered the room dressed in his Guards uniform. The contrast between the bemedalled colonel and the black-shirted architect was ominous.

A familiar cycle started once again. Charles hosted fundraising dinners for the rich, and in turn the foundation's new supporters were invited to give advice. Porter noticed 'a lot of manoeuvring around Charles. Everyone was jockeying for position. It wasn't double- but triple-speak.'

Among the new disputes was the prince's insistence that the new foundation promote his Poundbury philosophy. Yet another meeting was summoned at Highgrove. Charles, at least no longer in officer's dress, spoke about building houses that would liberate the common man with sunlight and fresh air without looking modern. His philosophy, complete with sacred geometrics and Sufi-inspired mysticism, permeated his description. Invited to participate, Porter was struck by how 'oblique it was. No one would talk straight. His officials were buttering Charles up and telling him what he wanted to hear.' Everyone was familiar with the Islamic art course included in Charles's foundation curriculum, but once he mentioned the relevance of Islamic geometry to traditional British buildings, there was silence. 'It was tremendously unclear what Charles wanted,' recalled Porter. 'He had a very short attention span and was surrounded by people who assured him that he was doing the right thing. And then Charles suddenly went quiet.' Porter witnessed a scene more akin to a seventeenth-century court as Bolland, Lunts and others struggled to find suitable words for what the prince wanted: 'It was immensely volatile. You were either for or against him.' The balance was in Lunts's favour. He not only organised conferences and introduced Charles to like-minded people, he also supported his ideas.

Hilary Browne-Wilkinson was troubled, but not disheartened. Over the previous months she had encouraged Gale to design a postgraduate course in the design of houses, homes and the environment. However, unknown to her, Bolland had already told David Lunts that Charles was uneasy about Gale. Then the axe fell.

'He's got to go,' Bolland was told. 'I don't want him.'

'It'll be very difficult for Hilary, sir,' replied Bolland.

'Well, it's my institute, not hers,' snapped Charles without hesitation.

Bolland's message to Lunts was equally tactless: 'We must get rid of the acolytes. It's reputationally damaging to the next king, and financially costly.'

In 1999, Browne-Wilkinson drove from London with Gale and Lunts to meet Charles at Highgrove to finalise the new course. After sitting down with the prince and Bolland, neither Browne-Wilkinson nor Gale anticipated Lunts's announcement: 'We're not doing the postgraduate course.'

'I was shell-shocked,' recalled Gale. 'I was silenced. I didn't have the higher, quick intelligence to see what was happening. I was blown apart by Charles.' The prince said nothing. Hilary Browne-Wilkinson felt stabbed in the back, but each of the visitors knew that protest was futile.

They returned to the capital before lunch. The institute's first seven students were about to pass the RIBA exams, the first success for the institute, and important for Gale. That afternoon, he was telephoned by Lunts. 'You're out,' he told him. Gale's course was duly cancelled, and Lunts took over as director. Porter was similarly dispatched. 'I was called in by Lunts,' he recalled, 'and told: "You've lost the confidence of the trustees.'" In hindsight he admitted, 'I could not modernise the prince or fit in with the court.'

David Lunts was perfect for the task. He made no attempt to change Charles's attitudes. Instead, he organised the prince's mission to persuade developers and planning authorities to adopt his Poundbury principles. Yet frequently Charles was disappointed. On a trip to inspect the incorporation of the Poundbury way into a Wimpey housing development in Jarrow, Charles became distressed. He fretted about the cheap finish – bad street lamps, cheap bricks, the wrong cement, and much more. Not prepared to compromise, he was angry that Wimpey had refused to pay for the high standards upheld in the Cotswold villages around Highgrove. Lunts could not help recognising Charles's limited understanding of the commercial reality of Wimpey's standard housing estate.

The same insularity emerged during a trip to Poundbury. Driving to Dorset in his Bentley, Charles told Lunts, 'I'm having trouble with Léon.' Lunts was surprised. Léon Krier was not only an accomplished architect, but was admired by Charles as a fellow ideologue.

'Léon is stuck in his ways,' the prince continued. 'Poundbury is wonderful, but we must be more contemporary.'

'What is it you want?' asked Lunts.

'I'd like more twentieth-century architecture.'

Lunts was surprised. 'What do you mean, sir?' he asked, wondering whether Charles was belatedly coming to appreciate Richard Rogers.

'I'd like some arts and crafts in Poundbury, but Léon is determined not to have them.'

Once they arrived, Charles was introduced to the owners of a new two-bedroom house. 'I have always stuck to the principle,' he told the couple, 'that I would not let anyone build a house here that I could not personally live in.' The occupant of six grand houses did not intend any irony. Nor did he appreciate the unintended humour of his argument that was to unfold with Krier. Standing in one of Poundbury's small squares, with a fountain gurgling in the background, the two men looked up at an ornamental street lamp. The design particularly pleased Charles.

Unexpectedly, Krier burst out angrily, 'They're electric, and we agreed they would be gas.'

Charles looked troubled. 'Léon can be so difficult at times,' he told Lunts during their return journey. 'But do you think he has a point?'

8

Teasing the Government

The announcement in May 1999 by John Cunningham, Labour's agriculture minister, to allow test planting of genetically modified crops, and his declaration that such crops were 'safe', challenged one of Charles's most cherished beliefs. As a result he decided to abandon any pretence of impartiality. Mark Bolland was instructed to find a newspaper that would publish the prince's denunciation of the government for allowing the cultivation of unsafe and unregulated produce. Normally Bolland would have chosen the *Daily Telegraph*, but on this occasion he decided the *Daily Mail* would provide a better platform. His choice earned a sharp rebuke from Charles Moore, the *Telegraph*'s editor, leading eventually to open warfare between Moore and the palace. 'Mark was feasting with panthers by getting too close to some newspapers,' said Moore, 'which was unprofessional and unwise for someone employed by the royals.'

In his *Mail* article, the prince deplored what he saw as the emotional blackmail of the government's insistence only GM crops could prevent global hunger. That policy, he wrote, would automatically lead to an Orwellian future that would produce contaminated soil. Worshipping uncertified GM technology rather than God would cause the same type of catastrophe as BSE's destruction of Britain's cattle. 'There would eventually be a price to pay,' he concluded. His article led the nation's news broadcasts.

'It's skewed reporting,' said Tony Blair scornfully. His irritation that Charles was anti-science and closed-minded was exacerbated by Alastair Campbell's denunciation of the article as 'dreadful'. Blair ordered him not to criticise the prince in public, but to accuse the media of hysteria and lament the danger of Britain's biotech industry losing out to the Germans. This tactful approach got nowhere.

The following day, after further criticising the absence of scientific research as unethical, Charles summoned the media to photograph him walking through a sunlit, buttercup-filled field in Wiltshire. Supported by the *Mail*, Charles was presented as the sane voice of opposition.

Through gritted teeth, Blair had no choice but to attend an event hosted by Charles in St James's Palace shortly afterwards. The timing was unhelpful – the government was already committed to contribute towards a £100 million expansion of the Prince's Trust.

The new money, according to the trust's publicity, was destined to create thirty thousand new businesses by 2005. While realising that criticism of the prince's work was impossible, the government's goodwill evaporated. A few days later Charles boycotted a reception hosted by the visiting Chinese president in honour of the queen, his protest against the maltreatment of Tibet.

To irritate the government yet further, Charles was soon selecting another contentious issue on which to pronounce – fox-hunting, a prime target of Labour activists. Natural conservatives in rural areas felt threatened by Labour's parody of their traditional way of life, in contrast to its espousal of Cool Britannia. Rather than Britain's history being a source of strength, Cool Britannia glorified a multicultural, classless society that was reluctant to acknowledge the nation's heritage. The proposed ban on hunting, Charles complained, symbolised the curse of Blairism. With a lame Tory opposition in Parliament and the dilution of the old political class, the prince appeared the most vocal protector of Britain's heritage.

The traditionalists' fears deepened in September 1999 when Blair's speech to the Labour Party conference decried the 'forces of conservatism'. In full flow, the prime minister trumpeted his 'patriotic party's' mission to sweep away discredited conservatism and set the people free. The result, he declared, would be 'a new Britain of true equality … free from the closed doors of snobbery and prejudice'. The casualties would be the 'old elites [who] hold people back. They kept people down. They stunted people's potential. Year after year, decade after decade … [they] chain us to an outdated view of our people's potential.' He pledged to make the Tories redundant, and to lead a government of national unity. Taking Blair's words at face value, Charles would have assumed that the prime minister was threatening to demolish the Establishment. However, unknown to him, the speech was actually designed to end a stand-off between Blair and the Labour Party.

Charles decided to retaliate. In defiance, he took seventeen-year-old William hunting with the Beaufort. Stoked up by the prince's spokesman, their participation attracted huge media attention. To incite more interest, he revealed that Charles would meet Blair the following day, 1 November 1999. The prince, his spokesman added, would inevitably discuss the threat to hunting. Stung, Blair professed himself 'pretty shocked' that Charles had appointed himself the people's representative. Alastair Campbell was even more irate, describing Charles's day of hunting as a 'political act ... to put himself at the head of the forces of conservatism'. Blair ordered Campbell to negotiate with Stephen Lamport that the disagreement should be played down. 'Charles,' Campbell noted, 'had to understand there were limits to the extent to which they could play politics with [Blair].' Lamport, however, possessed no magic wand to make Charles mend his ways, and Blair's message was dismissed. 'The government has made it political,' observed Charles to those in his office. Politicians, he insisted, needed to understand that he was not a puppet, and should be taken seriously. He was clearly irritated that Blair considered him whimsical.

Before the meeting at St James's Palace, Blair received a long letter from Charles outlining his opinions about the countryside, beginning with the benefits to the environment of hunting. Next, he explained why 'I cannot stay silent' about GM crops. And finally, 'I feel very strongly about [China].' The letter was leaked to the media before the prime minister had even left his office for the palace. 'He had people spreading stuff against us,' Campbell huffed. During ninety minutes of 'pretty hard talk' the prime minister was challenged about hunting, his antipathy towards traditional rural life, and the government's abolition of the automatic right of hereditary peers – who Charles felt had 'much to offer' – to sit in the House of Lords.

Dealing with Charles, Blair said on his return to Downing Street, was 'toxic'. The solution, he decided, was to treat his tormentor as simply an unavoidable element of the government's environment. 'The best is not to get into a stew about his opinions,' an official advised. By contrast, Charles judged the meeting a success. Not only had he championed traditional British values, but soon afterwards a government spokesman announced that Blair's next administration would create an improved Department for Rural Affairs. Once again, the heir to Britain's throne felt he had made a difference.

Blair took the opposite view. He no longer wanted either close involvement with or influence over the royal family. After two years as prime minister, he now understood that government and monarchy were not a common enterprise. He made no secret of his lack of interest in his weekly audiences with the queen. 'How are you getting on?' became his routine question to senior officials as he arrived at the palace. He rarely listened to the answer. Although he needed the queen to join the millennium celebrations at the Dome, he failed to persuade the prince to visit the giant tent.

Just as Charles disapproved of GM crops, he made it clear to Blair that Christianity would endure long after the wretched Dome had disintegrated. 'Britain's future king,' noted the republican Campbell with irony, 'not for the first time, is doing us all a favour.' To sympathetic journalists, Campbell did not hide his conviction that Charles ranked among the 'thick' royals, and was an 'over-privileged twit'.

The disapproval was mutual. Governments were elected on a minority of the vote, Charles believed, and unlike the royal family, they came and went. Through the Way Ahead Group, his family was modernising itself without Blair's help. The proof of their success was Australia's vote in November 1999 against becoming a republic. The royals' high profile, he believed, balanced the politicians.

Among Blair's agents assigned to reduce the tension between Downing Street and the prince was Richard Wilson, the cabinet secretary. In normal times, to resolve royal problems there was a golden triangle of the cabinet secretary, the queen's private secretary and the prime minister's principal private secretary (PPS). That traditional machinery had fractured. Blair's preference for 'sofa government' rather than the structures staffed by experienced civil servants had denied the royal family consistent support from Downing Street. In 1999 Blair had yet to appoint a new PPS, and Jonathan Powell, his chief of staff, was not only dismissive of the royals, but also markedly ineffectual. Unusually, there was only one helpful ally for both Buckingham Palace and Downing Street to speak to Charles, and that was Wilson.

His mission was temporarily complicated by the government's use of the prince as an instrument of British diplomacy. In March 1999 he was sent to Argentina. To improve relations he was asked to

shake President Carlos Menem's hand and, in a speech during an
official dinner at the Alvear Hotel in Buenos Aires, to pay homage
to Argentina's dead soldiers. He was also asked to keep faith with the
Foreign Office's assurance to the Argentinean government that he
would not mention the Falkland Islands. Twenty-four hours before
Charles arrived, William Marsden, the British ambassador, read the
draft of his proposed speech. One sentence praised 'a rather smaller
democracy just a few hundred miles off your coast'. He called the
Foreign Office. 'That is wrong,' he protested, 'and will spoil the
atmosphere.' He was told to consult Peter Westmacott, the FO's
South American specialist, who was travelling with Charles and was
the author of the draft. During a hurried conversation in the
embassy before the dinner, Westmacott insisted that 'speaking up
democracy is good for Argentina and helpful in the Falklands'.
Charles, he told the ambassador, had approved what he had written.
Together, the three headed for the hotel.

At the end of Charles's speech, some Argentinean politicians criticised him as a 'usurper'. British journalists reported 'a misjudgement and, at worst, extraordinary incompetence', and Labour was
blamed for a 'ham-fisted' diplomatic blunder. The prince was
derided as 'hapless … His attempts to rehabilitate himself after the
death of Diana seem to teeter towards clumsy.' BBC TV news
showed a protest outside the hotel, described by the reporter as
against Charles. In reality it was a demonstration about the
Argentinean government's discrimination against gays.

As the bad news ricocheted between Buenos Aires and London,
Charles finished dancing a hectic tango in the hotel's ballroom and
returned with Westmacott and Marsden to the embassy for a drink.
Westmacott was told to call John Kerr, the FO's permanent secretary
in London. Kerr was irate. 'Have you still got a job?' laughed Charles
as the FO man returned to the room. Westmacott had stood his
ground. The following day Charles played polo, then flew to the
Falklands to commemorate the bitter fighting at Goose Green. By
the time he returned to London two days later, Marsden had
reported that, despite the headlines, the visit had improved Anglo–
Argentinean relations. Neither the Foreign Office nor Blair thanked
Charles for his mission. Still smarting from their last conversation,
Blair realised that Wilson's advice to Charles to avoid controversy
had been ignored.

Charles refused to retreat from his stance on the environment. In May 2000 he grasped at an invitation from the BBC to present one of the Reith Lectures, an annual series of talks by a distinguished personality. He used the platform to denounce GM crops. The world, he said, had been turned into a laboratory, and 'literally nothing is held sacred any more'. He called for the renewal of a 'sacred trust between mankind and our Creator', under which man accepted a duty of stewardship for the Earth. 'We need to rediscover a reverence for the natural world, irrespective of its usefulness to ourselves, to become more aware of the relationship between God, man and creation.' Even committed environmentalists regarded Charles's attachment to the Deity as a step too far. Hundreds of millions of people were eating GM crops without side-effects. 'If scientists don't play God,' asked James Watson, the Nobel Prize-winning member of the team that discovered the structure of DNA, 'who will?' Cancer, he continued, was 'natural', but no one would forbid scientists from interfering with nature in their attempts to discover a cure. The way forward was surely to find a balance between mankind protecting the values it held most dear, in order to avoid a future catastrophe, while also examining the scientific evidence.

The research quoted by Charles and other opponents of GM crops was an Aberdeen University experiment in which rats were fed GM potatoes. The result, said the Hungarian biochemist Dr Arpad Pusztai in an ITV programme, was deformed rodents. Over the following weeks, Pusztai's methods were criticised as flawed by the Royal Society. Pusztai was suspended from the university, and later resigned. Charles disputed the criticism of the shamed academic but as usual refused to engage in further debate about the evidence. His credibility was undermined, especially in Downing Street. Knowing that only sympathetic experts were summoned to his court to confirm his opinions, government officials discounted his arguments as the product of emotion rather than intellectual analysis.

Their scorn was still evident at the start of a new crisis: the outbreak of foot-and-mouth disease. The infection had started among pigs in an abattoir in Essex on 19 February 2001. Before it had even been detected, the disease had spread to fifty-seven farms in sixteen counties, and had then multiplied daily. The outbreak was beyond the control of the organisation created during the Second World War to manage civil emergencies under the supervision of Cobra, the government's crisis committee. In a slow, uncoordinated response, officials began to cull six and a half million animals. Smoking pyres of corpses covered Britain, transforming the countryside into a killing zone. Meat exports were banned, and the rural economy was crippled. Farmers blamed metropolitan politicians' dislike of the countryside.

As rural Britain's self-appointed champion, Charles sent Blair a six-page letter blaming the outbreak on EU rules that had forced the closure of many local abattoirs. As a result, animals had to be transported long distances to super-abattoirs, spreading the disease. He also criticised the government's lack of understanding of the world outside the cities.

Charles's letter started with an apology for 'pestering' Blair while he was 'receiving copious quantities of briefing' from others: 'I am so grateful to you for being prepared to converse with an interfering busybody during this immensely difficult time.' The soft-soaping did not relieve Blair's irritation at Charles's partisanship – he replied that the culprits were not the EU, but farmers who didn't boil their pigswill. Also, he went on, Charles's advocacy of vaccinating animals rather than supporting the cull (which included millions of healthy animals) was opposed by the National Farmers' Union. The prince's complaint about closing local abattoirs ignored the government's duty to obey EU rules. For the prime minister, compelled by the crisis to postpone the planned general election by a month, Charles was encroaching on perilous territory. His simultaneous vocal opposition to a European army and criticism of Blair's support for Britain to become closer to the EU, and even part of a future EU superstate, had crossed the line into politics. Another discreet warning was delivered by an emissary from Downing Street.

Once again, Charles ignored the messenger. Amid a blaze of publicity, he gave £500,000 to farmers suffering financial hardship. In Downing Street, Alastair Campbell echoed Blair's anger: 'It's amazing he can lead the news with small change given their wealth and we can get fuck-all for spending billions.' In a more barbed response, Blair bemoaned Charles's initiative as 'deeply unhelpful'. Did he, Blair asked Campbell, contribute any money when six thousand jobs went at Corus Steel? 'This was all about screwing us and trying to get up the message that we weren't generous enough to the farmers.' Nevertheless, the master politician restrained himself from criticising Charles in public.

At their next regular meeting at St James's Palace, Blair and Charles again discussed the countryside. 'He's well-meaning but misguided,' Blair told Campbell, but added that once the prince got into an argument, 'he was not so well-meaning'. Using Peter Mandelson as a conduit was no longer possible after the politician's second resignation from the government over an alleged impropriety in obtaining British nationality for a rich Indian businessman.

'Best not to be in touch with Peter Mandelson any more,' Stephen Lamport had advised.

'It's stinky,' agreed Bolland. 'Peter has come to the end of his usefulness.'

Blair hoped that the appointment in 2002 of Christopher Haskins, a distinguished former chairman of Northern Foods, to review the government's rural policies might help calm matters. Instead, Charles told him that the choice of Lord Haskins was a mistake: his company personified the enemy. Blair asked Haskins to meet the prince. Arriving at St James's Palace at 6 p.m. for a thirty-minute meeting, Haskins entered a dark room lined with heavy red curtains and red sofas. Within minutes, Charles said that, as a beacon to the world, Britain should be transformed into an 'organic oasis'.

'We import 50 per cent of our food,' replied his guest. 'It's unrealistic to set up the procedures to ensure that even 50 per cent is organic.'

Charles became irate. As temperatures rose, Haskins began to feel that the prince was an evangelist who chose to ignore science and trusted his own gospel: 'My truth is the truth.'

Charles turned to Elizabeth Buchanan, who was sitting behind him. 'You agree with me, don't you?'

'Oh yes, Your Majesty,' she replied enthusiastically.

Ninety minutes later, Haskins departed. Charles called Blair. 'I told you he was unreliable,' he complained. Soon after, the former director of Friends of the Earth Jonathon Porritt phoned Haskins to report that the heir to the throne had been upset. Like Labour's parliamentarians, Haskins shrugged off the encounter.

Blair was so 'very pissed off' that he complained to the queen. Britain's interest, he told her, was to stay in the biotechnology race to produce GM crops. The queen's private secretary noted another example of the difference between the monarch's impartiality and her son's love of confrontation. By fuelling conflict, the prince was in danger of undermining the independence of the monarchy.

Ten years later, after his arguments with Charles were publicised, Blair was still courteous. All their discussions, he wrote in the *Guardian*, had been 'immensely helpful. I thought he had a perfect right to raise questions and did so in a way that was both informative and insightful. So I welcomed his contributions.' Memory evidently plays tricks. But neither Blair nor Charles could have imagined that a quixotic police investigation was about to propel the prince to the edge of a precipice, and even potential downfall.

Diana's 'Rock'

In early November 2000, Scotland Yard's Detective Chief Inspector Maxine de Brunner, one of Britain's most senior female police officers, and marked within the Metropolitan Police as a high-flyer, was given an unusual tip by a retired police officer.

A director of Spink, a respected auction house and fine-art showroom in Mayfair, had boasted while intoxicated at a party during an antiques fair in America that he was selling a two-foot gold-and-silver model of a dhow originally worth an estimated £500,000. The piece, he said, had been a wedding gift from the Emir of Bahrain to Charles and Diana. Just how Spink obtained the model was unclear, but its path from Kensington Palace to Mayfair was undoubtedly murky.

While de Brunner considered her next step, a national newspaper reported the story, illustrated by a photograph of the dhow in Spink's window. 'Our hand was forced,' admitted one of the officers on de Brunner's squad. They had to investigate.

The following day, de Brunner and other officers drove to Mayfair and seized the expensive piece. Spink's records showed that the dhow had been brought to the showroom on 11 November 1997, about ten weeks after Diana's death. The seller was Harold Brown, a butler at Kensington Palace. His contact at the showroom was one Jan Havlik. Further searches in the records showed that Havlik had previously bought, also from Brown, a diamond-and-emerald pair of Diana's earrings and a bangle. He had paid £1,200 in cash for the dhow; Spink was selling it for £30,000, as some of the precious stones were missing.

Days later, de Brunner led a raid on Brown's flat at Kensington Palace. They found that the apartment was filled with Charles and Diana's possessions, including the dhow's base. The butler was arrested. In his first interview, he said that the dhow had been sold on Diana's orders, and that he had passed the proceeds to her. That explanation, he later admitted, was untrue; the transaction had taken place after Diana's death. Brown next insisted that the jewellery had been a gift to him from the princess. The royal couple, he said, frequently gave unwanted presents to their staff, who would invariably sell them on and keep the money. The police doubted that the princess would give jewellery to a male employee, but did realise that there might have been a curious relationship between Diana and her servants. De Brunner asked members of Diana's former staff for guidance. All agreed that she did make gifts, but never of her jewellery or of something as valuable as the dhow.

To understand the palace's attitude towards Brown's apparent theft, de Brunner consulted Stephen Lamport. Their conversation revealed extraordinary relationships between the royals and their staff. The palace, explained Lamport, would support a prosecution if the alleged thief no longer worked there, but he was unsure about the position if the thief were still employed by the royal family. After Diana's death Brown had been taken on by Princess Margaret, meaning that the police faced the first of many unprecedented problems.

The butler's arrest was soon leaked, and the problem escalated. After reading a newspaper report, Kevin Ward, a police protection officer at Kensington Palace, called de Brunner's office to report that nearly a year after Diana's death, in the middle of the night – at 3.30 a.m., to be precise – he had watched Paul Burrell carrying bundles of dresses and a wooden 'presentation' box with brass fittings out of Kensington Palace and loading them into his car.

Since Diana's fatal crash, her thirty-nine-year-old former butler, described by the princess as 'my rock', had become famous for his care of his employer's corpse in Paris, and his emotional tributes to her over the following weeks. Employed initially at Buckingham Palace in 1976, Burrell had worked at Kensington Palace for Diana's last five years, and had become an intimate, confidential accomplice in her life. In the aftermath of her death, he was the natural person to help clear her apartment.

Unaware of that close relationship, PC Ward challenged Burrell, who replied, 'I'm removing some items that the family have asked me to destroy.' Uncertain about his position, Ward called his superior officer. 'Back off,' he was ordered. Burrell drove away with Diana's possessions.

Ward's report puzzled de Brunner. The best person to explain Burrell's position, she was told, was Sarah McCorquodale, Diana's eldest sister. McCorquodale was also one of the princess's executors, a role she shared with Richard Chartres, the Bishop of London, and Frances Shand Kydd, Diana's mother. As an honorary lady-in-waiting, McCorquodale often met her sister in the capital, and they occasionally travelled together.

In the months after Diana's death, McCorquodale and Shand Kydd had regularly visited Kensington Palace to weed through Diana's possessions. Some would be taken to McCorquodale's home in Grantham, others given to Diana's sons. To Burrell's dismay, the two women were also reading and destroying documents. They explained that many were intimate letters written during Diana's affairs. They also found records of her medical history, the destruction of which, they believed, would avoid future embarrassment. Burrell would later describe what he witnessed as 'shredding'. He did not realise that the two women, even as executors, did not necessarily have authority to act in the way they did.

Now, three years later, de Brunner and Detective Sergeant Roger Milburn visited Grantham, where they asked McCorquodale whether Burrell was authorised to take away Diana's possessions. 'No,' she replied in a shocked voice. The most Burrell would have received, she said, were small mementos like a pillbox and some photos – nothing more. She emphasised that he did not have permission to remove any of Diana's possessions, and recalled that when Burrell was offered more mementos while clearing Kensington Palace he replied, 'I can't take anything. I have enough. All of her memories are in my heart.'

The police mentioned that their next call would possibly be to Burrell. 'If you're there,' said McCorquodale, 'could you ask him for the contents of a large mahogany box? They're ours.' The locked box, she said, contained some of Diana's most precious secrets. On the advice of Richard Kay, the *Daily Mail* confidant of Diana, McCorquodale had found the key to the box hidden in a tennis-racquet cover. 'What were the contents?' asked de Brunner. 'Letters from Prince Philip, a signet ring belonging to James Hewitt, and some tapes,' McCorquodale replied.

'Why are you so worried?' de Brunner went on.

McCorquodale said that there had been a lot of newspaper articles at the time speculating that Harry was Hewitt's son, and that the press were trying to get a strand of Harry's hair to link him to Hewitt by testing its DNA.

She did not reveal her main concern, namely that the letters from Philip detailed his intimate thoughts about Diana's marriage to his son. Even more potentially damaging was a tape recording made by Diana of George Smith, a valet, describing his rape by another valet employed by Charles. The police remained unaware of those details that day, but Paul Burrell knew the dramatic contents of the mahogany box.

Three years earlier, as he and McCorquodale looked into the open box, he had said (according to her), 'I don't think we should leave it here. There are so many workers and strangers passing through.' McCorquodale had agreed. She was taking the train back to Grantham that day, but the box was too big for her to carry. 'Well, take it home for the night,' she had said, referring to Burrell's flat in Kensington Palace. Thereafter, she told the officers, he had been reluctant to return the box, and she had become anxious. Eventually he did return it – empty. She had pressed him for an explanation, but Burrell had prevaricated. 'He's refusing to give me the contents back,' she said.

Unaware of the sensitivity of the tapes and letters, the police returned to London to focus on Harold Brown and the dhow. In his third interview, on 28 November 2000, he offered yet another explanation. The dhow, he said, had been given him by Burrell, on whose instruction he had sold it to Spink. Afterwards he had given Burrell the paperwork for the sale and the £1,200 he had received, which he presumed would be put into the Diana Memorial Fund, of which Burrell had been appointed a trustee. Later, when the police checked the Fund's accounts, they discovered there was no such deposit.

More loose strings soon appeared. Shortly after, a curator from the Victoria and Albert Museum contacted the police. He revealed that a man named George Grimes, an amateur photographer attached to the museum, had been given a vase by Burrell after Diana's death; the butler had told Grimes that it had been a wedding present to Charles and Diana. Uncertain about the story, the police were next contacted by Louis Munday, a handyman living in

Bicester. Munday showed Milburn a photograph of an unnamed man wearing a dress owned, he said, by Diana. He refused to hand over the photo because he intended to sell it to a newspaper, but Milburn was allowed to take a photocopy.

Setting aside these seemingly random tips, de Brunner focused on the dhow. Finding the original copy of Spink's sale document was crucial. Accordingly, four police officers led by de Brunner arrived unannounced at Burrell's home in Cheshire at 6.50 in the morning of 18 January 2001. He was woken by his wife.

Standing by the front door, Milburn fired off the first question: 'Do you have the paperwork regarding the sale of a dhow which belonged to the Prince and Princess of Wales?'

'No.'

'Do you have any items from Kensington Palace in this house?'

'No.'

'Do you have the contents of a large mahogany box which belonged to Princess Diana?'

'No, I don't know what you're talking about.'

Milburn told Burrell he was under arrest, and that his house was to be searched.

What the detectives found was a surprise. The living room, study and other rooms in the house were filled with paintings, drawings, china and photographs that had clearly belonged to Diana and her children. 'Oh my God,' exclaimed de Brunner. In Burrell's study was an expensive inlaid mahogany desk inscribed 'Her Royal Highness'.

'How did you get all this?' asked de Brunner.

'The princess gave it to me,' replied Burrell, who then collapsed into a chair and began sobbing. As the search continued, the police discovered a pencil sketch of Prince William as a baby. 'Did Diana give you this?' de Brunner asked. Burrell's sobs intensified.

An officer opened a wooden bench in the butler's study: inside were two thousand negatives. A cursory look revealed Charles in the bath with his children, and many other photos of the young princes naked. Next, they found a box of thirty signed photographs of Diana, many empty silver frames, a box containing Diana's 'Wombat' postcards – her daily personal notes to William at school – and another box of intimate letters from Diana to William.

'Did Diana give you all this?' de Brunner asked again. 'Even these family photographs?' Dozens of cellophane and leather wraps containing photographic negatives of the royal family's intimate moments were an unusual possession for a butler.

While Burrell became convulsed by even louder sobbing, the police search continued. From the small attic an officer shouted, 'It's full of boxes, wall to wall!' The boxes were wrenched open: inside were clothes and other possessions that had belonged to Diana – bags, blouses, dresses, nightgowns, underwear, shoes, jumpers, suits and hats, including a blue-ribboned hat she had worn during her visit with Charles to Korea in 1992, their last official trip together. Her perfume, de Brunner noticed, lingered on the fabric.

Late that afternoon a truck sent from London was filled with two thousand items that de Brunner judged had been illegally removed. Diana, she believed, would never have given away such personal material, and certainly not in such quantities. The family photographs and letters, numbering in their thousands, could not be left unsecured and at risk of embarrassing the royal family. Nevertheless, a large amount of Diana's possessions remained in the house. Without orders from Scotland Yard either to seize everything that had belonged to the family or to seal the house as a crime scene, the officers departed with Burrell for Runcorn police station. 'I want white lilies on my coffin,' wailed Burrell as he was escorted to the waiting police car.

Tipped off by a member of the Burrell family, a *Mirror* journalist was waiting inside the station. The police's hope for discretion had been sabotaged by the inevitability of newspaper headlines about the arrest. (It was later established that Graham Burrell, Paul's brother, indirectly received money from the *Mirror*.)

In his interview under caution the next morning, accompanied by Andrew Shaw, a local solicitor specialising in crime, Burrell refused to explain why his house was filled with Diana's possessions. He did not even say that they were presents. He denied knowledge of the dhow, but admitted giving Diana's vase to George Grimes without authorisation. The police were naturally suspicious – Burrell had clearly lied at the outset of the raid by denying that any items from Kensington Palace were in his house. He was released on bail.

The following day's newspapers provoked Stephen Betts, an acquaintance of Burrell and his brother Graham, to sign a police statement that the brothers had travelled to America about ten times to meet Ron Ruff and Chuck Webb, a gay couple in Florida who were good friends of Paul Burrell, and who had made the butler's two children beneficiaries in their will.

The police report sheet was automatically forwarded to the Crown Prosecution Service. The CPS's lawyers, led by Michael O'Kane, an intelligent and articulate solicitor, were responsible for any prosecution. Since Burrell refused to explain fully why so much of Diana's property was in his home, the CPS's advice to the police was that he could be accused of theft. However, O'Kane added, 'it would be helpful' to prove a sale in order to challenge Burrell's defence that Diana had given him everything as presents. But to convict him of theft did not require evidence of a sale, as the case appeared to be sufficiently strong without it: he had taken items belonging to Diana, William and Charles, apparently without permission, to a transition point for storage, and months later had transferred them to his new home in Cheshire, where he had kept them for three years, apparently without telling any official or member of the royal family. 'They are very precious and very important for William,' Clair Southwell, an aide of Diana's, would later say about the letters and photographs. 'They should be with William.'

The news of Burrell's arrest reached Charles about a week later. Unaware of the scale of the alleged theft, he was wary at first. Considering their low pay, he was unsurprised and unbothered about pilfering by staff. Burrell probably did steal some things, he told Bolland, 'because they all do'. Within hours, however, he reconsidered. Police probes into murky palace habits could produce difficulties, and the arrests of Burrell and Brown were unprecedented.

At the end of January 2001, after discussions with Charles, Bolland asked Richard Kay to contact Burrell and suggest that he write to Charles. The butler's response was swift. In his letter he described his plight and the unjustified seizure of many gifts he had received from the royal family. He added: 'Most sensitively, [there is] some material which was entrusted to me. There is also a number of "family" items which quite simply I incarcerated in storage and then recently in my attic for safekeeping.' Significantly, he did not offer to return any of the property, but instead proposed that he and Charles should meet 'to resolve any misunderstanding and stop this sad episode escalating beyond control'. On Stephen Lamport's advice, and to keep him out of any investigation, Charles was not shown the letter, and it was returned to Burrell. Neither the police nor the lawyers at the CPS would ever read it.

The investigating officers were in uncharted territory. 'You've ruffled feathers at the palace,' Inspector Ken Wharfe, Diana's former protection officer and still a serving policeman, told Roger Milburn. 'The gay mafia are angry.' Wharfe's warning about a group of palace employees was recorded in writing.

On 27 February Burrell was again interviewed for an investigation now codenamed 'Operation Plymouth'. On the way to the interview room, Andrew Shaw said to de Brunner, 'You're making a terrible mistake. They won't let Burrell's secrets be splashed in the public domain. They'll never let this come to trial.'

'It's up to the CPS,' she replied.

'Did you tell anyone that you had the property?' Milburn asked Burrell in the recorded interview under caution.

'No.'

'Why didn't you tell Diana's two sons?'

Burrell did not answer the question directly, but instead said, 'She had a very generous nature. She received a very large number of gifts. She couldn't keep all of them. I wasn't dishonest in retaining them.' But that did not explain why he possessed two thousand photographs and hundreds of letters from Diana and Charles to their children, and all Diana's school reports – potentially a valuable hoard, the authorities believed, on the memorabilia market.

To prevent the situation spiralling out of control, Burrell was asked, 'Will you sign a disclaimer to the property?' The police tape recorder registered his laugh. He refused to return anything, repeating that the items were gifts. The interview was then halted by Shaw. Burrell, he said, was bound by the Official Secrets Act from giving further answers. 'We had that advice from Lord Carlile,' he added, referring to a senior London barrister.

Back in Whitehall, Lamport, looking beaten and downhearted, confessed to a colleague, 'We've got a terrible problem with this man Burrell. He's been taking things. The police are onto it. The Prince of Wales is distraught. The prince will say he gave the things to him and that Burrell's actions were all right.'

Lamport's anguish reflected his inability to take command. His confidant warned him that even Charles had to allow justice to take its course. But Lamport was not the man to persuade Charles to accept such advice. He may also have lacked the background to understand fully the quicksand surrounding the prince, but he did realise that Charles needed legal advice. The prince turned to Fiona Shackleton.

Just as Charles required of all his advisers, she had become devoted to his cause. Day and night, at weekends and on family holidays, she took his calls and obeyed any summons to travel to Highgrove, London or Scotland.

Aware that she was not a specialist in criminal law, she consulted Robert Seabrook QC, who had acted for Charles in his divorce. In the narrow terms set by Shackleton, the barrister's brief was limited to preventing Charles or William from stepping into the witness box. He was not consulted about any negotiations to recover property from Burrell. Like all the advisers, he knew only that Charles wanted to avoid any prosecution.

Faced with Burrell's attitude, Michael O'Kane, the CPS lawyer, and de Brunner arrived at St James's Palace on 3 April to brief the royal family's senior officials. Around the table were Robin Janvrin, Lamport, Shackleton, Michael Gibbins (an accountant who had been promoted to be Diana's last private secretary) and, representing the Spencer family, Sarah McCorquodale and her mother Frances Shand Kydd. Robert Seabrook was not invited to this first, critical meeting.

Soon after the meeting began, Diana's sister and mother showed that they were on a mission. There was a side to Burrell that Sarah McCorquodale had not grasped during the tumult immediately after her sister's death. But his over-the-top effusions of loyalty had gradually aroused her suspicions, and she no longer believed that he had been as close to Diana as he now asserted. Gibbins shared her disquiet. Before Diana's death, he knew, Burrell had secretly negotiated to buy a house in Cheshire in anticipation of leaving Kensington Palace and working in America; the new home was possibly intended to be a base in Britain for his wife and children while he worked abroad. The police had obtained a copy of his application for employment.

Gibbins had also been disturbed by Burrell's habit of stirring animosity in St James's Palace by suggesting that various employees might be dismissed if he, the all-powerful butler, reported adversely about them to Diana. Dishing out hints of royal displeasure was a potent destabilising force. All in all, Burrell no longer seemed to the family the saintly figure he had appeared to be immediately after Diana's fatal accident.

And there was another feature. Soon after Diana's death, the Spencers had obtained a court order to amend Diana's will to give Burrell £50,000, and had offered to buy a home in London so his children could continue at the Oratory school in Fulham. Burrell took the money, but refused the genuinely altruistic offer of the house, although he did become a trustee of Diana's Memorial Fund. Thereafter, to McCorquodale's irritation, he emerged as a brash celebrity, a frequent guest on TV shows and at parties, even posing for photographers at the Oscars. After a year, he had been asked to resign from the Fund's board. Following that acrimonious split, McCorquodale considered Burrell's possession of Diana's property totally unacceptable. At the meeting in St James's Palace, she had done little more than agree that he should be prosecuted. But thereafter, Burrell's friends believed, she pursued a vendetta rather than wanting justice. Neither de Brunner nor O'Kane – both straightforward public servants – had spotted at their first meeting with the royals the swirl of animosities between Charles, McCorquodale and Shackleton.

Nor did the police or O'Kane realise the poisonous disdain between the prince and the Spencers. Diana's brother Charles had not been forgiven for his speech at her funeral, and the legacy of that day lingered. Ever since the breakdown of his marriage, the prince spoke to Sarah McCorquodale only if there was no alternative; and he still loathed Robert Fellowes, Sarah's brother-in-law. For similar historic reasons, McCorquodale and Shackleton scorned each other, not least because McCorquodale wrongly assumed that Shackleton was associated with Diana losing the title 'Her Royal Highness'. The Spencers refused to accept that she had renounced the honour voluntarily. Finally, there was tension between Shackleton and Lamport. Charles had less trust in his private secretary than in Shackleton, and she in turn wanted Lamport excluded. Lamport, a decent man, assumed that Charles could rely on Shackleton's legal expertise, and appeared unaware of the animus against him.

Surrounded by those hostilities, the facts were outlined by O'Kane. An added ingredient to his briefing was that the police had become even more suspicious about Burrell. A *Mirror* journalist had called to report that she had overheard conversations at the newspaper that employees of the royal family had been selling items to a Dr Will Swift, a memorabilia trader in New York. When officers checked, Swift's website did indeed show several sales of royal items, but none were connected to Burrell.

After O'Kane had completed his briefing, McCorquodale and Gibbins repeated their belief that Burrell had no authority to take Diana's possessions, especially to his home. The same was said about Harold Brown.

'Brown could say the dhow was a present from Charles,' said Shackleton.

'That's not possible,' replied de Brunner, 'because it was not Charles's property, and Brown admits that it was taken – on Burrell's suggestion – from Diana's household and sold.'

Shackleton was not persuaded, and now delivered a surprise. Charles had told Lamport that he did not want Brown to be charged. 'The Prince of Wales,' she told the meeting, 'is distraught. He does not want it going any further, and is determined.' The prince, she went on, just wanted the property returned.

Lamport confirmed Charles's instruction. Burrell could argue in his defence that some of the items were gifts. 'Something,' he emphasised, 'which is common practice.' The prince would state as much. But Lamport retreated when the size of Burrell's hoard, especially the number of photographs and letters, was mentioned. That appeared to be far beyond the norm. Neither O'Kane nor de Brunner could believe that Diana would entrust to Burrell her personal letters to William, or photographs of her naked children.

Equally, the lawyers and police could not grasp the profligacy of Charles's lifestyle. Unlike the queen, whose household itemised and stored away every gift at Windsor Castle as part of the Royal Collection, forbidding any sales, Charles randomly allowed his staff to sell unwanted gifts and keep the money. Rewarding his butlers and valets, he believed, kept good staff loyal, and that could be equally true with Diana and Burrell. Outsiders might consider such a practice ill-advised, but royals made and lived to their own rules.

That habit was irrelevant compared to another revelation that emerged during the discussion. Shackleton told the meeting of the handwritten letter Burrell had sent to Charles, and which had been returned to him on her advice. She described the letter's message:

Burrell was willing to return some items if Charles agreed that he would not support any prosecution. In hindsight, the butler's attitude was confusing, not least because what Shackleton said contradicted what others recalled Burrell had told the police. However, what followed made the letter irrelevant.

O'Kane explained that Burrell's offer was not enough to bring matters to an end. The case could be closed only if Prince William and McCorquodale, who together inherited Diana's property, signed statements to drop their complaints.

Shackleton appeared surprised. Inexperienced in criminal law, she seemed unaware of the importance of the victim's opinions about an alleged crime. She now changed her mind. Agreeing to accept the return of some property in exchange for dropping the investigation, she said, would make it look as if Buckingham Palace were participating in a cover-up. Charles could not be party to undermining the legal system. 'It needs to be all or nothing,' she said. A partial return of the property 'would be a disaster both legally and for the family'. She and McCorquodale agreed that only a total return could stop the prosecution, which otherwise should go ahead. Having ruled out a compromise, Shackleton did not appear to consider that the absence of a wise manager in the royal palaces with the expertise to broker a deal with Burrell was a handicap.

The eight disparate participants – two lawyers, a policewoman, two former Foreign Office officials, an accountant and two aristocrats – stumbled to an uncertain conclusion. The meeting ended with Lamport and Shackleton agreeing to brief Charles, and Janvrin to inform the queen. In the light of what followed, this would be an important pledge. If the monarch had any knowledge of Burrell's legitimate safekeeping of Diana's possessions, her briefing by Janvrin would be her moment to say so. But she did not apparently say a word.

With the discussion concluded, Janvrin decided to have no more involvement with the Burrell saga. This was Charles's mess to solve; his priority was to oversee a perfect celebration of the Jubilee. Officially, the burden of managing the case would henceforth fall on Lamport. Soon after, the private secretary summarised the meeting for Charles. 'There is no alternative,' he wrote, 'but for formal charges now to be made against both men.'

On 23 April 2001, Lamport told Maxine de Brunner that the Prince of Wales supported the prosecution of Harold Brown, and the following day Brown was formally charged. Nothing was said about Burrell's fate. Diana's butler, Charles knew, had witnessed his secret meetings and phone calls with Camilla while he was married, as well as Diana's many rendezvous with her boyfriends. Such knowledge was a time bomb.

On reflection, Charles was unhappy with Lamport's report, in particular its conclusion that there was 'no alternative' but to prosecute Burrell. The prince believed that Lamport was too influenced by McCorquodale. He told his assistant to step aside and allow Bolland to navigate a way out of a prosecution. Bolland faced an awesome task. 'No one knew the truth,' he recalled, 'and the episode was damaging all the relationships.' There was, however, one truth: the intimacy among all Charles's friends and family was strained, not least because of their indulgent lifestyles.

10

A Family at War

Charles's lavatory at Highgrove was filled with cartoons featuring himself. In the guest's lavatory of Camilla's house, Ray Mill, were unflattering cartoons of Diana.

'That mad cow,' said Camilla, echoing the view held by her and Charles's friends. Camilla's denigration of Diana was unknown beyond their circle. The reward for her discretion was opinion polls that showed public feeling had moved in her favour. The latest finding was that 50 per cent of the British people supported her marriage to Charles, although 78 per cent opposed her becoming queen. Charles's ratings had also slightly improved. Seventy-six per cent now supported him as the next monarch. Few realised, however, that while Charles lived openly with Camilla, their domestic arrangements were unorthodox.

Seventeen miles from Highgrove, Camilla preferred to lead a separate life in the shabby farmhouse bought after her divorce for £850,000, half the proceeds from the sale of the family home, and registered as owned by a trust run by Lord Halifax. In the timeless network of their social class, Halifax was married to the former wife of Richard Parker Bowles, Andrew's brother. Living informally with her dogs, her garden and much cast-off furniture, Camilla was critical of Highgrove's tidy perfection. 'It's too small and too Charles,' she told her friends. 'I can't touch a thing.' The home of a fussy bachelor offered a 'lifestyle that doesn't suit me'. Life at Highgrove also frustrated her: 'Charles is always working, working, working.'

In their flexible arrangement, Camilla alternated between staying overnight at Highgrove or St James's Palace, and returning to Ray Mill. That also suited Charles. He was accustomed to living apart from rather than with a woman, and chose to sleep in a separate bedroom even when he and Camilla were under the same roof.

Both enjoyed regular separation. A creature of habit, Charles followed virtually the same routine every month in every year, allowing nothing to interfere as he moved his 'permanent' home between St James's Palace, Highgrove, and Birkhall, the queen mother's house on the Balmoral estate, with intervening stops at Balmoral itself and occasionally at Sandringham. When it suited her, Camilla followed. In a crisis, she would be summoned by Michael Fawcett to drive to join Charles regardless of the time of day or night. A sudden bout of melancholia or self-doubt required relief. Thankfully, she could always make him laugh or, in her words, 'jolly him along'. In return, money was no longer a problem. Charles paid off her overdraft, stabled her horses, provided a car and gave her increasing amounts of cash.

Camilla's public image was that of an undemanding mistress devoted only to making Charles happy, with no mention of marriage. 'She has never worked in her life,' commented Bolland, 'and is terrified of being on public display. A member of her family described her to me as "the laziest woman to have been born in England in the twentieth century".' As hard as Camilla tried to prove Bolland wrong, she remained 'nervy and lacked stamina'. The accepted view of a woman whose youth had been exclusively focused on social excitement, especially parties and hunting, making good in middle age was entirely accurate.

In the opinion of Tom Camoys and other like-minded courtiers, Camilla was not lazy in one respect: urging Charles to establish her own status. To oblige his mistress, he became careless about propriety. Yet another poll, this time by Mori, reported the public's continued belief in the royals as hardworking patriots who embodied British virtues and values.

Somewhat undermining that opinion, Charles flew to Greece in August 1999 with his sons for a cruise around the Aegean on Yiannis Latsis's yacht the *Alexander*. Two days previously, Camilla and her two children had been flown to Greece by private jet, paid for by Charles, from an RAF airfield near Ray Mill to await a large group of their and Charles's friends, including Hugh van Cutsem. The intention was to stage a public event as part of their continuing campaign.

To Charles's misfortune, the long-planned cruise risked being overshadowed by a scandal that had been bubbling for six weeks.

The spotlight was on Tom Parker Bowles, Camilla's twenty-four-year-old son, who had been exposed in the *News of the World* offering friends cocaine. Charles had good reason for concern. Although Tom Parker Bowles was seven years older than William, he had become his confidant. According to William's friends, Parker Bowles's behaviour posed a significant threat because Chris Morgan, a *Sunday Times* journalist, was keen to associate Charles's sons with cocaine. Another notable guest on the holiday yacht was Patty Palmer-Tomkinson, whose daughter Tara, a media personality and renowned publicity-seeker, had recently been admitted to an American clinic in the hope of curing her cocaine addiction.

Charles would not allow such embarrassments to ruin the cruise. On his instructions, the family get-together was presented to the media as William's idea, which had taken his father 'by surprise'. Few believed that, especially Charles's critics at Buckingham Palace, in whose opinion Charles was using William and Harry to paper over the scandalous behaviour of Camilla's son. Among those critics was Prince Philip, irritated once again by his son freeloading on Latsis, an unattractive character. The cruise was worth over £1 million, and Charles had recently accepted another £1 million from Latsis for his Youth Business Trust. Philip charged his son with damaging the public's trust by allowing the rich to buy access to him.

At the heart of that operation was the omnipresent Robert Higdon. In 1998, however, the American fell blind drunk from a boat in St Vincent into the Caribbean. 'I'm a wreck from alcohol,' he admitted, but nevertheless shortly afterwards he brought John and Caroline Kennedy to a dinner at St James's Palace that raised about £200,000. At another meal in Kensington Palace with the prince he introduced Ted Stanley, an American billionaire businessman, and other guests who each donated $250,000 to Charles's charities. 'Lamport and Bolland were freaked out by all the names I brought to London,' Higdon boasted. 'Their only problem was the placement.' But there was a second concern: his alcoholism. After an argument, the fundraiser returned to Washington prepared to resign.

'They flew me back to London for lunch with Charles, Geoffrey Kent and Bolland,' recalled Higdon. 'Charles asked me, "Are you being treated fairly?" and I replied, "Do you expect me to answer honestly in front of these two? Hell no, I'm not. I'm being treated very badly. I'm being lied to. You wouldn't be able to raise millions of dollars without me and you're not giving me anything.'" These were the rants of an unstable man who needed treatment and a fond farewell. Instead, in Higdon's version, Charles angrily exclaimed: 'No one's helping me. I'm being sabotaged. Tell me what you need and you'll get it.' In truth, he could not afford to lose such an outstanding source of revenue, and Higdon remained employed after receiving treatment. Together with Geoffrey Kent, he could entice a raft of American billionaires to finance Charles's charities.

In June 1999, eighty donors to Charles's American Foundation had booked to have dinner in Buckingham Palace. Knowing that the queen would be at Windsor, Charles intended to invite Camilla. That raised a double problem. The queen disliked the use of her home to raise money, and while she tolerated press photographs of Charles and his mistress at theatres and restaurants, Camilla's presence in Buckingham Palace was unacceptable. She usually just ignored such dilemmas, but this time she made one stipulation: while Camilla could be present at the party, she could not sit at Charles's table. The couple bit the bullet, and the evening went ahead.

Four months on, Higdon proved his value again. Forty Americans including the comedian Joan Rivers, Eileen Guggenheim of the wealthy mining family, and Carol Petrie, the billionaire widow of an American retailer, had dinner at Holyrood. Charles's Phoenix Trust was seeking £6 million to transform four deprived areas in Scotland – including a derelict industrial complex of nineteenth-century sandstone buildings at Stanley Mills, on the River Tay in Perthshire – into stunning housing estates. Higdon's introduction of Rivers, a close friend of his, strengthened Charles's profile in America and, helped by her amusing introduction, his speech of thanks to his guests after the dinner produced a gush of cash. He was now tempted to take bigger risks.

In May 2000, at the queen's request, Charles became the lord high commissioner of the Church of Scotland. Rather than copy the pattern of his mother's unpretentious engagements and modest dinner parties for a maximum of twelve, he was persuaded to arrange a week of high-profile events climaxing in a dinner for two hundred guests entertained by jugglers and fire-eaters. Bolland's motive was to promote Camilla. After endless prevarication and frets that 'We mustn't frighten the horses,' Charles agreed that without Camilla at his side he would risk looking furtive. The *Sunday Times* headline at the end of the celebrations rewarded Bolland's persistence: 'He Came. He Saw. He Conquered.' Thereafter, Charles disappeared from public life in Scotland for another year.

For about six months of every year, the heir to the throne enjoyed a unique lifestyle in beautiful places either in seclusion or with friends. Although his travelling staff (a butler, two valets, chef, private secretary, typist and bodyguards) could anticipate most of his movements between his five homes, the only definite confirmation of his final destination, especially to his hosts, would be the arrival of a truck carrying suitcases, furniture and food. Then followed endless telephone calls with his staff as he changed his mind about his future plans and projects.

Charles's demands were constant. An assistant was on call in his office until he went to sleep, and would be subject to familiar daily tirades: 'Even my office is not the right temperature. Why do I have to put up with this? It makes my life so unbearable.'

For four months every year he lived in Scotland, expecting people to visit him from London regardless of any discomfort – and usually at their own expense. When he emerged in public, he behaved impeccably and showed genuine interest in people and events. Few outsiders could guess whether or not, as one adviser commented, he was 'just putting on a game face'; insiders were similarly perplexed.

One of his habits was to have dinner served to guests at 8 p.m., but not to arrive himself until 8.15, because he had decided against eating the first course. The guests would be allowed to start without him, although visitors to Highgrove were cautioned by Camilla not to begin their breakfast before Charles appeared. Or he would arrive at a function with his policeman carrying a flask containing a pre-mixed Martini, to be handed over to the host's butler along with the glass Charles insisted be used. Hosts would be informed that an aide would deliver a bag containing the food Charles would eat. Unlike the queen, who ate the same food as other guests, Charles not only made it clear what he would consume, but if he accepted an overnight invitation, how and where he would sleep.

Each visit was subject to different requirements. At Chatsworth, the 175-room home of his beloved Debo, he and Camilla were assigned a whole wing for up to three weeks in the year for hunting. During the shooting season he enjoyed the company of Gerald Grosvenor, the Duke of Westminster, at either Eaton Hall, near Chester, or the duke's shooting lodge in the Forest of Bowland in Lancashire. In between, he stayed at Garrowby, the home of the Earl and Countess of Halifax in Yorkshire, and with Chips and Sarah Keswick in Invermark, Sutherland. Before a visit to one friend in nort-east England, Charles's staff arrived a day early with a truck carrying furniture to replace the perfectly appropriate fittings in the guest rooms: nothing less than Charles and Camilla's complete bedrooms, including the prince's orthopaedic bed, complete with his own linen. His staff made sure not to forget a small radio, the prince's lavatory seat, Kleenex Velvet lavatory paper, Laphroaig whisky and water in both rooms, plus two landscapes of the Scottish Highlands. The next delivery was his food. His hosts decided, despite their enjoyment of his company, not to invite him again.

Their experience was less distressing than the family asked to host Charles for a long weekend on the Welsh borders. In the preceding months they had invited many friends for the four meals, hired staff and ordered food and flowers. On the Friday afternoon of Charles's expected arrival, there was a call from St James's Palace to offer regrets. Under pressure of business, the prince could not arrive until Saturday morning. The following day, the same official telephoned to offer regrets for Saturday lunch, but gave the assurance that Charles would arrive for dinner. That afternoon, the whole visit was cancelled due to 'unforeseen circumstances'. The considerable waste and disappointment were not mitigated when Charles later revealed to his stricken hostess that the reason for his cancellation was that he had felt unable to abandon the beauty of his sunlit garden at Highgrove.

The prince was discourteous in other ways. After arriving punctually for the ceremony of the Order of the Bath in Westminster Abbey, the queen became irritated: Charles was late. Bad weather, she was told by an official, had prevented his helicopter from landing. Once he arrived, their performance was perfect. Each showed respect to the other, but as usual barely demonstrated any genuine affection.

Charles's lifestyle was unusually extravagant. With an annual income of £7.5 million from farmland owned by the Duchy of

Cornwall, he employed about ninety staff, including ten gardeners at Highgrove alone, at a cost of £2 million annually. He was unusually particular. Because he refused to use pesticides at his Gloucestershire home, he employed four gardeners to lie flat, nose-down on a trailer pulled by a slow-moving Land Rover to pluck weeds. Retired Indian servicemen were deployed to prowl through the undergrowth at night with torches and handpick slugs from the leaves of plants. Lewis Carroll had conjured a similar fantasy when the Red Queen in *Alice in Wonderland* demanded that her roses be of the right colour. The extravagance ran to his office, where he employed an individual private secretary for each of his interests, including the charities, architecture, complementary medicine and the environment. Visitors to St James's Palace were escorted to Charles's office by no fewer than three footmen, each responsible for a short segment of corridor. The reason for Charles's self-indulgence was often debated. The most obvious cause, speculated some, was his decision to defy his father's imposition of frugality at Gordonstoun.

Rather than appreciating his good fortune, Charles would frequently give vent to resentment, earning him one friend's accolade as 'an Olympian whinger'. Succumbing to pressure, in April 2000 he agreed to fly to Europe on a British Airways plane instead of by private jet. He returned vowing never to repeat the experience. The incident clearly had an effect. Soon after, at a dinner hosted by a billionaire at Klosters to raise money to restore a church spire in Prague, Charles was particularly maudlin. During the meal, the glossy women and their sunburnt husbands had been bantering in the braying tones unique to the super-rich.

One billionaire asked his neighbour, 'What did you do today?'

'I drank coffee, had a walk and not much more,' came the reply.

'Who are you?' the first man asked.

'I'm King Constantine of Greece.'

At the end of the meal, the king and Charles huddled in a corner. 'We pulled the short straw,' sighed Charles. Compared to others in the room, he complained, both he and the king were stuck for cash. The duchy administrators, he said, repeatedly told him what he could not afford to do. During a recent after-dinner speech at Waddesdon Manor, Jacob Rothschild's home in Buckinghamshire,

Charles had complained that his host employed more gardeners than himself – fifteen against his nine.

Fortunately, the public were unaware of such gripes, but Charles's lifestyle irked some of his senior staff, particularly Tom Camoys. The former banker argued that the estate should be run as a business, not as a self-indulgence. Camoys's fate was sealed during the investiture of Elton John for his knighthood. 'Mr John Elton,' he announced, seemingly unaware of who the singer was. In royal circles, careers could be wrecked by a single mistake, and Camoys was now a marked man. His misfortune, observed one courtier, was that even the queen disliked his attitude: 'He doesn't create a good atmosphere. Tom gave orders rather than using quiet persuasion.' Realising that even he, ranked among the most illustrious of the royal staff, was being 'hung out to dry', Camoys agreed to resign. To Charles, he had scored a victory over Buckingham Palace.

The millennium was approaching. To the queen's closest advisers, the planned celebrations were noticeably undermining her self-confidence. Even before the exhibition at the Dome celebrating twenty-first-century Britain opened, its contents were derided as tacky, and on the night itself the long queues and dreary show left the monarch looking glum. Her Jubilee, she warned, would be another damp squib. Bruised by years of media scrutiny, she relied for support on her daily phone call from the queen mother, during which she could also share her anxiety about her sister Margaret's declining health, the cost of a lifetime smoking and drinking. Her unhappiness permeated the household. The absence of leadership among the staff at Buckingham Palace was disturbing. 'I need them to work together,' she said to a senior official, 'so I can give my best.' After a pause, she also admitted her concern for her elder son's fragility.

Charles was even more wedded to the telephone. During his night-time and Sunday-morning calls to friends, he would wail about the stress of his semi-covert life, the tensions with his family, and Buckingham Palace's complaints about Mark Bolland. In that case, his predicament was insoluble. He needed his propagandist more than ever to legitimise Camilla, yet Robin Janvrin regularly complained that Bolland's activities were 'dangerous and irresponsible', dividing the two palaces. Bolland fought too hard, was the word. With skill and passion he was promoting Charles as the star, sometimes, Buckingham Palace believed, at the expense of the queen and other members of her family.

In their anger towards Bolland, Janvrin and other senior courtiers assumed that Charles was too gullible to ignore Bolland's advice. No one imagined that Charles and Camilla were approving or even directing Bolland's activities. To warn her son about the dangers, the queen agreed that an adviser should once again travel to Highgrove. The emissary was met with indifference as he described the 'bad atmosphere' between the palaces and the need for more genial relations. He then listened to Charles heap blame on Stephen Lamport. In truth, Charles's powerless but good-hearted private secretary was besieged by irreconcilable demands from the courtiers on the one side, and from Charles, Camilla and Bolland on the other.

The meeting of the Way Ahead Group chaired by the queen on 30 March 2000 reflected the family's year. Everyone was bad-tempered, and almost the only person not to raise his voice in anger – other than the queen – was Charles, who, fearful of a stinging rebuke from his father, remained silent. Eventually the tensions faded.

Only Camilla was satisfied. Her plan to be accepted by both monarch and public, she believed, was slowly bearing fruit. At Charles's behest she had met Robin Janvrin, David Airlie and Michael Peat, who had been praised for vastly improving the queen's finances. She had also been introduced to Scottish church leaders and to George Carey, the Archbishop of Canterbury, at the south London home of the clergyman's son. During those encounters she did much to detoxify her image.

Pressure on the queen was growing. At another fundraising dinner in Buckingham Palace organised by Robert Higdon, Camilla had fussed that she wanted to sit on the same table as Charles, but he was reluctant to antagonise his mother or Janvrin. While Bolland bore the prince's familiar complaints about the unfairness of life, Robert Higdon produced a solution: 'Why don't we keep Camilla "off-list" on the seating plan, then just put her in an unnamed "empty" chair on Charles's table?' While Charles greeted his guests at the door, Higdon approached the American socialite Betsy Bloomingdale and asked, 'Can you look after Camilla before dinner so she won't be alone?' 'Delighted,' she replied. Camilla ended up seated opposite Charles, between the husband of Patty Hearst, the renegade newspaper heiress, and Ted Stanley, a manufacturer of collectable coins and stamps. 'When Ma'am's away,' Charles told his guests, looking across at Camilla, 'the mice will play.'

The game plan was reaching another landmark. King Constantine of Greece had accepted an invitation to celebrate his sixtieth birthday in June 2000 at a barbecue lunch at Highgrove with many of Europe's royal families and the queen's close friends. Charles knew that his mother would be loath to miss the occasion. To his satisfaction, Janvrin told Bolland that the queen would go to the party, although she would refuse to be introduced to Camilla. 'For Her Majesty, she does not exist,' one courtier commented, adding that it was 'churlish of the queen'. Charles was told to arrange for the two women to sit far apart. Two days later, the *Sun* revealed that they would both be at the party. Camilla, 'a source' told the newspaper, had 'emerged into the sunlight. They are now free to marry if they want to.'

Bolland's optimism proved premature. Two weeks later the queen hosted 'the Dance of the Decades', a party at Windsor to celebrate the queen mother's hundredth birthday, William's eighteenth, Margaret's seventieth and Anne's fiftieth. The queen refused to invite Camilla, but sharing her mother's fondness for Andrew Parker Bowles, she welcomed the brigadier, by then hailed as the Guards' most popular commanding officer. Regardless of all the pressure, the queen did not believe that Charles would marry Camilla in her lifetime.

In the festering aftermath of the Windsor party, Robin Janvrin persuaded Stephen Lamport to make a formal complaint to the Press Complaints Commission about the *Sun*'s headline 'Marry Her', with the demand that Bolland receive a knighthood. Charles and Camilla, Lamport wrote to the newspaper, had no plans to marry. Strictly speaking, that was true, and was evidence of Janvrin's campaign against Bolland – and the prince.

Charles soon saw an opportunity to retaliate. He invited a galaxy of the rich to celebrate the opening of the Prince's Foundation in Shoreditch. The completion of the new east London centre had inevitably sparked arguments about some details, including where to locate a bar that would be open to the public. To resolve the issue, it was suggested that Charles be asked to mediate. 'This is ridiculous,' exclaimed Bolland. 'The idea that the Prince of Wales would have the faintest idea where to put a bar to entice the public is completely ridiculous.' To present a modern image, the stainless steel tables were covered in black rubber, and instead of flowers there were pots of cacti wound with barbed wire.

On the invitations to the dinner, Camilla was billed as co-host. To secure the media's attention, she arrived in a garish pink Versace dress (Donatella Versace was one of the guests), wearing the jewels given by King Edward VII when he was Prince of Wales to his mistress – and, not irrelevantly, Camilla's great-grandmother – Alice Keppel. The media were encouraged to report that Camilla had lost weight and was devoting attention to her appearance, with facials, manicures, a new hairdresser, and a reduced smoking habit. Unused to arriving at an event amid a blitz of flashes, she walked off from the car in the wrong direction. The media did not lampoon her mistake, nor mention that her outlandish dress had been worn in return for Donatella Versace's donation to the Prince's Foundation.

Publicising his feud with his mother overshadowed Charles's other work, in particular his creation of a school for British art students. For years he had deplored Britain's art colleges' refusal to teach traditional drawing and painting. By 2000 his irritation was no longer simply ideological, but was exacerbated by what he saw as the sheer inability of Britain's teachers to paint anything other than abstract art. Aspiring British painters were travelling to Italy to learn classical skills and work with life models. To Charles, the proof of the nation's inferior art education was the celebration of Tracey Emin – known for her sexually explicit autobiographical and confessional approach – as an outstanding artist. The new Shoreditch building, the centre of the Royal Drawing School and the brainchild of Adrian Gale, the man Charles had unceremoniously dismissed from his Institute of Architecture, was acclaimed by traditionalists as a considerable achievement.

Finding the money had been the work of three people. Hilary Browne-Wilkinson had enticed the philanthropist Drue Heinz to buy the building for £2 million. 'I'll give him the money if he comes to my home to ask for it,' said Heinz. Over lunch at her home in Hay's Mews, Mayfair, she said to Charles, 'I'll give you the money, but you didn't give me a receipt for the last lot I gave you.'

Charles grimaced. Heinz's first donation to the institute of £2.5 million had been wasted. 'I'm so grateful,' he said lamely.

The second donation was negotiated by Stephen Lamport, the Saudi government agreeing to translate an endowment into cash.

Thirdly, Robert Higdon had persuaded Joe Allbritton, the chief executive of Riggs Bank, to make a sizeable gift.

Securing the building meant a lot to Charles. He knew that his new school would not save the world, but at least it would win him the gratitude of artists. Inevitably, there were casualties. Charles did not endear himself to Tim Bell, the political consultant who had originally led Drue Heinz into his orbit: 'After I introduced her, Fawcett hustled himself into it and took my old friend to Scotland to meet Charles behind my back to get her money. Then they ignored me, which hurt my feelings. Charles never said a word of thanks.'

The controversial Turkish businessman Cem Uzan, another guest at the Shoreditch dinner, was more appreciative, and let Bell's consultancy, Bell Pottinger, know that he would pay generously to fulfil his social ambitions. In the parlance of the market, 'Uzan wanted to play with the big boys and get alongside the royal family. He wanted the photograph and the Christmas card.' Through Bell Pottinger, Uzan was introduced to Elizabeth Buchanan, who agreed to steer him into the prince's life.

At that point Michael Fawcett came into the picture again. Since, officially, Charles could not ask Uzan or anyone else for money, on his behalf Fawcett explained what size of donation would be expected: £200,000 would guarantee that Uzan's wife Alara sat next to Charles at a dinner. The appropriate payment was made, and the meal went off smoothly. The following day, photographs of both Uzans standing with the prince were posted on media sites across the world. Uzan was billed as a billionaire tycoon who had bought the famous In and Out Club on Piccadilly (in fact he never did so). Charles's relationship with Uzan aroused concern in Buckingham Palace, but the queen's advisers knew that he would ignore any warning from them.

A few weeks later, Charles and Camilla were cruising off Nice as the guests of Neimar Kirdar, an Iraqi-born banker and chairman of Investcorp, the owner of the motorway catering chain Welcome Break, Saks department store in New York, and Gucci. To secure Kirdar's donations, Charles had welcomed the Iraqi to Highgrove and accepted an invitation to his daughter's wedding. Sunbathing on Kirdar's yacht underlined the contrariness of Charles's life. While feuding with his family, he socialised with colourful donors to his charities, but did little to promote the monarchy. Some believed that his behaviour contributed to the decline of deference signalled by the BBC's refusal to broadcast the queen mother's hundredth-birthday parade in August.

Although the nation's enthusiastic celebration of that occasion exposed the BBC's misjudgement, respite was brief. In autumn 2000, the public mood again turned sour. Charles had been untouched by headlines about the use of illegal drugs by William's cousin Nicholas Knatchbull, and by Lord Frederick Windsor, the son of Prince Michael of Kent, the queen's cousin. These had distracted attention from the exposé of Tom Parker Bowles, but a new report created unexpected embarrassment.

In the past, Camilla had successfully isolated Charles from his old friends, including Nicholas Soames, and she now set her sights on Emilie van Cutsem. She suspected that van Cutsem disapproved of her relationship with Charles, and had heard that she had criticised her son Tom for taking William to unsuitable parties. She now complained that van Cutsem's son Edward, a close childhood friend of William, was also inviting the young prince to louche entertainments. But although, as one observer noted, 'Camilla poured her opinion into Charles's ear', the prince remained devoted to Emilie and Hugh van Cutsem.

In their prickly world, those who befriended the van Cutsems were ostracised by Robert Fellowes and his wife Jane. But any vitriol spread by the Fellowes enhanced Charles's warm feelings towards the van Cutsems, who years before he had spontaneously toasted at their wedding. However, events beyond his control would stretch that loyalty to breaking point.

Chris Morgan of the *Sunday Times* was still determined to unearth evidence that William and Harry were taking drugs. Having failed with several attempts, he approached Hugh van Cutsem and persuaded him that Mark Bolland was gossiping that the van Cutsems' four sons were drug-takers. Although the whole scenario had been fabricated by Morgan, van Cutsem – who was known to address underlings only if they could improve the breeding of his horses – became convinced that Bolland was guilty, and ordered his lawyers to write to Bolland accusing him of making 'highly damaging' remarks. Van Cutsem gave a copy of this defamatory letter, which Bolland believed was an attempt to bring about his removal from the palace, to the *Mail on Sunday*, adding for good measure that Camilla was undermining his friendship with Charles. In retaliation, to protect Camilla and embarrass van Cutsem, Bolland's irate reply was also leaked.

The public argument soon became uglier. Morgan (who for unrelated reasons eventually committed suicide) wrote in his newspaper that William had been caught using cocaine, but that Bolland had briefed journalists that it was in fact van Cutsem's son who had taken the drug, not William. That was also untrue – there was no evidence that either William or any van Cutsem had taken any drugs, or that Bolland had spread such a story. Nevertheless, to protect the royals, Bolland told the *News of the World* that Charles had summoned his sons from school to discuss the crisis. He also revealed that the prince had taken sixteen-year-old Harry to a rehabilitation clinic to show him the dramatic effects of addiction. Examination of the timing of all these events suggested multiple distortions of the truth – embarrassing Charles, Camilla, Hugh and Emilie van Cutsem, and the eight children of three families. All were tarnished.

'Everyone was livid,' recalled Bolland, aware that Janvrin had warned about this precise danger – of the royal family at the mercy of innuendo, scandalous accusations and his own manipulation of the media. At Charles's invitation, Hugh van Cutsem agreed to settle the argument between himself and Bolland at a meeting with the prince at St James's Palace. Stephen Lamport was also present. All four arrived convinced that they were the victim. At the end of the meeting everyone apologised, but the poison lingered. For the first time in about thirty years Charles did not invite van Cutsem to his annual shoot at Sandringham.

The unseemly spat between the friends coincided with the publication of *Shadows of a Princess* by Patrick Jephson, a former naval officer and Diana's one-time private secretary. The book's sympathetic description of Diana, and its revelations about the indignities inflicted on her by Charles, sharply contradicted Penny Junor's pro-Charles account.

To help his sales, Jephson hinted that at an early stage while he was writing the book, with the queen's approval, Robert Fellowes had offered to provide his confidential papers to him. 'Well, someone's going to do it, so it might as well be Patrick,' the queen allegedly told Janvrin. Later, Fellowes withdrew his supposed offer.

Added to that mix, Jephson also told journalists that he had not written about Diana's descriptions of Charles's unusual sexual life. Withholding that information did not protect the prince from the book's mass serialisation. Lurid headlines, sparked by intimate details, attracted the usual criticisms. Nicky Gavron, the former wife of a printer and multi-millionaire businessman who had donated £1 million to the Labour Party and soon after received a peerage, announced that Charles should have married a black woman. Mo Mowlam, a prominent, publicity-seeking Labour minister, declared that the queen should move out of Buckingham Palace and live in a small modern house. Once again, the monarchy's reputation began to slide.

Then it got worse. On 5 November the *Daily Mail* reported that Prince Andrew had befriended a drug dealer in Los Angeles, and next published photographs of the prince, during an official visit to New York, at a 'hookers and pimps' party with seedy characters. He had arrived with Ghislaine Maxwell, the daughter of the disgraced newspaper magnate Robert Maxwell, had been seen near a known prostitute, and soon after was photographed on a yacht in Thailand with topless girls linked to drugs.

Charles was not surprised by the revelations. He had long feared a fall-out from his brother's antics. Their relations had become fraught earlier in the year, after Charles refused Sarah Ferguson's invitation to her ex-husband's fortieth birthday party. Eight years after being photographed topless while her 'financial adviser' Johnny Bryan sucked her toes, Ferguson's vulgarity was still not forgotten. Charles's dislike of his one-time sister-in-law had escalated after she had chased him around Highgrove carrying a Bible, begging to be allowed to swear her innocence of her reported misbehaviour. In that unforgiving mood, he had listened at the recent meeting of the Way Ahead Group to Andrew's plan to become a British trade ambassador after leaving the navy the following year. Charles chose that moment to renew his attempt to remove the privileges enjoyed by Andrew's daughters and other minor royals. On that occasion he was thwarted by Andrew, who rallied support from the queen and Prince Philip. Charles argued with his father before, as ever powerless to defy him, walking out of the room.

At the same time, he also targeted Sophie Wessex, Edward's wife. He had warned her about the danger of accepting a contract to provide public relations services for Rover cars. Unwilling to forsake the £250,000 fee she had been offered, she had rejected his advice and took the money. In the face of such problems, Richard Luce, the new lord chamberlain and a principled former Foreign Office minister, had drafted rules for the royals to avoid compromising themselves with commercial connections. However, at Philip's insistence, Sophie's contract was not cancelled, although Luce did extract a promise from her not to use her position to attract business in the future. In Charles's opinion, the conduct of Sophie's husband was similarly unacceptable. In 1999 Edward had agreed with an American production company to produce and sell a TV documentary about the queen mother. At that point, he and Sophie were living in a fifty-seven-room house in Bagshot Park; they had made themselves vulnerable to public criticism.

All these perilous concoctions were brewing when Charles agreed with Mark Bolland's suggestion that he, Camilla and their children accept an invitation to celebrate the tenth anniversary of the Press Complaints Commission at Somerset House in February 2001. Their presence, said Bolland, would repair relations. The event, with five hundred guests, was a success, but six weeks later another crisis arrived.

In just the sort of scandal Charles had feared, Sophie Wessex was caught in a *News of the World* sting. A two-hour taped conversation recorded her flaunting her royal connections in order to secure a £500,000 publicity contract, unaware that she was speaking to the undercover journalist Mazher Mahmood, alias 'the Fake Sheikh', who was supposedly representing a Dubai investment company. The encounter had been arranged by the notorious publicist Max Clifford. That breach of Wessex's promise was made even worse by her reference to the queen during the conversation as 'the old dear'. She also disparaged Tony Blair as 'ignorant about the countryside', described Cherie Blair as 'absolutely horrid, horrid, horrid', William Hague as 'deformed', and predicted that Charles and Camilla would marry, but not until 'the old lady dies'. What reputation she still possessed was not enhanced by her business partner's boasts about his use of cocaine and rent boys.

The timing would never have been ideal, but it now proved doubly unfortunate. Robin Janvrin had recently mentioned to another courtier that Buckingham Palace was thankfully immune to the scandals battering St James's Palace, and in that benign mood he had replaced Simon Lewis with Simon Walker. The former journalist and publicist, after a stint employed by John Major in Downing Street, was to focus on arranging the Jubilee celebrations. After Sophie appealed for help, he appeared sufficiently experienced to manage the maelstrom, made all the more significant because, once the queen mother died, Sophie would become Britain's second-highest-ranking woman in order of precedence after the queen.

Walker negotiated a deal with the *News of the World*. The paper agreed not to publish Sophie's comments about the queen and the Blairs in return for an interview with her about Edward's sexuality. Naïvely, Walker did not ask himself why the paper was so cooperative. Nor did he demand a transcript of the Mahmood tape, relying instead on Sophie's emotional outburst to him admitting her sins – although in the familiar way of royal conversations, she failed to reveal all her embarrassing comments. Thus Walker did not realise that Rebekah Wade, the *News of the World*'s editor, had agreed not to use the taped conversation only because it lacked, in her opinion, 'a killer line'. By contrast, the agreed interview produced a sensational headline on April Fool's Day: 'Sophie: My Edward is Not Gay'. Sophie was quoted as saying, 'I can tell you he is not gay', and describing the couple's use of IVF.

That seemed, in all its tawdriness, to be that. But Sophie got stung a second time. On the same day as the publication of the interview in the *News of the World*, the *Mail on Sunday* published all her dismissive comments about the queen, the Blairs and Diana. Unknown to Walker, the *Mail* had somehow obtained a transcript of the conversation. Panic hit the palace. 'That's made it ten times worse!' cried one official. Thrashing around for a culprit, Buckingham Palace officials assumed without any evidence that since Sophie's embarrassment could only benefit Charles, it was Mark Bolland who had handed the scoop to the *Mail on Sunday*. Extraordinarily, no Buckingham Palace official dared challenge Bolland to his face. 'You had to tread carefully,' admitted one. 'He had a Rasputin-like reputation. There was a risk that to make an enemy of Bolland would make an enemy of Charles.'

While Buckingham Palace sniped at Bolland, the *News of the World* blamed Walker for breaking their agreement. The following weekend, the newspaper published the full transcript of the interview. Self-righteously, the *Sun* joined the fray, describing Sophie as 'nothing but an ambitious PR on the make. We know her sort. We know her game. We have no respect for her or her husband.'

There was a naïvety in believing that Bolland was to blame for everything which was echoed by Prince Philip's blame of media intrusion. In truth, the mess was caused by Sophie's greed. The queen accepted the advice of Janvrin and Richard Luce: Sophie was ordered to resign from her PR job. She blamed Simon Walker for her predicament, and was supported by Lord Wakeham, the chairman of the Press Complaints Commission, who told Luce, 'Walker let it happen.' Charles, the only winner from the imbroglio, was content for Luce, his temporary ally, to launch an investigation into the minor royals undertaking commercial work and whether they should be expelled from the official family. Unsurprisingly, under the headline 'Reform or Die – Tony Blair Had Warned the Royals', the *News of the World* supported Charles's proposal that the palace should be cleansed. 'Only Charles is talking sense,' commented its editor.

The prince's three siblings were furious. While he pocketed nearly £8 million that year from the Duchy of Cornwall, which would increase by £2 million the following year, and each of his private-jet flights between London and Scotland cost nearly £20,000, he offered no solution to their financial plights. Philip shared their anger. All four children, he said, should be treated equally. 'We have different attitudes,' he said, persistently irritated by his eldest son's behaviour. Why, he asked, did Charles undermine his parents' frugal lifestyle as an example to the nation? And why did he continue his affair with Camilla, whose former husband was a brother officer? And why did he cultivate trashy American billionaires?

Charles would not tolerate such criticism. With disdain, he sat through another family meeting, knowing that Philip would be annoyed by his silence. The tension between father and son did not die down. Charles rejected his father's pleas that he, Philip, was a loving parent. Both preferred to communicate by letter. Some still excused Charles's churlishness as the unresolved result of the misery of his childhood. Others, quoted by Graham Turner, a journalist with access to Philip, would say that a fifty-three-year-old man was no longer of an age to scowl about being 'quite frightened by his father who dominates the family by being bullying and loud'.

Preoccupied by his own emotions, Charles showed no sympathy for Philip's own torrid childhood as an exile, forced to move home constantly without a father, while his mother was confined in a Swiss clinic for eight years with paranoid schizophrenia. And he resented what he regarded as his father's hypocrisy. Throughout Philip's marriage there had been rumours of affairs with aristocrats, actresses, and even a waitress at Fortnum & Mason. Admittedly, if the gossip was true, Philip had been exceptionally discreet, and none of his dalliances could be irrefutably proven.

Any chance of brokering peace between father and son was disturbed by Graham Turner's semi-authorised biography of Philip, serialised in the *Daily Telegraph*, in which he quoted Philip's judgement of Charles as 'precious, extravagant and lacking in the dedication ... to make a good king'. Shortly after the book's publication, Philip wrote his son an apology.

Charles's perpetual squabbles with his parents were aggravated by their tolerance of his brothers' follies. The latest of these was Edward's planned TV documentary about Charles's life with Diana and Camilla. Janvrin hesitated to seek a directive from the queen to tell Edward to halt the production. Despite Charles's warnings, Edward then began a documentary about Prince William. Without permission, his crew filmed around St Andrews University, where William was enrolled as a student, in the hope of finding him or interviewing his friends for a £50 fee. After learning about the film, Charles refused to take Edward's calls. Even Philip was irritated, and his anger boiled over when he heard that Andrew had just passed an entire week playing golf, and had spent £500,000 on private jets that year. 'You're lazy and selfish!' he shouted. 'Just lounging around!' But neither younger son had a profession he could fall back on. To conceal the wounds, Richard Luce issued a statement that, subject to consultation, the royals 'should be allowed to pursue careers, including in business, if that is what they wish to do'. Within the palaces, no one was deceived.

The wisest of the queen's advisers had watched the slow train crash knowing that 'it was going to end in tears'. The queen, as so often where her children were concerned, prevaricated. Torn between duty and her love of family, she asked Philip for his opinion. The duke wanted 'action', and agreed to a conference at Windsor about Edward's future. In advance, officials composed a written description of Edward's predicament. An added complication was that his production company had debts of £2 million. The solutions proposed were either that he could keep his title but be restricted to work as an unpaid royal, or that he be allowed to earn a living but become a private citizen.

While he awaited his parents' decision, Edward spent much of his time in his house playing computer games. During the ensuing frosty discussion the queen and Philip were clearly dejected. By its end, she had decided to give Edward £250,000 annually in compensation for not working. Then, in a rare moment of frustration, she tore up the discussion document and threw the scraps of paper into the fire. Soon after, Simon Walker left Buckingham Palace. Charles had got what he wanted, although his own mismanagement was propelling him towards yet another showdown.

11

A Butler's Warnings

The outbreak of royal embarrassment struck Don McKinnon, the new secretary general of the Commonwealth, as unfortunate. The sixty-three-year-old former deputy prime minister of New Zealand had arrived in London the previous year. In his first private meeting with the queen he had been impressed by the importance with which she, as head of a family of fifty-two nations, regarded the Commonwealth. Equally, he knew that while all those governments, regardless of their political colours, respected her leadership, such sentiments did not apply to her eldest son.

'You'll have to work hard to keep Charles as the next head of the Commonwealth,' Emeka Anyaoku of Nigeria, McKinnon's predecessor, had told him. Charles wrongly assumed that he would automatically inherit the right to leadership, warned Anyaoku, but he failed to appreciate how many Commonwealth leaders, especially in the conservative Caribbean and Africa, were shocked by reports of his extramarital affairs and by his treatment of Diana. Additionally, it had been noticed that, while Charles travelled frequently, the only Commonwealth countries that he had regularly visited were Canada, Australia and New Zealand. He was prepared to fly off to see President Bush to maintain Britain's special relationship, but rarely his non-white Commonwealth brethren. 'Commonwealth leaders say that they don't know Charles beyond the salacious stuff they read in the newspapers,' McKinnon told Janvrin and Lamport. Neither denied the criticism. 'Charles must do his bit,' he went on. 'He needs to focus on Commonwealth affairs.'

Lamport was reluctant to assist, and McKinnon discovered that senior officials in Whitehall were no better. John Kerr, the permanent secretary at the Foreign Office, tolerated Charles's demands for 'a bit of a glamorous jolly' on foreign trips, but made no attempt to persuade him to visit the non-white Commonwealth more frequently. There would also be no help from Tony Blair to encourage Charles to 'do his duty visits'. The prime minister, McKinnon realised, was not interested in the Commonwealth: 'To him, it belonged, like fox-hunting, to another age.' He appealed to the queen. The Commonwealth's existence, he emphasised, was in jeopardy. She agreed to persuade her son to visit countries selected by the Foreign Office rather than picked out by him for his own pleasure. McKinnon was grateful, but remained dissatisfied. To rush Charles into visits would be unwise. 'We need to hold meetings between Charles and the high commissioners in London,' he told Lamport, 'so they can send positive reports back to their governments.'

Charles resisted the idea. Conversing with diplomats appalled him. After pressure from Buckingham Palace, he finally relented and agreed to meet the high commissioners from the Pacific countries at New Zealand House. McKinnon was unimpressed by the reports of the encounter.

Charles was about to become immersed in more 'salacious stuff' that would threaten a great deal more than his leadership of the Commonwealth.

At 3 p.m. on 30 April 2001, Detective Chief Inspector Maxine de Brunner and Detective Sergeant Roger Milburn arrived at Fiona Shackleton's office. Waiting in the conference room were Sarah McCorquodale and Michael O'Kane, with an assistant to take notes.

Shackleton started the discussion. Mark Bolland, she said, had taken responsibility for the Paul Burrell issue. She also revealed that Charles was 'very determined' that the march towards prosecution should be halted. De Brunner and O'Kane did not know on whose advice the prince had made that decision. Both could only assume that Shackleton had been consulted.

Shackleton now revealed that Prince William had received a letter from Burrell dated 19 April, six weeks after the butler's second police interview. Unknown to de Brunner or O'Kane, Burrell had written this letter on the advice of Bolland, who in turn was acting on Charles's instructions. Unread by William, the letter had been forwarded to Shackleton.

'There is much to explain,' Burrell had written. 'Items [that] have been taken from me, many of which were given to me for safekeeping, should be returned to you ... I know that you realise that I would never betray the trust your mother placed in me and I remain the person you have always known.'

After she read the letter, Shackleton realised that Burrell had changed one aspect of his story since his first two interviews. Six weeks earlier, he had refused to return all the items he had taken. He had also admitted that he had not told the princes that he was 'safe-keeping' their property. Now he was offering a partial return of William's possessions, but did not mention the items belonging either to Charles or to Diana's executors. She had not given the letter to the police.

To the officers present, Burrell's intransigence was inexplicable. Beneath a straightforward allegation of theft were layers of recrim-ination and suspicion. As outsiders, they sensed impenetrable machinations among those surrounding Charles. Then, out of the blue, the meeting became electrified.

In passing, McCorquodale mentioned the missing contents of Diana's mahogany box, including 'a tape which is sensitive'. To the evident surprise of the police and O'Kane, Shackleton blurted out, 'If you're talking about the rape, I know all about that.* I was given written instructions by my boss to make the whole business go away, which I did, but it was one of the lowest points of my twenty-two-year legal career.' She added, 'By the way, who has the tape now?'

'Paul Burrell has it,' McCorquodale replied. She understood the Medici-like atmosphere of Charles and Diana's court. She did not bother, however, to explain those relationships to the police officers or to O'Kane. Rather, she focused on the facts, and particularly her recollection of seeing the small tapes held together with a plastic band inside the mahogany box. She, like the police, was convinced that they were still in Burrell's possession, although in Charles's camp there were doubts. 'We didn't know if a tape existed,' said Bolland. 'It became a psychodrama because Charles just wanted to protect Fawcett. We changed our minds every day about the rape.'

In the tense minutes that followed Shackleton's outburst, McCorquodale added: 'The rape was covered up by palace officials.'

---

* Based on O'Kane's notes, Michael Peat would report that McCorquodale was the first person to use the word 'rape' (Peat Report, pp.35–40, 46). Both police officers insist it was Shackleton.

O'Kane assumed that Shackleton's admission about 'one of the lowest points' implied that Smith was telling the truth, and that she had been asked to cover things up. Regardless of the tapes, the conundrum was whether Shackleton's description of her devoted service to Charles five years earlier, when Smith's allegations surfaced, had crossed the line or was merely incautious language. Potentially she might have committed a crime, and so might her boss. After the meeting ended, O'Kane consulted David Calvert-Smith, the director of public prosecutions, to establish whether Shackleton's generous redundancy payment to Smith to make the matter 'go away' could amount to a criminal act. Calvert-Smith would rule out any criminality.

Shackleton then explained the background. On the tape was the voice of George Smith, a former Welsh Guardsman. He had been traumatised during the Falklands War watching his comrades burn alive on board the *Sir Galahad* after it was bombed by Argentinean aircraft. In 1986, he became a valet to Charles. Nine years later, by October 1995, he had become an alcoholic and suffered a nervous breakdown. At Charles's expense he was admitted to the Priory Hospital in south London, where he received a handwritten note from the prince that expressed his sorrow 'about all the agonies that have accumulated throughout your life and which have now come to the surface with such explosive force. I could not be more sympathetic and feel for you greatly.' Charles assured Smith that his job would be waiting for him when he was 'properly mended'.

Unknown to her ex-husband, Diana visited Smith at the Priory. 'She looked stunning,' the valet would later say. 'She was very happy and jovial. She cheered me up.' Accompanied by Victoria Mendham, her timid assistant, she then made a second visit, this time with an ulterior motive. She coaxed Smith, who was married, to retell his account of a drunken evening in 1989 in Michael Fawcett's flat. Smith described how he had awoken to discover that his trousers were down and that he had been raped while he slept. 'I was totally ashamed. I felt sick,' he told Diana. 'Terrified' of Fawcett and anxious to keep his job, he did not complain, but returned to St James's Palace. He would later say that as he told his story, 'The princess was shocked. She looked stunned.' Unknown to him, Diana had recorded everything he told her.

On returning to Kensington Palace, she discovered that her tape recorder, borrowed from Richard Kay, had malfunctioned. Undaunted, soon after Smith left the Priory she invited him to Kensington Palace, where he repeated his narrative for thirty minutes, directly into the same recorder. He then added a twist: he described seeing Fawcett in bed with Charles in the midst of a sexual act. At 3 a.m., Smith was driven home. Diana locked the tapes in a large mahogany box and hid the key.

Up to that point, most of those in Shackleton's office were aware of Smith's account. What happened afterwards, once Diana had the tapes, was known at the time to Shackleton, but not to either the police or O'Kane until later. Soon after the meeting with Smith, with Paul Burrell apparently standing at her side, Diana called Charles. After describing Smith's allegations, she urged him to dismiss Fawcett, whom she had never liked. 'Charles, are you listening to me?' she asked. 'This man is a monster.' According to Burrell, Charles urged her 'not to listen to staff tittle-tattle'.

Despite his concern, Charles disliked Smith, and overwhelmingly trusted Fawcett. Royal courts, the prince knew, attracted a certain kind of man who enjoyed the theatricality and pomp of the monarchy. Dedicated flatterers, they were comfortable in unreformed and unaccountable palaces. One aspect of their employment was the gay scene in Buckingham Palace's servants' quarters, but although some considered it debasing and predatory, employees generally chose either to participate or to leave. In that world, Burrell had been seen by some men as a trophy, but his wife Maria seized an opportunity to escape the situation by moving to Highgrove. There Burrell met Fawcett. In Diana's opinion the two men enjoyed intriguing together, and a bond was formed. Somewhere in that mix was George Smith. As Charles admitted to Bolland, Fawcett had probably bullied Smith, or something similar. As for the alleged rape, he gave Bolland the firm impression that 'he did not really believe Smith', although occasionally he changed his mind.

The mood was different in Kensington Palace. 'The tapes had become Diana's nuclear weapon,' reckoned Patrick Jephson, who judged Smith to be 'a decent, nice man who was naïve and easy to exploit'. One of Diana's virtues, he believed, was 'seeing through liars. She could suss truth and danger whereas the Windsors could not read people.' By contrast, Michael Gibbins, the accountant promoted to be Jephson's successor as Diana's private secretary, considered Smith 'incoherent and unreliable'. In the peculiar world of Kensington Palace, Gibbins concluded, hearsay was being treated as if it were fact, so everyone believed Smith; while in St James's, where no one in Charles's camp believed the valet, facts were turned into hearsay. The tapes were just one of many battlegrounds between the two palaces.

At the heart of most of these clashes was Michael Fawcett. 'He did have a hold over Charles,' observed Robert Higdon, 'but it wasn't sexual. Fawcett is asexual, and Smith's accusation was bullshit.' Bolland agreed that Fawcett was no rapist, but felt that his fate was entwined with that of Burrell, who had become Diana's weapon in the war between the two factions.

Among Burrell's skills was his ability to use and misuse the court's highest-value currency – information. Both Jephson and Gibbins believed that Burrell had devoured Diana's secrets, not least by read-ing letters and documents in her desk. Once he became the secret conduit into Kensington Palace for her lovers, the Faustian pact with Diana precluded his removal. Her dependence upon Burrell mirrored Charles's on Fawcett.

Charles's motives were complicated. Back in 1996, Smith's allega-tions had surfaced at the worst moment in the prince's life. In the aftermath of Squidgygate (a tape of a bugged conversation between Diana and her secret lover), Camillagate, the Dimbleby and Morton books, Diana's *Panorama* interview and so much more, he suspected his former wife of using a vulnerable man to invent a story just to cause him trouble. He feared that Smith, egged on by Diana, would repeat his allegations to the media. 'Diana has been interfering and visiting George Smith,' Shackleton had noted after a conversation with Charles. More bad publicity was his worst nightmare, so he had asked Richard Aylard to investigate. The result was unambigu-ous. Smith told Aylard that he did not want to make a complaint, while Fawcett vehemently denied the allegation.* The private secre-tary's report seemed to end the saga.

Charles's misfortune was that Smith's accusations had surfaced just as Aylard was handing over to Stephen Lamport. With the management of his office in disarray, Charles relied upon Shackleton.

---

* Smith would later deny that Aylard had questioned him.

After several conversations with Smith, she told Charles that 'there may be truth in some of the allegations' because, she added, 'There is no smoke without fire.' However, on the basis of Aylard's investigation, she advised that there was no need to inform the police about what Smith had said, even though the palace needed to establish the truth about his 'very serious claims'. Without a criminal expert in Charles's office, Shackleton's judgement produced a convenient solution: everyone at St James's Palace agreed to disbelieve Smith and deny a rape had occurred. In a crisis, perceptions counted. On Charles's instructions, Lamport also sought to avoid a proper investigation.

Weeks later, the crisis flared up again. Smith's mental condition had deteriorated, and Charles decided he should resign. Taking instructions from her employer, Shackleton made a note that Smith should depart 'without explosion'. Before Shackleton visited his home to discuss a redundancy payment, independent solicitors, paid for by Charles, were retained to advise Smith. A note by a colleague records Shackleton saying before her visit, 'I'll tell him that if he brings it into the open, then we look v. heavily into his background etc. Ruin chances of getting another job.' During her visit, she offered him £38,000, a generous amount, on condition of his silence. Smith took the money, and soon found a new job.

Over the following months, neither Diana nor Charles would be sure whether Shackleton fully understood everything that had happened. Diana would insist that she was not blackmailing Charles, but was only seeking to destroy Fawcett. She had told Bolland that she and Charles had discussed the gay staff employed in the palaces, and that both enjoyed identifying who was in a relationship with whom, and speculating about the sex below stairs. Both were intrigued by homosexual practices. Whether Shackleton (who did not share their enthusiasm) understood those bizarre dynamics was debatable. Some would later say that she was out of her depth.

Briefed by O'Kane, David Calvert-Smith had referred his concerns to Lord Williams of Mostyn, the attorney general, who in turn spoke to Jeremy Heywood, Tony Blair's principal private secretary. What had started with the theft of two small ornaments had reached the prime minister and the queen's private secretary. Since the alleged rape was a separate crime, Commander John Yates, de Brunner's superior officer and in overall charge of the Burrell investigation, assigned the case to another team under Detective Superintendent Steve Gwilliam and Detective Sergeant Mark Hodges. They would follow Burrell onto the cruise ship the *QE2*, where he gave lectures about his life as a royal valet and promoted his book *Entertaining with Style*. He was questioned about the missing contents of the mahogany box, and especially the rape tapes. He professed complete ignorance. By then his denial had been contradicted by Ken Wharfe, for six years Diana's protection officer and still a serving policeman.

On 2 May, Shackleton, by this time much concerned, called O'Kane. The CPS's note of the meeting in her office, she protested, was incomplete. The references to the rape, she said, ignored her explanation that in distressing circumstances she had been compensating the victim of a crime. During that call and a subsequent conversation about Burrell, she added (according to the police record), 'Charles doesn't want to prosecute and wants it all to go away. It must be stopped.' Some of those directly involved in the case would judge that Shackleton was well-meaning but at times too sure of herself. Others thought she was panicking.

Following her call to O'Kane, he in turn phoned de Brunner and told her of the conversation. In her notes about the call, made at the time, de Brunner wrote, 'Prince Charles didn't want to prosecute and wanted it all to go away and be stopped.' Two years later, O'Kane could not remember speaking to Shackleton after their meeting on 30 April – or, by implication, reporting the conversation to de Brunner.

On the same day, the CPS's case against Burrell became more assured. Included in the police haul from his house were two china plates which Sir Hugh Roberts, a curator of the Royal Collection, confirmed were from the Collection. As Burrell would have known, nothing from there could have been gifted away. More plates from the Collection would later be found under a sofa in Graham Burrell's home during a police raid. A watercolour by Charles was also recovered, stashed in Graham Burrell's attic.

The suspicions snowballed after the police watched six videos found in Paul Burrell's house. They featured Diana talking about the most intimate details of her relationship with the royal family, her sex life with Charles, and her affair with the police protection officer Barry Mannakee. They had been recorded by Peter Settelen, a speech coach hired by Diana in 1992 to improve her self-confidence in public. Pertinently, when soon after her death Settelen had asked for the return of not six but sixteen tapes, Michael Gibbins had replied, 'I am advised by Mr Burrell that he has been unable to trace them.' Yet on the day of this latest police raid, Milburn had asked Burrell about 'the tapes', meaning the rape tapes. 'What tape?' Burrell had said, and denied possessing any such thing. The police could only guess at the fate of Settelen's missing ten videos.

O'Kane, however, was no longer working on assumptions. Burrell, he realised, possessed many letters and cards from Diana to William, but none of the hundreds she had written to Harry. In the memorabilia market, letters to William, the heir to the throne, were valuable, those to Harry less so. The investigators drew one conclusion: Burrell's defence that he was holding William's cards to protect them from destruction by Diana's executors was questionable. Sarah McCorquodale was unlikely to shred a mother's letters to her son, and William had clearly not given them to Burrell.

In early July, de Brunner and Milburn flew to New York, Florida and San Francisco to search for evidence of any sales of Diana's possessions by Harold Brown and Burrell. The trip had been sparked by an informant in London. Jan Havlik, the Spink dealer, had claimed that Brown had certainly sold some of Diana's items in New York, and speculated that Brown and Burrell 'did this sort of thing together'. Another informant had suggested that Burrell and his brother had flown 'at least ten times' to America for exactly that purpose. Burrell had refused to comment about his trips. A later investigation showed that he had criss-crossed the Atlantic to give lectures and promote his book.

The two British officers met Jane Kerr and Dr Will Swift, dealers who were actively selling royal memorabilia. Swift's company, HRH Photographs, had dealt with Brown, but not with Burrell. The police returned to London disappointed. Another object of their visit had been to find out whether the FBI would help the investigation, but the FBI's input was limited, and without their influence Burrell's friends in America could not be persuaded to say anything.

In the middle of what had become a global investigation, any police pessimism was offset by the discovery that in 1999 Burrell had taken two diamonds to be remodelled as cufflinks. He had told the jeweller that they were a present from Diana, an explanation that could not be disproved. Equally intriguing, the police had also obtained a statement from Gregory Pead, a gay Australian living near Surfers' Paradise on Queensland's Gold Coast, who described his close sexual relationship with Burrell before the butler's marriage, and handed over forty letters from his ex-lover describing intimacies in the palace. Since the early 1980s, said Pead, Burrell had given him various objects taken from Kensington Palace. The butler's secret yet profligate homosexuality further complicated the investigation. Darren McGrady, Diana's chef, had called him 'Barrack-Room Bertha' because of his frequent affairs with guardsmen. By any measure, the circumstances facing the prosecutor were unusual.

By then, Burrell's lawyers had given the police a psychiatrist's report following a session with their client. His homosexuality was not mentioned, nor was anyone alerted to the psychiatrist's description of Burrell having met the queen at Buckingham Palace. The butler had spoken about his 'relationships' with Elizabeth, but did not mention a discussion with her about the safekeeping of any property. It was a vital omission, but easy to miss. Threads of evidence spread in all directions, and some were not being woven together, even by Burrell's lawyers. Andrew Shaw was visibly destabilised after Milburn showed him Burrell's love letters. The solicitor appeared to the police officer 'shocked and surprised'.

At the same time, the police were becoming more confident about their investigation. In a telephone call to de Brunner on 19 July 2001, Inspector Ken Wharfe repeated what he said was the latest gossip: the rape did happen, and Burrell was putting pressure on St James's Palace not to prosecute by mentioning the tapes, 'which he has got'. De Brunner recorded the policeman's message in writing.

The call coincided with Alex Carlile and Andrew Shaw meeting Shackleton and Robert Seabrook. Burrell's two lawyers issued a warning: the police investigation should be stopped, to avoid their client embarrassing the royal family. If Burrell were prosecuted, he would have to describe from the witness box not only details of Diana's sexual life, but also quote letters from Prince Philip allegedly threatening Diana – although no one besides Burrell and Prince Philip knew the contents of these letters. 'We hope we can get all this sorted out,' Bolland told Higdon, 'so Charles and Camilla can get married.'

At this point, the CPS and the police planned a 'victims' consultation meeting', in order to obtain the direct approval of Charles, Prince William and Sarah McCorquodale to prosecute Burrell. In anticipation of a police visit to Highgrove, Charles appealed to Bolland: 'Mark, this is crazy. You must do something.' The prince was willing to approve anything to avert a trial, especially with William a potential witness. The ideal solution, Bolland agreed, was for Burrell to return all the property and avoid a trial. He simply knew too much that could harm the Prince of Wales, so the errant butler needed protection.

A meeting was arranged through the journalist Richard Kay, by then Burrell's trusted confidant. It was set for the afternoon of 24 July at Balls Bar in St Martin's Lane in London, but at the last moment, nervous about being compromised, Bolland was reluctant to turn up. Kay pleaded with him, 'You must understand that Paul didn't steal anything.' The police, he said, had underestimated Diana's generosity towards Burrell: 'They're missing a trick about royal largesse to their staff.'

Persuaded to keep the appointment, Bolland intended to encourage the butler's belief that Charles cared about him. That proved unexpectedly easy. Over coffee, Burrell told Bolland, 'I'm sorry.' He wanted to let Charles know that he would return the property, but to tell him so in person. Bolland agreed to pass on the message. Throughout, he was appalled by Burrell's 'creepy manner'. The royals' staff, he thought, were 'a slimy, weird group with odd relationships'. He ended the encounter after twenty-five minutes, and duly reported back to Charles that the butler wanted 'a big hug and an offer of a job at Balmoral. He doesn't want to be cast out.'

'He doesn't want to be cast out,' repeated the prince thoughtfully.

One truth occurred to Bolland: 'No one cares whether Burrell is guilty or not.' Charles's fear was the butler's knowledge of Diana's reported drug abuse. Would he dare describe in court her use of cocaine, or would he disclose something worse, like the tapes? The combination of sex, drugs and thefts was all so grubby. 'Let's have a meeting with him,' Charles decided.

Bolland arranged the encounter between the prince and Burrell for the early evening of 3 August at the house of Amanda Hornby, the widow of Charles Hornby, a controversial businessman who lived in Tetbury, a short distance from Highgrove. Charles had already agreed for the police to visit Highgrove earlier the same day.

In anticipation of the 'victims' briefing', Commander Yates had spoken to Shackleton and Seabrook on 31 July. Yates arrived with the purpose of securing their support, and therefore Charles's, for a prosecution. In the two lawyers' opinion he kept his cards close to his chest, openly admitting that he feared that any information given to Charles would be leaked to the media by Bolland. 'Everyone has it in for Mark,' Charles exclaimed when he learned this. The police, he believed, were being self-important. Yates's take was more generous. In his opinion, Shackleton was charming, sought to please everyone, and told him what he wanted to hear.

The facts that Yates used to describe the results so far had been prepared with de Brunner's help and signed off by Assistant Commissioner David Veness, an experienced Scotland Yard troubleshooter noted for his loyalty towards the monarchy. Knowing that he would be addressing the future king, Yates believed that he should be particularly careful. His intentions backfired. In the aftermath of their conversation, Seabrook and Yates disagreed about what had been said. Seabrook recalled Yates confidently asserting that 'large quantities of items had been sold abroad and there was compelling evidence that there had been a big shift in Mr Burrell's standard of living, including the acquisition of two properties'. As a result, there was a strong case against Burrell. Contradicting this, Yates recalled that he had emphasised that he was 'optimistic' that the police would find evidence of foreign sales, and was 'hopeful that there would be a strong case against Burrell'. There was, he insisted, nothing conclusive. Once again, truth was a disputed commodity.

At lunchtime on 3 August, Burrell was driving south from Cheshire. In the serpentine arrangements demanded by Charles, Richard Kay was waiting in Cirencester to take Burrell to the Snooty Fox pub in Tetbury, where they would wait until told to drive to Amanda Hornby's house. At that same moment, at Highgrove, Mark Bolland became suspicious. 'The police know about the meeting,' he warned Charles. He suspected the informant was a police protection officer who he felt was loyal to the police rather than to Charles, not least because he had a difficult relationship with the prince.

There was no alternative, said Bolland – the meeting should be cancelled. Charles agreed.

Yates, de Brunner and O'Kane arrived at Highgrove at 3 p.m. There was a tense relationship between Yates and de Brunner, not least because Yates had previously always served as a uniformed officer, and lacked any relevant investigatory experience as a detective. The visitors were given a briefing about etiquette. Everyone was to stand in line for the formal introduction. Initially Charles was to be addressed as 'Your Royal Highness', thereafter as 'sir'.

As they were climbing the stairs to the first floor, the police met a casually dressed young man chewing gum: Prince William. 'All right?' he asked easily. Two Jack Russells padded along the corridor. Charles had once been asked whether he was not part of a 'corgi family'. 'I can't stand them,' he replied. He now came down the stairs somewhat dishevelled. 'Sorry we're late,' he said, 'I couldn't get Harry out of bed. The normal parents' problems.'

Formality further disappeared as the heir to the throne, sitting in an armchair, described his polo ponies being prepared for that afternoon's match at Cirencester. William smiled but said nothing. Nearby a palace official took notes, while Bolland, Shackleton and Seabrook sat in the background. The atmosphere seemed unreal. The royals, the visitors understood, were not a whit put off by having two investigating officers in their home.

Charles had prepared himself to speak as if he were not unduly worried by anything Diana's former butler might have done, so as to persuade William that he should agree that any prosecution should be abandoned. 'Does this really matter?' he was intending to ask. He assumed that Burrell, like all the royal butlers, pocketed odd items without anyone complaining, and received gifts as part of the compensation for his poor pay. 'Yes, some items may have been pilfered,' he would say, 'but just how serious is it? Not very.' That attitude, he hoped, would not be seen as interfering, but would place the police in a difficult position: it was not within their remit to bring a case on their own initiative.

Ever since he had studied *King Lear* at school, Charles had understood that a monarch's survival depended on displaying royal power; but outside his immediate circle, he was uncertain whether he showed sufficient resolution. Although he knew that the subterfuge about his personal relationships had cost him public trust, he occa-

sionally behaved as an absolute monarch for whom truth appeared
irrelevant. Charles was not, as Bolland knew, 'a terribly strong
person ... he lacks a lot of confidence and he does not have a lot of
self-belief. He doesn't have a lot of inner strength. It's one of the very
sweet and lovely things about him that he's a humble man.' Yet now
everything depended on Charles manoeuvring around the police
and prosecutors.

Yates spoke from a prepared seventeen-point script, all on a
single page, drafted to prevent Charles saying anything that might
cause him to become a witness in a court case. But as he listed the
items seized from Burrell's home, Charles exclaimed, 'He's taken the
lot!' Behind him, Bolland was equally surprised at the revelation
that the butler's pickings had been 'on an industrial scale': over two
thousand items.

Yates continued: 'The police are in a position to evidence large
quantities of items which have been sold abroad.' He mentioned in
particular Harold Brown, who by this stage had been charged with
the theft of the model dhow. The police also had a statement from
Will Swift that he had bought royal items from Brown. But Yates did
not tell Charles that they had no independent confirmation that
Burrell had ordered Brown to sell the dhow, nor any evidence that
the butler had sold any royal possessions. He could barely say there
was 'intelligence' or 'information' about Burrell's sales, and certainly
he could not say there was 'evidence'.

As a layman, Charles would not have recognised the distinction,
but his lawyers did. The prince would later insist that Yates's briefing
had 'strongly influenced' his decision to agree to prosecute. His
recollection, highlighted in a subsequent internal report, would be
used by the palace to disparage the police for 'deceiving' Charles
into believing that the case against Burrell was strong. As always,
each assertion could be persuasively contradicted.

Any sales of Diana's possessions were not crucial to the prosecution. Burrell had lied to Detective Sergeant Milburn when the police
arrived at his home; he had refused to return all the items they had
found; and the prosecutor would claim that he had shown an 'intent'
to steal by having failed to tell anyone for three years about his
possession of the royal family's intimate belongings.

And there was another complication. Burrell's lifestyle and
finances, said Yates, had 'altered drastically' after Diana's death.

Before her fatal accident, the butler's bank account was overdrawn and showed little activity. However, soon after, 'a large movement of funds' had passed through his account. Yates left the impression that the butler was spending more than he was earning, despite his increased income from his lectures and book sales.

Since Diana's death, Burrell had acquired two houses, Yates said. This was not an accurate description: he had in fact bought a new house before selling his old home, and had arranged a bridging loan. That police error was compounded by Yates telling Charles about Louis Munday's photograph, which showed, said the officer, that 'a butler was wearing Diana's clothes'. Charles presumed that by 'a butler' Yates meant Burrell. In reality the photo was of Timothy Bowyer, who had been smuggled into Kensington Palace in 1998 by Harold Brown and allowed to take away a hat and a dress of Diana's, and had posed in them at a New Year's Eve party in New York. By then Munday had sold the photograph to the *Mail on Sunday*. Yates did not say 'Burrell', but nor did he identify Bowyer. He was to say later that he was unaware of Charles's mistaken belief that it was Burrell in Diana's clothes.

At the end of his presentation, Yates asked Charles whether he would support a prosecution. If the case were dropped, he said, the police would find it difficult to restore the property found in Burrell's house. 'This is terrible, appalling behaviour,' murmured Charles, without disguising his wish both that everything should be returned and that the prosecution should disappear. 'We mustn't meet Burrell,' he said. By the end of the interview, he appeared to support the police. 'We've got no alternative,' he sighed.

William also appeared uncomfortable. He had arrived worried about any disclosures about his mother but wishing to protect Burrell, whom he had known well. His mood changed as Yates spoke. Noticeably, he also patted his father, urging him to calm down. Before leaving, presumably alerted by Charles's protection officer, Yates asked Charles not to have any contact with Burrell, though he did not mention that he knew a meeting had been planned.

After the police left, Charles and William were visibly upset. Both believed Yates had described Burrell wearing Diana's clothes in order to help him sell them. 'We were horrified and disgusted,' recalled Bolland. 'William moved from being concerned about

Burrell – he thought the police were against him – to being worried about what Burrell would say about his mother. The meeting had changed his view.'

Protecting Diana's reputation was only part of Charles's agenda. His priority was to protect William and himself. Somehow he had to get Burrell to return all the property and persuade Sarah McCorquodale to drop the prosecution. That was unlikely. She appeared unconcerned about any fallout, and her anger would be assuaged only if Burrell returned everything he had taken. One barrier to getting her on board was Charles's decision not to negotiate with her personally. Any approach, he feared, would be scorned. 'I haven't got any power at all,' he lamented before disappearing upstairs.

As the prince set off to play polo, Burrell was still on his way south from Cheshire, unaware that his journey was now pointless. At the same time, Yates and de Brunner were driving back to London in a mixed mood. Yates was delighted to have secured the princes' support, while de Brunner remained uncertain about what she called 'the politics'. Back at Highgrove, Bolland was briefing Richard Kay on the telephone about the police's presentation. 'It's just not true,' responded Kay, still convinced that the butler was not a thief.

One hour after the polo game started, Charles fell heavily and was taken to hospital with a severely injured arm. In a second phone call, Bolland mentioned the injury to Kay as the reason the meeting had to be cancelled.

At the polo ground, Robert Higdon saw Michael Fawcett 'running mad because Charles's team was sponsored by Porcelanosa [the Spanish tile manufacturer] and there was no prince'. At Fawcett's behest, William stepped in to take his father's place as the host of a dinner for Manuel Colonques, Porcelanosa's owner, and the company's hundred guests. Among them was the supermodel Claudia Schiffer, paid to be present. Shots of the meal, taken by Porcelanosa's photographer, appeared in ¡Hola!. 'They paid more than money,' Bolland told Higdon cryptically.

Five days later, Detective Sergeant Milburn arrived at St James's Palace to meet Bolland. In the wake of the conclave at Highgrove, the same protection officer who had passed on the news of Charles's planned meeting with Burrell had warned Milburn that Bolland was speaking to *News of the World* editor Rebekah Wade, and was 'dangerous'. Milburn feared that Bolland might also have recounted Yates's briefing to the wary butler. To cap the Yard's disquiet, the *Daily Mail* had reported the cancelled meeting between Charles and Burrell. 'You've got to play these people carefully,' an officer observed, without irony. Disputes about the truth were common currency for the police, but the complications in this case were off the scale.

Milburn confronted Bolland, with Shackleton listening. 'Have you met Burrell?' he asked.

'Yes, I have,' replied Bolland.

His admission confirmed Milburn's suspicion that Bolland was Charles's agent of sabotage to ensure that no prosecution took place. The policeman asked him to sign a formal statement as a potential prosecution witness, which would legally prevent him from further contact with the suspect. Shackleton looked surprised. Like the CPS, she had not been told about Charles's attempt to meet Burrell.

Cutting off Bolland may have suited the police, but not Burrell's defence lawyers. Soon after, Andrew Shaw expressed his anger to Milburn that Bolland could no longer broker a deal between Charles and his client. For his part, Bolland was relieved to be excluded.

In theory, constitutional machinery exists to protect the heir to the throne from exposure to dangerous situations, yet Shackleton, Bolland and Lamport all lacked the specific skills that in 1937 Edward VIII's adviser Walter Monckton had deployed during the abdication crisis. Imperfectly guided, Charles was left hanging. If Sarah McCorquodale agreed not to prosecute, Burrell would be free to sell not only the possessions seized by the police, but also those that were still in his house. If she refused to cooperate, Charles could not be seen to interfere with any future prosecution. Faced with this dilemma, he was dependent on the advice of Shackleton and, more importantly, on Lamport and Bolland. But relations between the prince, Shackleton and Bolland were being poisoned by mistrust. In particular, Shackleton's attitude troubled Bolland. While he and Charles wanted the prosecution stopped, she seemed to waver. Many of her comments, particularly about Bolland's personal life-style, had been unhelpful, and this influenced his view of her. They could no longer rely on the lawyer, he told Charles.

The focus was on Stephen Lamport. At the best of times, courtiers under pressure are not good administrators, and he now stepped back from applying any pressure to convince his royal employer about possible dangers. The three advisers might consult and discuss, but they offered no unequivocal recommendation on how to negotiate with the CPS. Constitutionally, Lamport bore the blame for the incoherence, because as private secretary he was responsible for the management of Charles's affairs.

'All the trust had broken down,' recalled Bolland. 'There was chaos. Lamport was weak and tired, Shackleton ambitious to retain her position, Buckingham Palace disconnected and I was out of control. We weren't on the same page. Everyone had a different agenda.' Bolland's official job was to care for Camilla, while Shackleton wanted to defend Charles, his sons and Diana's reputa-tion. 'We were all to blame for the drift towards a trial that everyone wanted to stop. It was a mess.'

Officially Charles had to support the CPS's charge that Burrell had stolen the items. Prosecuting Burrell depended upon the CPS. To support the prosecution, Michael O'Kane could rely upon Lamport's signed statement that no one was authorised to take Charles's possessions, namely his family photographs and water-colours. O'Kane had decided that there was sufficient evidence to charge Burrell with theft – a 95 per cent threshold to secure a conviction, he would later explain.

Burrell was summoned to West End Central police station in London, and arrived there with Andrew Shaw on 18 August. By then he was heading towards a nervous breakdown, and was taking medication to mitigate his depression. In an attempt to avert pros-ecution, Shaw gave the police a thirty-nine-page statement signed by his client. The first part described the reason for Burrell's posses-sion of each of the 310 items formally identified as stolen. Providing this information was difficult because, Shaw argued, after a 'shoddy investigation, the police list was inaccurate'. As an example he cited a straw hat, allegedly owned by Diana, which Maria Burrell said she could prove she had bought at Marks & Spencer. Shaw expected both the police and the CPS to study the statement for one month, and then to decide to abandon the case.

In the second part of the document, Burrell described his close relationship with Diana: how he would smuggle her boyfriends into Kensington Palace; how he would cancel public engagements so she could stay with her lovers; how he provided meals for the princess and her lover of the moment; and he further hinted that he would tell what he knew about Diana's nocturnal visits around Paddington to persuade prostitutes to give up their trade by plying them with gifts. 'The threat was obvious,' concluded Edmund Lawson QC, the legal adviser subsequently retained by Charles to investigate the affair.

'Unpalatable to the royals' was Roger Milburn's conclusion after reading the statement, which was relevant to Burrell's defence but also clearly amounted to a threat. If Burrell described Diana's sex life as part of his testimony at trial, Charles and the monarchy would be seriously harmed. Yet nothing in his statement undermined the charge of theft.

Burrell was then questioned formally by Milburn. During that recorded interview, he claimed that the items found in his house should be seen either as gifts, taken by mistake or handed over to him to be destroyed. Once again, he did not offer to return anything. He had been prompted to take Diana's papers, he said, after watching the shredding of her archives by Sarah McCorquodale and Frances Shand Kydd. In particular, he did not state on whose authority he was 'safekeeping' Diana's letters to William or the family photographs. There was no mention of any conversation with Diana's executors, her sons or the queen.

Burrell's statement had been passed on to the CPS, and Michael O'Kane read it at the same time as Burrell was being interviewed. At 2.40 p.m., after hearing from Milburn that Burrell had not offered any new information, O'Kane ordered that he should be charged with three counts of theft. 'I was genuinely shocked that he was charged on that day,' said Andrew Shaw about what he believed would be a 'trophy' trial for the police, who appeared to be unconcerned about any repercussions for the royal family. 'I couldn't understand why they didn't spend more time considering and investigating the statement.' When Maxine de Brunner asked for Burrell to be remanded in custody, Shaw realised that he was dealing with 'hard-nosed police officers. There's a line in the sand and you're on the other side of it.' The only light moment was when he smelt de Brunner's perfume. 'You're using Escape,' he said, laughing. To his surprise, de Brunner was not amused.

One month later, Shaw wrote to Charles asking for an audience so he could explain 'the extreme delicacy of the situation' should

Burrell testify. The letter was given to Shackleton, after which he heard nothing. Dissatisfied, he sent further warnings about Burrell's intention to speak about events of 'extreme delicacy' and 'matters of a very private nature', and how his enjoyment of Diana's 'intimate' trust would require 'close examination' at trial. Shackleton consulted with Robert Seabrook, and together they assumed that Burrell would testify about Diana's affairs, Charles's relationships with both Diana and Camilla, and possibly mention the contents of the fated mahogany box. They could not make a judgement about the embarrassment value of Prince Philip's letters to Diana, as no one on the prosecution side had seen them.

Unknown to everyone, Burrell had copied Philip's letters and sent the duplicates to a friend in America. Unknown to the police, Diana had shown the originals to several members of her circle before they were temporarily stored in the Brazilian ambassador's safe by his wife, one of her close friends. Thereafter, they were placed in the mahogany box. (Long after the trial was over, the letters were revealed to be no more than affectionate messages.)

Burrell also possessed a letter from Diana sent to him in October 1993, ten months after her separation from Charles was announced. It stated: 'My husband is planning an accident in my car, brake failure or some serious head injury, in order to make the path clear for him to marry Tiggy [Legge-Bourke, her sons' nanny]. Camilla is nothing more than a decoy, so we are being used by the man in every sense of the word.' The embarrassment if Burrell was allowed onto the witness stand had been ratcheted up another notch – not least because in her wild imaginings Diana had openly alleged to Tiggy Legge-Bourke at a party in December 1995 that the nanny had aborted Charles's child, which was grossly untrue.

Potentially, the most damaging of all these threats was still the rape tapes, although Charles did not know whether Burrell had told his lawyers about them.

There was another person to consider: William Boyce, recently named as crown prosecutor. The appointment was unexpected. Boyce was not one of Britain's top lawyers. His courtroom speeches were, according to one person who had heard them, 'like being hit on the head with a dead fish. Boring.' Boyce would have to take a view about the tapes. Unfortunately for Charles, the prosecutor adamantly refused to speak to Robert Seabrook or any other lawyer representing the different players. That unusual decision prevented Charles from knowing whether Boyce intended to allow the tapes to be admitted in evidence. His silence bewildered and frustrated the other lawyers. Seabrook could not guarantee that Boyce would ask the trial judge to decide that the rape scandal was irrelevant, nor could Charles know whether the judge would decide that the rape tapes, and so much else about Diana in Burrell's statement, was being presented to bamboozle the jury or cause embarrassment.

The unknowns gnawed at Charles, the more so as he lacked control over his own destiny. On his lawyers' advice, he chose not to respond to Shaw's latest approach. This provoked Burrell's lawyer to threaten to summon the prince as a witness. When that suggestion was also rebuffed, Shaw presented Shackleton with a potentially devastating allegation. To justify the prosecution, he said, the police had misrepresented the evidence at Highgrove. Yates, he submitted, had wrongly claimed that Burrell had sold items in America, and had further deliberately deceived Charles and William by suggesting that Burrell was the man photographed in Diana's clothes. He based his allegations on Yates's own note used at the meeting. Far from being over, the whole sorry story had just got worse.

12

A Struggle for Power

Towards the end of 2001, Robin Janvrin, with the queen's support, persuaded Michael Peat, the keeper of the privy purse, to replace Stephen Lamport as Charles's private secretary. Although Peat's range of conversation was limited and his manner slightly robotic, his successful reorganisation of the queen's finances had won plaudits. Charles's instinctive resistance to his nomination was largely dissipated by David Airlie, whom he trusted.

The queen's motives were understood in both palaces and in Downing Street. Peat was tasked to bring order to Charles's world. In the queen's opinion, the collection of advisers around her son, still empowered by their knowledge of secrets about his faltering marriage, needed to be removed.

Unfortunately, Charles had been persuaded by the queen mother to trust these people, but in the hysteria since his marriage collapsed too many had become privy to confidences, and hence unduly powerful. Even Lamport acknowledged that he was overstretched. Others would say that the emollient official was out of his depth, especially in his handling of Bolland, who reported directly to Charles and Camilla. 'He never did anything right for me in eight years,' Charles said ungenerously of the loyal retainer who had never failed to bow. The prince's scheming courtiers subsequently mentioned that Lamport's exit was helped by Fred Goodwin, the chief executive of the Royal Bank of Scotland, who had made a job available for him not long before he began steering RBS into bankruptcy.

Peat's qualifications for his new post were mixed. At Buckingham Palace he had cultivated a parsimonious image by cycling to work. He had removed the minor royals from the civil list and reduced the monarchy's costs by 50 per cent in real terms over just five years. The media headlines praising his financial acumen had sealed his reputation as a moderniser. Educated at Eton and Oxford, he had surpassed both his father and grandfather, who had been merely auditors of the privy purse, and proved that he was not just a good accountant: he had mastered Buckingham Palace's sensitive tax affairs, negotiating adroitly with Tony Blair and Gordon Brown about the civil list, and delivered an assured performance in front of the House of Commons' Public Accounts Committee.

But his critics were sceptical. In the opinion of one prominent courtier, Peat was 'a fiddler, a cunning accountant who can dress things up'. Others, like Patrick Jephson, believed that he had fortuitously secured an apartment in Kensington Palace that had been expensively refurbished and filled with paintings and antiques selected from the Royal Collection. His weekly rent was a mere £880, including gardeners and maintenance. Although that was more than Prince and Princess Michael of Kent's weekly rent of £67 for a sixteen-room flat, it was still far less than the market rate of approximately £4,000 per week.

In 1996, soon after arriving in Kensington Palace, Peat had asked Jephson whether Diana would agree for his wife to exercise her dog in the courtyard, to avoid the less convenient trip to Kensington Park. 'No,' he was surprised to be told. Diana's reason was her dislike of the social ambitions of Peat's wife. Peat's own aspirations had spurred his move five years later. Activity at Buckingham Palace, he saw, was declining. Power was gradually shifting to Charles's court. The promise of political influence alongside an active heir was attractive for a slightly bored accountant. When the queen died, he believed, he would be in the right place. Those ambitions disturbed some officials in Buckingham Palace and Whitehall. Their suspicions were fuelled by the cost-cutter's arrival on his first day at St James's Palace in a new claret Bentley Arnage worth £165,000. Most assumed Peat owned the car, but in fact he had arranged a three-month loan of it. Even so, there was bewilderment about what he was trying to prove.

To Charles, Peat's self-confidence was a positive. With some private wealth, the accountant had sufficient privilege to pledge independent loyalty. An added attraction was his commitment to improve the Duchy of Cornwall's income. David Lansdale, the existing land agent, in charge of the duchy's commercial properties and farms of about 120,000 acres, had not radically reformed their management. Peat intended to recruit an agent from Savill's to increase the rents and produce more income from investments. These would finance Charles's increasingly expensive lifestyle.

To those few Whitehall officials who understood St James's Palace, Peat was the wrong appointment. Without the experience of a civil servant – the Foreign Office was particularly useful – they doubted whether he understood the difference between account-ancy and giving advice based on a deep grasp of constitutional and political history. He was undoubtedly reliable and decent, but there was no evidence that he was astute or imaginative enough to guide an activist prince. After all, Whitehall's masters had watched Stephen Lamport failing to challenge Charles's rebellious outbursts.

'You need someone who will tell you the truth,' the prince had been told.

'I agree,' came the reply. 'I need strong advice.'

That exchange was purely theatrical. Charles wanted an adept servant who would follow his orders, regardless of his own inde-pendent judgement.

Peat's first task immediately challenged his new employer. On the queen's behalf, Robin Janvrin wanted Bolland controlled or, better still, got rid of. 'You're too divisive,' he had told Bolland, 'and you're too much in the spotlight.' To remain in the palace, Bolland under-stood, would require reinvention of his role. That was achievable in theory, but impossible in reality. Every day and every night, Charles telephoned him with new demands, and after nearly five years Bolland's personal relationships were suffering from the pressure. Peat's arrival was an opportunity for him to disengage. Only Camilla's fear of her vulnerability delayed his departure. Both she and Charles still relied on him to steer them clear of dangers and ultimately towards marriage.

Peat was keen for Bolland to leave, although neither he nor Janvrin fully understood that the initiative for his ingenious manoeuvres often originated from Charles and Camilla, and were certainly approved by both. Moreover, Bolland was skilled in arts quite foreign to the two courtiers, not least in firefighting.

Not all his ideas to steer the tabloid newspapers away from expos-ing embarrassments had been successful: on one occasion, Camilla had walked away after a car crash, unwittingly abandoning the woman driver of the other car. He had also been helpless when seventeen-year-old Harry confessed to smoking cannabis with girls in Highgrove's cellar, an incident leaked to the *News of the World*, which led to the headline 'Harry's Drug Shame'; but he did manage to turn that scandal into praise for Charles's behaviour. 'Today we commend the refreshing courage and honesty of the Prince of Wales,' sermonised the paper, adding sympathetically, 'As a shining and enviable example of wisdom, he emerges as a modern king in the making.' Bolland had negotiated a deal in which the *News of the World* agreed to conceal Charles's failure to spend sufficient time with his vulnerable son. 'There is no point in hiding the truth,' the worried father told the paper, without irony.

Bolland was not surprised by Peat's appointment. 'We went too far – sometimes,' he admitted. His deals on Charles's behalf had alienated purists like Charles Moore, the *Daily Telegraph*'s editor, a permanent critic. Moore preferred to ignore Charles and Camilla's support for their spin doctor; just as he apparently preferred to forget that his refusal, in 2000, to share photographs of William's trip to South America with other newspapers would lead Sandy Henney, Charles's deputy press secretary, to resign. Even when, the following year, Bolland had himself offered to quit his post as a full-time employee and become a consultant, Charles and Camilla had resisted that option. His departure, they said, would be a betrayal.

At the outset, Charles, Camilla and Bolland accepted Peat as an alternative to Lamport. The mood changed after the new consiglieri introduced himself at the outset of the long transition. 'I must control every aspect of this organisation,' he told his staff. 'There can be no vacuum. I must be in every space.' His insistence on total control changed Bolland's attitude. 'Peat was going to be difficult to work for,' he concluded. 'His initial views were wrong. I could see that we would go through a lot of pain and difficulty before he got to the right place.' Bolland again offered his resignation, and was again urged to stay.

Both Charles and Camilla had every reason to cling to their oft-time saviour. A succession of celebrity dinners promoted by Bolland was strengthening their position. In March 2001 Camilla had hosted a dinner for eighty at St James's Palace to celebrate the twenty-fifth anniversary of the Prince's Trust. The presence of Mick Jagger, Geri Halliwell, Elton John, Sting and Joanna Lumley guaranteed copious headlines. Two months later, Bolland generated more publicity for a dinner at Buckingham Palace hosted by Charles and Camilla to raise money for the Samaritans. That night the queen was in the building; there was no stipulation about where Camilla should sit.

Five weeks later, Robert Higdon arranged for 120 super-rich American supporters of the Prince of Wales's Charitable Foundation to be hosted in Buckingham Palace's picture gallery. Charles's favourite billionaires and other celebrities including Lily Safra, Betsy Bloomingdale, Blaine Trump (the future US president's sister-in-law), Lynn Wyatt, Patty Hearst, Joan Rivers and Shirley Lord milled around the smiling prince as *Vanity Fair* recorded the scenes. Once again Fawcett had invited the Turkish tycoon Cem Uzan, lauded by the magazine for owning three yachts, two helicopters and flying in on his own Boeing 747. Unmentioned in any of the press coverage was a new investigation in America into Uzan's possible racketeering after a complaint by two companies seeking the return of $2.7 billion. Despite that irritation, Uzan's £200,000 contribution again secured Fawcett's agreement for his wife to sit next to Charles at the dinner.

The following day, the entire group travelled across to Highgrove to join another two hundred guests including aristocrats, actors and rich C-list celebrities for dinner in the Orchard Room, a large ballroom built by Charles near the house, where they were entertained by Shirley Bassey and Joan Rivers. In his speech of welcome, Charles thanked Fawcett for creating 'such a fantastic evening'. Some minutes later, Higdon was found hysterical in the garden. 'Charles called them "donors" and it should be "friends"', he wailed. 'They think they're his friends. I'm so embarrassed.'

Those two parties on consecutive days would contribute £3 million to Charles's charitable foundation, a spokesman announced. The exaggeration could not pass unchallenged: the published accounts showed that in 2001 Robert Higdon had raised $2,622,981 for the foundation and distributed $1,912,273, less than half the sum claimed. His administrative costs and salary were $716,000, an unusually high amount, leading to renewed friction with the prince.

'Charles and I had a dysfunctional relationship,' recalled Higdon. 'He would phone on Thanksgiving and Sundays, which was disturbing. But we did laugh a lot. But Charles never said thank you.' Yet after one particularly awkward moment Camilla told him, 'You can never leave him. He couldn't do without you.'

Two days after the double beanfeast, photographers were summoned to a reception at Somerset House for five hundred guests to celebrate the National Osteoporosis Society, chaired by Camilla. The charity's trustees could never have anticipated the enormous interest, but the media had been tipped off by the usual reliable source that Charles and Camilla would greet each other with a kiss.

As a climax to this frenetic offensive, on the eve of the long royal summer holidays, Bolland arranged for Charles to be interviewed by the *Daily Mail*. Asked whether he was considering marriage, he replied, 'Who knows what the Good Lord has planned?' Delighted by this salvo, he and Camilla then retreated to Scotland.

They were leaving a major problem behind. Throughout the year's fundraising, Higdon and Fawcett had argued. Their disagreements centred on who should control the foundation's dinners and money. Since Higdon arranged the Americans' donations and entertainment, he wanted to supervise their visits. But Fawcett wanted to push him out, complained Higdon: 'He not only provided bad food and horrible sweet German wine but deducted the cost of the food from my raised money, and he organised the dinners like a Barnum & Bailey circus.' Higdon became yet more agitated about the accounts after he was billed an unusually large amount for a tent. Then they argued about the seating plans for guests. Fawcett had perfected the art of ignoring Higdon's scheme, and placed women of his own choosing next to Charles – either because they were particularly good-looking or because they had promised significant cash.

Minutes before the guests arrived for Higdon's lunches or dinners, almost farcical arguments would erupt, with each man grabbing or clutching a name card to place next to or away from Charles. In the case of Eva Rausing, the American wife of the Swedish billionaire Hans Rausing, their argument became particularly unseemly. Higdon had originally persuaded Rausing to support Charles's charities but discovered that at one American dinner Fawcett placed her next to Charles, apparently in exchange for a donation of £500,000, thus outdoing the American woman who Higdon had promised would sit next to the prince – for $250,000.

To challenge Fawcett, Higdon discovered, was a self-inflicted wound. Since neither Lamport nor Peat liked either man, the two were scrapping among themselves, and Fawcett displayed his canny tactics. That had been evident ever since Charles agreed to host a charity event at the opening of the Mariinsky Theatre in St Petersburg, with Valery Gergiev conducting. A crowd of donors were already seated as they waited for Charles to enter, but Conrad Black, then the proprietor of the Telegraph newspaper group, refused to sit down – he intended to snatch a place next to Charles. Fawcett knew how to deal with that tactic. Walking behind Charles as he entered the room, Fawcett brought with him two men carrying a large chair. Under his direction they placed the chair between two seated donors of whom Fawcett approved, and soon Charles was sitting in it, while Black found himself cast to the periphery.

The frantic pace of bidding for access to Charles raised new alarms in Buckingham Palace. In the queen's opinion, her son ignored the boundary between his charities and his constitutional position. 'Charles cannot see beyond the horizon,' complained one official. 'He's working hard but clearly cannot understand the conflict with propriety.' While they acknowledged that Fawcett had the knack of approaching the right rich people and spreading his network to raise money, Lamport and then Peat found themselves being asked 'How did that person get in?' more frequently. Both may have tried to bar a 'suspicious person' only to discover that the guest had Fawcett's blessing.

The phrase 'rent-a-royal' began to circulate. Robin Janvrin suggested guidelines for officials to implement, but he was resisted – not least by Fawcett who, while producing donors for Charles, was simultaneously receiving gifts from those he facilitated. When Charles ignored such conflicts of interest, a Whitehall official again reminded him what was permitted and what conduct was off-limits. Such a warning so soon after the new private secretary's arrival was unexpected.

Peat's former colleagues noticed a change in his attitude towards them. His appointment had been linked to Janvrin's plan to build better relations between Charles and Buckingham Palace. Instead, Peat took an independent line. 'How very odd,' thought Malcolm Ross, comptroller of the lord chamberlain's office in Buckingham Palace, during one meeting with Peat. 'That must be at Charles's request.' Within weeks, the gulf between the palaces was even greater than before. 'Peat was a changed person,' recalled Ross. 'He was contemptuous towards us and soon resisted attending some meetings. Charles wanted a strong manager and got a control freak. "Leave it to me," Peat would say to assert his command.'

However, the moment Charles entered his office, Peat would melt, rushing to put on his jacket rather than be seen in shirtsleeves. Once properly dressed, he would bow deeply. Although there were fewer staff at St James's Palace than at Buckingham Palace, they did not eat together. The result was an atmosphere of fear that Peat did nothing to dispel. Some in Buckingham Palace, Ross observed, became 'upset because he was so difficult. He was more a loner than a team player. The atmosphere was so different in St James's.' Ross concluded that Peat had gone native. He had shifted his loyalty to Charles, and been briefed to continue the war against Buckingham Palace. Any proposal for repairing relations would be abruptly responded to with 'I'm too busy.'

'On every issue he had strong views,' said Bolland. 'There was never a discussion. Instead, he would say, "This is how it is," and there would be a bitter argument. Then he would rethink and might agree to the original suggestion. It was an unusual way of working.'

Only one topic was off-limits: Camilla. Knowing that Charles's loyalty to Bolland appeared solid so long as the journey towards public acceptance of his relationship remained unfinished, Peat did not share his opinions about his employer's partner with his staff. But he assumed that Bolland's final exit, so long discussed, could be completed in the near future.

13

A New Era Begins

The death of the queen mother on 30 March 2002 altered the lives of both the queen and Prince Charles. Until the eve of her death, the queen mother had telephoned her daughter every day. Her voice alone reminded the seventy-four-year-old monarch about the stoic values inherited from her father. As she held the hand of her mother at her death she knew that such support was gone forever.

'What we really need is a good funeral,' Bill Heseltine, the queen's former private secretary, told Roy Strong. A big show, he implied, would encourage support for the crown. Heseltine had good reason for concern. The BBC's news coverage was distinctly non-deferential, and the government's recall of Parliament in recognition of the queen mother's passing was scorned by republicans as 'an embarrassing spectacle'.

In the event, the sceptics were proved wrong. Public grief for the queen mother was widespread. Two hundred thousand people filed past her coffin as she lay in state in Westminster Hall, and over a million lined the streets for the funeral procession. Few of the mourners appreciated the late queen's part in persuading Charles to marry Diana, or her ruthlessness with those she disliked – according to one courtier her eyes would go 'dead, ice cold'. The queen's advisers noted that the public's affection for her mother lightened her own gloom about the monarchy's unpopularity.

The mood, captured by Charles's emotional reaction, influenced the queen's decision over whether Camilla should be invited to the funeral. Her immediate response had been 'No,' because her mother had so disapproved of Camilla. That decision, she knew, would be challenged by Charles, who when told of his grandmother's death had rushed back from a skiing holiday in Switzerland. In a televised address he expressed his profound sorrow at the loss of a woman who was more than a grandmother. Throughout his life, especially when he was a young child and his parents were away for months touring the Commonwealth, his 'darling magical grandmother' had been his friend, confidante and supporter. She had been especially kind during his frequent depressions.

To his surprise, after his TV tribute his mother called and thanked him. Probably she did not agree with the criticism that in his address Charles had spoken about his own grief rather than about the subject of that grief. She had decided that Camilla could be at the funeral as 'a friend of the queen mother', but not as Charles's partner. In truth, she had little choice. The latest opinion polls showed that the majority of Britons were now in favour of Charles and Camilla getting married.

There was no doubting Charles's deep grief. During the funeral ceremony he was openly distraught. He stared at the coffin, his lips trembled and he was close to tears. A solitary figure, he travelled with the coffin to Windsor Castle and watched its interment in St George's Chapel. Then he flew to Scotland to meet Camilla at Birkhall. By then speculation about his future, encouraged by Bolland, was rife. On the back of his tearful speech, the *Sun* urged him to marry: 'Follow Your Heart, Charles'. Camilla's position was sealed when it was agreed that later in the month she and Charles would meet the queen for thirty minutes before a concert by the cellist Mstislav Rostropovich at Buckingham Palace. The objections to normalising their relationship were finally peeling away. Everything was in place for Buckingham Palace's modernisers to rebrand the monarchy. The queen mother's death, combined with that earlier in the year of Princess Margaret, had removed two obstacles to reform.

Charles's complaints about the conduct of the minor royals were reinforced when Princess Michael of Kent allowed her children to host a party for more than a hundred friends at Kensington Palace until 5 a.m. while the queen mother was still lying in state. That was quoted as another example of exploitation of their privileges. Without any formal announcement, the queen agreed that the official line-up on the balcony of Buckingham Palace for future state occasions would be limited to five royals – the queen, Prince Philip, Charles and his two sons.

A few days later, Charles flew to Greece to stay for three days on his own in a monastery on Mount Athos. In the aftermath of his grandmother's death, that seemed reasonable. However, a newspaper photograph showed the prince stepping off a boat with a butler in tow. The contrast between the bereaved royal carrying out his duty, and his lifestyle – billionaires' yachts, private jets, six homes, shooting, a huge staff, all funded by the duchy, and a remarkable amount of luggage for a few days of meditation – sat uneasily with the theme of the imminent Jubilee celebrations: to emphasise the monarchy's relevance in modern Britain. Julia Cleverdon, one of his charity's executives, stuck the photograph on her office wall and wrote, with risky irony, 'We're off to Mt Athos with 43 pieces of luggage.'

On Charles's return, in time for Princess Margaret's memorial service, Roy Strong recorded, 'The Prince looked awful.' During the countdown to the make-or-break Jubilee celebrations, 'the queen became less relaxed', noted one adviser. Five years' planning was coming to a climax, but she remained uncertain about the public's response. Naturally sympathetic to the lives of her people, she had earlier opposed the suggestion by a senior official that she should emerge from Buckingham Palace to watch the Changing of the Guard and observe a minute's silence with the crowds after the Islamic attacks in America on 11 September 2001. Such an action, she replied, could be seen as a gimmick; but after a reasoned discussion she agreed, and was surprised by the success of her appearance. Similarly, she overcame her initial reluctance to fly by helicopter to a hospital, land on the roof and visit some patients. That too met with an enthusiastic reaction, encouraging her to trust her advisers' radical suggestion: a speech to both Houses of Parliament to celebrate her Jubilee. She would start by refuting any speculation about abdication, rejoice about the nation's continuing support for the monarchy, and set out her manifesto for the future.

On 30 April she stood in Westminster's Great Hall as the pillar and protector of Britain's 'enduring' and 'timeless values', as she named them. 'We in these islands have the benefit of a long and proud history,' she read (credit for drafting the speech was given to Robin Janvrin and Richard Luce):

> This not only gives us a trusted framework of stability and continuity to ease the process of change, but also tells us what is of lasting value. Only the passage of time can filter out the ephemeral from the enduring. And what endures are the char-

acteristics that mark our identity as a nation and the timeless values that guide us. These values find expression in our national institutions, including the monarchy and Parliament, institutions which in turn must continue to evolve if they are to provide effective beacons of trust and unity to succeeding generations.

The magic was restored. An early-evening reception for two hundred journalists at Windsor Castle soon after converted many remaining republicans into admirers.

Charles could not have made a similar speech. As a rebel, he was unsuited to unite political foes with an appeal to Britain's traditional values. Whatever the latest opinion polls said about his possible marriage to Camilla, only a minority of his country respected him, and few felt affection for him. Until he reframed his challenges to the government in less sermonising tones and resolved his domestic status, his succession might be unopposed, but it would not be welcomed.

Camilla's fate remained problematic. Charles was spotted making an extravagant show of affection to his mother during her visit to his 'healing garden' at the Chelsea Flower Show, which he had dedicated to the late queen mother. Under pressure, mother and son had evidently come to an arrangement, or at least a truce brokered by Janvrin for the Jubilee: during the parades in front of Buckingham Palace, Camilla would sit in the royal box.

Over the first weekend in June, two sunny days, more than a million people gathered around Buckingham Palace to watch spectacular classical and pop concerts, highlighted by Queen guitarist Brian May playing from the palace's roof. The whole event was 'a masterstroke' judged the cabinet secretary Andrew Turnbull. Few had anticipated the extravaganza: a choreographed five-hour march by twenty-two thousand people up The Mall, appearances by Cliff Richard, Paul McCartney and Rod Stewart, a dramatic fly-past and three tons of fireworks exploding for fourteen minutes over London. Amid astonishing scenes of affection, ecstatic crowds waving Union flags sang 'God Save the Queen'. As indeed He had. All the queen's doubts about the country's loyalty vanished.

The following day, a further million followers lined the City's streets to watch the royal family gather at the Guildhall for lunch.

Tony Blair spoke for the majority when he said, 'Affection is earned and the affection this country feels for you is real.' The queen in her reply said to the people of Britain, 'I'm so proud of you,' and praised Charles's 'gratitude, respect and pride' for his country. In his tribute, catching the mood and watched by Camilla, Charles was more effusive than usual: 'I am so proud and grateful for everything you have done for your country and Commonwealth over fifty wonderful years.' He was loudly cheered.

Celebration led to opportunity. Three weeks later, the afterglow of the celebrations still lingered. Ninety American multi-millionaires were brought to Buckingham Palace by Robert Higdon. The cast for the five-day visit included Blaine and Robert Trump, Betsy Bloomingdale, Kip Forbes, Perry and Nancy Bass from Texas, Steven and Kimberly Rockefeller, Queen Noor of Jordan, King Constantine of Greece, Cem and Alara Uzan – and Lily Safra, whose third marriage, like the previous two, was about to end in unusual circumstances. Charles paid particular attention to Joe and Barbara Allbritton, in spite of recent accusations that the chief executive of Riggs Bank had overseen illegal financial transactions.

Each couple had paid $20,000 for dinner with Charles and Camilla in the Buckingham Palace ballroom, lunch with Camilla at a polo match featuring Charles and Harry in Cirencester, drinks with Princess Margaret's son Lord Linley in his furniture showroom, a day's racing at Ascot, and finally another dinner, this time in a marquee at Highgrove, with 150 additional guests. Those at the Highgrove event would sit on silver bamboo ballroom chairs, while Charles was ensconced on a gilded armchair covered in crimson brocade. 'If you grew up in Hobo Town,' explained Higdon, '$20,000 means nothing to you. And then you drive to Highgrove and see Elton John or Rod Stewart, and it's special. Charles was so gracious, that's what he's trained to do, and so in the end you agree to offer the $250,000 donation.'

The target was $3 million, with the promise that small amounts of that sum would be passed on to three American charities: the Phoenix Trust, the New York Academy of Art and the Harvard Aids Institute. One unfortunate hiccup for Higdon was the hosts: 'Charles and Camilla didn't like all the people who gave them money. But they'd say, "We'll get through."' Getting to that point always required an effort. The meals, orchestrated by Michael Fawcett, featured organic food either from Highgrove or from suppliers approved by Charles. The tables at Highgrove were lit by twenty-candle candelabras that Fawcett had brought from Buckingham Palace. The dinner in London was eaten off china from Highgrove.

Such glitzy fundraising annoyed Prince Andrew. In his opinion, his elder brother was promoting himself in the name of duty, while spending huge sums of money on himself. Charles's decision to move into Clarence House after his grandmother's death was understandable, but the estimated cost of refurbishment had soared from £3 million towards £6 million, all funded by taxpayers. More millions would be spent by the duchy. Charles had also taken over Birkhall, a fourteen-bedroom house, from the queen mother, and held in trust the Castle of Mey, her fifteen-bedroom house by the sea at Thurso in Scotland. His sixth home would be rebuilt with the aid of a £1 million gift from Julia Kaufmann, a Canadian-born heiress living in Kansas City. Charles's extravagance passed unnoticed by the public, but it was only grudgingly tolerated by civil servants in the protocol department of the Foreign Office. The same officials were less understanding about Andrew.

Within months of his appointment as the special representative for British trade and investment, the younger royal had attracted complaints. Too often, objected the Foreign Office's protocol department, he refused to stick to the agreed itinerary and 'left a trail of glass in his wake'. 'Andrew's relations around the world,' commented one official at the weekly heads of department meeting, 'are dicey. He's showing bad judgement about people. He's rude, lashes out to lay down the law, and it's so difficult to sell him.'

'You can call me "Andy",' Andrew told one British rear-admiral.

'And you can call me "sir",' was the stiff reply.

Complaints from British embassies about Andrew were now never in writing. Ever since a British multi-millionaire had obtained a critical, classified embassy report from Belize about himself and successfully sued for libel, diplomats had been warned by the Foreign Office not to include adverse comments about people in their dispatches. Thereafter, anything unfavourable was conveyed in telephone calls. These included comments about Andrew. The public only became aware that 'Air Miles Andy' refused to fly on commercial airlines after the government published a list of his destinations. Included were a golf tournament, a football match and social visits across the globe to beautiful girlfriends.

An example of Andrew's capricious behaviour was overheard in an early-morning exchange in his ski chalet in Verbier. A young guest was making his breakfast tea when Andrew suddenly appeared. 'Andrew, would you like a cup?' asked the guest.

'I'm Prince Andrew to you,' snapped the host, and walked off.

Initially, the FO relied on Charlotte Manley, Andrew's private secretary, to ask him for better behaviour. She failed. Following complaints from embassies in the Middle East and Chile, Janvrin discussed 'the Andrew problem' with his senior officials. The queen, it was agreed, needed to be told. As usual, she prevaricated and suggested that Philip be consulted. If he agreed the problem needed to be dealt with, she said, she would make a decision. Unusually, Philip was annoyed, and suggested that Andrew be officially told to 'sharpen up his act or lose his job'. An official met Andrew and issued the warning.

Don McKinnon, the secretary general of the Commonwealth, felt that Charles needed the same medicine. One year after his unimpressive encounter with the high commissioners from the Pacific countries, Charles – again reluctantly – agreed to meet the high commissioners of Africa and the Caribbean. Ever since he had spent five days trekking across an isolated area of Kenya with Laurens van der Post in 1975, digging his own latrine and swatting mosquitoes, his opinion of Africa had been jaundiced. Nevertheless, diligent as ever, he briefed himself about the difficulties created by the EU to the exports of sugar, bananas and other agricultural produce from Commonwealth countries. Come the meetings, to his irritation, the diplomats were only interested in arranging photographs of themselves with Charles to send home. As they spoke, Charles rolled his eyes. The diplomats, he signalled, were 'dead wood'.

Bruised by the prince's anger, Michael Peat mirrored his employer's attitude towards Whitehall's next suggestion: a long-distance Commonwealth trip. The mechanism was well-tested: an FO committee considered the requests for all royal visits to promote Britain, but they knew that negotiating with Charles would be difficult. 'Unlike the queen,' recalled a palace official, 'who was open-minded, he argued about all the options, and any resistance by the Foreign Office provoked his anger.' In red ink, Charles firmly wrote

'No' or 'Maybe' but rarely 'Yes' to the first suggestions, other than the Middle East, where his sympathy towards Islam was welcomed. Even then, he demanded refinements.

'He would drive me bananas,' admitted a former head of protocol.

'Can't you see?' Charles shouted in disapproval at Peat. 'You're stupid!'

Quickly identifying the unacceptable destinations, Peat bluntly told the FO emissaries, 'You're wrong about the choice of countries His Royal Highness should visit.'

Don McKinnon experienced the private secretary's prejudice head-on: 'He effectively said, "I don't know anything about abroad and I'm not interested. I refuse to discourage the prince from his selfish behaviour."' The Commonwealth leader's reaction was blunt: 'Peat was so English, an old-fashioned British bulldog. He was the opposite of unassuming. As an accountant he wanted to show that the prince was good value for money, and that was arrogant.'

To remain in control, Peat always hovered when Foreign Office officials called to re-present their proposals. 'Charles usually headed towards a compromise,' recalled one official. 'He would agree to visit one place identified by the Foreign Office on condition that the FO would organise an "add-on", a place he wanted to visit. So he would agree to visit the Middle East if the plane would then go on to India, where he wanted to check out a local wheat for his Duchy Originals.'

Steadfastly, Charles refused to fly commercial, and insisted on a private Airbus. 'That's outrageous,' Michael Jay, the new permanent secretary at the Foreign Office exclaimed, but before long he too climbed down.

Reflecting Charles's preferences, Peat became more uncompromising towards McKinnon. 'He did not like being told what to do,' realised the diplomat. 'And Charles refused to engage with me. I met the queen once a year, but never Charles.' If McKinnon had represented fox-hunting rather than the Commonwealth, he grumbled, he would have enjoyed greater access.

That very cause, so important to Charles, resurfaced in the summer of 2002. While Tony Blair was preparing for the invasion of Iraq, Charles and many in the countryside hoped that the government would implement the carefully crafted compromise presented by Terry Burns, the former Treasury permanent secretary, to avoid a ban on fox-hunting. Blair seemed inclined to accept the deal despite his party's opposition. His neutrality provoked protests. But then Iraq scuppered any chance of a compromise. To secure parliamentary support for the war, Blair could no longer sit on the fence over the divisive sport. That left everyone dissatisfied. Labour's supporters were furious at the prospect of war, while country folk, still raw about the foot-and-mouth outbreak, remained angry about the metropolitan Blairites' animosity towards rural communities.

The Countryside Alliance's planned protest in London on 22 September was supported by Charles. To those marching, Labour's encouragement of immigration and the criminalisation of fox-hunting reflected the Blairites' self-hatred at being English, and Blair's betrayal of British values. Nearly two years earlier, Charles had agreed to become a patron of the Alliance, but withdrew after being advised to do so by both Bolland and Lamport. While he reluctantly resisted any public endorsement of the 400,000 people marching through London, he did personally repeat one farmer's complaint to Blair: 'If we as a group were black or gay, we would not be victimised or picked upon.' He then authorised the leak of that riposte to a journalist. Charles's contemporaneous letter to Blair, accusing the government of 'destroying the countryside', was also published. If hunting were banned, Charles threatened, he would spend the rest of his life skiing.

The prime minister had good reason to be shocked by such uncompromising conservatism. The prince appeared to believe the scurrilous story that Blair had sought a prominent role in the queen mother's funeral in spite of resistance from Sir Michael Wilcocks, Black Rod. Regardless of the truth, in a speech to celebrate the Jubilee, Charles had mentioned the seldom-sung second verse of the national anthem, as a dig at the government. The verse asks God to 'scatter [the monarch's] enemies and make them fall, Confound their politics, [and] frustrate their knavish tricks'. The prime minister's advisers, Charles said to an aide, should understand that 'they need to take my opinions into account. Why can't they understand this all means a lot to me?' Supporters of fox-hunting hailed him as a hero.

Out hunting, jumping the highest fences, if not always successfully, Charles had won respect for his bravery. On one occasion the master of a Staffordshire hunt had rapped on Camilla's car window to say, 'Ma'am, I hope you've got some sharp teeth tonight. His Royal Highness has just pulled himself out of a hawthorn bush.'

Later that afternoon, Charles sat in a dilapidated barn eating pheasant stew with local farmers and listening to their problems, many caused by Whitehall. Those who knew his fondness for walking with his dogs in the Lake District would have recognised his genuine pleasure at being among country people – even sleeping once in a B&B with strangers was part of his rural lifestyle. 'We have to do something,' he said as he finally got up from lunch at 5 p.m. 'I must return to London. I'm speaking at the Mansion House in three hours.'

Charles's opposition to the government extended from the environment to urging Blair to confront Robert Mugabe and help Britons fleeing Zimbabwe. He had also raised concern about inadequate equipment for the military, poor roads, the pollution of the sea with plastic bags, and government programmes to de-radicalise extremist prisoners. His influence, he continued to fear, was negligible. On China, GM crops and foot-and-mouth disease, he had been ignored. 'I'm not going to change my mind,' he would say stubbornly. The government, he believed, should attempt to persuade him, but Blair refused to engage, suspecting that Charles had been captured by the right wing. However, he had little choice other than to indulge the prince in private, and oblige Peat's requests to protect him in public.

In the real world, to help secure his party's support for the Iraq war, Blair finally betrayed his own convictions and supported a fox-hunting ban. That left Charles exposed, especially to his Labour critics. Tony Banks, a vocal London MP, spoke for many when he accused the prince of 'getting into dangerous waters'. Others believed that his letters to ministers – he was suspected of writing about a hundred of them in recent years – were 'extremely ill-advised and foolish'. Undeterred, Charles wrote to Blair that hunting was 'environmentally friendly', and good for foxes. The opponents, he claimed, were 'driven by agendas other than the welfare of the fox'. He added, 'There is bewilderment that the government is responding to calls to ban something which uses no modern technology, which does not pollute the countryside, [and] which is completely neutral in that it relies entirely on man's ancient and, indeed, romantic relationship with dogs and horses.'

To embarrass Charles just after the countryside march, someone in the office of Derry Irvine, the lord chancellor, leaked the correspondence between him and the prince. Since Charles's handwritten letters were kept in Irvine's locked safe, the culprit could have been identified, but no one was ever named.

In these letters, Charles had protested about the Labour government's welfare policies, political correctness, and red tape. Irvine did not dispute the prince's right to engage, but complained to his officials about feeling 'bombarded', a strange lament for the physically imposing, exuberant lawyer.

In the first leaked letter, dated 26 June 2001, Charles railed against the growth of American-style compensation payments: 'Such a culture can only lead ultimately to an atmosphere of distrust and suspicion let alone the real fear of taking decisions that might lead to legal action.' He condemned the decision by Norwich council to chop down some chestnut trees because people might be injured by falling conkers. New laws and over-regulation about hygiene, he continued, were preventing volunteers cooking and reheating meals for the elderly in their own homes. Good volunteers were being excluded by health and safety laws and the 'blame' culture. The imposition of so many rules, he wrote, echoing the opinion of many, had 'the potential to be deeply corrosive to the fabric of our society'. Even the army's capability was being reduced because, to minimise risk and remove the threat of a commanding officer being sued for negligence, live ammunition was not used during training.

Convinced that the leak had been orchestrated from Downing Street, Charles published the letter in full. 'It does seem to be that over the past few years,' he wrote, 'we in this country have been sliding inexorably down the slope of ever-increasing petty-minded litigiousness.' He complained about the 'remorseless obsession with rights without there being any corresponding requirement of obligation'. Challenging Irvine's argument about the value of human rights legislation, he said, 'I simply do not accept, as you suggest in your last letter, that rights and responsibilities are marching forward hand-in-hand ... That's rubbish – we're a society based on rights alone.' The law, he insisted, did not focus on the individual's responsibilities, and that was a threat to society.

Six days after the letter was published, Charles spoke at the re-dedication of a vandalised war memorial and mentioned the 'lawless youths' responsible for the damage. In his judgement they were 'shallow-rooted and bereft of a spiritual and moral dimension'. They represented, he wrote, the blighted product of Labour's human rights laws. Again, he spoke for many Britons. Irvine replied forcefully but politely. His fundamental disagreement with Charles was unshaken. The prince would not retreat, but was charmless in defeat by the unyielding politician.

In normal times, such an exchange would have been barely noticed; but in the wake of Labour's second landslide election victory the previous year and the Tory opposition's continued hopelessness, Charles appeared to be the government's single significant opponent. Peat should have reminded his employer about the requirement for impartiality, but he wilted when Charles raged that, to counter the government's leaks, he would reassert his right to send letters to ministers.

Peat was struggling with many problems. Unsurprisingly, on his arrival at St James's Palace he had not announced, 'I'm here to kill Bolland,' whatever he may have felt, but Bolland harboured suspicions. Unlike some of his predecessors employed as Charles's spokesman, Bolland was not unctuous, and on many occasions had been helpful to journalists. Peat was well advised not to challenge those relationships. To conceal his hostility, he had told journalists, 'I'm just a boring accountant, here to look after finances.' That approach changed as Robin Janvrin and others in Buckingham Palace suspected that Bolland had aggravated the scandals involving Prince Andrew, Prince Edward and Sophie Wessex, and even William and Harry, in order to protect his master.

By spring 2002, Janvrin and Peat wanted Bolland out. Both had apparently forgotten the palace's cack-handed management over a decade of disasters including *It's a Royal Knockout* (the humiliating TV show featuring Edward, Sarah Ferguson and other junior royals), Camillagate, Squidgygate, Sarah Ferguson's toe-sucking and the War of the Waleses. They resented giving any credit to Bolland for rescuing Charles. His punishment for being effective was to be crushed.

The public charge against Bolland, dubbed 'the puppet master of St James's', was led by Charles Moore, the editor of the *Daily Telegraph*. He echoed the anger of Janvrin and Peat. In a battle between the three privately-educated (Eton and Marlborough) and

Oxford orthodox conservatives and the Middlesbrough schoolboy, the latter was doomed to lose. 'The big guns are now turned on Bolland,' wrote Richard Kay, by this time a friend of Bolland. In December 2001, under the headline 'Revenge of the Old Guard', Kay wrote in code about the 'weak and ineffective courtiers who have done so much to harm both the monarchy and Britain over the past thirty years', and now had their 'knives out for Bolland'. The result, he warned, would be regretted: 'There will be a rapid resurgence in everything we have come to despise about the misuse of royal privilege.' Unable to resist the pressure, Charles and Camilla finally agreed that Bolland should leave St James's Palace, although he would continue to provide advice as a consultant.

Kay himself could never have foreseen the accuracy of his warning. Nor, more importantly, did Janvrin or Peat particularly anticipate the effect of Bolland's departure on the Paul Burrell saga. As Robert Higdon summarised from the sidelines, 'Peat came in to control Bolland. The result was turmoil.'

14

Shuttlecocks and Skirmishes

Over Christmas, after reconsidering his position, Paul Burrell and his lawyers put together another statement, which was delivered to the police on 13 February 2002. They rated it as a bombshell:

> The defendant will say that in a private conversation with the Queen she indicated to him that his relationship with Princess Diana was unprecedented. The defendant will also say that he received private counsel with the Queen which was in part a harbinger to future problems which may have been directed towards him … He remembers spending three hours with the Queen when he sat with her on her settee shortly after Princess Diana's death. The Queen was telling him that she had tried to help Princess Diana. She warned the defendant to be careful. So many people were against Princess Diana and he had sided with her.

If Andrew Shaw and Alex Carlile, Burrell's lawyers, calculated that the revelation of a three-hour conversation with the queen would alarm the prosecution and provoke new inquiries at the palace, their expectation was misplaced. Michael O'Kane was on the eve of leaving the CPS, and Patrick Stevens, his successor, appeared not to have fully mastered the case. The CPS's lawyers decided that since Burrell's statement did not mention Diana's property, it was not relevant to the charge of theft. After all, even Shaw and Carlile had not suggested that anything relevant to the prosecution had been discussed.

In normal circumstances, John Yates and Maxine de Brunner would have interviewed any potential witnesses at the palace, but without an explicit directive from the CPS the police did not react.

Taking the initiative had been firmly ruled out by Assistant Commissioner David Veness, Yates's superior, who was close to palace officials. The traditional investigator's practice of closing every possible avenue of escape was abandoned. 'We got caught in the headlights of dealing with royalty,' said one police officer, ruefully recalling the awe of Scotland Yard's chiefs towards the monarchy.

By then the police were more influenced by the discovery that two of Burrell's contacts in America, Ron Ruff and Chuck Webb, had in their safe a watercolour by Charles which appeared to have come from one of the Burrell brothers. They also claimed to have found evidence in Burrell's home of his meeting Ruff and Webb in New York. But the investigation could go no further. Since the decision had been made that Charles could not be called as a witness, he could not be interviewed as a potential victim of a crime. Accordingly, nor could he be asked whether he had given any of his paintings to Burrell. So that trail of evidence had to be left unexplored.

In April, Detective Sergeant Roger Milburn flew to America. He returned with a signed statement by the memorabilia dealer Dr Will Swift that Harold Brown had sold him items from Diana's household for between $2,000 and $3,000 a time. Swift's website showed frequent trade in royal items, so he seemed a credible source. Milburn also reported that after Diana's death Burrell had given some of her possessions to associates in America, including key rings (silver 'Ds' attached to a leather fob) and a religious medallion that had been a present from Mother Teresa. However, in the most important purpose of the trip, Milburn had failed – he found no evidence of Burrell selling items. Soon after his return, he visited Fiona Shackleton to report his lack of success. 'I told my boss [i.e. Charles] that the police had no evidence of sales,' Shackleton would later tell Milburn. The prince did not react to the news. Nor did Shackleton.

Unseen by outsiders, the partnership between Charles and Shackleton was fraying. Under pressure, her assertive reassurances had been replaced by a tendency to take every complaint or problem as a personal attack. 'I'm just protecting my client,' she would reply huffily. 'I want to do what's right.' Those so addressed wondered whether she was playing her part in a team or angling for power.

Charles's reduced faith in her was fanned by Camilla's conviction that Shackleton was not an ally, but rather than voice personal ill will, she criticised the quality of her advice. 'Fiona's strength was her self-confidence,' observed an official, 'and by then her self-confidence was misplaced.' This had its repercussions; to say that the deterioration in the relationship was unhelpful would be a massive understatement.

In an unexpected sign of Burrell's increasing concern, Andrew Shaw again approached the police. His client, he said, was offering to return all the royal items in his possession if the prosecution was dropped. The police, he was told, were no longer in control – he should approach the CPS. As a lawyer, Shaw would have been aware of that, but he bizarrely insisted that the offer should be passed directly on to Charles. The waters were truly muddied, with the result that the proposal never reached its intended destination.

Burrell's trial was due to start in six weeks' time. His latest threat to make embarrassing revelations from the witness box coincided with the publication of *Diana: Closely Guarded Secret*, Ken Wharfe's memoir about his thirty-three years in the Metropolitan Police. The heart of his book was the six years he had spent with Diana. Breaking the confidentiality expected of a royal protection officer, Wharfe described Diana's love affairs in detail, her possession of a vibrator, and how Britain's intelligence service had bugged her telephone calls because 'the Establishment was out to get her'. Portraying his charge as a helpless but perfectly sane victim, Wharfe revived public anger against Charles and Camilla, who was now dubbed 'the Rottweiler' because of her fierce attacks on Diana.

Upset by the effect of Wharfe's revelations, Charles had also become aware of Burrell's offer to return all the property. He hoped that the proposal would stop the trial, although legally that was impossible. Burrell should have formally declared his position before he was charged. Ignoring both the law and the CPS's sole responsibility for the prosecution, Charles ordered his private secretary to tell the police that the prosecution was a lost cause.

Michael Peat had only formally taken over his new role on 12 August, and as would become clear over the following years, he was occasionally underprepared. In the Burrell case, he knew little about the background, he was not a lawyer, and without any experience of a police investigation he had an unhelpful temperament when managing sensitive issues. 'I warned Peat that the police were not always 100 per cent truthful,' recalled Bolland, who was willing to contribute to his new colleague's steep learning curve. 'But he wouldn't accept an anti-establishment view without a huge confrontation. He believed in the hierarchy.' Peat's natural inclinations thus conflicted with his employer's instructions.

By the time Peat, on Charles's orders, summoned Maxine de Brunner and Roger Milburn to St James's Palace on 30 August, he thought he understood his brief. With Shackleton and Colleen Harris, Charles's press secretary, present during the two-hour meeting, he adopted his favoured manner. At the outset he directed de Brunner to a low chair so he could look down on her – a higher chair was noticeably moved away – and thereafter spoke only to Milburn.

'How can you be sure that these items were not gifts?' he asked the junior officer.

Milburn redirected the question to de Brunner. Not persuaded by her answer, Peat was emphatic that the prosecution should be stopped. 'You have not got enough evidence,' he said. 'We want the property back without a fuss.' In his concern to protect Charles, he forgot that Burrell had been charged with stealing property belonging to Diana's executors, not the prince, and that the fate of any prosecution rested with the executors, the CPS and ultimately David Calvert-Smith, the DPP, who was sure he could prove Burrell's guilt.

'He wants the case stopped,' the two officers agreed afterwards, both of them disturbed by Peat's performance, 'but the train has left the station.' The meeting ended inconclusively.

There was much that still baffled Scotland Yard, not least the CPS's strategy about which case to bring first. In the straightforward prosecution of the alleged theft of the model dhow, Harold Brown's conduct could be more easily established than Burrell's. But the CPS chose to prosecute the more difficult, more controversial case. Charles was well aware of the inherent dangers, and again directed Peat to remove them.

Even for the secretive House of Windsor, the meeting between Peat, Shackleton, Sarah McCorquodale and Michael Gibbins in St James's Palace at 5 p.m. on 11 September 2002 was unusual. All three visitors knew the topic for discussion, and that the initiative had come from Charles. 'The police,' Peat told the executors, 'don't have enough evidence to mount a successful prosecution and the case must be stopped. There is a risk of acquittal.' His disdain for Yates and de Brunner was obvious, and Gibbins shared some of his doubts. As an accountant, he had been Peat's superior at KPMG, and he was equally not accustomed to managing the political pressures swirling around the royal palaces. The police, he thought, were enjoying their involvement in the case too much, and had failed to appreciate the nuances. Considering the unique circumstances, that may not have been surprising, but Scotland Yard had a credible track record. The same team had successfully prosecuted both the novelist Jeffrey Archer and the politician Jonathan Aitken for perjury. Nevertheless, Gibbins was uncomfortable.

By contrast, McCorquodale was absolutely focused. She told Peat that she wanted all the property returned, and that she had sought the advice of John Nutting, a senior criminal barrister who was close to the royal family (he was the queen mother's godson). Nutting had approached William Boyce, but like Robert Seabrook he had been rebuffed. His first advice to McCorquodale was not to interfere. Nutting would be criticised by Burrell's lawyers for being too close to the coterie around Charles, and for failing to put clear water between McCorquodale and the royal family. He would dismiss the accusations. His advice to McCorquodale echoed Seabrook's to Charles: Burrell's latest offer was too late to stop the prosecution.

The meeting had just got under way when Peat came to the point. Charles, he said, feared Burrell testifying in detail about the rape tapes, Diana's anger at her treatment by the royal family, and her love life. But it was no good. After two hours of discussion, he had failed to persuade Charles's sister-in-law to change her mind. 'Sarah McCorquodale wanted Burrell to get his come-uppance,' said Gibbins. 'She was convinced that he had made away with the property. She wasn't interested in deals.' After the meeting McCorquodale called de Brunner, with whom she had built up a working rapport. The trial, she warned, would be thwarted in some way. At that time, supervising more than ten other investigations, de Brunner decided there was nothing more she could do.

With the same objective as Peat, Alex Carlile met Robert Seabrook. A conversation between two criminal lawyers representing different sides was not unusual, but the content of their discussion was unprecedented in modern royal history. Carlile repeated his belief that the police briefing at Highgrove had misled Charles, and that since then the prosecution had failed to understand the relationship between Burrell and Diana. According to a subsequent report for Charles by Edmund Lawson QC, a criminal barrister hired by Peat to investigate the accusations, Carlile threatened that Burrell's 'embarrassing revelations' would cause the three princes 'distress and embarrassment', and described the case as 'a disaster waiting to happen'. He said that Charles might be called as a witness, and added that the prince had been 'deceived by the police'. He urged Charles and McCorquodale to intervene to protect the royal family.

Seabrook was in no mood to agree. Carlile, he said, was making a 'huge assumption' that Yates had persuaded Charles to support the prosecution. Whatever Yates said about the sales had not influenced the prince's decision. Charles, he said, could not interfere, but he would support McCorquodale if she decided to stop the prosecution. The shuttlecock fell to the ground.

15

The Queen's Recollection

On Monday, 14 October 2002, Paul Burrell, forty-four years old, stood in the dock of Court Number One at the Old Bailey, accused of stealing 310 items together worth £4.5 million. To be acquitted, he would need to show the jury that, from the outset and during the three years he possessed the items, he never intended to steal them.

Nearly a dozen famous people had been listed to testify on his behalf. The celebrities would enhance his reputation as Diana's 'rock', praised for his seventeen years' loyal service and for his public pledge to preserve her memory 'as decently and as respectfully as possible'. None of Burrell's witnesses was aware that he had planned to resign from Diana's service and move to the United States.

After the first jury was discharged because one member was the wife of a policeman, a second jury was addressed by William Boyce. The prosecutor was competent, but with questionable self-confidence, and his unusual unwillingness to discuss the case with other lawyers suggested that he did not fully appreciate Burrell's threats, nor understand the implications of Alex Carlile's accusation of police deception, nor Burrell's unproveable 'sales' in America. Apparently unaware of what had been going on behind the scenes, he did not anticipate the traps that Carlile would spring during his cross-examinations of Maxine de Brunner and Roger Milburn. Both officers assumed that Boyce would protect them; they were wrong.

In his opening statement, Boyce told the jury that the prosecution would seek to prove that Burrell had not informed anyone that he was holding property belonging to the executors of Diana, the Prince of Wales, or Prince William. Before the police arrived at his home, no one knew about the hundreds of items he had taken from Kensington Palace. Further, after his arrest he had refused to return them. His subsequent letters to Charles and William about 'safekeeping' proved only that he had been holding their property without permission.

The prosecution's case rested on the evidence of Sarah McCorquodale, Frances Shand Kydd and the main police officers in the inquiry, particularly Milburn, whose most important piece of testimony was recounting his first question to Burrell after arriving early in the morning at the butler's home in Cheshire.

'Do you have any items from Kensington Palace in this house?' Milburn had asked.

'No,' was the reply.

Burrell's lie, and his obstructive answers during two subsequent police interviews, were crucial, yet Boyce chose not to ask Milburn for any details about those exchanges. The officer was puzzled. After all, in each of the interviews Burrell had said that he was unwilling to return Diana's property, even those items that he later told William he held for safekeeping. Equally bewildering was Boyce's silence during Carlile's cross-examination of Milburn.

Towards the end of the day, Burrell's counsel produced into court Diana's large mahogany box. Burrell would subsequently write in his autobiography that, according to the police, the box's lock had been 'forced and broken'. That was untrue, as both de Brunner and Milburn insisted after the trial.

Lifting up the box for the jury to see, Carlile asked Milburn to describe what had been inside. Milburn knew that a full answer would terrify Charles, and also that the box's contents, not being part of the charge, were irrelevant to the trial. He looked at Boyce for help. The lawyer's rotund face remained expressionless. Instead of protesting to the judge that the defendant was not accused of their theft, so the box's contents should be excluded, he said nothing. A chance of protecting Charles from Burrell's threats was lost. Milburn was on his own.

To avoid falling into Carlile's trap, he refused to answer the question, and instead asked the judge, Anne Rafferty, for guidance. As an experienced criminal lawyer, Rafferty was trusted by both sides. She ordered Milburn to write down one single item found in the box – he noted James Hewitt's signet ring. Rafferty was handed his piece of paper and announced that she would decide whether that detail should be disclosed to the jury. She then adjourned the hearing until the following day.

Charles's legal advisers were nervous. They assumed that once in the witness box Burrell would mention both the rape tapes and Prince Philip's letters. Here they may have misread Carlile. The barrister and his defence team would later say that at this point they didn't know what the box contained, and that they were simply hoping to discover whether the prosecution had withheld any evidence that might help their client. They would also claim they were unaware of McCorquodale's allegation that the box's contents had been stolen by Burrell. Milburn doubted both claims. After all, Burrell could easily have told his defence team what the box contained – and they must surely have asked him. In a courtroom trial, lawyers of Carlile's experience rarely pose any question without knowing the answer.

The following morning, Rafferty allowed the jury to hear Milburn's testimony about Hewitt's ring. Carlile did not ask any further questions, and the box was taken out of the courtroom. Despite that piece of good news for Charles, there was panic in St James's Palace. Assuming that the defence lawyer had fired a warning shot, the prince's legal team could not guarantee that the judge would exclude evidence of other scandals, and Boyce was steadfastly refusing to discuss the case with Robert Seabrook.

Charles's fears grew during the cross-examination of Maxine de Brunner. Carlile ridiculed the notion that the original reason for the police raid was merely to find the paperwork for the model dhow. They were fishing. In their blunderbuss approach, he alleged, they couldn't decide what to take and what to leave, as was illustrated by a video of Burrell's house after the raid. A huge number of items taken from Kensington Palace remained there. De Brunner was asked whether she had entered the loft. No, she replied; she disliked heights. Carlile openly mocked her, as if her faint-heartedness proved Burrell's innocence.

Next, he sought to persuade the jury that Charles and his sons had been misled by de Brunner during the meeting at Highgrove, although only John Yates had spoken on that occasion. First, because the police had implied that the man in the photograph wearing Diana's dress was Burrell; second, more importantly, because de Brunner had failed to understand the source of Burrell's income.

In his briefing to Charles at Highgrove, Yates had described how the butler's bank balance had soared after Diana's death. One reason was undoubtedly his book sales and lectures: he was a man in the news. However, before the trial, forensic accountants employed by the Fraud Squad had examined his bank account. Their report, in two large green volumes, showed that a credit of about £30,000 remained unexplained. The jury would have to decide whether the police had misled Charles about Burrell's wealth.

Next, Carlile asked de Brunner whether she had told the princes that no evidence had been found of Burrell selling any items in America. 'No,' she replied. Carlile accused her of having grossly misled the royals. She was then addressed by the judge. 'Is it right that you allowed the two princes to remain under that misconception?' 'Yes,' she replied. As she watched journalists leave the courtroom to report this dramatic news, de Brunner realised too late what she had failed to mention.

Milburn had told Fiona Shackleton on 30 August that there was no evidence of Burrell selling anything, and Shackleton had duly passed the message on to Charles and his sons; so at least one of Carlile's criticisms of police misconduct could have been rebutted. De Brunner had every right to expect Boyce to pick up on her forgetfulness on re-examination, but he never did. The impression was established that the police investigation had been botched. In the prosecution's opinion, that was irrelevant to proving Burrell's guilt or innocence on the actual charge, but the blaring media headlines disturbed St James's Palace.

On that Friday afternoon, proceedings ended unusually early, the judge sympathising with Carlile's plea that he was tired. The trial, it was assumed, would resume after the weekend.

Just after 8.30 on Monday morning, 28 October, Boyce was reading his papers in a small exhibits room adjacent to the court when John Yates unexpectedly joined him. 'I've just had a conversation with Michael Peat,' the policeman said, then repeated the private secretary's exact words: 'Her Majesty has had a recollection.'

On the previous Friday, Peat had explained, the queen had recalled a meeting one afternoon five years earlier, soon after Diana's death. Paul Burrell had come to the palace to tell her about preserving some of Diana's papers. 'The queen agreed that he should care for them,' said Peat. According to Yates, he had replied, 'Michael, that clearly scuppers the prosecution.' Peat had said, 'Oh, surely not?'

Boyce visibly paled as he heard the news. Taking off his wig, he seemed to shrink. For a barrister who would later boast on his website, 'He fights every case with tremendous passion,' one eyewitness recalled, 'He looked crushed. A vibrant man was shellshocked, destroyed. The little courage he had disappeared.' Boyce's panic infected others – lawyers and police officers – who had arrived in the room for that day's trial. He appeared to believe the case was as good as lost.

Eventually he explained his reasoning. In his opening statement, Boyce had said that Burrell had been silent about taking Diana's possessions. During the years after her death, no one had been told about any 'safekeeping' role her former butler might have assumed. Now Burrell would testify about what he had told the queen and how he received her approval. He could quote her 'recollection' in his defence. Only by questioning the queen in court could Burrell's version of the conversation be rebutted, and that was constitutionally impossible; no reigning monarch could appear in 'Her Majesty's' court. 'That's the end of the trial,' Boyce told his perplexed audience. Next, he texted de Brunner, who was drinking tea in the canteen: 'I'm sorry for what is about to happen.' With that, he went into the courtroom to continue what was left of the prosecution.

During that same day, the circumstances of the queen's recollection emerged. Peat revealed to the CPS lawyers that the previous Friday, she, Charles and Philip had driven together to St Paul's for a memorial service for the victims of the Bali bombings. Driving past the Old Bailey, she asked why a crowd was standing outside. Charles answered that Paul Burrell was on trial. The queen was apparently unaware that he was being prosecuted. Then she mentioned that, some years before, Burrell had sought an audience with her to explain that he was caring for some of Diana's papers, and she had agreed that he should do so.

After the royal family returned from St Paul's, there was unusual activity in St James's Palace. Lawyers were summoned for a conference to discuss the queen's recollection. Peat was told that Boyce should be informed immediately. Next, Robin Janvrin was called. Told about the new evidence, the queen's private secretary expressed his astonishment. 'Oh my God,' an eyewitness heard him exclaim. Thereafter Janvrin did nothing, allowing Peat to continue managing the crisis on Charles's behalf.

Then something very strange occurred. Contrary to Seabrook's advice, neither Boyce nor the CPS was told on that Friday afternoon about the 'recollection', and the lack of communication continued through Saturday and Sunday. According to palace rumours, however, Peat did tell Peter Goldsmith, the attorney general, that the recollection was a 'golden opportunity to get rid of this embarrassment'. Early on Monday morning, Peat called Yates to report the queen's remarks.

To some in the prosecution team, and to the police at the Old Bailey, Peat's version of the circumstances connected to the trial, subsequently described in the written report by Edmund Lawson QC commissioned by Peat and submitted to Charles (the Peat Report), lacked credibility.

First, Janvrin, an assiduous official, had been regularly briefed about the investigation, not least because William and Harry were involved. He would certainly have fulfilled his duty and reported the main details of the case to the queen during their daily meetings.

Second, the queen was known to read the newspapers regularly, and for over a year Burrell's plight had been widely reported. The trial itself had dominated the front pages for the eleven days before her drive to St Paul's.

Third, it was unusual for the monarch and the heir to travel in the same car, for security reasons. The coincidence that mother and son, who seldom spoke to each other, should have been so publicly united on that particular day while driving past the Old Bailey was a coincidence that raised questions.

Fourth, the version offered by Peat contradicted that of others in the palaces. He failed to explain why the prosecution was not told about the queen's recollection for two and a half days; he failed to report his own consultation with a lawyer to understand the significance of the recollection; and he omitted to explain why he, rather than Janvrin, asked the queen about her suddenly jogged memory. The reason for that at least was clear to observers inside the palaces: Janvrin wanted no part in the undertaking.

All those inconsistencies led to one question: who had masterminded the operation over the weekend? Amid the speculation there was also admiration. Using the queen to halt the trial was a masterful tactic. The police and the CPS were unprepared for a challenge at that exalted level. Both had been naïve to believe that they could prosecute without the Establishment's wholehearted support. 'Stardust clouded our judgement,' confessed one stunned officer.

Inevitably, some of those involved in the case questioned whether the queen had ever met Burrell in the 'three-hour' audience he had described in his statement of 13 February 2002. After all, even Peat would claim to have been unaware of the statement in which Burrell mentioned the meeting. But three witnesses would have been available had the police sought that information. First, Michael Gibbins had been asked by Burrell in December 1997 for permission to visit the queen to complain about 'the activities of the executors'; second, a palace page told Richard Kay about accompanying Burrell to the queen's sitting room, where he remained for between forty-five and ninety minutes; and finally, soon after that audience, Burrell told Kay that he had met the queen to complain about how the Spencers were destroying history, and to tell her he wanted to save documents for posterity. The queen had, he said, replied, 'How interesting. Good idea.' Pertinently, in Kay's version Burrell mentioned only 'documents'.

The police failed to seek those witnesses, and in hindsight allowing Burrell's disclosure to remain unquestioned appears inexplicable. In their self-interest, both palaces blamed the police and the CPS for failing to follow up. But in reality, Peat and others knew that each organisation was under orders to limit its access to Charles, while the police were forbidden to interview the queen. And both the police and the CPS harboured doubts about Burrell's crucial meeting at the palace.

Few believed the butler's version of spending three hours with the queen, and in any event his description of their conversation – about documents and not hundreds of Diana's personal possessions – was irrelevant to the charges he faced. Similarly, none of the prosecutors or police expressed at subsequent meetings their outright belief of the Buckingham Palace spokesman's explanation that 'the queen did not realise that her evidence was important, and no one told her'.

Nevertheless, that explanation could well have been true. The queen, by nature a reactive person who absorbed enormous amounts of information, would not have taken any initiative after meeting Burrell. The surprise was the timing of her revelation, coinciding with Charles's increasing despair and the palaces' highly convenient interpretation of that meeting. 'An act of genius,' was the judgement of one Whitehall observer, 'a machination to solve desperation. Only a golden bullet could have stopped the trial. And they invented it.' A senior police officer was more succinct: 'The palace lied.' The sceptics could not name the mastermind of any conspiracy, but they assumed that Charles participated in the crucial discussions. Identifying the other participants, and establishing the timeline of their conversations, was impossible. When required, members of the royals' inner sanctum were masters at protecting their secrets.

At 8.30 a.m. on Tuesday, 29 October, Boyce chaired a meeting with de Brunner, Milburn and two CPS lawyers, Patrick Stevens and Sue Taylor, at the Old Bailey. The prosecutor had decided to ask the judge to stop the trial, but he added a peculiar twist. He intended to ask for the court to be cleared of everyone, including the police, the defence lawyers, the jury and even the stenographer. To suspend proceedings, he would apply for a Public Interest Immunity hearing – although without any intention of pursuing that application. The ruse would conceal the true situation from the outside world while the prosecutors secretly sought a way around the queen's intervention. To protect himself, Boyce asked the police to hide two tape recorders in a briefcase that would be placed on his desk in court. The tapes would then be kept under seal by the CPS. He did not reveal who had advised him to follow this extraordinary arrangement.

Next, Boyce explained why the queen's 'recollection' had skewed the trial and would help Burrell. By telling the queen that he was caring for 'documents' he had covered everything, including two thousand sensitive photo negatives, Diana's 'Wombat' cards to William, and the family photo albums. 'Why?' a police officer asked. Sarah McCorquodale would never have destroyed family photographs or Diana's letters. On the contrary, the evidence was that all such items were to be sent to Highgrove.

Boyce ignored the question and said, 'Burrell wants to keep Diana's underwear and clothing, which will make him a multi-millionaire within one month. The only way out is to negotiate with the defence.' For his audience, to start such a negotiation in the middle of a trial was uncharted territory.

'Princes Charles and William need protection from threats,' said Boyce. He mentioned 'Joseph', another defence lawyer, who in a private conversation had said that Burrell was 'anxious to talk and be indiscreet'. Boyce continued, 'We must protect the source from the media frenzy if the recollection is released.' 'The source' was his way of referring to the queen.

Boyce's defeatism stung Patrick Stevens: 'Surely it's not as bad as you think. Surely we can carry on. We can't put a lid on this. We'll just put a statement about the queen's recollection to the court and leave it for the jury to decide.'

'Yes,' replied Boyce, 'it's not hopeless. The jury will come to the right decision.' Then suddenly he somersaulted. 'My gut feeling is that after hearing about the recollection, the jury will not convict.' After wondering how the queen should be approached, he said, 'I need to speak to the attorney general.'

At exactly 10 a.m. Boyce walked into the courtroom, asked the judge to halt the trial and send the jury home, then disappeared for the next ninety minutes.

Neither the defendant nor his lawyers had any idea why the trial had been halted. Burrell hadn't told his counsel any more about his conversation with the monarch than his mention in his statement about her warnings during 'three hours on the settee'. Andrew Shaw was certainly unaware that his client had supposedly mentioned to the queen that he was 'safekeeping or acting as a custodian of any of Diana's possessions'.

At 11.30 the same morning, Boyce returned to his small office and dictated a list of questions for the queen. Who else was present at her meeting with Burrell? What was said at the meeting? Why was the meeting not revealed before? How many meetings did she have? Were any entries made in the Buckingham Palace diary?

At 4.35 that afternoon, de Brunner and Milburn met Peat, Seabrook and Shackleton at St James's Palace to present Boyce's questions. Two hours later, Peat handed over the written answers provided by the queen. 'You're overreacting,' Seabrook told the officers. 'This is a storm in a teacup. The case can continue.' He added, 'Someone's fingerprints are all over this to disrupt the prosecution.' He did not identify the culprit, but the officers wrongly assumed he meant Mark Bolland.

For their part, the police regarded Seabrook as part of the Establishment conspiracy to end the trial. Again, they were mistaken. Like other criminal lawyers, Seabrook could not understand Boyce's dogmatic pessimism. There was nothing, he would later say, to prevent the prosecutor from describing the queen's recollection to the jury, obtaining a ruling from the judge that Peat's statement could not be challenged, and allowing the trial to continue. Any references in the charges to Burrell stealing Diana's 'papers' would be dropped, and the trial would carry on.

After Seabrook's intervention, Peat explained the background to the queen's intervention to the police and lawyers. The palace, he said, was concerned that any failure to disclose Burrell's meeting with the queen would reflect badly on the royal family if he were convicted, or if he harmed himself because of his depression. None of his audience was disposed to accept this explanation. Moreover, the police were struck by Peat's incredulity about the consequences of the queen's action. Shackleton shared his amazement. 'The prosecution lawyers,' she told Milburn, 'are reacting too quickly to the information.' Milburn and de Brunner returned to the Old Bailey in a state of bewilderment. As an independent institution, Scotland Yard could have pushed for the truth, but Assistant Commissioner David Veness told them, 'We must protect the monarch,' and ruled against any further activity. Charles and William similarly required protection. Yates passed the order down. 'I think the prosecution left a number of open goals,' he said ruefully in the aftermath.

The first crisis meeting of the prosecution lawyers was held at the offices of the CPS on Tuesday evening. The principal players present were the prosecutors William Boyce and Richard Whittam; David Perry, a criminal lawyer and constitutional expert invited by the CPS; John Yates; and Maxine de Brunner. In the chair was the CPS lawyer Patrick Stevens; David Calvert-Smith, the director of public prosecutions, who should have been present, was away on holiday in Greece.

'Why are you doing this?' Perry asked the prosecutors and the police. 'You should let it go away. It cannot be in the interest of the monarchy to pursue a simple theft.'

'We have enough evidence,' replied Boyce, 'but it's not my call.'

In the brainstorming session that ensued, there was even discussion about whether a new trial could be convened inside Buckingham Palace, with a jury of courtiers and peers empowered to hear the queen's testimony. That fantasy was discarded after it was generally agreed that there was no legal reason to stop the trial.

The following day, the same group met again. Decisions were needed. To bring the issue to a conclusion, Peter Goldsmith, the attorney general, and David Calvert-Smith, now back from holiday, joined them. Richard Whittam, the junior prosecutor, again suggested that the prosecution could withdraw the charge of the theft of 'papers' or documents and continue with the theft of the remaining items. Boyce ignored him, and repeated his opinion that proceedings must end, without any prospect of a new trial. David Perry agreed: 'The queen cannot provide evidence in her own court and the queen can do no wrong. No chance of rebuttal or contradiction.' The prosecution, he continued, would have to accept that there had indeed been a conversation, and could not disprove whatever Burrell testified that he and the queen had discussed. The decision about Burrell's guilt or innocence would then be left to the jury, as it always had been.

Only two people could order the trial to end: Calvert-Smith and Goldsmith. Calvert-Smith prevaricated, speaking 'on the one hand and on the other', so Goldsmith took the lead. He went to see the queen to explain the consequences of what he termed the 'fiasco', then consulted Tony Blair. Robin Janvrin had also called Downing Street. At that moment, Blair was immersed in deciding the size of Britain's military commitment for the invasion of Iraq. Once again he was being asked to consider how to save the monarchy. His decision was that the trial should be brought to an end.

Goldsmith reappeared at the meeting of lawyers. Understandably, he did not want to direct Boyce to stop the prosecution – technically that was the responsibility of the director of public prosecutions. Accordingly, Calvert-Smith had invited Milburn and de Brunner to the final stages of the meeting. 'If the coffee pot is half empty,' Milburn told de Brunner, 'it means they've made up their minds before we got there.' On entering the room, Milburn looked at the cafetière. Half full.

Little was discussed. At midday, Yates said to Milburn, 'Give me six good reasons why the case should go ahead.'

'I can give you thirty, sir,' replied Milburn.

Thereafter, according to a hostile eyewitness, Yates was 'as useful as a chocolate fireguard'. Late that afternoon, Milburn and de Brunner were asked to meet Calvert-Smith in his office. Over a glass of cheap wine he asked them why the prosecution should continue. After they had again given their reasons, the DPP said nothing except to bid them farewell.

Reflecting on the mismanagement of the royal interests over the previous two years, not one of those involved – Janvrin, Peat, Shackleton and all the lawyers who regarded themselves as among the finest in London – appeared to consider what Burrell would do after the trial. None openly discussed how the former butler might make his fortune by doing precisely what they had sought so hard to avoid – selling royal secrets. Led by Goldsmith, an insecure attorney general, the seemingly blinkered satraps composed a statement for Boyce to announce in the courtroom on Friday, 1 November: the complete end of the prosecution. His statement, expressly mentioning the queen's recollection, took everyone in the court by surprise. The trial was over. Charles and Peat breathed sighs of relief.

So did Burrell. Crying on Carlile's shoulder in the gloomy corridor outside Court Number One, he exclaimed, 'The queen came through for me.' In the excitement, his brother Graham told a journalist, 'He will have his revenge, but he will do it with dignity.' After repeating to the crowds outside the court that his life had been ruined, Burrell headed off towards Covent Garden to celebrate. Among those drinking with him was Richard Kay, who had cared for Burrell for two years, especially during his nervous breakdown and a drug overdose. In return, Kay expected that Burrell, steeped in debt, would sell his story exclusively to the *Daily Mail*. Instead, as he had always planned to do, Burrell offered his revelations to the *Daily Mirror*, which had secretly paid money to his brother Graham and had broken the story of Burrell's arrest. His agent mentioned £1 million as the possible fee. The *Mail* was not given the opportunity to make a counter-offer. Not only Kay felt double-crossed: all of Diana's famous friends who had been prepared to testify about her butler's loyalty would be shocked by his duplicity.

While Burrell drank champagne, Maxine de Brunner was hiding in the Landmark Hotel in Marylebone. Unrelated to the trial, she faced a serious threat to her life from a known terrorist living in London who was involved in another of her investigations. He had recognised her from the media coverage. Isolated in her room, she feared criticism in the following morning's newspapers.

The comments were even more vitriolic than she could have anticipated. 'The police have covered themselves in disgrace,' said the *Daily Mail*, referring to 'a black farce'. In a withering attack on the CPS and the DPP for having 'shown an incompetence that beggars belief', the paper accused de Brunner of lying about the 'Burrell photograph' and the CPS of concealing his conversation with the queen. Both accusations were unjustified. Other papers charged Shackleton and McCorquodale with ignoring Charles's wise judgement and pushing for a prosecution that was doomed from the start. Bolland was reported to have threatened Shackleton that he would have 'her legs blown off'. Everyone was blamed except Charles. On 4 November he had flown to Italy, and he returned four days later determined to ensure that responsibility for the embarrassment fell upon the police. In his reception room at Highgrove he emphasised to selected newspaper editors the folly of Scotland Yard.

Simultaneously, palace officials aggressively briefed journalists about the officers' deception. Leading the charge was Stephen Pollard, a respected commentator who had not previously written about the royals. His article, prominently featured in the London *Evening Standard*, eviscerated the police. There was 'no crime and no victim', he wrote, only a conspiracy to put Burrell behind bars. The prosecution was 'a result of a potent mix of malice and quite astonishing incompetence'. The entire case was based on 'the idea that Mr Burrell was flogging the Princess of Wales's possessions in the US'. To implement that conspiracy, wrote Pollard, de Brunner went to 'quite extraordinary lengths to obscure this lack of evidence'. He continued, 'At no stage did she inform the Prince of Wales or his solicitor of her "mistake"'. De Brunner, he wrote, had either been lying or had been 'grotesquely incompetent'. He concluded that the world had witnessed a 'once-in-a-generation, high-profile prosecution which defines the reputation of the police for years to come. And they have blown it quite spectacularly'.

Given the source of his information, Pollard's invective was inevitably based on multiple errors. The media's humiliation of the police nevertheless failed to suppress entirely the suspicion that it was Charles who had orchestrated his mother's 'recollection'. A handful of perceptive journalists conjured up a scenario of courtiers inventing the ruse to stop Burrell describing a palace riddled with staff who indulged in cross-dressing, selling official gifts, theft and rape. At the centre of this narrative was The World versus Maxine de Brunner, with the police officer the inevitable casualty.

At 2.30 on the afternoon after the trial, de Brunner's mobile rang. 'I'm so sorry,' said Sarah McCorquodale. 'They shouldn't have done that to you. It's disgraceful. We're totally behind you. This investigation has been sabotaged. A deal was struck by Paul Burrell and the Prince of Wales.'

As McCorquodale went on, de Brunner made sure she wrote down all that was said. 'They agreed that the trial would be stopped if three things happened,' McCorquodale continued. 'First, Burrell would not mention certain things in his book; second, William's property will be given back to William; and a third thing which I don't know. Once the deal was agreed, Fiona contacted the police to tell them about the queen's recollection of events.' She concluded, 'They couldn't afford for Paul Burrell to go into the witness box. Burrell had told the Prince of Wales that he would tell all unless the trial was halted. The palace have maintained that they didn't know about the queen's and Burrell's conversation.'

McCorquodale agreed to sign a note describing the meeting organised by Peat on 11 September to end the trial. At de Brunner's suggestion she met Milburn for coffee on 12 December and signed the handwritten account on an A4 sheet of paper that he had prepared for her.* Michael Gibbins signed the same note a week later, agreeing that Peat, on Charles's behalf, had sought to stop the trial. In Milburn's words, 'I was protecting my back.'

'Let's nick Peat for seeking to pervert the course of justice,' Milburn said to Commander John Yates after showing him the signed note. After apparently consulting David Veness, Yates agreed, telling Milburn, 'You've set off an Exocet.' Milburn believed that Yates had given the note to Patrick Stevens to consider whether Peat should be formally cautioned and interviewed. Later, he assumed that the CPS lawyer decided that a prosecution was not in the public interest. He was mistaken. Yates had done nothing to stir that pot.

That same week, still isolated in her hotel room, de Brunner answered a call from Stuart Osborne, one of Charles's protection officers. 'You can't fight the Establishment,' said Osborne sympathetically. 'That press statement [about the recollection] from the palace

---

* Edmund Lawson mistakenly states in Peat's Report (para 2.80, p.69) that the note was made on 19 December, whereas it was made on the 12th, the same day that Milburn and McCorquodale met. Gibbins would subsequently deny that he was at the meeting on 11 September, deny that he signed the statement, and deny that he was questioned by Lawson. The evidence suggests that his memory was mistaken.

was a lie, but the police view is that the House of Windsor must be protected at all costs.' De Brunner wrote down what Osborne had said on the Landmark Hotel's notepaper.

By this time, she and Milburn were feeling so battered that both were convinced by an official at the Scotland Yard's Department of Professional Standards that a police group was on standby at Putney police station to await an official complaint from Buckingham Palace that would trigger their arrest for perverting the course of justice. The truth about the existence of such a group has never been established.

Charles, despite his immediate relief, was similarly beleaguered. Burrell had apparently agreed not to embarrass the royal family, yet the publicist Max Clifford had obtained not only his original thirty-nine-page statement but also his proof of evidence. That document, composed by his lawyers, described in explicit detail Diana's relationship with many boyfriends, including Hasnat Khan, a Pakistani surgeon who more than once had been smuggled into Kensington Palace either under a blanket or in the boot of a car for night-time encounters. Burrell described cancelling Diana's public engagements so that she could stay with Khan, even specifically so that she could stay in bed with him.

To add spice to such revelations, Burrell presented Charles as a pampered, absolute monarch similar to France's notoriously self-indulgent kings before the Revolution. In his statement, he revealed that the prince had ordered him to lie to Diana about his movements, and once, after the butler had inadvertently told the truth, had thrown a book at him; how Charles insisted that his own crystal goblets and silver cutlery be brought to the hospital after his polo accident so he would not have to use institutional crockery; that the prince had ordered staff at Highgrove to burn a crafted table presented to him by South Sea islanders; and that he would sneer at Diana about her clothes, describing her on one occasion as looking like an air stewardess and on another as a member of the Mafia. In graphic detail, he described how Michael Fawcett had held a specimen test tube for his master to pee into. (He did not mention that at the time Charles was handicapped by having one arm in plaster.)

Clifford obtained £300,000 for the two statements from the *News of the World*, undermining Burrell's relationship with the *Mirror*.

The paper splashed headlines about Diana's sex life, including Burrell's breathless account of her seduction of Khan wearing just sapphire-and-diamond earrings and her fur coat, and about serving the Pakistani doctor breakfast in bed on one occasion after Diana had left Kensington Palace early.

Burrell cashed in further in the following day's *Mirror*, this time giving a taste of his cast of mind as directed against the Spencers. Depicting the grieving family as a collection of snobs and predators, he targeted Charles Spencer for his refusal to rent his sister a cottage at Althorp in the summer of 1997, ostensibly to avoid public intrusion. 'The Spencers found Diana unacceptable in life,' wrote Burrell, 'but after her death they found her very acceptable at £10.50 a ticket,' referring to the price the public were charged to visit Diana's grave at Althorp. He held back a letter Spencer had written to Diana on 4 April 1996 in which he branded her as manipulative, deceitful and mentally ill. That titbit was saved for his book. Amid the tsunami of media vilification aimed at Charles and his family, such an omission was barely a mercy.

The royal palaces were being plagued by recriminations about the trial. The internal furore was concealed from the world outside by discreet courtiers – with one notable exception. At 8.30 a.m. on Thursday, 7 November, Fiona Shackleton telephoned de Brunner and in the course of a tirade said that Mark Bolland had organised the queen's recollection. 'He's the head boy, he's evil and he hates the police,' she ranted. 'Bolland has infiltrated the whole system. He knew about it [the recollection] on the day it happened. You cannot let that man win.' After confessing that her own position was now in jeopardy, she ended up: 'It's disgusting and unjust. Why couldn't they have seen it through? At least Burrell wouldn't have sold his story.' But despite her fury, no evidence existed that Bolland, by then a consultant to Charles, had been involved in the 'recollection' or in any strategic discussions that fateful weekend. Moreover, he denied any participation.

Days later, during the opening ceremony of the Field of Remembrance in Westminster Abbey, the queen looked unusually morose. At the Cenotaph later that week, Charles barely spoke to his mother, and avoided lunch with his family. Palace officials warned them both that there was much worse to come. For once they were right.

16

A Private Secretary Goes Public

The calamity Charles feared had materialised. Despite his generous pay-off, George Smith sold his story to the *News of the World*, waiving his right to anonymity. For the first time, the media could explain some of the background to the royal machinations over the previous years. One week after the Burrell trial, the *News of the World* published Smith's allegation that an unnamed man, an employee of the royal family, had raped him. Referring to the mahogany-box tapes, Smith also revealed that he had recorded a secret about a family member so devastating it could destroy the monarchy. The newspaper described the 'rape tape' and allegations of a cover-up by Charles. The headlines ensured that five years of hard labour to restore the public's trust in the Prince of Wales disintegrated.

With Charles's financial help, Michael Fawcett sought an injunction to protect his identity, while simultaneously denouncing Smith through an expensive firm of solicitors as an 'unreliable alcoholic' whose allegations included 'demonstrable discrepancies' about when and where he was raped. In retaliation, Smith claimed that there had been a second rape. Constrained by the threat of an injunction and the laws of defamation, the media could still not reveal the full story behind Smith's confession – and that ignorance was precisely what Charles was relying on.

Pressed to explain the outcome of inquiries into Smith's original rape allegation, Scotland Yard issued an unconvincing reply. After a 'full' investigation, it declared, the investigating officer had submitted a report to the CPS recommending that no prosecution be brought. That explanation would be contradicted by a subsequent admission that Hounslow police had in fact abandoned their review after Smith refused to make a complaint. Neither statement was accurate; the truth had been buried. (In 2016 Detective Superintendent Steve Gwilliam would say that he could not recall the case, and a similar memory loss affected the CPS lawyer responsible for the file.)

In the same issue of the *News of the World* that featured Smith's allegations, the paper revealed for the first time that Paul Burrell was gay. The comedian Michael Barrymore, who was known to have had homosexual affairs, described how the butler had attempted to seduce him three days after Diana's death by showing him three of her diamond rings then lunging at him. Burrell denied the story. His wife did not comment. Amid more revelations about his sexuality, Burrell had flown to America to sell some of his secrets to all three major TV networks for huge fees. 'Telling my story was never about money,' he said, omitting to mention that he had previously pledged not to betray Diana's privacy. 'It was only about truth and justice and telling it honestly and properly.' He left behind a furore about Michael Fawcett's conduct.

At the very moment that Burrell was making his announcement on American television, Fawcett was supervising arrangements for a dinner at Windsor Castle for Charles's American Foundation. By then, his hold over the prince was well known. Although George Smith did not name Fawcett, media allegations linking him to the misuse of Charles's property under the headline 'Fawcett the Fence' had surfaced. Before the end of the day, Charles was forced to condemn his trusted employee to 'indefinite leave' and exile from the castle. In a foul mood, he now had no one on whom he could rely to rebut the consequent gossip about his paying Fawcett off, or dampen the speculation about whether his valet would be forced to give up his rent-free home in Richmond.

For very different reasons, three men – Burrell, Fawcett and Smith – were all creating major problems for Charles. The combination of adultery, alleged gay rape, drugs, sex orgies, thefts and the unprecedented end of a criminal trial was no longer a soap opera, but had escalated into a real crisis. Charles considered appearing on TV to deny that Smith had been raped, then abandoned the idea, not least because Fawcett obtained an injunction to prevent anyone linking his name with Smith's allegations. 'It is impossible to exaggerate the devastation wreaked on the House of Windsor in the last week,' wrote Trevor Kavanagh in the *Sun*, adding ridicule by revealing that one of Fawcett's responsibilities was to squeeze the tooth-paste onto Charles's brush. 'There is a cesspit of intrigue at the heart of the realm.'

The thunder of derision heaped upon the royal family appeared to bemuse Peat. Asked if Charles was shocked by the uproar, he replied, 'Yes, I suppose so, to the extent that you can believe it.' He added that Fawcett, despite the public accusation of taking commis-sions both on the sale of gifts to the royals and from suppliers, 'is here and is working'.

Peat's air of nonchalance angered Whitehall. A senior official suggested to him that only an inquiry could end the frenzy. The appointment of a High Court judge was instantly discounted as dangerous. Instead, Peat announced on television, on the advice of Lord Stevens, the Scotland Yard commissioner, that he personally would conduct an inquiry. Four issues required investigation: whether Smith's allegation of being raped had been covered up; whether Charles had sabotaged Burrell's trial; whether official gifts to Charles and his family had been sold by his staff; and whether Charles's staff had received improper payments.

'I, and more importantly the Prince of Wales,' said Peat, 'are totally committed to openness and accountability.' He did not trou-ble to explain how he, as Charles's private secretary, could be truly independent when conducting an inquiry into the conduct of his employer and his own staff, including himself. 'Anyone who says it is going to be a complete whitewash doesn't know me very well,' was his glib justification. Hours later, he undermined his own independ-ence. 'I don't think any of us are going to take [the rape allegation] seriously,' he said. 'What can one do, except to laugh?' He added, 'I can give you my 100 per cent assurance that there was no interfer-ence in the trial.' Similarly, the allegations against 'Fawcett the Fence' were dismissed by Peat before his inquiry began. 'We have abso-lutely no evidence of it,' he declared. 'I think it's very unlikely. What people have told the press that he has done, no one told us. We have no allegations at all about Mr Fawcett's behaviour.'

Peat also displayed his prejudice against the police. At the same time as the inquiry was being announced, Burrell was claiming that he had not been charged with the theft of the hundreds of items belonging to Diana that had been left in his house by de Brunner after his arrest. The police, said Burrell, accepted that they had been

genuine gifts to him. At that moment the police were so overcome
by criticisms of their conduct that Burrell's assertion passed unchallenged, but eventually Maxine de Brunner explained that her priority had been to seize everything that might embarrass the royal
family, and that she would have removed more, but ten hours after
their arrival at Burrell's home the police could not load any more
items onto the lorry sent from London after the local police trucu-
lently refused de Brunner's request to provide a truck. Her mistake,
she and Yates would later admit, was not to seal off the house as a
crime scene.

Peat immediately exploited that error in an interview with the
Evening Standard: 'The police well know that high-value presents
had been given to Paul Burrell because they didn't charge him with
stealing a large number of items of considerable value, because they
accepted that they had been given to him by the Princess of Wales
… It was totally clear to everybody that the Prince and Princess of
Wales gave gifts, and valuable gifts, to their staff.'

Peat was dancing on a pinhead. In the end, the CPS and not the
police had decided to charge Burrell. Moreover, some of the alleged
thefts had not been listed because the items belonged to either
Charles or William. To link either of the princes with allegedly
stolen property would have required them to give evidence at a trial,
and that had been ruled out. Peat appeared to be spreading
confusion.

In a lengthy interview with the media, he angrily complained that
the police had failed to listen to a long briefing about the gifts
donated to Burrell. The law officers said that was not true. 'The
denial,' said Peat, 'is difficult to understand … There is no question
of the CPS having been misled.' Scotland Yard had heard enough.
While Peat was proving to be protective of Charles, the Yard's chief
showed his robust support for de Brunner: she was heading for
promotion to deputy assistant commissioner.

In that retaliatory atmosphere, William Boyce made another
announcement in court: the charge against Harold Brown had been
dropped. Once again, the police were surprised. There was clear
evidence that Brown had sold the dhow after Diana's death, had lied
in his statements, and that the money from the sale had disappeared.
Those facts were not mentioned in Boyce's court declaration. Brown,
the lawyer explained, possessed a note from Charles which read:

'There is a very good gold wedding ring here which someone in the office might find useful.' The valet had then sold the ring. Although that piece and the dhow were unconnected, Boyce said that Brown could have relied on Burrell giving him permission to sell the dhow in 'good faith'. Brown was also formally acquitted by the court over the sale of Diana's earrings in January 1998, and his offering for sale of her emerald-and-diamond bangle and a diamond brooch.

The most vulnerable person was still Charles, approaching his fifty-fourth birthday. His defencelessness was increased by his separation from Bolland, who told a friend, 'Peat never misses an opportunity to trash me. He wants to destroy my relationship with Charles.' The prince's two foremost henchmen now openly detested each other.

The final breach between them took place in the wake of Burrell's acquittal. Peat received a warning from a trouble-seeking lawyer that the *News of the World* was planning a honey trap for Charles's younger son in what had become an unceasing quest. Using a girl to forge a relationship with Prince Harry, the newspaper hoped to obtain a sample of his hair. According to the lawyer, the hair's DNA would be tested to establish whether Harry's father was not Charles but James Hewitt. Peat's solution was to alert the police and call Rebekah Wade at the *News of the World*.

Bolland opposed both calls. 'Let's find out first,' he told Peat. 'I just don't believe it.' He said that Hewitt and Diana had not seen each other for a full year before Harry's birth, and that to date the media had abided by the strict guidelines that forbade any breach of Harry's privacy: the *News of the World*, he was convinced, would not publish such allegations. Peat ignored the advice, and called Wade anyway. In a heated exchange, he warned her that publication would result in dire repercussions, and despite her advice not to put anything in writing, he sent her a formal letter of complaint.

Inevitably, under the headline 'St James's Palace Goes Mad', a full account of the conversation appeared in Wade's paper, along with a quotation from 'a senior palace aide' that Charles was 'furious … to have been bothered by such a ludicrous story'. Peat assumed the 'senior palace aide' was Bolland, and encouraged Charles to reprimand him.

For more than a year Charles had been under pressure from his private secretary to fire Bolland. That had been one of Peat's priorities on arriving at St James's Palace. He had resisted because he needed Bolland's special talents, but now, utterly dependent on Peat to save him from the Burrell and Fawcett calamities, he felt he had no choice. Charles called Bolland at the adviser's Clerkenwell home at lunchtime that Sunday, 15 December. After listening to the complaints, Bolland replied, 'This man [meaning Peat] is destroying everything. It's ridiculous.'

'How do you know it's ridiculous?' asked Charles.

'Because I'm having lunch here with Rebekah Wade, and she tells me it's ridiculous.'

'We can't go on like this,' said Charles after a pause. 'You have other consultancies. It's time for you to go.'

The call ended on a sour note, and a productive six-year relationship was over. The following day, Bolland formally resigned. 'To survive and thrive you need to be there to see the knives coming out,' he mused, 'so the part-time consultancy had to end.'

Over the following days, he reflected that Peat had never wanted their extraordinary relationship to work. He knew better than most how vicious the palace could be, but even he was unprepared for what appeared in the *Daily Telegraph* that Friday, and two days later in the *Mail on Sunday*. First, the papers published a story that he was disgruntled not to have succeeded Stephen Lamport as Charles's private secretary. He blamed Peat for that piece of untrue mischief. The *Mail on Sunday* also quoted Charles – his words relayed to the journalist, Bolland assumed by Peat – dismissing Bolland's work for himself and Camilla as 'dirty deeds'. 'Their betrayal,' said Bolland, 'upset me.' He knew all too well that few left the Prince of Wales's employ happily. 'There's an absurdity about him,' said the dismissed retainer. 'Charles cares about no one other than himself.'

Not for the first time with an employee, Charles mismanaged Bolland's exit. In their irritation, neither he nor Camilla bothered to show any gratitude. Charles did not host a farewell party, nor did he recommend Bolland for any honour. He never even said goodbye. Nor did Camilla, who, as a friend explained regretfully, 'did what she was told'.

Stung, Bolland agreed to write a regular column for the *News of the World*. Under the pseudonym 'Blackadder', for many months he vented his spleen against the courtiers in the three palaces, Princes Andrew and Harry, and above all Peat and Charles. In retaliation, and to prove that Bolland's services were not missed, Charles attempted to win over the *Daily Mail* by giving the newspaper an interview, and inviting its editor to a state dinner at Buckingham Palace.

One week later, he invited Tony Blair for lunch. The scene at Clarence House was surreal. The host was struggling in a swamp of sleaze, while the prime minister was in the midst of his own scandal: his wife Cherie had been exposed as having lied when she denied a financial relationship with an Australian conman who had arranged her purchase of two flats in Bristol. Blair was also under pressure to explain his relationship with Carole Caplin, his 'lifestyle' adviser. In that familiar predicament, he could hope only that his accusers would eventually give up.

Charles could hope only for the same respite. But there was no relief. In a poll by BBC's Radio 4, listeners were asked which British personality they would most like to deport. Charles ranked fourth. He had had enough. At a dinner party, he hurled a plate to the floor, complaining that everything had gone wrong. But now he had only Peat to protect him.

Money Matters

Charles was worried about money. With his reputation once again in tatters, American donors were cancelling their appearances at his fundraising events, making a nonsense of Robert Higdon's target of raising $5 million a year. Similar difficulties faced his British charities. His saviour was Michael Fawcett. Based in Clarence House despite the public announcement of his suspension on 'indefinite leave', Fawcett continued to gather the donors, organise the parties, and decide who to admit to Buckingham Palace, St James's Palace or Highgrove.

When Fawcett took against a person, Charles echoed his judgement. One casualty was John Studzinski, a sophisticated American-born investment banker and a generous donor to British causes. After Studzinski delivered a finely worked speech at a lunch at St James's Palace to raise funds for the homeless, Charles told an organiser, 'John shouldn't have made the address, because Michael says that he doesn't give me enough money.' Although that rebuff did not diminish Studzinski's continued work with the prince, Fawcett was inclined to value the size of a donor's cheque rather than his sincerity.

The management consultants from Bain and McKinsey were more popular than some individual donors. In return for their pro-bono work, Fawcett organised a dinner with Charles. 'It was red-carpet fever,' said one consultant. In their excitement, the consultants speculated that a big donation might secure a knighthood personally from Charles. Nothing appeared too vulgar for consideration, including Fawcett's taste in entertainment. One performance by the Irish dancer Michael Flatley was accompanied by a troupe of female dancers who whipped off their robes to reveal skimpy bikinis, with violin music coming from their crotches. Aides noticed that Charles did not comment about such tawdriness; Fawcett was too valuable.

The master valet had encouraged the flamboyant Turkish businessman Cem Uzan to give another donation, although in early 2003 this profitable relationship soured when Uzan was accused of non-repayment of loans, and in the follow-up was sentenced by the High Court in London to fifteen months in jail for failing to be present at a hearing.

Some reproached Charles for ever having welcomed Uzan to Buckingham Palace, but that criticism paled into insignificance when set against his relationship with the American oil tycoon Armand Hammer. 'Hammer had no morals of any kind,' wrote his biographer, Neil Lyndon, of an international criminal whose death in 1990 had removed the legal constraints that prevented writers and journalists from revealing the truth. He described Hammer's criminal greed as the cause of 167 men dying as a result of the explosion on the North Sea oil rig Piper Alpha, and how, as a Soviet agent in the 1920s, the tycoon had made billions of dollars by illegally trading in food and oil with Lenin and Stalin. In an attempt to rehabilitate his reputation Hammer had contributed about £40 million to Charles, either to his charities or his personal expenses. Among the gifts was £2 million in return for being allowed to stand next to the prince while the Tudor warship the *Mary Rose* was raised from the Solent in 1982; and at a charity gala in Palm Beach he pledged $50,000 each time Diana danced with one of his friends, mostly Mafia bosses.

Lyndon had found in Hammer's archives a bundle of handwritten letters from Charles overflowing with thanks for money, flights on his jets and hospitality. 'My Dear Dr Hammer,' read one letter, 'We were both enormously touched that you should have thought of sending us that beautiful Christmas present.' He signed another thank-you note, 'With warmest best wishes and everlasting gratitude'. The death of Hammer, and of Yiannis Latsis in 2003, deprived Charles's charities of millions of pounds, and the prince himself of free holidays on their yachts.

Charles's understanding of money was rudimentary. Despite a good education and contacts with a succession of rich businessmen, he remained determinedly ignorant about financial matters. He was happy to assume that, under his control, much happened without his knowledge. His response when a duchy accountant told him that a proposal was unaffordable was characteristic.

'Why is it unaffordable?'

'Because you haven't got the money.'

Charles left the room and told an assistant in his office, 'I never want to see that man again.' Michael Peat was asked to negotiate with the Cabinet Office for more money to sustain Charles's official duties.

To some in Whitehall, Charles's passion for his charities showed his unselfishness and integrity. Others felt uncomfortable about his concern for the disadvantaged while he himself enjoyed so extravagant a lifestyle. The contradiction was revealed in early 2003, when his stable of charities came in danger of stumbling into another crisis.

The most exposed was the Prince's Trust. A few years earlier, Fred Goodwin, the rapaciously ambitious chief executive of the Royal Bank of Scotland and the chairman of the Prince's Trust in Scotland, had sought to fire Tom Shebbeare, the trust's director. Goodwin had complained to Elizabeth Buchanan, the assistant private secretary recruited by Tim Bell, that the trust was badly managed, and it was 'time for him to go'. The plot to remove Shebbeare was aborted by Bolland and Lamport. Goodwin's criticism remained unanswered: Shebbeare was, he said, 'charismatic, but his skill was not the boring management of an organisation and he was powerless to contradict Charles'.

By 2003 the trust's problems had worsened. Staff redundancies were inevitable. Its plight was to be considered at the charity's annual board meeting. On 17 July 2003 the businessman William Castell formally retired as chairman. After five years leading the charity, he had assented to Buchanan's nudge that Goodwin should inherit his post. 'He's bringing in a lot of money,' said Buchanan – Goodwin was personally giving about £250,000 a year, by far the biggest contribution of any trustee. He had also committed his bank to making a £5 million donation after he became chairman.

Castell had joined the trust after meeting the prince in a fish-and-chip bar in Aberdare in 1990. Charles was visiting on behalf of the trust. His mission was to persuade a group of drug addicts to improve their lives. The charity, he felt sure, could help them. 'Charles,' Castell observed, 'had real passion, and the young people loved him.' To the prince they represented the lost generation of a million young people who preferred welfare benefits to education and work, and who had been abandoned by those in power. Ten years later, Castell was proud that he and Angus Ogilvy had managed to persuade Tony Blair to contribute £50 million to the trust; but that money alone could not resolve an increasing hazard shared by all of Charles's charities.

At its best, the Prince's Trust could provide instant help to the disadvantaged young. An applicant asking for money to improve his employment chances, or needing a musical instrument, could watch as the chairman wrote a cheque on the spot. The trust's remit was expanded to help unemployed school-leavers undertake twelve-week courses to develop their self-confidence. Through the trust, half a million children at the bottom of the social heap had been helped by courses financed by private employers and the government. Then in 2000 Charles agreed to devolve management to the regions, and centralised control was lost. Within three years, the flagship charity was stumbling. Critics questioned why Charles was competing with the more successful Duke of Edinburgh Award. Too often the trust was helping less vulnerable children, while the most desperate cases were left to other organisations. It was accused of adopting a fortress mentality, and of being unwilling to cooperate with other charities. And, on the eve of his retirement, Castell acknowledged a pressing financial problem.

The 'Skilled City' exhibition for vocational skills, hosted in Birmingham by the trust, had lost about £2 million that year, contributing to a £3 million deficit, an unacceptable situation for a royal charity. 'It was a true shock,' Castell acknowledged. An internal investigation by David Brooks, a local businessman, blamed Shebbeare's lack of management skills and his disregard of risk assessment. Shebbeare's vagueness, said his critics, had caused the financial hole. The next item at the trust's board meeting after Castell announced his departure was the unexpected mention of Brooks's report. One trustee suggested that Shebbeare should go. Feeling ambushed, Castell listened as the majority fell into line against Shebbeare. He was horrified by what he characterised as a 'bitterly divisive meeting. They had agreed to cut off Tom's head without consulting me.' Shebbeare, in Castell's view, had 'for years success-fully raised funds to make sure the trust was not insolvent'. But having left his post, Castell was powerless to intervene.

In a normal organisation Shebbeare would have been asked to step down, but he was the face of the trust, and close to Charles, so the trustees reckoned his dismissal would be a self-inflicted wound. 'The Prince's Trust had allowed Charles to reinvent himself after 1997,' recalled one of the trustees, 'and it would not have been helpful to sack the man associated with that success.' Instead, the trustees' unhappiness was passed on to Charles through Elizabeth Buchanan. He was torn. Battered by the Burrell saga and bewildered by the financial disarray among his charities, he was in a state of shock. Although Shebbeare was mocked as a court jester, he was also a loyal supporter who worked well with the prince. He could tease, praise, entertain and motivate Charles to help young people, and most vitally to restore his lost self-esteem.

'Let's look at all the positive things you've done, sir,' said Castell sympathetically during a post-mortem dinner. Unspoken in the wake of the Burrell crisis was Charles's use of his charities to improve his profile and buttress his self-belief. Accordingly, Shebbeare's mistakes needed to be concealed, despite his honest confession: 'I'm culpable for the loss and I'm vulnerable.' 'What would you like to do?' Michael Peat asked Shebbeare. Instead of the director departing, Peat proposed what one trustee called an elegant solution. Shebbeare was promoted upstairs to oversee all the prince's charities and to 'big-up' the prince as a 'charitable entrepreneur'. But to critics, Shebbeare's new responsibilities were fanciful; the charities needed reorganisation, not expansion.

Driven by his sense of mission, Charles was still dabbling in too many ventures, and directing staff to create new charities on little more than a whim. After a trip to Japan he established the Prince's Trust Volunteers, without realising that a similar organisation already existed. New ventures overlapped with identical set-ups elsewhere. The Prince's Drawing School and the Prince's Teaching Institute, dedicated to encourage 'real' teaching and the understanding of literature through weekend schools, were both on the verge of insolvency. A well-constructed smokescreen concealed the truth.

Peat put out three promotional brochures to publicise the prince's initiatives. One, 'Working for Charity', described his patronage of 350 organisations and his successful raising of £70 million that year. In parallel, high-profile events featured Charles at their centre. The first was a star-studded Shakespeare gala; the next was 'Fashion

Rocks', a spectacular entertainment at the Royal Albert Hall attracting five thousand people and financed by Lily Safra. By then Safra had become famous after the mysterious death of her fourth husband, a billionaire banker, in a fire in Monaco. (A previous husband had died after shooting himself, twice.) She wanted to be accompanied to the event by Robert Higdon, but Peat excluded the American and inserted Jacob Rothschild as her companion instead. To avoid any distraction from the publicity coup of an event that eventually raised over £1 million, Peat also sought to prevent Camilla from accompanying Charles; he lost that battle. In retaliation, Camilla's friends bad-mouthed Peat to the *Daily Mail*. Higdon joined the carping after Peat arranged a third event, agreeing during a chance meeting at Wimbledon with Anna Wintour, editor of American *Vogue*, for the magazine to have exclusive photographs of Charles's next fundraising dinner in Buckingham Palace. That agreement undercut Higdon's identical promise to *Vanity Fair*. 'I got screwed again,' complained the fundraiser. 'Peat was acting big pants. He had the political sense of a hamster.'

Charles's secretary could not so easily override opposition from Whitehall. After the three fundraising events, a senior civil servant again called Peat and in an exasperated tone told him that Charles's trading on the allure of the royals was open to corruption. Buckingham Palace was no longer for sale.

Peat responded by circulating new rules of engagement. Fawcett and Higdon were told that they could no longer sell seats at dinners in a royal palace to the highest bidder. Instead, donors would be asked to buy a table for around £20,000, with an unwritten understanding that they would also be expected to make a hefty donation. To prevent the entry of dubious characters into the palaces, Shebbeare was tasked to oversee both men – in addition to his supervising approximately twenty charities and his patronage of 350 organisations. The empire was running out of control.

Fred Goodwin was uninhibited in his complaints to Charles. As he was the chief executive of RBS, the director of each of Charles's charities would call and ask him for money. 'We need to put a lid on things,' he said of the multiple approaches to the same banks and corporations. Charles's charities, he warned, were also in danger of attracting renewed criticism for inadequate governance, poor management and substandard trustees.

Peat agreed. 'Don't we need some reorganisation?' he asked Charles.

'It's not going to happen,' chimed the charities' chairmen in reply.

Peat was reluctant to challenge Shebbeare directly. Each charity had its own chairman, board of trustees and administrators, and each resisted reform, mergers and loss of control.

Presentations to the prince followed a predictable pattern. Shebbeare, Peat, Julia Cleverdon, Buchanan and invited heads of his charities would gush about the joy and privilege of working for His Royal Highness. In his own presentation, Shebbeare fluently described his progress towards making Charles's charities super-efficient. Sensible rationalisation would have reduced the charities to just four – for the arts, business, the environment and the Prince's Trust – but that was opposed by the charities' directors, and, shuddered Shebbeare, would be an insult to Charles. Instead, he merely offered a hymn of praise, and after finishing his review sat attentively to listen with his A4 notebook open. Invariably, Charles started with a lament about so many of the good things he'd done going unrecognised. His audience cooed in sympathetic agreement.

When occasionally during these meetings the prince directed that another charity be created, Shebbeare never said 'No' or 'Hang on a moment.' Instead, critics described his responses as 'soft drivel to justify his salary'.

'There was a lot of muddle,' Shebbeare later admitted to a friend, grateful at least that Elizabeth Buchanan 'fought my corner' to win Charles's agreement to accept dinner invitations to thank donors. Charles concluded every session with polite thanks to his employees.

'I got the sense that the whole stable was not being pulled together,' observed Mike Lake, an experienced charity director for Help the Aged who was recruited by Shebbeare as his deputy, and to be groomed as his successor. Lake had first met Charles through Prime, which had been set up by Charles in the late 1990s to develop opportunities for old people. Like some other charities, Prime had lost its way. 'I saw signs of a financial situation being allowed to continue,' said Lake, 'which beyond the palace would have created alarm.'

To avert the crisis, Charles summoned Jacob Rothschild and Hayden Phillips, the retired permanent secretary at the lord chancellor's office and later at the Department of Culture. Both were trusted administrators and skilled problem-solvers. The arrival of two such heavyweights did not disturb Shebbeare. Instead, he mini-mised Phillips's role, not only ignoring his advice to reduce the number of charities but, at Charles's request, creating new ones in Afghanistan, China, Burma and Romania. 'I was better at starting organisations than running them,' he admitted. At the same time, Lake was asked to implement Phillips's recommendations. No one appeared to consider the possible consequences of the two incom-patible objectives.

Aware that Charles's public image was under threat, Peat planned to publish a mission statement. In advance, he briefed a Daily Mail journalist that 'Charles does not enjoy a champagne and caviar life-style.' Contrary to the public's perception, he continued, the prince possessed only one car, and did not even own his own home. In reality he owned at least six cars, including two Aston Martins, a Bentley, an Audi, a Range Rover and a Land Rover, while Peat's quibble about the legal ownership of the six homes variously occu-pied by Charles (Clarence House, Highgrove, Birkhall, the Castle of Mey, Balmoral and Sandringham) was clearly disingenuous. The newspaper report was met with derision and the publication of the 'mission statement' was abandoned.

Other events forced Peat's hand. Pressure for more candour started after Buckingham Palace revealed that the royal family had avoided the payment of inheritance taxes after the death of the queen mother because her jewels, antiques and art collection – including a Monet valued at over £50 million – had been given to her daughter and grandchildren in 1993. By law, gifts made seven years before death are not liable to inheritance taxes. Although the 'gifting' was suspicious, because the queen mother's collection of jewels was found in her cupboards after her death, the Inland Revenue did not challenge the queen's claim for tax exemption. The convenient settlement nevertheless raised suspicions about the royals' finances. Although the accounts showed that the monarchy cost each British person just 61 pence a year, the revelation that Andrew had spent £3,000 on a flight from London to Oxford, and that eighteen journeys on the royal train by various members of the family had cost £750,000, persuaded the National Audit Office to undertake the first official investigation of some of the royals' accounts, including those of the Duchy of Cornwall. The agency's conclusion that the duchy's accounts were 'not crystal clear' prompted MPs on the Public Accounts Committee to announce the first ever parliamentary investigation of Charles's finances.

Peat was summoned by MPs to be publicly questioned in Westminster. With some urgency, he composed a new brochure presenting Charles as a hard-working, modest man. The statistics, he believed, would sway MPs and the public. In the previous year (2003), he wrote, Charles had undertaken 517 engagements, met ten thousand people, received nine thousand guests, written two thousand letters, visited eighteen regiments and raised £109 million for charity. (Peat omitted to mention that about half of that money was contributed by the taxpayer, in the form of government contributions.) Fifty-two photographs of Charles in the review's first thirty-six pages represented him as 'the greatest charitable entrepreneur in the world'.

Michael Fawcett echoed Peat's pitch to one donor: 'His Royal Highness lives modestly. He hasn't got a yacht and doesn't eat lunch.' In both instances that was true, but he failed to add that beyond the £4.1 million Charles received from the government for his official duties, his personal annual income from the duchy for the year in question was £11.9 million.

Unlike other members of his family, since 1337 the heir to the throne had enjoyed a guaranteed stream of income from the Duchy of Cornwall. Created by Edward III, the duchy owned about 57,000 hectares of farmland and commercial property across the country, including shopping centres and offices, worth £463 million. Financially independent of any state control, Charles did not have to answer to anyone over his use of the money, which included his employment of 124 staff, eighty-five of whom worked full-time. Among them were four valets, so that two would always be available to help change his clothes, which he did up to five times every day.

The duchy's finances were deliberately opaque. The country's fourth largest landowner selected various descriptions of itself to suit each audience: it was a private trust, a private estate, a part of the crown, or a 'legal entity' (except when circumstances made it advantageous to say the opposite). Payment of taxes was expected, but was still entirely voluntary. By developing a mystique, Charles's various managers used the duchy's immunity from income tax, inheritance tax and capital gains tax to increase its value from £110 million in 1996 to £463 million in 2003. The only constraints were that the duchy was obliged to reinvest any capital gains in England and Wales, and that any investment over £500,000 required Treasury certification that the arrangement was commercial.

The Prince of Wales was entitled to the duchy's income, but was not allowed to spend any of the capital (that is, by selling any of the duchy's assets) on himself. To comply with that rule, Highgrove had been bought by the duchy, then rented to Charles for £336,000 a year. In a quaint arrangement, he paid that rent out of income he received from the duchy – all without paying taxes.

Before the hearing at Westminster, Peat's cleverly worded review persuaded the MPs on the committee of Charles's good intentions; but he failed to dampen their curiosity. Not least because, under Peat's supervision, the duchy's income was due to rise by 11 per cent over the next twelve months, to £13.2 million, and Charles would increase his personal spending from £4.4 to £5.2 million. Considering the prince's conduct over the previous fifteen years, the MPs were hardly sympathetic, and decided to probe further.

After conversations with the Treasury official responsible for the duchy, the MPs' researchers concluded that the estate had increased in value every year, and was expected to be worth £505 million in 2004. Discovering the reasons for that success was difficult. Accountants employed by the National Audit Office found 'obscurities and potential conflicts of interest' in the duchy's scant accounts. One example was the sale, for £2.3 million, of trees planted by Charles on duchy land to the duchy itself. In that circular deal, the prince pocketed the money without paying any tax. What he did pay after deducting his expenses remained entirely voluntary. Free of any scrutiny, his advisers had boosted his income by moving money from the duchy's capital account to the revenue account, refusing to explain their reason adequately. Everyone understood the real purpose of the manoeuvre: Charles wanted more money, not least to pay his staff. The more he claimed as official expenses, the less he voluntarily paid in income tax.

At their public hearing, the MPs asked Peat how many of Charles's staff of 124 were genuinely working in an official position. The duchy's accounts described ninety-four people as 'official' employees, but the MPs were suspicious. They also wondered whether

Camilla's personal upkeep – including her hair, clothes and jewellery – should be set off as a tax-deductable item on the grounds that the costs of her appearance were incurred for her official engagements. After all, they said, she undertook very few public duties.

Peat resisted giving detailed answers. The secrecy of the arrangements, he told the MPs, had existed for seven hundred years; and since the duchies of Cornwall and of Lancaster (the queen's estates) were private, outsiders had no right to know specifics. 'They are not public bodies,' he said. 'They are well-run private estates specifically created to provide income for the sovereign and [for the] heir to the throne.' Echoing David Airlie's justification for the queen not paying taxes, Peat noted that the monarch's and the heir's private fortunes were protected from taxes and from investigation in order to protect their impartiality and financial independence from the government.

The MPs were not convinced. The duchy, some concluded, was a tax fiddle, and should be made clearly legitimate and more accountable. Irritated by their scepticism, Charles authorised his spokesman to describe the MPs' report as a 'travesty' and 'fundamentally wrong'.

His refusal to release his personal accounts for scrutiny was supported by Gordon Brown, then chancellor of the exchequer. 'He does not deserve to be the target of these shoddy and underhand tactics,' said Brown. Events would show that the masters of such shoddy and underhand tactics were Charles's own staff.

18

Whitewash

Michael Peat published his report about Prince Charles and the Burrell trial on 13 March 2003, the eve of the invasion of Iraq. With luck, Charles's advisers calculated, media interest would disappear within a day. People's expectations were muted. Announcing his inquiry four months earlier, Peat had promised that there would be 'no whitewash'. That assurance was challenged within his report's first pages.

In a joint conclusion, Peat and Edmund Lawson declared that they would not 'express any view about the truth' of George Smith's allegation that he had been raped by Michael Fawcett. The report summary, however, judged: 'No one believed Mr Smith's rape allegation,' and because Smith 'declined to pursue his complaint' with the police, he was therefore lying. That conclusion was clearly questionable. Victims of sexual abuse often fear confessing an attack to officials, and Smith's own explanation about avoiding embarrassment in front of his children was credible. Moreover, some in Highgrove did believe Smith, as had Diana and her staff at Kensington Palace, but the report minimised Diana's involvement.

Interpreting Fiona Shackleton's expression of remorse at the meeting with the police on 30 August 2001 was another potential trap for Peat. Shackleton's comment, 'I'll tell [George Smith] that if he brings it into the open, then we look v heavily into his background etc. ruin chances of getting another job,' incriminated Charles. Peat took an opposite line. In his report, he simply denied that there could have been 'an improper motive (that is, to suppress the truth)' about Charles's £38,000 payment to Smith. But he gave no credible explanation for that denial.

On the question of whether it was Shackleton or McCorquodale who first said 'rape' at the meeting with the police, Peat and Lawson decided, based on Michael O'Kane's notes, that it was McCorquodale, and rejected the two police officers' testimony that Shackleton broke the silence. Either way, it was immaterial. Their forensic examination of that unimportant question obscured the relevance of Shackleton's outburst: 'I was given written instructions by my boss to make the whole business go away, which I did, but it was one of the lowest points of my twenty-two-year legal career.' This appeared to imply that Charles had ordered her to suppress Smith's allegation, a serious matter. That was the interpretation made by Michael O'Kane after the meeting. But for obvious reasons he decided to take it no further.

Peat and Lawson dismissed O'Kane's straightforward conclusion. Instead they wrote that they were 'puzzled' how the reference to Charles could be misinterpreted – and said nothing more. Except, they pushed the blame onto Shackleton, who, they wrote, could not make 'an admission of impropriety' because that would be untrue, since Charles was indisputably innocent. From that circular argument they concluded that the issue 'remains something of a mystery'. Charles was exonerated and Shackleton portrayed as unreliable, a judgement that she regarded as a betrayal of her selfless devotion to Charles's cause and a personal insult by Peat, an old family friend. Distortion, Peat's critics said, had suffocated fidelity.

Moving on, the report considered the allegation that Charles had improperly influenced the aborting of Paul Burrell's trial. Since Peat had been involved in those discussions, he asked Edmund Lawson QC to investigate that accusation without his participation. His conclusions were incorporated into the report.

Lawson, well-known at the Bar as a chain-smoking bully, was an unfortunate choice. He lacked both the skill and the reputation to produce a convincingly independent result. As it was, he relied on a memorandum from Stephen Lamport to Charles following the first police briefing about Burrell and Brown, on 3 April 2001: 'There is no alternative but for formal charges now to be made against both men.' Charles, wrote Lawson, 'accepted that advice for the time being', but still wanted to explore 'whether a prosecution could be properly avoided'.

Lawson's premise was deliberately misleading. On several occasions either Lamport or Shackleton, acting on Charles's behalf, sought to prevent a prosecution. Before 3 April, Lamport had told the police that Charles was keen to stop Brown being charged. On 2 May, Shackleton's message to the police and prosecutor was emphatic: 'The Prince of Wales is distraught. He does not want it going any further and is determined.' Three months later, before the police briefing at Highgrove, Charles had tried through Bolland and Shackleton to bring proceedings to a halt. Lawson ignored Shackleton's messages. Instead, he concluded that Charles considered it 'inappropriate for there to be interference in the prosecution process'.

Adjusting the evidence to suit his narrative, the lawyer duly reached his inevitable conclusion. Charles, he admitted, was 'concerned' and 'worried' about revelations. His mention of the defence's 'threats' would offend Andrew Shaw and Alex Carlile – 'It's drivel and defamatory,' Carlile would later say, insisting that the defence was seeking only to protect the royal family and was certainly not threatening Charles. Pertinently, Carlile was not asked personally about his 'threat' by Lawson, who instead focused on justifying Charles's concern.

To avoid the intense media interest, Lawson wrote, Charles had asked Peat to summon the meeting on 11 September 2002, the eve of the trial. Lawson admitted that the private secretary's task had been to persuade McCorquodale and Gibbins to withdraw their complaint, but what followed was fiction. To disguise the pressure that Peat unsuccessfully exerted on both executors, Lawson distorted their statements to the police and dismissed their criticism of Peat. The executors' accounts, he wrote, were 'consistent' with Shackleton and Seabrook's descriptions of the same meeting, and 'generally with Sir Michael's recollection'. That again was not true.

To seal his apparent intention of acquitting Charles of any blame, Lawson quoted Carlile, who had spent many hours warning the prince's advisers to stop the prosecution: 'The suggestion that there was any attempt to interfere in the prosecution [by Charles] is absurd.' Lawson failed to elicit a similar quotation from Shackleton, Lamport, Bolland or others who, unlike Carlile, were in actual contact with Charles.

That left the most important mystery – the queen's 'recollection'. To demolish the account that the queen had enquired about the crowds outside the Old Bailey as she was being driven towards St Paul's, Lawson described how, before they set off from Buckingham Palace, Philip had allegedly told Charles that the queen's recollection had been triggered a few hours earlier by the publicity about the trial. Apparently, it was only on that morning, eleven days after the trial had started, that she considered the relevance of her conversation with Burrell. Lawson did not adequately explain why she had not revealed the meeting earlier (he mentioned a conversation between the queen and Philip before they drove to St Paul's), or why Charles had never spoken to her about Burrell or the trial.

Lawson's description of what followed the queen's recollection made little sense to the police or to some of the lawyers involved. He wrote that Charles had told Peat about the recollection only on Saturday, 26 October, the day after the St Paul's service. This time-line was inaccurate. Robert Seabrook had been told about the recollection the previous day, and had immediately gone to Clarence House with Shackleton to advise Peat to inform the prosecution as a matter of urgency. Yet William Boyce was told only on Monday, three days later. Lawson also reported that Shackleton had given the news to Commander Yates, despite being told by Yates that it was Peat who had telephoned him with the news, and that he was '100 per cent certain of that'. The effect of Lawson's apparent distortion was to impugn Shackleton.

Towards those suffering 'cynical suspicion' that the queen's recollection had been invented in order to prevent the royal family's embarrassment, or was in any way improper, Lawson was witheringly dismissive. Their suspicion, he concluded, 'finds no support in the available evidence' because 'there is simply none'. At no stage, he wrote, did Charles or anyone on his behalf try to stop the prosecution.

That was plainly untrue. Bolland, Shackleton, McCorquodale and Gibbins all described various such attempts, as did Lamport, O'Kane and the police officers. McCorquodale's conversation with de Brunner after the trial drew a direct link between the meeting on 11 September – when Peat failed to persuade McCorquodale and Gibbins to withdraw their complaint – and the manoeuvres by Charles and his officials to end the proceedings.*

The police's investigation and subsequent conduct were criticised by Lawson's report, but consistent with the whole exercise, Scotland

---

* Peat's Report states (para 2.80, p.69) that Lawson did interview Gibbins, but Gibbins denies that.

Yard would successfully persuade the *Guardian* to write, wrongly, that neither Peat nor Lawson had criticised its officers. To achieve what many royals considered the police's own 'whitewash', Scotland Yard produced a thirteen-page report by William Taylor, a former commissioner of the City of London police, which cleared de Brunner of having misled Charles and William at the meeting in Highgrove. 'It's water under the bridge,' Taylor said on the day his report was published. 'Nothing radical or unexpected was found.' Regarding the briefing at Highgrove, he reported that he had 'no opinion ... because that issue was not addressed by me'. He blamed his inability to interview Charles for that omission. Taylor's faintest criticism was confined to the comment, 'some issues arising from the investigation remain unresolved'. Sir John Stevens, Scotland Yard's chief, added, 'The officers concerned in the inquiry have my full support ... I suspect that a lot of people are looking for blood on the carpet. But I'm afraid that sometimes the facts are things that have to be accepted.' Charles and William were reported to be 'very disappointed'. Burrell described the report as 'scandalous', because it 'ignores appalling blunders ... Everyone wants the fiasco of my court case to be forgotten about.'

Lawson's fee for compiling his report was never disclosed. He died six years later, without receiving an honour, which he could normally have had expected. The next section of the report, an investigation into the sale of gifts to Charles, was completed by Peat. He described his inquiry as 'comprehensive'.

The rumours about 'Fawcett the Fence' were denounced by Peat, who stated that none of Charles's staff, especially Fawcett, had 'received improper payments or other benefits'. Although he revealed that Fawcett had been given valuable 'benefits' by suppliers – including a Rolex watch worth £2,500, membership of Mosimann's Dining Club worth £3,000 per annum, a Tiffany watch, a Pasha pen and several consignments of champagne, as well as other unknown gifts – he blamed such errors on a few officials' casual understanding of the lax rules in Kensington and St James's. Those had been 'infringed', he conceded, but Fawcett had sold official gifts only with Charles's authorisation. Any mismanagement was 'limited'. The headlines about Fawcett had been inflamed by rumours caused by 'jealousy and friction', and not by any hard evidence.

The report was handed out at a press conference for fifty journalists at St James's Palace. Those present were given no time to examine the dense text about an intricate saga before Peat pleaded *mea culpa* on his employer's behalf. Lessons would be learnt, he said, and the management of Clarence House was changing. Charles's household was 'under-resourced' for an executive that raised millions of pounds every year, and employed seven hundred people in the Prince's Trust. Charles was 'incredibly busy', and to improve the management Peat would hire more people, to be financed from the duchy's income. He linked the reorganisation to the exit of Bolland and the imminent resignation of Fawcett. To those journalists who connected the departure of the two men to Peat's revenge against those close to Camilla, Peat scoffed, 'Ridiculous.' Instead he blamed Bolland for disturbing relationships among the royal family, and censured Fawcett for organising extravagant parties. That was all.

In his own statement, Charles, who was visiting Bulgaria on the day of the report's publication, declared: 'The review does not make comfortable reading in some parts but I accept full responsibility for all the recommendations.'

Peat could congratulate himself. Ignorant of the many intricacies of the saga, the media overlooked Charles's culpability. The 'whitewash' was masterful. As intended, journalists focused on the alleged rape of Smith. Most news stories included the 'allegations of a cover-up of a homosexual rape' and Fawcett's departure after twenty-two years in royal employment.

By the time Charles returned to London, the worst was over. The only unfortunate repercussion, for Charles in particular, was Fawcett's departure. His one-time valet was irreplaceable – and in truth unsackable. More even than Burrell, Fawcett knew secrets that might endanger Charles's succession. Accordingly, his exit package was sufficiently generous to avoid any temptation for him to sell his story. He received £500,000, the right to remain in his grace-and-favour home in Richmond, and a three-year contract for his company, Premier Mode Events, to work for Charles from a newly decorated office in Clarence House. The first commissions were for William's twenty-first birthday party for three hundred people at Windsor, and a contract to supervise the rebuilding of Clarence House. No one at Fawcett's farewell party in St James's Palace doubted Charles's intention to keep his fixer close.

19

Revenge and Dirty Linen

The publication of Paul Burrell's book *A Royal Duty* on 20 October 2003 caused an even greater earthquake than expected. The *Mirror*'s ten-day serialisation started with Diana's handwritten letter to Burrell in 1993 predicting that there was a plot by Prince Philip to kill her in a car crash, possibly 'by brake failure … in order to make the path clear for Charles to marry'. The image of the unloved princess isolated in Kensington Palace, writing that she was 'longing for someone to hug me and encourage me to keep strong', was a devastating indictment of the royal family. Charles was portrayed as a heartless schemer who had married a twenty-year-old virgin in order for her to bear him an heir while he continued his affair with Camilla.

In her letter, Diana accused Charles of putting her 'through such hell' with the 'cruel things' he had done to her. 'I have been battered, bruised and abused mentally by a system for fifteen years now,' she wrote, and as a result had 'cried more than anyone will ever know'. Suddenly, Mohamed Fayed's ludicrous conspiracy theory about an Establishment plot masterminded by Prince Philip to prevent the pregnant princess marrying his Muslim son by arranging the fatal car crash in Paris gained credibility. By the end of the first day of serialisation, Burrell's eyewitness account of Diana's battle was generally accepted as truthful. But no one could explain why Diana would commit such thoughts in a note to her butler. Her close friend Lucia Flecha de Lima believed all the letters were fake. Burrell, she would say, was 'perfectly capable of imitating' Diana's handwriting, a charge that Burrell would deny.

The following day, the *Mirror* published Philip's letters to Diana. In one, he reflected that Charles would not be 'in his right mind' to leave Diana for Camilla. In another, he denied that he had encouraged Charles to return to Camilla should the marriage to his young wife fail after five years. Diana had written back, 'That made me feel like being offered to your family on a sale-or-return basis.' The correspondence between the two, described in detail by Burrell, included Diana's comment: 'I have a husband who does not love me any more and by his own admission never has. And he resumed his relationship with Camilla rather sooner than you might have imagined. He was never emotionally divorced from her.' Quoting intimate letters between Charles and Diana, Burrell reported in Diana's own words her despair and her fears about Charles's demand for a divorce. Painted as a traitor to Diana, Charles was once again accused of being unfaithful first. Overall, the serialised material cast Charles and Camilla as ruthlessly selfish plotters against a vulnerable young mother.

'I do not have in my possession the letters Prince Philip wrote to the Princess,' Burrell claimed. But Sarah McCorquodale had always suspected that he had taken those letters from the mahogany box and made copies. He would later admit that he had indeed done so, and had then sent the letters to America for 'safekeeping'. He clearly did not 'possess' Diana's original letters, and Philip's were never recovered.

By any measure, Burrell's book was a catastrophe for Charles. Citing the worst ever opinion polls for the royal family, Bolland wrote in his *News of the World* column: 'I warned Charles that the Burrell trial would lead to disaster and revelations and I urged him to stop the trial.' Had Bolland not been dismissed, St James's Palace could have made further attempts to negotiate an arrangement with Burrell, a possibility apparently not considered by Peat.

Burrell's own hypocrisy was plain. Although his book was presented as a tribute to his beloved princess, he betrayed her secrets for about £4 million, the amount he would have received from the book's global sales, newspaper serial rights, and interviews. In his account, he ridiculed the police for failing to understand that 'gifts were an unwritten perk of the job' and 'sentimental symbols of time spent working for a senior royal'. But the negatives of intimate family photographs, the photo albums and Diana's letters to William were not proven to be gifts, nor had they been handed over to Burrell for safekeeping. He never adequately dealt with those inconvenient truths, while his assertion that 'twenty telephone lines of my closest family and friends were bugged, as documentation later proved' was denied by the police, and never substantiated.

Burrell's defence of Diana's reputation appeared self-interested to anyone who recalled his pledge in a letter to William: 'I will never betray you. My middle name is loyalty.' In a published comment after the serialisation started, William castigated Burrell: 'We cannot believe that Paul, who was entrusted with so much, could abuse his position in such a cold overt betrayal. It is not only deeply painful for the two of us ... it would mortify our mother if she were alive today.' His statement ended with a plea to Burrell to stop his revelations, a request to the public to boycott the book, and a suggestion that he and Burrell might meet. 'The princes can't take any more,' Richard Kay was told by Colleen Harris, who had drafted William's declaration. The meeting never happened.

To Burrell's good fortune, the general public ignored his sophistry amid the renewed ridicule of Charles. The prince told friends of his fear that his visits to the theatre with Camilla would no longer be greeted with affection. A fundraiser at Holyrood organised by Higdon attracted fewer Americans than before the trial.

Mark Bolland echoed the public's distaste with the royal family: 'They did nothing to help [Burrell] after his arrest and many who work for them actively sought his prosecution.'

The consultant turned columnist blamed 'forces' among the courtiers for preventing Burrell and Charles from meeting to resolve the fate of Diana's property. Their 'reward', wrote Bolland, was now to read about the royal family's cruelty towards Diana: 'Their treatment of Burrell was an own goal of astonishing proportions.' Damaged and hurt, Charles and Camilla avoided meeting the queen and Philip when they next stayed at Birkhall, two miles from Balmoral, and they also stayed away from Sandringham.

Even Charles Spencer joined in the reproaches. Prince Charles employed incompetent or dishonest staff, he told a journalist, also claiming that during the first days after Diana's death, while Kensington Palace reeled in anguish, Burrell was searching for valuable items to sell.

Burrell's book had sparked a new frenzy. In return for payment, George Smith too was persuaded to extend his allegations. The former junior butler was angry about the Peat Report, especially its protection of 'a much more powerful member of the Royal

Household than I was'. Under the headline 'Charles and His Valet: The True Story', Smith claimed in the *Mail on Sunday* to have witnessed a 'shocking incident' between Charles and another unnamed royal servant while he served Charles his breakfast in bed. His account was not credible, not least because Charles did not eat breakfast in bed.

One week earlier, travelling in the Gulf, Charles accepted questionable advice from aggressive solicitors that Michael Fawcett should try to prevent the publication of Smith's new allegations in any more detail. Fawcett's lawyers, paid for by Charles, obtained an injunction and, to preserve their client's anonymity, also obtained an order forbidding the media from reporting that the injunction existed. As a libel injunction the court would have needed to be persuaded that it was likely, based on all the evidence, that there was no truth in Smith's allegations. This 'super' injunction provided another reason for the media to inundate Charles with questions. His spokesman, as expected, denied Smith's story, but since Charles's office had also denied Andrew Morton's accurate description of his marriage in *Diana: Her True Story*, and had also ridiculed so much more that eventually proved true, the new denial was generally disbelieved.

Instead, the credibility of Smith's allegation was given fresh life by Bolland, who described how Peat had telephoned him on holiday to ask whether Charles could be bisexual: 'I was astonished at the question. I told him the prince was emphatically not gay or bisexual.' Peat reportedly denied ever having asked the question, but the additional slur stuck – Bolland's denial had raised the possibility of the heir to the throne being bisexual, and that was enough. Amid talk of a witch-hunt and a vendetta by critics and the media against every cast member – Charles, Fawcett, Smith and Diana – the monarchy's future was again brought into question.

Fawcett's super injunction riled supporters of media freedom. Applying to another judge, the *Guardian* had the ban overturned. That enabled the newspaper to reveal that Fawcett had won the injunction. However, at 6.50 p.m. the same day, Mr Justice Henriques, sitting in a traffic jam on London Bridge, reinstated the injunction without allowing the *Guardian* the opportunity to argue its case. In the familiar madness of British justice, Henriques's ruling was overturned the following day by Mr Justice Tugendhat. With the super injunction removed, Fawcett was not only named, but was linked to a sex incident with Charles. Once again, the prince had brought on himself the worst of all outcomes.

The resulting burst of derision spurred Peat, with Charles's approval, to re-enter the fray to deny the unspecified allegation against Fawcett. He proceeded to produce an artless own-goal by arousing the public's curiosity about an allegation that until then had been unexposed. 'The story,' said Peat to TV cameras, without explaining what he meant by 'story', 'is totally untrue and without a shred of evidence.' He named three reasons for discrediting the calumny. 'Firstly, because the Prince of Wales has told me it's untrue and I believe him implicitly. Second, anyone who knows the Prince of Wales at all would appreciate that the allegation is totally ludicrous and indeed, risible.' Third, the man who made the allegation had 'suffered from health problems', and his other allegations had been investigated by the police and found to be unsubstantiated.

Singlehandedly, Peat inspired a major crisis. Across the world, the super injunction had never been obeyed. Beyond Britain, Charles was being explicitly linked to a homosexual act with a named member of his staff. The salacious rumours and outlandish conspiracy theories started by Diana's death now extended to her ex-husband, portrayed as a scandalous adulterer surrounded by perverted men. Charles, always an easy target, had been stripped bare by his consiglieri.

'He poured a tanker-full of petrol on to the embers,' commented the *Daily Mail*. By choosing a policy of concealment, 'at every stage the royals have made a bad situation worse'. Echoing the opinions of its readers, the newspaper blamed the royal family's 'barbaric treatment of Princess Diana ... that reduced this vulnerable woman to the state where she tape-recorded lurid allegations by one of her husband's servants about goings-on in the royal household'. Peat's attempts at ending all the speculation had brought his employer's slow resurrection to a grinding halt. Charles returned home from the Gulf and India (his first visit to Delhi since Diana sat alone on a bench in front of the Taj Mahal for the cameras) to find all the old feuds and past indiscretions once more dominating the news cycle.

None of the principal participants could stop themselves. Peat's ally the *Daily Telegraph* criticised Bolland for meeting Burrell, and mocked his recent comments as sour grapes for failing to receive an honour or even a farewell party. Bolland duly replied in the *Guardian*, depicting Peat as a crank, spendthrift and meddler. In the *Daily Mail* he said that Peat represented the 'faceless, antediluvian, snooty men in suits' responsible for the Burrell debacle and the shipwreck of Charles's reputation. To underline his anger at Charles's attack on him, he described Clarence House as 'a very medieval environment full of jealousies and intrigues and backstabbing and plots'. Readers may have wondered why he needed to point that out – it was how the public at large now viewed Charles's world.

To capitalise on the renewed warfare, Burrell joined in, writing in the *Mirror* that his book was but 'the tip of the iceberg', and that if the 'dark forces' threatened him or his family he would publish more revelations. 'There are many, many more secrets I have not written about,' he hinted. 'Very personal, very damaging … not very pleasant.' As he had told Richard Kay before the end of the trial, 'It's not what I put into the book, but it's what I keep out to protect Diana's reputation.' Much more, Kay knew, could be included in another book, including revelations about incidents during Burrell's twelve years' work for the queen at Buckingham Palace. That fertile area was off-limits, but only for the moment.

Bereft of substantial allies in the media, Charles adopted Bolland's tactics. Since Burrell was writing for the *Mirror*, it made sense for Peat to approach Rebekah Wade, later to become Rebekah Brooks, and newly moved from the *News of the World* to become the *Sun's* editor. Peat explained that Charles was open for business, and over the following months the *Sun's* journalists enjoyed an easy relationship with the heir to the throne. In particular, Arthur Edwards, the paper's royal photographer, became the emissary to promote a positive profile of the prince. Charles was praised for supporting the police bravery awards and endorsing 'Help for Heroes', the *Sun's* embrace of the armed forces. And it would be the *Sun* that produced a secret video of Burrell admitting that he lied at the Diana crash inquest. 'I didn't tell the whole truth,' he was heard saying. 'Perjury is not a very nice thing to contemplate.'

Disenchanted by the doubts cast on his credibility in Britain, he then snapped, 'Quite frankly, Britain can fuck off.' 'A plague on all your houses' was Britain's riposte. Charles's popularity fell back to the dismal levels reported in the days after Diana's death.

20

Drowning Not Waving

The aftermath of the serialisation of Burrell's book was painful, and eroded any goodwill Charles had generated over the previous six years. Camilla disappeared from public view. By the time she surfaced again, in February 2004, she was still being portrayed as a kept woman who preferred to do as little work as possible. Cocooned from the outside world, she glided between London, Highgrove and Birkhall in her expensive jewellery and fine new clothes, while making it clear that she 'could not stand abroad'.

To fuel the poor press, a story surfaced that she disapproved of Charles's friendship with Antonia Wellesley, the attractive younger wife of the heir to the Duke of Wellington. Camilla was credited with having introduced Antonia to David Somerset, the Duke of Beaufort, with whom she felt she had more in common. Miranda Beaufort, the duke's second wife, was not grateful. Christopher Wilson, a journalist who covered the royals, described Charles's fury that a whispering campaign to destabilise Camilla had started.

Without Bolland's protection, the gossips, especially Charles's old friends, angered at being excluded by Camilla, dug up the deathbed confessions of 'Kanga' Tryon about her long affair with the prince. Kanga's graphic account of their romance during Charles's stopovers while driving between Highgrove and London was sold to a newspaper. In the wake of that revelation, the chatterers revived stories about his affair during the 1980s with Eva O'Neill, a German divorcee to whom he had been particularly generous. None of this was pleasant; but then came something truly damaging.

Peter Settelen, the former actor employed by Diana between September 1992 and December 1993 to improve her confidence while making public speeches, had decided to profit from the recordings of her confessions to him during their sessions. The tapes

– found in Burrell's attic during the police raid and recovered by Settelen from the police after his victory in a court battle launched by Sarah McCorquodale for them to go to Diana's estate – were sold to the American TV network NBC for a reported £700,000.

In the first broadcast from beyond the grave, Diana spoke about her misery, her suicide attempts and her confrontations with Camilla: 'I had so many dreams as a young girl … hopes that my husband would look after me, he'd be like a father figure, he'd support me, encourage me, say "Well done." But I didn't get any of that.' In the next instalment, she confessed to her affair with her police bodyguard Barry Mannakee. At that time, she revealed, 'Charles only wanted to make love once every three weeks.' After Charles discovered the relationship, 'He [Mannakee] was chucked out. And then he was killed [in a motorcycle accident in 1987]. I think he was bumped off. He was the greatest fellow I've ever had. The biggest blow of my life.' Nearly twenty years after the event, Diana described her sobbing pleas for help to 'the Top Lady. And I said, "What do I do? I'm coming to you. What do I do?" And the Queen replied, "I don't know what you should do. Charles is hopeless."'

If it were possible, the prince's stock fell even further in America, while his humiliation in Britain was complete. A meagre respite was the support from George Carey, the former Archbishop of Canterbury, for Charles and Camilla to marry. In his disclosures, revealed while promoting his memoirs, Carey sniped at Diana's 'cunning' use of the media and, after revealing his meetings with Camilla in the late 1990s, contradicted the public perception of an 'ogress' or 'temptress': 'I came to the conclusion she cannot be like that.' He wrote, 'The present situation is unsustainable and hypocritical … We need to put the case for a marriage with Camilla. She'll be splendid as a king's consort.'

Carey's lone voice did not influence Hugh van Cutsem, one of Charles's oldest companions. In October 2004 the van Cutsems sent out invitations to 650 friends announcing the marriage of Edward, their eldest son, to Lady Tamara Grosvenor, the daughter of another of Charles's great friends, the Duke of Westminster. The queen, Philip, Charles, William and Harry were all invited to the wedding at Chester Cathedral. Naturally, the monarch and her family would sit at the front. The van Cutsems explained that Camilla, although invited, would have to sit at the back, and could not enter the cathedral through the main door. Charles was outraged. He interpreted the seating plan as a continuation of the feud started by the false accusation about Edward van Cutsem being implicated with Tom Parker Bowles over taking cocaine. For Camilla, to be cast into the cathedral's outer reaches was the outcome of Emilie van Cutsem's pique that Camilla threatened her long relationship with Charles and his sons. The ill feeling between the two women had deepened since Hugh van Cutsem tried to restore his friendship with Charles. To Camilla, the van Cutsems' sentiments were irrelevant. She refused to be marginalised. Neither she nor Charles troubled themselves to understand the dilemmas caused by their relationship.

Camilla had become accustomed to her life of luxury. At her behest, Michael Peat provided a chauffeur-driven car, while at Charles's insistence she flew only on private jets. This lifestyle only encouraged her habit of unpunctuality. Frequently Charles shouted from the bottom of the stairs at Clarence House, 'Come on, get a move on.'

'Where are we going?' she would ask as she rushed down.

'Haven't you read the brief?' he would snap, as if to a slow learner.

Emilie van Cutsem naturally heard on the grapevine about this wine merchant's daughter's struggle to get to grips with her duties. The stories reinforced her resistance to Charles's demand that Camilla's status should not be diminished in the cathedral. In the end, to placate Camilla's fury, Charles sent his apologies: on the day of the wedding he was required to visit the families of troops of the Black Watch. The snub to Camilla fed the rumour machine. Her 'rusting reputation', carped her enemies, was not going to be saved by the appointment of Peter Mimpriss, a lawyer, to build up her charity work.

This second spat with the van Cutsems also revealed the state of Charles's relationships with his family. For months, his staff at Clarence House had noticed that William and Harry entered the building through the servants' quarters, so as to avoid Charles and Camilla. In their opinion, Charles's lifestyle had blinded him to his sons' personal troubles, as well as to their coolness towards Camilla. Harry was the more worrying. Ever since his confession two years before to smoking cannabis in Highgrove with people he met at a local pub, Charles had struggled to control 'the party prince', as the media had dubbed him. Paparazzi had sold photographs of Harry emerging bedraggled with a topless model from Bouji's nightclub in South Kensington; then chasing Chelsy Davy, his Zimbabwean girlfriend, across Africa; and finally being ordered to return early from a holiday in Argentina for misbehaving at endless parties. Just six weeks after arriving back, on the eve of going to Sandhurst, he appeared at a fancy-dress party in Nazi uniform. The photographs were published just before a commemoration service for the more than one million people murdered at Auschwitz. 'Prince Harry,' said Colonel Bob Stewart, a popular army commander and future Conservative Member of Parliament, 'must be an enormous idiot with minimum common sense.'

Apparently oblivious to his younger son's continuing misery over Diana's death, Charles focused on countering the bad publicity. He appointed James Lowther-Pinkerton as his sons' private secretary. Acting as a guardian, the former SAS officer was expected to care for the two boys around the clock, and supervise their visits to nightclubs.

Charles's treatment of this domestic turbulence appeared perfunctory. It was mirrored by his maladroit attempt to remedy constitutional problems. Despite his best efforts, Don McKinnon had failed to convince the prince that he would not automatically become head of the Commonwealth on his mother's death: 'I didn't get through to Peat about the importance of Charles showing that he understood the Commonwealth. The well-dressed, well-spoken flunkies around him never had an answer except, "He has a very busy schedule."'

Peat's indifference was aggravated by Charles's official visit with Camilla to Jordan in 2003, and by another trip to Saudi Arabia with a last-minute stop in Bam, a city in north-eastern Iran, after an earthquake had killed forty thousand people. This was home territory for Charles: he wanted to highlight a joint charities' appeal for the seventy-five thousand people left homeless and to praise Iran for opening up its nuclear programme for inspection. In return, his hosts lauded his pro-Islamic sentiments and presented him with a sack of pistachio nuts.

McKinnon heard that Jack Straw, the foreign secretary, had encouraged the visit as a way to improve relations with Iran, so he asked Straw to goad Charles into showing the same enthusiasm towards the Commonwealth. 'He doesn't listen to us at all,' Straw replied. Charles, he explained, had not even visited the USA for four years, because his Arabist sympathies made him critical of American policy. McKinnon turned again to Peat. 'We'll look into it,' said that important functionary, in what McKinnon described as his 'mirror policy', namely 'looking at himself'. Charles's private secretary, McKinnon had found, was 'never the easiest man to deal with'.

Unsurprisingly, the combative New Zealander found it even harder to arrange the next meeting between Charles and the high commissioners. 'We'll give you dates when we're available,' Peat replied. McKinnon interpreted this as 'Charles is at the centre of the world and he will be chosen head of the Commonwealth regardless of the circumstances.'

'They don't know him,' he again told Peat.

'I know the prince better than you,' came the reply, 'and he knows the Commonwealth. And they know him, particularly that he's funny.'

'Look at his travel schedule!' McKinnon produced a list of Charles's foreign trips over the previous ten years. 'He only goes to Canada, Australia, New Zealand, plus many visits to Transylvania and the Middle East. It looks ugly and it is ugly. It's all to Arab countries so he can collect money for his charities. They're dictatorships. Why does he prefer to meet dictators and not democratically elected leaders of the Commonwealth?'

'He doesn't like long-distance flights.'

'All the Commonwealth is long-distance,' replied McKinnon. 'What about going to Sierra Leone?' He pointed out that a visit to a country where a brutal civil war had just ended thanks to British intervention would show the prince's sympathy for its people's suffering.

'No,' said Peat. 'He has a very busy schedule. And it's all decided by the Foreign Office.' His manner seemed calculated to make McKinnon feel an idiot.

'It's the ghastly British brush-off,' the New Zealander decided. It wasn't just Peat. Foreign Office officials, he knew, would tell him, 'The prince decides where he will go, not us.'

He next played a trump card. Within twenty-four hours of the queen's death, he told Peat, the government would authorise a proclamation that Charles was her successor. He would be the new king.

But, he warned, the government could not include in its statement that Charles was also the head of the Commonwealth, as it could not assume his acceptance by all fifty-two countries. At least one unidentified government or party, he predicted, would publicly repudiate Charles for political reasons. 'We need to mitigate the risks by removing the Commonwealth from the proclamation.'

Jolted by this suggestion, Peat reported the conversation to the Foreign Office. McKinnon was summoned by Straw and asked to confirm that Charles would automatically become the head of the Commonwealth. McKinnon said he could not do that. 'This is what you're facing,' he explained. 'You need to work off the shoe leather to get acceptance of Charles.' Under pressure in the aftermath of the Iraq war and the allies' failure to find evidence of Saddam Hussein's supposed weapons of mass destruction, Straw's interest faded.

Next, McKinnon approached Downing Street. Preoccupied with his own survival, Tony Blair agreed that the Commonwealth should be omitted from the proclamation. On hearing the news, Charles was shocked, and the queen surprised. How much time might they have before they reached the precipice and were embarrassed? Elsewhere in Buckingham Palace, a committee chaired by the Duke of Norfolk was scheduled to refine plans for 'London Bridge', the code name for the queen's funeral. Charles risked a smooth succession slipping from his grasp.

Another unresolved constitutional obstacle was his relationship with the Anglican Church. Repeated attempts to persuade him to repair the damage caused by his comments to Jonathan Dimbleby about his Accession Oath had been rebuffed. Unhelpfully, Charles still insisted on making a pledge to be defender of faith rather than of *the* faith. Rowan Williams, the new Archbishop of Canterbury, had been one of many to remind him publicly that, despite his adultery, he would be expected to pledge himself to be the defender of one faith and, as head of the Anglican Church, to assert the primacy of Protestantism in England.

Charles's refusal to retreat on that fundamental issue irritated Downing Street. Compared to Robin Janvrin and others at Buckingham Palace, Charles was seen, according to a senior government official, as 'a millstone and a dragging anchor and not a driving force'. Until he agreed to the usual wording, his ambition to marry Camilla would be stymied by Whitehall.

To negotiate a solution, Downing Street established a committee, described as a 'workstream', under the civil servant Anthony 'Wally' Hammond. During the negotiations, Charles finally realised that pursuing this fight was damaging. He retreated and agreed to say the historic oath. As consolation, he would be free to hold a multi-faith ceremony after his coronation. The committee was disbanded.

Removing that obstacle did not improve relations with Buckingham Palace. Taking his lead from his master, Peat urged his officials to avoid fraternising with the queen's staff. 'You're wasting your time,' he said. 'There are a lot of fuddy-duddies over there. They don't know what's happening in the real world.' Charles particularly disliked symbolic customs such as the gentlemen at arms and the yeomen. Their ceremonial parades with pikes and axes pleased the queen, but he regarded them as evidence of Buckingham Palace being stuck in the Dark Ages. He dismissed the monarch's birthday parade as a waste of money. Inspecting the guard was, for him, a chore to be got rid of despite the traditionalists' protests. He had even laughed when a historian suggested that the coats of arms on Windsor Castle's ceiling should be repainted. His disdain divided his household.

The conundrum about whether Charles was a moderniser or an autocrat was aired in public at an employment tribunal hearing in November 2004. Two years earlier, Elaine Day, Mark Bolland's assistant, had complained about her promotion prospects. In a memorandum, she had expressed her dismay that after five years' employment she was undervalued. Bolland forwarded her typewritten complaint to Charles. The prince was unimpressed. As an outspoken opponent of the modish prizes-for-all philosophy, he supported success based on talent, aspiration and work. 'What on earth am I to say to Elaine?' he had replied by hand to Bolland. 'She is so PC it frightens me rigid.' Predictably, he vented his anguish. 'What is wrong with everyone nowadays? What is it that makes everyone seem to think they are qualified to do things far beyond their technical capabilities?' After denouncing the ideological corruption of proper education, he continued: 'This is all to do with [the] learning culture in schools. It is a consequence of a child-centred system which admits no failure and tells people they can all be pop stars, high court judges, brilliant TV personalities or even infinitely more competent heads of state without ever putting in the necessary effort or having natural abilities.'

To Charles's misfortune, Day had spotted the prince's reply on Bolland's desk, and used it to support her case that humiliation and sexual discrimination were common at St James's Palace. Charles only later became aware that, when sending his formal replies to letters, Day occasionally enclosed a photocopy of his notes on the original message in the same envelope. Her employment, he realised, had been a mistake.

Day had filed her complaint the previous April, and now published Charles's handwritten note. The media blasted the heir's elitist attitudes, cosseted as he was by valets, butlers, cooks, secretaries, gardeners and chauffeurs. Day's complaint appeared to be given added weight by the abrupt departure of Rupert Lendrum, an equerry, and other staff. Charles's focus switched once again to Michael Fawcett. 'I can't do without him,' he told Sarah Goodall, who was employed as his clerk for twelve years but was later also fired – because, she believed, Camilla suspected that she had become too close to Charles. The blame for managing the 'shambles' fell on Peat, who according to Malcolm Ross, the comptroller in the lord chamberlain's office at Buckingham Palace, offered Charles solutions without properly considering the human and financial cost.

Day lost her case. In every case that came before judges or tribunals in the period covered by this book, Charles was always the successful party, suggesting an inherent royalism amongst England's judiciary. To the prince, with the public as unrelentingly hostile as ever, they appeared the exception.

21

New Enemies

'Nobody knows what utter hell it is to be Prince of Wales,' Charles said in November 2004. He had just spoken at the memorial service for the poet Kathleen Raine, who had died at the age of ninety-five. Her mystic philosophy had encouraged him throughout his adult life to proclaim his intolerance towards the materialism of the modern world and to 'fight the battle' to advance ancient insights. 'Wisdom,' he said in his address, 'is born not of reductionist analysis but of contemplation and ultimately revelation.' Spiritualism, encouraged by Raine, was guiding his life. 'May God rest her dear departed soul,' he ended, 'and may flights of angels sing her to her rest.' He did not seem concerned that his reference to himself, an outcast prince unsuccessfully rebelling against the state of the world, was at that moment, amid all the scandals, singularly inappropriate. Regardless, he carried on with his causes.

Those same mystic sentiments encouraged his faith in complementary medicine, although he no longer had confidence in the management of his Foundation of Integrated Health, fearing it had not made a significant impression – not least because Michael Fox, its chief executive, had failed to raise sufficient money, and had employed some unimpressive people. To solve what he described as a crisis, Michael Peat arranged to be appointed the foundation's chairman to oversee Fox. 'His standards of attire,' Peat complained, 'leave much to be desired. He forgets that he represents HRH.' Like Peat, the majority of board members were dissatisfied with Fox, not because of his appearance, but following an unfortunate controversy.

Largely due to Charles's aggressive campaign, complementary medicine's status had markedly improved. In May 2003 his foundation hosted a relaunch addressed by Nigel Crisp, the permanent secretary at the Department of Health. The antagonism towards alternative medicine within some NHS circles was diminishing slightly. Charles wrote an article in the *Guardian* to assert with some confidence that the NHS should provide such treatments to prevent and cure allergies. He urged the government to research coffee enemas and carrot juice for the treatment of cancer, but at the same time cast doubt on nanotechnology, a method to manipulate materials one-millionth the size of a pinhead. Scientists, he added, did not know everything, and should be challenged. His disapproval of orthodox medicine provoked Michael Baum, a cancer specialist, to advise that the ignorant should remain silent. 'My twenty-five years in cancer research,' wrote Baum, 'are just as valuable as the prince's power and authority, which rest on an accident of birth. If homeopathy is correct, much of physics, chemistry and pharmacology must be incorrect.'

The criticism bounced off the prince. Boldly, he urged the government to oppose EU directives that banned the sale of untested herbs produced in China and sold as homeopathic remedies in Europe. The shrubs, according to the EU's experts, could cause serious harm. Initially, Charles's private protest to John Reid, the health secretary, was rebuffed. Reid sent him an advance copy of a paper that endorsed the EU rules for the statutory regulation of herbal medicine and acupuncture. Undeterred, Charles met Tony Blair, and after their meeting wrote that the Brussels directive requiring medicines to be licensed would have 'a deleterious effect on the complementary medicine sector … I think we both agreed that was using a sledgehammer to crack a nut.' Blair replied sympathetically, 'The implementation as it currently stands is crazy … We can do quite a lot here: we will delay implementation for all existing products.' He weakened the rules so as to delay the new laws until March 2011, and praised the prince for his contribution.

Charles tempered his successful lobbying with self-deprecation: 'I think you will know by now to your cost!' he wrote to Blair, 'that there are matters about which I care deeply. But perhaps now I am too dangerous to associate with …' Such humorous sign-offs were the nearest he got to self-criticism.

The following year, 2005, Charles individually encouraged both Michael Fox and Michael Dixon to approach Alan Johnson, the new secretary of state for health, to provide government finance for the foundation. Johnson, a supporter of complementary medicine, agreed on the eve of the general election to give £900,000 over three years to two universities to study the benefits of such therapies, and to organise the self-regulation of ten thousand practitioners of complementary medicine. The foundation also received funds from the Prince's Charities Foundation, giving it an annual turnover of about £1.2 million.

A further £90,000 was donated by Robert Wilson, chairman of Nelsons, a manufacturer of complementary medicines. At the time, Wilson was financing a campaign to promote his company's products intended for use during childbirth – 'The use of Bach Flower remedies is another way of helping to reduce maternal anxiety in pregnancy,' ran one ad. Although there was no scientific proof to support that assertion, Charles approved the advertisement and, to show his appreciation for Wilson's donation, invited him to dinner at Clarence House.

Emboldened by government support, he also stepped up his promotion of complementary medicine as a cure for cancer. His favourite remedy was called the Gerson Therapy, advertised as 'a natural treatment that activates the body's extraordinary ability to heal itself through an organic, plant-based diet, raw juices, coffee enemas and natural supplements'. At a healthcare conference he told two hundred professionals, 'I know of one patient who turned to Gerson Therapy having been told she was suffering from terminal cancer and would not survive another course of chemotherapy. Happily, seven years later, she is alive and well. So it is vital that, rather than dismissing such experiences, we should further investigate the beneficial nature of these treatments.'

Prodding doctors to reconsider their use of chemotherapy as a treatment for cancer, and instead to offer their patients thirteen glasses of fruit juice and five coffee enemas per day, and weekly injections of vitamins, raised inevitable criticism. Charles made no distinction between leading a healthy lifestyle in order to prevent cancer, and the use of nutrition to cure the disease. Most doctors believed the Gerson diet probably hastened death. His embrace of the 'blood flow' theories advanced by Andrew Taylor Still, the inventor of osteopathy, raised yet more doubts. 'Charles is a master of quackery,' maintained Edzard Ernst, who classed Still's opinions as pseudo-science. Fox was asked by Charles to neutralise Ernst's defiance, so in 2005 the foundation published *Complementary*

Healthcare: A Guide for Patients, which recommended the use of acupuncture to cure addictions and osteopathy to cure asthma, as well as listing homeopathic solutions for other complaints.

The publication sparked a further riposte from Ernst. He had just completed a study for the World Health Organization analysing the cost-effectiveness of natural cures. On the basis of twenty-seven economic evaluations, he concluded that there was no proof that the therapies provided any value. In a bitter exchange with Fox, he criticised the foundation's new brochure as 'misleading' and failing to provide any information about the effectiveness of the treatments. 'I knew I was declaring war against Charles,' admitted Ernst. His battle isolated him throughout Exeter University.

Stung by his own appointee's opposition, Charles encouraged Peat to mount a challenge. Peat commissioned the company Fresh Minds to produce a series of interviews promoting non-chemical therapies. Fox opposed the idea. 'It isn't the right approach,' he told Peat. He feared a damaging debate.

Peat simply ignored the chief executive of the prince's own foundation, and two young researchers began interviews with experts, including Ernst. But their work was abruptly halted by Charles. Rather than producing more advertisements, he said, the foundation should gather research to persuade government ministers of the value of alternative treatments, and directly challenge Ernst's negative reports. This new directive, Peat and Tom Shebbeare agreed, could threaten the foundation's charitable status, but neither chose to question the prince. Instead, Peat recommended that Charles appoint Christopher Smallwood, the former chief economic adviser for Buckingham Palace and Barclays Bank, to report on the cost-effectiveness of natural cures for the NHS. The report, Charles directed, would be presented to the government to support his argument that the NHS's use of complementary medicine would save taxpayers billions of pounds.

Once again, Fox opposed the appointment: 'Peat was talking about "Marketing the Foundation", and I didn't understand where he wanted to go. It was more important to secure more money for research to produce the scientific evidence in favour of complementary medicine.' Fearful that the foundation was heading in the wrong direction, he continued, 'Peat didn't understand healthcare delivery, how to get change in the NHS or the complicated, fragmented world of complementary medicine.' Nor, he believed, did the accountant understand Fox's own efforts to introduce better regulation of practitioners of alternative cures.

Peat ignored Fox's criticisms. Their relationship finally came apart over the private secretary's aim to make the charity financially self-sufficient, regardless of where the money came from. He accepted a further donation from Robert Wilson, which Fox opposed as a conflict of interest. They agreed that Fox should resign. 'I'm surprised you're leaving,' Charles said. After seven years, Fox knew it was pointless to explain why. He was followed by the charity's accountant, who, in what proved to be a fateful decision, Peat replaced with George Gray as the foundation's finance director.

Naturally, Charles did not consider offering any payment to Christopher Smallwood for his work, and, delighted by the commission, Smallwood did not ask for a fee. The Fresh Minds research, partly funded by Dame Shirley Porter, the controversial former Conservative leader of Westminster council, was limited to a survey of the published literature and interviews with six experts. 'That was the best we could do,' Smallwood would later concede. There was no other data he could use.

Homeopathy was an easy target for the critics, and Smallwood played to the enemy's strength. Endorsing the placebo effect, he had recommended in his draft the value of the watery mixtures because some people felt better even if water produced no medicinal benefits. As a newcomer, he emailed Ernst the drafts of the relevant chapters, asking him to read them in confidence. Ernst assured him that the contents would not be disclosed to anyone.

In his draft, Smallwood suggested that about £480 million could be cut from the NHS's prescription drugs bill if 10 per cent of GPs offered homeopathy rather than standard drugs, even for asthma; a further £38 million could be saved by prescribing the herbal remedy St John's wort to 10 per cent of depression patients; and that milk thistle could treat liver problems. Smallwood did not cite any medical tests as proof. A pilot study, he wrote, showed that the use of complementary medicine had cut the number of consultations with GPs by 30 per cent, and the prescription drugs bill by 50 per cent. He concluded that the national use of homeopathy would save £4 billion from the NHS's drugs bill. After reading that, Charles would feel vindicated.

Smallwood and Ernst met before Ernst had read the material, and his mood changed during their conversation. He disagreed with Smallwood's conclusions that complementary medicine was effective in three areas, including acupuncture, and was appalled by Smallwood's endorsement of homeopathic mixtures. 'The bottles,' he complained, 'are mostly filled with water.' Smallwood, a reasonable man, departed acknowledging that he and the fiery German would never agree.

Ernst, however, was indignant. In an increasingly acrimonious email exchange following their meeting, he told Smallwood that his draft was strewn with errors. By focusing purely on value for money and ignoring whether people's health benefited from complementary medicine, the report was worthless. He added that his own report for the World Health Organization showed that this form of medicine was not cost-effective, and had actually added to the NHS's bill. Moreover, a dozen scientific reviews had shown that homeopathic remedies were useless, especially in the treatment of asthma. The solution to rectify all the mistakes, he suggested, was that he should write the report for Charles.

Smallwood, with Peat's support, rejected that offer. In response, Ernst asked for his name to be removed from the final document, adding, 'You wrote the conclusions before you looked at the data.' The dispute should have ended on that note, but in August 2005 the outraged professor spoke to *The Times*. Somehow the paper had obtained a copy of the draft chapters. Despite agreeing to Smallwood's request for confidentiality, Ernst volunteered his comments. Aiming directly at Charles, and intending to 'destabilise' Smallwood's conclusions, he told the paper: 'These are outrageous estimates without any strong evidence to support them. The report glosses over the science and its methodology is deeply flawed. It is based on such poor science, it's hair-raising.' He added that Smallwood had 'selected all the positive evidence and he left out all the negative studies'. He concluded, 'The Prince of Wales also seems to have overstepped his constitutional role.'

Smallwood was furious that his uncorrected drafts had been leaked and his reputation publicly trashed. 'Ernst broke our confidential agreement and was absolutely outrageous,' he fumed, before emailing the professor that he would 'regret' his behaviour. He wanted Ernst's head. So did Peat, and so did Charles.

A few days later, Steve Smith, Exeter University's vice-chancellor, received a written protest from Peat. Acting not only as Charles's private secretary but also as a foundation trustee (and its chairman), he complained about Ernst's 'disreputable breach of confidence', and enclosed a letter just published in *The Times* from Richard Horton, editor of the *Lancet*, which echoed his outrage. Horton's anger was unexpected, since the *Lancet* had just published a commentary by Ernst on another draft report about complementary medicine.

Equally surprising was Peat's reliance on Horton, who had stated in his letter that 'complementary medicine is largely a pernicious influence on contemporary medicine, preying as it does on the fears and uncertainties of the sick'. He would subsequently write that Smallwood's published report 'contains dangerous nonsense'.

Smith telephoned Peat. For Clarence House to interfere in a spat between academics, he said, was unusual. He asked whether Charles really wanted an investigation into a minor breach of etiquette that was not a sacking offence. After consulting the prince, Peat replied that he did. Accordingly, Smith asked the university's Research and Ethics Committee to investigate whether Ernst had breached Smallwood's requirement of confidentiality. The German rejected the allegation and, in his defence, argued that Charles was both challenging academic freedom and denying that 'a doctor had a public interest not to be silent'. Thirteen months later Ernst was found culpable, but the offence was deemed too trivial to merit even a reprimand. He would remain at Exeter until his retirement seven years later – with full permission to criticise the prince.

As usual, Charles divided rather than united. Peat's 'usual snakepit stuff', according to one eyewitness, pushed Smallwood to the sidelines, and palace politics took over. To assert Charles's primacy, Peat and Shebbeare asked the prestigious King's Fund to host a conference to discuss Smallwood's report. The opening speaker was Peter Hain, the Labour secretary of state for Northern Ireland. To Charles's satisfaction, Hain had announced his intention to introduce complementary medicine in Northern Ireland through the NHS. In turn, the King's Fund endorsed some alternative therapies and urged the government to finance more research and to promote cooperation with NHS doctors. The Department of Health agreed to study whether Hain's initiative in Northern Ireland should be copied in England.

The foundation appeared rejuvenated. Part of the credit, Charles acknowledged, was owed to Kim Lavely, the new chief executive appointed by Peat. Lavely, a former director of consumer organisations including Which, was, like Peat, unfamiliar with the NHS. She was also not a professional fundraiser. Nevertheless, she was told to find donors and to follow Peat's mantra to 'get a more balanced look at alternative medicines'. Peat's new direction presented Lavely with a divided board. The diehards wanted the foundation to focus entirely on promoting complementary cures to the public, while others offered their support of Charles's ambition to integrate natural remedies into the NHS.

After successfully reasserting Charles's cause in Whitehall and in some universities, Lavely encountered another problem. During her quarterly meetings with Charles, the prince would support both strategies, but would then veer off to talk about some particular passion. 'We must push Gerson,' he said over cups of tea. Lavely was not surprised. At meetings with health ministers, Charles would ignore the agreed agenda and switch to preaching about the importance of Gerson's Therapy. Usually in these sermons he referred to some personal experience of the previous twenty-four hours. Lavely's scepticism about Gerson, she could see, did not please her employer. Without any scientific evidence that coffee enemas would cure cancer, she told Charles, the foundation's credibility would suffer. 'Well, get the evidence,' Charles spluttered. Patiently, Lavely explained that only controlled trials could produce scientific proof, and that finding cancer sufferers prepared to risk their lives to justify Gerson would be difficult. Charles's anger mounted. Hovering over every discussion was Professor Ernst's public rebukes about homeopathy. The German's criticism, Lavely discovered, 'drove Charles crazy'.

'There are different types of evidence,' retorted Charles, 'and the evidence of experience is just as important as scientific evidence.' To calm his irritation, he regularly lapsed into reflections about the 'harmony' of the projects and places he knew, before ending the meeting. Clearly, he was reluctant to discuss the charity's administration with Lavely. For him, the natural world was much more relevant than the practical one.

As the standoff continued, Charles was unwilling to approve the additional money Lavely repeatedly requested to keep the foundation from insolvency. Any hope that Peat might support the practical agenda evaporated. At board meetings, he closed down any discussion that contradicted Charles's convictions. A look of iron resolve would cross his face as he protected his employer. At her meetings with the prince, Lavely encountered the same resistance.

'How do you get to their offices?' Charles had asked Peat, seemingly unaware where the foundation had relocated after leaving Holloway, a seedy north London area disliked by Peat.

'By bike, of course, sir,' replied Peat.

'Oh,' said Charles, wincing. 'I would so like to do that.'

His hands were clutched tightly, hiding his chewed fingernails, as he drifted into a description of his visit to the Physic Garden in Chelsea. With sudden animation, he described the plants growing there for use in complementary medicine. 'You see, it's not just me who believes in this,' he sighed. Lavely departed without any agreement about finding money. Sensing the direction of the tide, Peat lost interest and resigned as chairman, to be replaced by Tom Lynch, an Irish businessman who promised cash. Like so many donors, Lynch had been enticed to 'keep an eye' on the charity, but Clarence House transferred his donations to other trusts and not to the foundation.

Charles's campaign had reached a crossroad. His support for treating the 'mind, body and soul' was undermined when, addressing an audience in May 2006, he referred to the origins of diabetes and heart disease as a disturbed flow of blood. The 'sacred geometry' of the body, he continued, composed by a 'spiral' of numbers called the 'Fibonacci sequence', was his diagnosis for the cause of those illnesses. Complementary medicine, he said, including Gerson's Therapy, provided the proper cure. 'Harmony' was the answer.

His suggestions were ridiculed by doctors and scientists alike. 'Homeopathy,' admitted Michael Dixon, 'was Charles's Achilles heel. There was so much more that was credible.' The herbal practitioner Simon Mills had become disillusioned. The complementary medicine team, he lamented, had 'failed to get their act together'. Instead, they had engaged in pointless territorial and professional disputes. 'There is an absence of leadership,' said Mills. 'There's no Mr Complementary Medicine.' Charles could not fight the battle alone, but his frustration that his wishes were not being obeyed paralysed the foundation. 'In the vacuum,' recalled Mills, 'we didn't deliver a fully argued opinion against Ernst, and so there was no lobby to bridge the division between complementary and orthodox medicine.' He abandoned the foundation and the campaign.

By 2007, the beginning of worldwide financial turbulence coincided with the crisis at the foundation, just as David Brownlow, a self-made entrepreneur and publicist known in Clarence House as a 'king of donors', was appointed as president of the Prince's Foundation for Integrated Health. To Kim Lavely, Brownlow showed little interest in his new fiefdom.

The absence of leadership had weakened virtually all of Charles's charities, by then heading towards twenty-five separate organisations. Each chief executive was still chasing the same sources for funds, and the duplication included needlessly rented offices and other overheads. To reduce costs, Shebbeare was once again told that merging was the answer, but as before the chief executives and their boards refused to sacrifice their independence. Charles, they knew, enjoyed saying 'all my charities I've created'. Numbers were important to him. Unable to overcome these objections, Shebbeare struggled to achieve a single economy.

Among those who supported a merger to solve their own charity's financial crisis was Lavely. Charles begrudgingly met her plea for money, persuading Robert Wilson to pledge a further £150,000, making a total £194,000 for the year 2007, while the government contributed an extra £110,000, bringing the taxpayers' stake to £1.1 million. In Lavely's opinion that was still insufficient, yet no one offered more. Mark Leishman, Charles's deputy private secretary newly responsible for the medical charity, focused entirely on implementing Charles's wishes to promote Gerson and other therapies. Lavely was bewildered. 'It's driving me crazy,' she told Leishman. 'Close the foundation down. You aren't providing the money to make it work.'

Leishman too was powerless. He could only refer it 'up'. Proper management was impossible. Lavely resigned. Automatically, she was removed from Charles's Christmas card list. She was not replaced. Instead, George Gray, the finance director, was made temporary chief executive.

Disaster struck the following year. The audit of the 2008 accounts revealed that the financial director, George Gray, had stolen nearly

£253,000 from the foundation. He would be convicted of theft and jailed. The foundation, Charles and Michael Dixon agreed, could no longer continue with the prince as sole standard-bearer. The £1.1 million donated by the Department of Health had been spent. The collateral damage to Charles's reputation was a warning about the result of mismanagement.

'The fraud was a shock,' admitted Dixon. 'The brand was sullied.' He and the other trustees resigned from the board, and the bankrupt foundation closed. Not only was Charles embarrassed, but the 'Pathway in Integrated Health' course at Exeter University was wound up. Edzard Ernst was, as usual, available to comment, particularly about the prince. 'Under the banner of holistic and integrated healthcare,' he told the *Guardian*, 'he promotes a quick fix and outright quackery.'

Charles found the renewed criticism 'very difficult', said Dixon. The prince 'was surprised by the vindictiveness making him out to be a monster. There was a feeling of hurt about the way he was being attacked, like an academic jihad against him and complementary medicine. He found it strange that just a few people could so loudly denounce his ideas to promote the importance of lifestyle, social relationships, daily exercise and healthy living.' But, Dixon concluded, 'the attacks made him more determined to make his case. He had courage to stick to his guns.'

22

For Better or Worse

To resolve Camilla's status once and for all, Charles proposed marriage. 'Charles went down on his knee,' said Camilla, describing the scene at Birkhall. She was fifty-seven and he one year younger. Their first dalliance had begun thirty-three years earlier. Their second, in the late 1970s, satisfied a woman spurned by her husband. Their third affair, starting in the mid-1980s, was a union of two unhappy middle-aged souls seeking relief from broken marriages. Nearly twenty years later, their relationship had survived exceptional obstacles. 'She suffers indignities and vilification,' said her promoters, 'because she loves Charles.' Her reward for decades of frustration, Charles reasoned, would be a blissful traditional wedding.

To Charles's fury, the *Evening Standard* ruined his careful preparations. On 11 February 2005, the *Standard*'s front page boasted an old-fashioned scoop. Robert Jobson, the paper's royal correspondent, never revealed his source. Charles was indignant. Instead of announcing the forthcoming wedding, a personal triumph for the prince, with a dignified flourish, Clarence House was forced to rush out an untidy press release. The *Standard*'s editor was crossed off the royal invitation list.

In St James's Palace, Michael Peat stood in front of oil portraits of Charles's predecessors dressed in their military uniforms. 'All the ducks are in a row,' said the ruffled private secretary with a grimace. Over the previous three years, during conversations with journalists, he had cultivated the image of a self-confident Establishment fixer. Standing stiffly before those same people, he now explained the procedure that would enable the two divorcees, one of whom was the heir to the throne, to do as they wished. The marriage would be a civil ceremony at Windsor Castle, followed by the Archbishop of Canterbury blessing the newlyweds in the castle's St George's

Chapel. Certain of his preparations, he then handed out a short statement by Charles: 'Mrs Parker Bowles and I are absolutely delighted. It will be a very special day for us and our families.' Their engagement was 'welcomed' by the queen. Peat returned to his office, anticipating a smooth climax on the wedding date of Friday, 8 April.

To his staff, he presented himself as the marriage-broker. Charles and Camilla, he told colleagues, had been content to 'muddle along'. The prince was not 'keen', but, Peat puffed, 'My job was to get them married.' Many of his staff doubted that he wielded such decisive influence, but his self-importance reinforced the impression of a loyal courtier who had successfully masterminded a blend of the civil and church ceremonies to make the day palatable to Charles and his family.

Within days, Peat's plans had unravelled. It seemed that every hour after the announcement some learned lawyer or religious scholar would bring up another insurmountable obstacle. The first was the Marriage Act of 1836, which specifically forbade the marriage of any member of the royal family in a civil ceremony in a register office. Two subsequent acts, in 1949 and 1953, upheld that law. The intention was indisputable. In a memorandum written in 1948, a Home Office lawyer recommended that the ban on civil marriages for royalty be kept in the 1949 Act. His recommendation was accepted. According to the 1949 law, Charles could be married only by Anglican clergy, and the advice the prince received when he divorced Diana confirmed that. The ceremony for members of the royal family had to take place in a church. Subsequently, the Anglican Church reaffirmed its 'moral obligation' to refuse to unite two divorcees.

Peat had not only ignored the three Marriage Acts, but also the law about weddings conducted in a register office. Civil marriages had to be held in public places, and Windsor Castle was the queen's private home. If Charles requested a registrar to officiate in the castle, the queen would be obliged to allow access to the public, which was out of the question. Peat and Charles were comprehensively trounced. Peat blamed his deputy Kevin Knott, who resigned shortly afterwards. Charles Falconer, the lord chancellor, was also accused of providing inaccurate legal advice. Peat asked Downing Street for help.

Tony Blair was preparing for his third general election. Although the opinion polls were favourable, saving Peat was not a priority. However, he felt there was no alternative. To limit the royals' embarrassment, and without sufficient time for new legislation, Falconer and Blair decided to overlook the statutes. Just as Henry VIII expected his lord chancellors to change the law or face execution, Falconer took it upon himself to declare that the three Marriage Acts could be ignored. The advice written in 1948, he professed, was 'too cautious', and the Act had anyway been overruled by Labour's human rights legislation. The royals could after all be married in a register office. Charles was saved, but he failed to savour the irony: he had denounced that very human rights law as a 'threat to sane, civilised and ordered existence'.

St James's Palace's mistakes were protected by a cover-up. Citing public interest, the government refused to release the 'legal advice' underlying Falconer's decision to override the established law. The final hurdle was the venue. Since Windsor Castle could not be opened to the public, Peat was told that the ceremony should be held at the register office in the Guildhall, Windsor.

Two weeks of turmoil had somewhat bruised Peat's self-image, but another irruption was still to come. A YouGov opinion poll confirmed that Charles's reputation had not recovered from the Burrell saga. The majority of Britons, 60 per cent to 21 per cent, reluctantly accepted that tradition would prevail when the queen died, but preferred William as king; and only 16 per cent welcomed Camilla as the next queen.

Within Clarence House, there were fears that the newly married couple would be booed on a cold morning outside the Guildhall register office. Anticipating the public's animosity, Peat had originally announced that after Charles's accession Camilla would be named princess consort rather than queen, and until then she would be Duchess of Cornwall. His self-esteem was again dented when government lawyers quietly admitted that the marriage would not be morganatic (that is, a marriage between people of unequal social rank, which prevents a husband's titles and privileges passing to the wife) – and that Camilla could and would become queen. 'The shambles Peat has presided over,' Mark Bolland wrote gleefully in the *Sunday Times*, 'brought shame and ridicule' on the couple. The final ignominy was the queen's unexpected disclosure, while hosting a dinner for Charles and Camilla at Buckingham Palace, that she would not be present at the Guildhall ceremony.

Charles was inconsolable. In spite of having finally achieved his ambition, at every spare moment he would telephone friends and sympathetic officials to complain about his fate. He believed he was at the mercy of history, events, his family and his advisers. 'He needed to get things off his chest,' recalled one person on the list for regular tirades. 'He needed to let off steam. He would go on forever, far into the night.' To alleviate the tension, one confidante half-jokingly asked whether the queen might abdicate. 'No,' replied Charles, taking the question at face value. 'Can you imagine her looking out of the window of Clarence House and waving to me as I paraded in a carriage down The Mall?'

He was also upset by the absence of any media excitement about his wedding. His feelings did not remain private for long. Asked by news photographers to pose for them while skiing in Klosters on the eve of his wedding, he complied, and behind a forced smile whispered to his sons, 'Bloody people. I hate doing this.' In the front row of journalists crouched Nicholas Witchell, the BBC's royal correspondent. The prince's personal dislike of Witchell matched his anger with the corporation as a whole. 'I can't bear that man,' he muttered, unaware that a live microphone was nearby. 'He's so awful, he really is. I hate these people.' Reluctant to remove his sunglasses or to answer Witchell's inoffensive questions, Charles asked William, 'What do we do?' 'Keep smiling,' replied his son, whose relationship with Kate Middleton had just been revealed. Charles did not apologise to the journalist.

The queen was anxious to avoid unnecessary controversy, so rejected her son's proposal for a glittering dinner party for 650 guests at Windsor. She also vetoed the employment of Michael Fawcett to supervise a modest celebration at her home. Her frostiness towards Camilla continued even during the weeks leading up to the wedding: she excluded her future daughter-in-law from both royal ceremonies and official dinners.

To minimise public displeasure, palace briefings described Camilla as an 'unwilling bride' and 'a bundle of nerves' who would gladly remain in the shadows – silent and supportive – with no ambition to be queen. Since most Commonwealth countries, including New Zealand, disliked the prospect of Queen Camilla, an inaccurate impression was promoted. 'When he becomes king,' wrote Charles's long-time supporter Jonathan Dimbleby in the *Guardian*, 'she will not be queen. The essence of her role is not constitutional but personal.'

In the same vein, courtiers gave the impression that Charles had dithered about marriage until he was persuaded by the queen of the importance of averting a constitutional crisis if he were still unmarried at time of the succession. The protocol problems about seating Camilla on state occasions would have been even more embarrassing than they had been at the van Cutsem wedding. As supreme governor of the Church of England, Charles could not 'live in sin'. One of those influencing him to overcome his reluctance, it was hinted, was his old friend Richard Chartres, the formidable Bishop of London.

The wave of disinformation about Camilla being a protesting bride was soon ridiculed. This was a woman, her critics riposted, who had always posed as reluctant. To get her way, she had feigned resistance to marrying Charles; then she had hesitated about accepting a royal title; and finally she was pretending to oppose being crowned queen. That was all nonsense. She relished the prospect of the title of princess consort. As Duchess of Cornwall, she would rank above Princess Anne and Sophie Wessex, both of whom would be expected to curtsey to her and to acknowledge that Camilla could choose who to speak to and expect no one to leave a room before her. To modify her expectations, a courtier let drop that the queen, referring to Camilla's wedding ring, made from special Welsh gold, commented, 'There is very little of it left – there won't be enough for a third wedding.'

The guest list for the reception at Windsor included those loyal friends – the Palmer-Tomkinsons, the Marquess of Douro, the Earl and Countess of Halifax and the Duchess of Devonshire – who had allowed their homes to be used by the couple during their secret affair. Among those who declined the invitations were members of several European royal families, in retaliation for Charles's past refusal of their own invitations. The excuse of one Swedish royal was a trip to Japan to open an Ikea store. Among the guests who eventually declined were the van Cutsems – Hugh van Cutsem wrote that they were committed to a prior engagement.

Mark Bolland was not invited. 'Honesty about their relationship,' he wrote just after the wedding, 'did not come naturally, even with each other. It was forced upon them by Diana's revelations.' He continued, 'While the royals pretend to work hard, they holiday for nearly half the year and only put in a three-day week. Camilla does not even pretend. With limited stamina, she has never worked and hates being on public display. Now Charles and Camilla must persuade the public that they can be satisfactory monarchs.'

There were invitations for the comedian Joan Rivers and for American financiers of Charles's charities. But there were concerns about the American fundraising operation. For the first time questions arose about Robert Higdon's expenses. The running costs of the foundation were 52 per cent of its income, rather than the customary 10 to 20 per cent. A scandal had also arisen at the New York Academy of Art, supported by a $100,000 grant from the foundation. The Academy was charging $1,000 a head for dinner in 'Charles's Room', and one director was suspected of fraud. There was also unease about the American Young Presidents' Organization, a group recruited by Higdon to pay a minimum £30,000 per person for a tour of Clarence House and Windsor Castle, ending with dinner with Charles.

The absence of popular excitement was capped by anti-climax. On 2 April, six days before the planned wedding date, Pope John Paul II died. Under pressure from the queen, and after the Archbishop of Canterbury decided to fly to Rome for the pope's funeral, Charles agreed to postpone the ceremony for one day so that he could be in Rome as her representative.

The next morning, a small, enthusiastic crowd cheered modestly outside Windsor's Guildhall before the marriage, which was witnessed by Charles's three siblings. He and his new bride returned with some tears of joy to the castle for the archbishop's blessing in St George's Chapel. Few monarchists were placated by Charles's promise to 'acknowledge and bewail our manifold sins and wickedness'. The queen looked serious as the archbishop asked, 'Do you, his relatives, his friends and supporters, will you support the prince in his marriage vows and his loyalty for the rest of his life?'

The guests roared, 'We will!'

As the queen emerged into public view, she smiled then walked briskly to a side room invisible to the celebrities, writers, charity workers and Charles's old girlfriends filing into the state apartments. She was, as planned, just in time to watch the Grand National with

Andrew Parker Bowles and other racing enthusiasts and then enter the reception. Charles looked warily at Andrew Parker Bowles. There was a call for silence.

'I have two important announcements to make,' said the queen. 'I know you will want to know who was the winner of the Grand National. It was Hedgehunter.' After the laughter subsided, she continued, 'Secondly, having cleared Becher's Brook and The Chair and all kinds of other terrible obstacles, they have come through and I'm very proud and wish them well. My son is home and dry with the woman he loves. They are now on the home straight; the happy couple are now in the winners' enclosure.'

Amid the cheers of approval, few noticed that the queen did not mention Camilla by name; nor did she speak to her during the party. 'I can't believe it,' the new bride repeated to her friends in the room. 'I can't believe it.' The queen was also noticeably cool towards her son. She had given him a brood mare as a wedding present, and a promise to cover her and pay the expenses for the foal. Not interested in racing, Charles had not appreciated the gift. When the queen telephoned a few days later, he ordered his valet, 'Tell her I'm busy having a dinner party.'

After her speech, the queen re-entered the side room to watch a replay of the big race. To her irritation, the event had not been recorded. 'Someone forgot to push the right button, Ma'am,' explained a nervous courtier.

The queen curtailed her stay and headed for the exit, passing Michael Fawcett on the way. 'Oh look,' she said loudly to Philip, 'there's Fawcett. He's got so fat.'

Charles was waiting for her on the steps outside. 'That went rather well,' she said, according to a lip-reader hired by the *Sun*.

'Yes,' he replied.

'We're leaving now.'

'Oh, I really want a picture of us all.'

The queen stood for just fifty-two seconds, then, without another word, walked away.

Back inside the castle, Charles turned to Billy Tallon, known as 'Backstairs Billy', the queen mother's favourite steward. 'If only Grandmama could have been here and seen this.'

'If she'd been alive,' Tallon replied, 'you couldn't have married.'

23

Resolute Rebel

Marriage changed Camilla. Responding to Charles's order that she receive special treatment, the staff in Clarence House learned to bow to 'Your Royal Highness', always to reply 'Yes, Ma'am', and to ensure that all her demands were satisfied. Before visiting friends, she adopted Charles's habit of sending her hosts a list of her likes and dislikes, especially foods. On her arrival, she might expect a curtsey. In the splendour of choosing to live in any of her husband's six homes, she was not concerned that his annual household costs had risen to over £5 million. (When choosing where to stay, she described the Castle of Mey on the north coast of Scotland as gloomy. She could just tolerate Birkhall, but preferably without guests, not least because she had been forbidden to change anything. To overcome Charles's order, she had scanned the Farrow & Ball colour chart for identical matches so that Charles would not notice any new paint.) She was not heard to commiserate with the queen, who she knew could not afford to redecorate and rewire dilapidated parts of Buckingham Palace and Windsor, although some of the interiors of both buildings, beset by leaky roofs, crumbling masonry, antiquated plumbing, draughts and asbestos, had not been repainted since the coronation in 1953.

Instead of her usual pub lunches, she enjoyed driving with an armed escort to meet friends in expensive restaurants. She was a happy woman in control of her life, married to the queen's heir. She imposed limits on the number of her solo public engagements – her principal task, she would say, was to keep Charles happy. No one doubted that since their marriage her husband looked more relaxed. With a tease or a chide, without stirring his anger, she supported his ambition to win public acceptance. To reinforce his wife's higher profile, Charles requested that flags should fly on public buildings on her birthday. Soon after their wedding, they stood together at Trooping the Colour and at a ceremony to commemorate the fallen in the world wars.

Unfortunately, despite Clarence House generating favourable media comment about Camilla, the polls were still against her becoming queen. Beyond Charles's control, two downmarket TV dramas based on his infidelity were in production. According to the eager promoters, Camilla would feature in one as a 'screaming bitch' and would describe herself as a 'slut', while Andrew Parker Bowles would be presented as a philanderer and Princess Margaret as an alcoholic, bisexual nymphomaniac. Even Gyles Brandreth, a monarchist former Tory MP, had proposed a documentary to Channel 4 based on the Camillagate tapes, portraying her as Charles's 'surrogate mother'. The popular quip that the age of deference had been replaced by soap opera was being reinforced in the most literal way.

Charles as usual appeared undaunted and undeterred. He unexpectedly agreed to the Foreign Office's proposal that he and Camilla make an eight-day state visit to New York, Philadelphia and Washington to meet President George W. Bush. The government needed to promote British tourism following the foot-and-mouth outbreak and in the aftermath of the bombings in London in July that had killed fifty-two people. Bush was receptive to the idea. In the wake of the Iraq war, his tardy response to Hurricane Katrina and the rising price of oil, he hoped that a royal visit might improve his own low ratings. The mutual interests of the British and American governments meant that the minimal affection between the two men was ignored. For four years, Charles had deliberately not visited America. Only two years earlier, angry about the Iraq war and Bush's dismissal of climate change, he had stayed away from the state meal at Buckingham Palace during the president's visit. That snub was disregarded, and the Foreign Office reluctantly agreed to charter a large jet. To offset Camilla's fear of boredom, Robert Higdon promised her 'a good time'.

Rightly concerned that the media would compare their visit to the epic White House dinner twenty years before, featuring Diana's memorable dance with John Travolta, Camilla insisted on tipping the programme in her favour as much as possible. In addition to a combined twelve Foreign Office members and police protection officers, Charles and Camilla brought sixteen staff, including Hugh Green, Camilla's hair stylist, Julia Biddlecombe, her make-up artist, and a wardrobe assistant to care for the fifty dresses selected from hundreds sent to Clarence House for approval. Camilla was determined that she should look her best.

No one expected America's arbiters of style to become excited about the middle-aged couple. The country's anger about Charles's mistreatment of their beloved Diana was easily reawakened, and Charles suspected that he had ceased to be of great interest. But no one anticipated New York's merciless response to the duchess's physical appearance.

By comparison with Diana, carped the city's stylists, Camilla was Frump Tower versus the Fashion Princess. Rupert Murdoch's *New York Post* was particularly vitriolic. Amid remarks about horses, mutton and dumplings, there was not a kind word for Camilla's dresses or teeth. Mark Bolland, still in attack mode, joined the chorus. 'She's a horsey home-wrecker,' he wrote, observing that Camilla had an unsuitable hairstyle, too much make-up, and overdid the jewellery. An old and not particularly attractive couple, wrote another columnist, was hardly likely to encourage tourism to Britain. Higdon's 'spectacular reception', held at New York's Museum of Modern Art, was mentioned only to list those celebrities who chose not to appear. At best, the media reaction was somewhere between lukewarm and indifferent.

Their next stop was Washington. Higdon's presence alongside the prince was alarming the Foreign Office. Charles's emissary, the diplomats heard, had alerted his network of ninety donors to keep the weekend free. Contrary to the FO's wishes, Charles planned to use his trip to raise money for his charities.

Higdon was already unpopular among British officials and charity executives in London. While one former British ambassador in Washington dubbed him 'the Loiterer', another senior official called him 'Creepy, because he was getting a high salary and not raising enough to justify himself.' In 2004, Higdon's personal income increased by 33 per cent in one year to £310,000 (£194,000 in salary, £106,000 in bonuses, £10,600 in benefits), yet the foundation had given only £1 million to charities in America. That left £3.8 million in the American Foundation's bank account. No one could explain why Charles had not distributed more.

So far, Higdon's proximity to the royal couple had protected him. His perfect manners, charm and good looks disarmed would-be critics. Nevertheless, to reinforce any supervision that Tom Shebbeare was able to impose, Leslie Ferrar, an accountant, was appointed to oversee his activities. But Higdon had more worrying enemies. The *Daily Mail* probed his background to discover the family home in Florida, a shabby building inhabited by his father and mother, respectively a car salesman and a bank clerk: far from the plush Ivy League background their son had always suggested.

Among America's meritocrats, Higdon's rags-to-riches story was laudable. After all, he had raised money for Ronald Reagan's presidential library, and he remained Nancy Reagan's preferred social escort. On that basis, he managed Margaret Thatcher's international travel and raised money for her foundation too. But those relationships were no more than past glories when he arrived with Charles and Camilla in Washington expecting to escort Nancy Reagan to President Bush's state dinner in the White House. Searching the seating plan, he could not find his name. 'It blew my mind,' he said, 'that I wasn't invited. They didn't want to acknowledge my role. I was so humiliated.'

Bolland, as ever, felt he knew what had happened. 'Higdon was cut out because Buckingham Palace people are mean. The system doesn't encourage people to be nice to each other. Someone said, "Who's Robert Higdon? Let's keep him out."' The insult was made worse when President Bush's wife Laura asked Camilla, 'What would we do without Robert?' Her guest agreed, but proved powerless that night against what another victim called 'the cruel snobs around Charles'.

Higdon was left to pick up scraps: 'It was a horrible guest list. Most of those invited were undistinguished unknowns.'

Among the 'unknowns' was Joseph Allbritton, the former chief executive of Riggs Bank, which had recently been fined $25 million for its disregard of money-laundering laws. The bank also later pleaded guilty to a series of illegal transactions with the former Chilean dictator Augusto Pinochet. Allbritton had, however, given a £190,000 donation to Charles's foundation, and loaned his Gulfstream jet. In return, thanks to Higdon, he had spent a night at Highgrove.

Without any true stars at the dinner, most agreed that the event was dull. That was not the fault of the guests of honour. Over the previous five years, President Bush had hosted just five state dinners (compared to the Clintons' thirty-one in eight years), because he did not drink, did not dance, and preferred to be in bed by 9 p.m. Everyone departed relatively happy – although neither Charles nor Camilla commiserated with their prize fundraiser.

Instead, the prince was puzzled by two newspaper breaches of his privacy. First, the *News of the World* had discovered that Harry had banned Camilla from being present at a parents' night at Sandhurst, where he was training to be an officer. Charles was surprised that a journalist could somehow know about his private phone discussion with Harry. Second, the *Mail on Sunday* had obtained nine of his private journals, which recorded his thoughts about a range of subjects. The newspaper's source was Sarah Goodall, an ex-personal assistant in his private office, angry that she had been summarily dismissed. The paper planned to publish one of the journals, about his 1997 trip to Hong Kong for the transfer of power to China, which was titled 'The Handover of Hong Kong or The Great Chinese Takeaway'. In the journal, Charles referred to the Chinese leaders he met as 'appalling old waxworks'. The paper justified the breach after Charles missed the state banquet that was being hosted by the queen for Hu Jintao, the Chinese president.

Charles's excuse for that absence was the delayed departure on his chartered jet from Washington. Few in London believed the clash of timing was a coincidence: his track record with China was well known. Two years earlier he had refused to go to the state banquet at Buckingham Palace for President Jiang Zemin. Shortly before, contrary to Tony Blair's wishes, he had met the Dalai Lama, a sworn enemy of China. Charles's preoccupation with the lack of democracy in the country ignored the protocols of government. As king, he would be expected to visit China or host its president, regardless of his opinions. More important, he also ignored the rapid economic growth and social progress in China and Tibet under Jiang's and Hu's governments. Stuck with opinions forged twenty years earlier, Charles was not recognising the new social harmony that Mao's successors were introducing to forge better relationships with other countries. If his behaviour continued, relations with China would suffer.

Peat heard about the *Mail on Sunday*'s intention to publish the Chinese journal and called Peter Wright, the editor, to protest that it could not appear without Charles's agreement. Wright mentioned the legal arguments in favour of publication in the public interest. They disagreed whether the journal was private or not, although neither disputed that at least thirteen copies had been distributed and read by some forty people – later estimates were that seventy-five politicians and media figures had in fact already read the journal.

After their conversation, Peat did nothing to stop the newspaper's plan. On 13 November 2005, millions of people read Charles's denunciation of the Chinese leaders and his dismissive remarks about Tony Blair's focus groups. Only after the prince's confidential thoughts had been broadcast around the world did Peat consult lawyers. 'It's a matter of principle,' he said belatedly. 'Like anybody else, the prince is entitled to write a private journal without extracts being published.' He was advised to apply for an injunction to stop publication of future extracts as 'a breach of copyright and breach of confidence'. Once again, he failed to anticipate the potential damage of a courtroom battle.

In his submission, Peat explained his employer's role: 'The Prince of Wales avoids making public statements on matters which are the subject of disagreement between political parties. He does not campaign on contentious issues but occasionally raises questions about matters which he regards as being of public concern.' The prince had not, he emphasised, 'bombarded ministers with his views but has written to them from time to time on issues which he believes are important'.

The *Mail on Sunday* possessed evidence to contradict that statement. Not only did Charles's journals substantiate the description of his duties on his own website – to 'protect national traditions, virtues and excellence' – but his letters to ministers clearly sought to change policy. In its defence, the paper denied that Charles was entitled to prevent legitimate scrutiny of his secret defiance.

The moment Mr Justice Blackburne, in charge of the hearing, began speaking in the courtroom, the *Mail*'s lawyers assumed defeat. The judge suggested that Charles's privacy had indeed been infringed. Fighting against an apparently royalist judge, the newspaper argued that the public had the right to know about Charles's attitude towards China. To support that argument, the paper delivered a bombshell.

In a statement offered to the newspaper, Mark Bolland delivered his payback for all Charles's ingratitude. 'The prince,' he said, 'was aware of the political and economic importance of the state visit.' Charles was motivated to make a public stand 'against the Chinese – hence the decision to boycott the banquet'. Driving in the dagger, he drew a parallel with Charles's 'deliberate snub' of a 1999 state banquet 'because he did not approve of the Chinese regime and is a great supporter of the Dalai Lama whom he views as being oppressed by the Chinese'.

To inflame the wound, Bolland described how Charles routinely meddled in political issues, and wrote in extreme terms to ministers, MPs and others in power. The prince, he said, saw himself as a 'dissident working against the prevailing political consensus'. While employed in St James's Palace, Bolland had read 'highly politically sensitive correspondence' from Charles that denounced elected leaders 'in extreme terms'. The prince 'bombarded' ministers with letters, and secretly briefed the media on delicate matters of diplomacy – or, to cite a particular instance, on GM foods through the *Daily Mail*. 'The prince's very definite aim in all this activity, as he explained to me, was to influence opinion.' Although Charles knew that he ought to avoid contentious subjects, he ignored that requirement 'if he felt strongly about particular issues or government policies'.

In order to promote himself, said Bolland, Charles had asked Richard Aylard when he was private secretary to portray him as 'a wise man, a thinker and a changer of views'. Later, he had ignored Stephen Lamport's cautionary advice to be silent, and instead had either 'authorised friends and employees such as myself to make the prince's views known'. Masterful in news management, 'the prince was delighted at the coverage' he had engineered in 1999 to publicise his boycott of the Chinese president's visit. 'In a democracy,' Bolland concluded, 'the price of political activism must be transparency.' The public, he believed, was entitled to know Charles's opinions.

The judge was not convinced. Moreover, in restricting the evidence of Charles's interference in British politics, he prevented the newspaper offering as further proof of the heir's calculated political warfare his opposition to various government policies in fields including education.

Since the early 1990s, Charles had publicly criticised the 'intellectual fanaticism' of political correctness. He openly accused 'fashionable theorists' of peddling trendy dogmas, ignoring Shakespeare and creating a cultural and moral void where children were not taught the three Rs. Thirty per cent of school leavers were either illiterate or innumerate. 'Our language has become so impoverished, so sloppy and so limited,' he said in 1999, 'that we have arrived at a wasteland of banality, cliché and casual obscenity.' Criticising Tony Blair's government, he compared the virtues of traditional educationalists to 'the new Establishment' that was 'overbearing, arrogant and destructive'. The result was 'an entire generation of culturally disinherited people'.

Praised by conservatives, Charles was derided by the left. 'He is talking rubbish,' said Labour's London mayor Ken Livingstone. 'This is *Sun*-speak,' scoffed Labour cabinet minister Clare Short.

Instead of retreating, Charles intensified his criticism. The Labour government's education policies, he riposted, represented the 'brutal vandalism' of the 'roots of our tradition'. The result was the 'destruction of our cultural, historical and moral heritage'. No hardbitten Tory could have been more damning.

'I think he should think carefully before intervening in that debate,' said Charles Clarke, the Labour secretary of state for education, in 2004. 'He doesn't understand what's going on in British education.' Because of his class and privilege, Clarke added, alluding in part to Charles's support for fox-hunting, the prince was 'old-fashioned and out of time'.

Charles immediately counterattacked. In a speech at Lambeth Palace he criticised the 'travesty of the truth' of Britain's 'demoralised' education system. 'For the last thirty years,' he said, 'I have done all I can to give young people who have limited opportunities a chance to succeed. That is what my Prince's Trust is all about.' Which politician, he asked, could claim to help hundreds of young people every day, benefiting 500,000 of them over thirty years? The Labour Party, he said, had failed the working class: 'There has often been a very patronising view, an old-fashioned view, that says that certain people can't do certain things.' In his efforts to show that there was an alternative to uninspired teachers burdened by red tape, excessive testing and constantly changing curricula, Charles had for some years invited a hundred English and history teachers to a summer school in Devon to instil pupils with the value of good manners, reading and the classics. 'I know that my ideas are sometimes portrayed as old-fashioned,' he said. 'Well, they may be. But what I am concerned about are the things that are timeless, regardless of the age we live in. Also, I have been around long enough to see what were thought of as old-fashioned ideas have now come into vogue. Ambition is a good thing.'

Up to that point, he was echoing traditional Conservative policy – and winning public support. But then he overreached himself. Bad education, he said, resulted from 'a profound malaise, a deep disease, a disintegration and disfunctioning of the natural harmony in the human existence [because] the soul was declared as a moribund and derided concept'. Such proselytising was relevant when assessing Charles's impartiality, especially once he became king.

In the *Mail on Sunday* case, the trial judge restricted any exposure of that bias, and rejected Mark Bolland's evidence. Both Mr Justice Blackburne, and subsequently the judges in the Court of Appeal, ruled that Charles's copyright and confidentiality of a 'private' document had been breached. His personal rights, said one judge, 'outweighed the significance' of the newspaper's right to freedom of expression under the same Human Rights Act that Charles had called 'rubbish'. Few others in Britain would have been similarly protected; but despite the ruling the damage was done.

Three months later, Charles was the subject of a Channel 4 documentary, *The Meddling Prince*. The accusation stung. On the night the programme was broadcast, he hosted a dinner at Clarence House. The contrast between the rarefied atmosphere in his home on The Mall and the tough counterattack orchestrated by his new spokesman Paddy Haverson, formerly employed at Manchester United FC, reflected Charles's unapologetic rejection of his critics. Michael Peat issued a lengthy statement denying that the heir to the throne was a meddler. The prince, he said, 'cares deeply about the well-being of the United Kingdom and everyone in it, and wants to add value to his position by helping people and making a difference'. Some, he went on in a statement crafted by his employer, sought Charles's silence, but he wanted to 'make an active contribution to national life' for those who 'might not be heard'. There was a difference, he said, between being the sovereign and being the heir, and between political issues and public policies linked to Charles's charities: 'It would in my view be more damaging if the Prince of Wales did not take advantage of his position to help with issues which matter to ordinary people but which have not found their way on to political agendas.'

Within Clarence House, the statement seemed reasonable, but beyond the palace, officials and politicians were not impressed. Unlike any other political player, Charles demanded the right of influence, but refused to be held to account. Sometimes his meddling led to significant change. His agitation against GM crops had contributed to the multinational biotechnology corporation Monsanto's termination of GM research in Britain. His condemnation of modernist architecture had also borne fruit. Other interferences had accomplished little or nothing. In a letter to the environment minister, he urged the Royal Navy to patrol areas where the illegal overfishing of the Patagonian toothfish was starving the 'poor old albatross'. More pertinently, he asked another minister to finance the preservation of two Antarctic huts built by Shakleton and Scott. But there were also political protests – some winning popularity with the public. He asked the education minister to improve the standards of school food, and Tony Blair about the limitations of Lynx helicopters operating in high temperatures in Iraq. The delay in the helicopter's replacement, he complained, because of 'significant pressure on the defence budget, is one more example where our Armed Forces are being asked to do an extremely challenging job (particularly in Iraq) without the necessary resources'. In his reply, Blair admitted the helicopter's 'limitations' – which he had failed to do in Parliament.

In another letter to the prime minister, Charles supported the controversial badger cull, intended to combat the spread of bovine tuberculosis. 'I for one cannot understand how the "badger lobby" seem to mind not at all about the slaughter of thousands of expensive cattle and yet object to a managed cull of an overpopulation of badgers – to me this is intellectually dishonest.' Disregarding the prince's familiar lament about the farmers, Blair did not support the cull. In another letter to Downing Street, Charles expressed his anger that the Office of Fair Trading was a 'serious obstacle' to developing dairy cooperatives 'of the necessary size and influence'. Unlike the equivalent agencies in Denmark and Germany, he believed, the OFT had misinterpreted EU competition rules. (British civil servants were regularly accused of 'gold-plating', or unnecessarily adding to the complexity of directives from Brussels.) The supermarkets' stranglehold was reducing the prices paid to farmers. 'It would be splendid,' Charles wrote, 'if the government could find innovative ways to give the necessary lead' to encourage the purchase of British agricultural produce to support British farmers 'so the countryside will survive'.

As ever unapologetic about his campaigns, Charles admitted in a television interview that he was a nuisance: 'I mind deeply about this country and the people here.' But often his attempts to galvanise interest in his work were fruitless. After Blair won his third election victory in May 2005, Charles's hope for forging a better relationship with the government foundered on the prime minister's unpopularity over the Iraq war. Blair was fighting his own battles, particularly to resist his chancellor Gordon Brown's demands for his resignation, and had little interest in managing a smooth succession from the queen to Charles.

Even less important was the prince's precarious relationship with the Commonwealth. But the queen had become concerned. After another conversation with Don McKinnon in late 2005, she summoned her son, who had just returned from a fundraising trip in the Gulf, to a meeting with Robin Janvrin. The issue was duly discussed, after which Janvrin told McKinnon, 'We've been thinking that he might visit Malta.'

'Malta's down the street,' snapped McKinnon. 'He needs to go further.'

Janvrin asked whether Charles should host the banquet at the next Commonwealth heads of state meeting in Uganda in 2007.

'That's going too fast. He'd irritate everyone. He can go to receptions but not replace the queen.' McKinnon's impatience was aggravated by the announcement from Clarence House of another foreign trip by Charles and Camilla – but not to a Commonwealth country. On their first wedding anniversary, Charles had agreed to visit Egypt and then, in a familiar deal, to travel on to India. The agreement papered over strained relations between him and the Foreign Office officials appointed under Blair. Reflecting the prime minister's own attitude, the new breed considered the royals a waste of time. Often appointed on the grounds of politically correct diversity rather than exceptional talent, the new officials clashed with the older, tradi-

tional FO staff about Charles's insistence on private planes, especially for flights to Europe. After one particularly nasty spat, he had
reluctantly agreed to fly commercial in Europe. On his return, he
refused ever again to take a BA plane. 'He wanted the convenience
and not to mix with hoi-polloi,' observed one mandarin.

Charles nevertheless did make some concessions. In 2006 Clive
Alderton, the FO's representative in Calais, was appointed to arrange
his foreign trips rather than Peat. To 'slowly' introduce the prince
across the Commonwealth, civil servants from India and South
Africa were seconded to work in Clarence House. Charles's charities
were also to be used to ease his introduction to Commonwealth
countries. Finally, he agreed to visit Pakistan with Camilla in late
2006.

Just as they arrived in the region, Pakistani forces attacked a
suspected terrorist base. Diverted to a safer area, and accompanied
by boorish officials and indifferent journalists, Charles was greeted
by few local people for a tour of an organic farm and an archaeolog-
ical site. McKinnon was unimpressed. 'That was for the Foreign
Office, not the Commonwealth,' he said. Soon after, Charles briefly
visited Sierra Leone. 'That trip spread the angel dust for Britain, not
the Commonwealth,' McKinnon noted this time. Eleven weeks later,
Charles and Camilla started a ten-day trip to five countries in the
Arabian Gulf.

Charles's sympathy for Islam was well established. In 1986 he had
written to Laurens van der Post after a visit to Saudi Arabia and
Qatar: 'This tour has been fascinating and have learnt a lot about the
Middle east and Arab outlook … Also begin to understand their
point of view about Israel. Never realised that they see it as a US
colony. I now appreciate that Arabs and Jews were all Semitic people
originally + it is the influx of foreign, European Jews (especially
from Poland, they say) which has helped to cause great problems. I
know there are so many complex issues but how can there ever be
an end to terrorism unless the causes are eliminated? Surely some
US president has to have the courage to stand up and take on the
Jewish lobby in US? I must be naïve I suppose!'

Seven years later, in a speech in Oxford, he had expressed the
hope that the West could overcome its 'unthinking prejudices'
against the Muslim religion. After describing Islam's mystical power
to unify man and nature, religion and science, mind and matter, he

For nearly a decade, Charles fought bitterly against his mother's opposition to his relationship with Camilla. The queen's disdain was evident after she posed with the couple for just fifty-two seconds for their marriage photo in 2005. Camilla's appearance on Buckingham Palace's balcony after Prince William and Kate Middleton's wedding in 2011 reflected Charles's insistence that despite public disapproval, his wife would be the next queen.

The trial of Paul Burrell, Diana's butler (opposite page, top left), in 2002 and its aftermath wrecked Charles's attempts to rehabilitate himself. Scandalous allegations against Michael Fawcett (top, right) were investigated by Michael Peat, Charles's private secretary (below). Caught in the middle were Mark Bolland (bottom left), employed by Charles to make Camilla acceptable to the queen and the country, and Fiona Shackleton, Charles's devoted solicitor (bottom right).

Michael Peat's report on the Burrell affair was criticised as a 'whitewash' by both Sarah McCorquodale, Diana's sister (above right), and by Scotland Yard's investigators of Burrell's alleged thefts, Detective Chief Superintendent Maxine de Brunner and Detective Sergeant Roger Milburn (below). Like Fiona Shackleton, the police officers were caught in the crossfire of the trial's sensational aftermath.

Marriage to Camilla transformed Charles, and cleared his path to become king. Excluding the minor royals from Buckingham Palace's balcony was his initiative to diminish the role of his siblings, and to parade in 2017 the succession of the next three sovereigns after the queen – himself, Prince William and Prince George.

Loyal palace employees rarely leave the palaces content. Tom Shebbeare, Charles's charities supremo (above left), Robin Janvrin, the Queen's private secretary (above right), and Stephen Lamport, Charles's private secretary (below right), were all bruised by serving the prince. Only Michael Fawcett (below left), rewarded with a generous departure package before his re-employment, appeared to be satisfied.

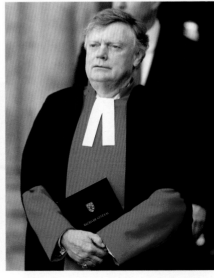

Entertaining celebrities and the rich to raise money for Charles's charities was orchestrated for over twenty years by Robert Higdon (left), supported by the American comedienne Joan Rivers (far left). Despite the opprobrium as a 'rent-a-royal', Charles raised millions of pounds to improve the lives of the disadvantaged.

Charles's critics were occasionally outspoken. Don McKinnon (above) was furious about Charles's attitude towards the Commonwealth, while Malcolm Ross (below left) disapproved of his self-indulgence. Christopher Geidt (below right), the queen's private secretary, resigned in 2017 after disagreements about Charles's role during the remainder of the queen's reign.

Highgrove and its spectacular garden is Charles's sanctuary. Controversial and conflicted, his passions arouse both admiration and anger, fuelling speculation that as king he will be a meddler who could jeopardise the monarchy.

said that it 'can teach us today a way of understanding and living in a world which Christianity is poorer for having lost'. He appeared particularly to commend those aspects of Islam that influenced European society before the Enlightenment in the seventeenth century, despite European rulers' deliberate impoverishment of Muslims. In Charles's admiration of the pre-industrialised world, he was not bothered that, whereas 68 per cent of Englishmen were literate when Napoleon invaded Egypt in 1798, an era when only 3 per cent of Muslims could read. The reason was that ownership of a printing press in Egypt, and across the Ottoman Empire, was a capital offence. To stifle democracy, a new means of communication had been suppressed, casting doubts over Charles's admiration for Islam. At the same time, both the prince and Michael Peat rejected invitations to visit Israel.

While Charles had often spoken about resolving the 'misunderstanding' between the three Abrahamic faiths, Judaism, Islam and Christianity, he seemed willing to ignore Islam's rejection of Western ideas of liberty and equality and, more important, the separation of religion from the state. He had even proposed to build a mosque near a new duchy development of 1,200 homes in Cornwall – even though no Muslims lived in the area. His uncritical sympathy alarmed the Anglican Church. Dr Michael Nazir-Ali, the Bishop of Rochester, cautioned that the heir to the throne should recognise the value of Britain being a Christian country: 'You cannot defend every faith, because there are very serious differences between them.' His objections were ignored.

Charles was enthralled by the Arab world, and particularly by the Saudi royal family. In Riyadh his fellow royals hailed him as a trusted friend, especially Prince Khaled Al-Faisal. In 2001 the two princes had jointly exhibited their paintings, and Khaled had been invited to dinner at Highgrove to raise money for the Oxford Centre of Islamic Studies. To Britain's Arabists, Charles was a hero who compensated for Tony Blair's indifference towards the Gulf rulers. Whereas the prime minister disliked autocratic monarchs, Charles made a distinction between Chinese and Saudi Arabian oppression. Unlike others in the West, he had refused to support Salman Rushdie, the author of the novel *The Satanic Verses*, after his life was threatened by a fatwa imposed by Iran's Ayatollah Khomeini. Charles not only disapproved of liberals' defence of Rushdie's perceived jeer at Islam, but in August 2005 he had flown to Saudi Arabia for King Fahd's funeral, even though the monarch had done little to stop Saudi-financed terrorists murdering Europeans and Americans.

Charles's influence was clearly limited. He had failed to persuade the Saudi government to release Sandy Mitchell, a British medical technician imprisoned and tortured for thirty-two months on trumped-up charges of planting terrorist bombs. Nevertheless, he was entranced by membership of the Club of Kings, and by his hosts' generosity. On a previous trip, Prince Khaled had given Charles a Rolex Daytona watch, which he duly turned over to Michael Fawcett; Camilla received jewels including a ruby-and-diamond necklace. During the same visit he also accepted a multi-million-pound donation for his foundation.

Charles was aware that winning similar popularity among Britons would be more difficult. One year after the wedding, less than 20 per cent approved of Camilla becoming the next queen, while another poll showed that 53 per cent would prefer William to succeed as king.

But then there was a ray of hope, as twenty years of tabloid persecution abruptly ended. On 9 August 2006, Clive Goodman, the *News of the World*'s royal correspondent, was arrested for phone hacking, and shortly afterwards the source of his scoops about Charles, Harry and other royals was exposed – namely, listening to the recorded messages on their mobile phones. Goodman would eventually be convicted and jailed. Charles stopped offering cups of tea or lunch to the editors of the *Mirror*, *Sun* and *Mail*. Without fear of exposure, the royal family would have a chance of appearing quite normal.

The improvement had started four months earlier. On 21 April 2006 the queen celebrated her eightieth birthday with twenty-six members of her family at a dinner party in Kew Palace hosted by Charles and organised by Fawcett. The tensions between the queen and her eldest son had subsided. His tribute at the meal to 'darling Mama' and the 'many wonderful qualities she has brought to almost an entire lifetime of service and dedication' was reported without the simultaneous publication of awkward revelations.

Similarly, in a television tribute Charles reminisced about his childhood and how his mother had visited him in the nursery at Buckingham Palace wearing her crown as she practised for her coronation. The programme was well received. Building on that slim success, Charles's spokesman revealed that he had invited two hundred victims of terrorist attacks, including the survivors of the London bombs on 7 July 2005, to a reception at Highgrove. Charles had written personally to each family – as he had to the grieving relatives of victims of the Islamic attacks in New York in September 2001, and in Bali in 2002 and 2005.

This was often his way. One night after dinner in 2011, he and Camilla would fly from Scotland to London to tour the riot-damaged streets of Tottenham. At the request of William Castell, the former chairman of the Prince's Trust, they met in a debris-strewn pub with broken windows. Two glasses of double malt whisky awaited the royal couple on the bar. Emerging from the wrecked building, they walked down Tottenham's main street through the very groups of black youths who had wrecked the neighbourhood. 'You come to this shit-hole after the riots!' shouted one. 'We love you!'

As always, however, it was a case of two steps forward and one back. In August 2007 Camilla informed Peat that she intended to be present at a memorial service in London's Wellington Barracks to commemorate the tenth anniversary of Diana's death. Once the news leaked, there was uproar. All the old stories of adultery were recycled in the media until, five days before the service, she pulled out, releasing a statement that her presence would 'divert attention from the purpose of the occasion'. Charles and the rest of the royal family flew from Balmoral to London, to be greeted by a silent crowd. To avoid joyless solitude in Scotland, Camilla asked Fawcett to contact Sir Donald Gosling, the former co-owner of National Car Parks. Fawcett's personal relationship with the multimillionaire had provided many donations to Charles's charities, and on this occasion he asked whether Camilla and three girlfriends could spend a week cruising the Mediterranean on his 250-foot yacht. Gosling rarely declined Fawcett's requests, nor did he this time.

During the cruise, Camilla was said to grumble about the restrictions of married life. All week she had to listen to Charles's laments about the world going wrong, and how he was either ignored or misunderstood. For relief at weekends she escaped to Ray Mill while Charles remained in Highgrove; only there could she feel comfortable.

That running sore, Diana, had repeatedly intruded into her life. Camilla wanted closure, and the opportunity suddenly arose. In October 2007 an inquest under the appeal court judge Lord Justice Scott Baker met to hear Mohamed Fayed give evidence that Diana and Dodi Fayed had been murdered by conspirators organised by Prince Philip and the royal family.

To avoid any accusations of prejudice, the exhaustive investigation of the crash by French officials had been ignored, and a new investigation headed by Sir John Stevens, the former head of the Metropolitan Police, was presented to the court. It concluded that the accident was caused by the car's speeding drunken driver. Nevertheless, the judge gave Fayed licence to rummage through Diana's love life and her miserable relations with her brother Charles Spencer. Fayed even mentioned her anger with Charles for hosting a fiftieth birthday party at Highgrove for Camilla in the summer of 1997. He also wanted the world to know of Diana's gratitude to him for an invitation to holiday that summer in the south of France.

Fayed's wholesale trashing of reputations climaxed with Paul Burrell telling the court about a handwritten letter Diana sent him in October 1993. It included once again the outlandish claim that Charles was plotting to kill her in a car crash so he could marry their sons' nanny. Those suspecting that Burrell might have forged the letter were outflanked by a note by Lord Mishcon, Diana's solicitor, in which he recorded that the princess had repeated the accusations at a meeting in October 1995, although Mishcon had waited until eighteen days after her death before informing the police. Nevertheless, after a six-month hearing, the jury would unanimously reject both Diana's accusation and Fayed's conspiracy theories – not least because, as the judge said, Fayed had not produced 'a shred of evidence' to support his slurs. The Egyptian was condemned as a fantasist.

The judgement about Diana was similarly divided. To some, she was the manipulative schemer described in Tina Brown's recent biography, *The Diana Chronicles*. To others, she remained the victim of Charles's cruelty. Either way, after the verdict Charles and Camilla hoped for the first time in over twenty years that her ghost had been laid to rest. But any respite was temporary.

24

Rules of Conduct

'You must be quite mad,' exclaimed the queen. 'Work for Charles?' After a brief silence, the monarch's evident surprise disappeared. 'Well …'

When she found herself under pressure, she rarely uttered more than a few words, and in this case she appeared to resign herself to the news. The audience in the sitting room in Buckingham Palace was over. Malcolm Ross, the comptroller in the lord chamberlain's office, took his leave. The queen would customarily give a parting smile, a gesture that many in Buckingham Palace treasured, but on this occasion it was absent.

The summons to Ross had come not from the queen but from her eldest son, in a late-night telephone call. 'I need you,' said the Prince of Wales. Ross's protests were brushed aside: 'No, I need you,' repeated the pained voice. He wanted Ross to be his master of the household. As Charles well knew, a royal command was rarely ignored. Over the years he had enticed some of the cleverest and richest of his kingdom to serve him; some had been bruised by the experience but departed in silence, others remained loyal but critical. An important minority, mostly women, were permanently devoted. Ross accepted the job out of duty, and because he expected to forge a good relationship with Michael Peat. His confidence was misplaced. Within a short time he became alarmed by Peat's denigration of the queen's staff as 'dinosaurs' and 'old has-beens'. Shaped by his eighteen years' service in Buckingham Palace, Ross had anticipated personal support from Charles. Instead he became isolated.

Peat had proved himself to be a talented financial manager. In 2005 the Duchy of Cornwall made a record £14 million in profits. The following year he could quietly boast that Charles's personal income had risen to £15.1 million, and in 2007 to £16.3 million.

During 2007 Charles's advisers sold most of his shares before the stock market crash, and also sold commercial property at the top of the market. Since the duchy did not pay capital gains tax, its value had risen to £647 million. With more income, Charles could increase his staff to 146, including nine media specialists, eleven gardeners at Highgrove and over thirty employees to support his private secretaries.

To minimise his own achievement, Peat issued a statement in praise of Charles for costing the taxpayer just 3.5 pence per person every year. To placate the prince's critics even further, he announced that he had given up polo for the sake of the environment (because he usually travelled to matches by helicopter). To economise on water Charles placed bricks in the lavatory cisterns of his homes, and as proof of his code of duty he had sent 2,247 letters, raised £110 million, £119 million and £122 million for his charities over the past three years (receiving about half from the taxpayer), and voluntarily paid £3.3 million in tax every year, rising to £4.2 million in 2006. The low tax rate reflected his deductible expenses of travel, his homes and staff.

Charles's employees no longer included Peat's former deputy Elizabeth Buchanan. Her departure was not associated with the prince's 'economising': rather, her unconcealed hero-worship of Charles and her frequent appearances alongside him in photographs had infuriated Camilla.

Understandably, Peat omitted from his latest report the information that one trip on the royal train from Highgrove to Penrith simply to visit a pub had cost £18,916, and that Charles had spent £20,980 for a day trip by plane from Scotland to Lincolnshire to watch William receive his RAF wings. Such costs were food and drink to republican MPs. By contrast, the queen would travel by train to Sandringham at Christmas on First Capital Connect. Her ticket cost £50, instead of £15,000 had she taken a royal carriage.

To emphasise his employer's benevolence, Peat produced another sixty-page brochure, the fifth in five years, illustrated with forty-three photographs of Charles and Camilla. The text celebrated the prince's championship of his green agenda. 'Our animals,' the brochure revealed of the royal cattle, 'release less methane because they have better feed and eat more grass.' Peat also wrote: 'Charles is the world's most successful philanthropic entrepreneur.' Clearly he had forgotten others, not least Bill Gates. But only Peat would have measured Charles's achievements by mentioning that he had shaken more hands than in the previous year.

These presentations masked Charles's continuing patchy understanding of finance. Always eager to increase the duchy's income, especially from its investments, Peat occasionally summoned successful fund managers to explain the world's economy to the prince. In 2007 he invited Ronnie Cohen, the creator of Apax, Britain's largest private equity company, to meet Charles alongside Jacob Rothschild. Another guest, a respected economist, was invited to start the meeting with a 'state of the world' presentation.

'What's happening across the globe?' asked Peat.

'How long have I got?'

'Five minutes,' came the reply without a blink.

Five minutes later, Charles nodded. 'Excellent,' announced Peat. 'Now,' he asked Cohen, 'what return do you get on your investments?'

'About 11 or 12 per cent.' Peat and Charles seemed impressed.

'How much do you want to invest?' continued Cohen.

'£6 million,' replied Peat. Charles smiled in agreement.

Cohen's face fell. He dealt only in hundreds of millions.

At precisely 6 p.m., Peat gushed, 'Your Highness, we have taken far too much of your time. I'm sure you have more important things to do.' The three visitors departed with the impression that Charles had done them a favour by listening to their advice. In reality, he had little understanding of his own numerous and complex investments – not because of the limits of his education, but due to a lack of interest in matters he considered unspiritual.

Overall, the prince's good intentions remained frustrated by disharmony. During the previous four years, Tom Shebbeare had struggled to assert control across his unruly empire. While assuring Charles that all was well, he encountered opposition from the charities' directors to rebrand the corporate centre, or to accept any plan to save money. Supervision, he discovered, was difficult because the charities were similar to a federation, and 'no one was in charge'. Because every charity was different, the chief executives resisted mergers of their administration. In 2006 Shebbeare began looking for a building to house all the charities at a low rent. Fred Goodwin told Charles that the Prince's Trust could not afford to move. In a familiar pattern, the prince accepted this, and so the cost-saving scheme was abandoned.

The following year, Charles created a new crisis. During a dinner at Windsor Castle he was told about the fate of Dumfries House, a Palladian mansion in Ayrshire, designed in the 1750s by John and Robert Adam. The building, partly boarded up, its gardens overgrown, was located in a coalfield far from any desired destination and without a view. For two hundred years it had been in the possession of the Marquesses of Bute, but the family was about to sell up to a local hotelier and auction its unique collection of early Chippendale furniture at Christie's.

For Charles, the house and its effects were an opportunity to prove that heritage projects could transform a derelict area. Although he had never visited the mansion, and his charities did not have sufficient money for the purchase, he invited the marquess to Clarence House to negotiate a deal.

Michael Peat was under pressure from Charles to buy the house and its furniture. The original valuation of £25 million, he knew, reflected the inflated levels of the property boom. In normal circumstances, even under orders to buy, he might have advised Charles to resist the temptation to rush in, and instead drive a hard bargain; but, meeting the marquess late at night, Peat lacked any leverage. The Chippendale furniture, said Bute, was at that moment packed in lorries and heading south for the sale in London. Peat agreed to buy everything for £43 million. The lorry drivers were told to make their way back to Ayrshire. The following morning, Charles was delighted. He was assured by Peat that the money could be found.

As usual, his staff obeyed the order without objection. A new charity was established which would initially borrow £40 million. The loan, Peat calculated, would be partly repaid by building and selling 770 houses on neighbouring farmland that he had bought separately for just £268,000. With planning permission, the land's value would rise to £15 million. Just as he foresaw, after the purchase East Ayrshire council rezoned the farmland for housing. The land's value soared – to collapse only weeks later as the global financial crisis hit. Charles's new charity was engulfed by interest and loan repayments.

'We were a little unlucky,' Peat admitted. 'But we were not the only property developer caught out by the crash.' Although Charles's income from the duchy had increased to £15.1 million, Peat refused to spend that money on Dumfries. Instead, he and Charles targeted rich donors to raise £20 million to pay off part of the debt and to finance the first renovations of the overpriced hulk.

Charles and Fawcett approached a galaxy of property developers, bankers, lawyers, accountants and foreign billionaires from both sides of the Atlantic, Saudi Arabia, Latvia and Kyrgyzstan. Favours were asked from landowners such as the Earl of Leicester, who agreed to host overnight at Holkham Hall, his stately home in Norfolk, a group of Americans arriving by private plane before travelling on to Dumfries the following day.

Implicit in the request for donations was the opportunity of a lunch or dinner with Charles, and an assurance that a sizeable donation would be rewarded with a room in the mansion named after the sponsor. Among those approached were hedge-fund manager Michael Hintze, Sheikh Hamad of Qatar, and Knanysher Alefza, who reportedly gave £1 million each. A group of rich Canadians introduced by Amanda Sherrington, an employee of the billionaire Canadian Weston family, also contributed.

By then, there was a pattern to Charles's fundraising events. If they were to be held in someone else's home, the hosts were told the food he would like. If he chose lamb, they were instructed to contact Barrow Gurney, the suppliers of organic meat produced on the duchy's farms. The richest person present would be seated next to Charles – 'Look, I think you should write a cheque for this,' the heir to the throne would murmur. During the meal, each guest was given a pledge card. After Charles's speech about Dumfries, many wrote '£5,000'; but a frisson went around the room when they noticed Charles ostentatiously examining each card, and suddenly pens were retrieved and £5,000 became £50,000.

The casualties of this frantic scramble for money were the other charities. Since 2003, Tom Shebbeare had been unable to deliver fully on pledges of additional funds that had been made to newly recruited chief executives. Some were surprised when promised support failed to materialise. In the opinion of one trustee, 'Without embarrassment, Shebbeare reneged on his promise of money. He wasn't a villain but a courtier who played by the court rules.' Another trustee described Shebbeare as 'festering on the sea bed, living off the detritus of others'. In those circumstances, Mike Lake, hired to become Shebbeare's successor as chief executive, resigned.

The ripples spread further. Julia Cleverdon, the chief executive of Business in the Community since 1992, left in 2008. Described by one courtier as the 'obstacle in Clarence House', she was criticised for 'flabby thinking'.

The disarray reflected Charles's increasingly insensitive attitude to public opinion. Earlier that year he had been invited to New York, along with Camilla, to collect a Global Environmental Citizen award from Harvard Medical School. At the Foreign Office's insistence, he was told to fly on BA. Camilla demanded a private plane. The FO mentioned to Peat that the sight of Charles arriving on a chartered jet to receive an environmental prize would be unhelpful. The impact, the official went on, would be similar to Charles's Bentley being driven from London to Prague for his visit there, despite the embassy owning a perfectly good new Jaguar.

On Peat's recommendation, Charles agreed to BA, only to be met by Camilla's stubborn resistance. She was proving a demanding spouse. Although Peat had written in his published report that she cost taxpayers a mere £2,000 a year, he omitted to mention that the taxpayer had spent £1.8 million on security around Ray Mill, and a further £200,000 on Camilla's various travels. She also remained vulnerable to the criticism of being work-shy. During the previous year she had fulfilled thirty-eight official duties on her own; the queen mother had completed 130 when she was eighty years of age, and 118 at ninety.

Charles resented the criticism. Camilla, he explained, was not a solo royal but had appeared as his consort at 196 public events. That barely chimed with her excuse that a cut hand would prevent her travelling to New York. After a fierce argument, she retreated and agreed to fly on the BA plane with Charles – along with fourteen staff including her hairdresser, two valets, a butler, a dresser, press officers, a doctor and five police protection officers. 'We told the prince his entourage was too big but he ignored us,' recalled an FO official. Even then, Charles could not resist complaining to Higdon about BA's 'incredibly uncomfortable first-class seats'.

To allow time for Camilla to recover from the journey, the group flew first to Philadelphia, where Higdon had arranged a fundraising dinner. Charles and Camilla headed for the city's concert hall to meet Leonore Annenberg, the eighty-nine-year-old widow of media billionaire and former American ambassador in London Walter

Annenberg. Higdon forgot to mention that the reception would be on the eleventh floor. To avoid claustrophobia in the lift, Camilla walked up the stairs wearing a chandelier necklace of thirty-seven rubies and many diamonds, a recent gift from the King of Saudi Arabia. As she shook Mrs Annenberg's hand, an oxygen tube stuck up the elderly woman's nose blew out and disconnected from the bottle, spewing oxygen around the room. Camilla looked at Higdon and burst out laughing. 'We had a great time together,' said Higdon later.

The presentation of Charles's award, by Al Gore, was greeted as an accolade for twenty years' pioneering work. Nevertheless, the trip offended environmentalists, cost-conscious critics and those urging Charles to show more interest in the Commonwealth, the risk to his status among whose countries had not diminished – the governments of New Zealand and Australia were considering whether to remove the Union Jack from their national flags. Charles and Camilla's presence at the Commonwealth Heads of Government meeting in Kampala alongside the queen in November 2007 barely affected their reservations. Despite his smiles and earnest conversations, he was told that he would again be a bystander at the next summit in Trinidad in 2009.

'It would be too early to do more,' his staff was told by Simon Gimson, a senior member of the Commonwealth Secretariat. 'He can't breeze into the CHOGM leaders' banquets with the queen. He'd be resented. He'll have to work his passage.'

As his retirement as secretary general of the Commonwealth approached, Don McKinnon was as irritated as ever that, while he had had thirty audiences with the queen during his eight years in London, Charles had refused to meet him privately even once. Camilla was not helping. She disliked hot countries, she said, and could not cope with jet lag. She refused to compete with Diana.

On the eve of his sixtieth birthday, Charles overtook his great-great-grandfather Edward VII as the longest-waiting heir to the British throne. As was his habit on such anniversaries, he contemplated the future. As the queen aged, he had hoped that more frequent appearances at events would win him greater public acceptance; but beyond the genuine respect he often won during personal encounters, his people remained sceptical. The scorn provoked by controversies over the previous twenty-five years had barely subsided. Charles's uphill progress was still impeded by many of the old obstacles. Although at times downcast, he refused to admit defeat, and searched for new opportunities to win support. Casting himself as a misunderstood prophet, he appeared in *The Passionate Prince*, a BBC documentary explaining his insatiable idealism. 'I don't call it meddling,' he told his audience. 'I call it mobilising.' So many of his causes had been unpopular at first, he said, but became justified over time: 'Perhaps, though, after all this, eventually people might realise some of the things I have been trying to do aren't all that mad.'

Grudging acceptance was the best he could expect. Stability, and no more scandals, would secure a bedrock of support. All too aware of his troubled relations with his parents, he knew he needed to heal those wounds. The best place to do so, he decided, would be at the headquarters of the Prince's Trust. Just before his sixtieth birthday party, he welcomed the queen and Philip there. 'May I say,' said his mother to the staff, 'that we are both enormously proud to have been reminded here today of his personal contribution to this remarkable organisation.' Ten years earlier, that scenario – followed by a birthday party at Buckingham Palace for four hundred guests, including kings, queens, singers, actors and Camilla – would have been unimaginable.

By the third anniversary of his marriage, Charles's domestic life had settled into a happy routine. Although his staff occasionally heard arguments, Camilla had become his anchor and his protector from his eccentricities. 'I've been on the Tube, you know,' he once told a friend after they returned from the theatre to Clarence House for dinner.

'Yes, but only to open a line,' was the accurate riposte.

Even Camilla could be amused by Charles's loftiness. That same evening, she had told the staff to leave salads and cold cuts of meat on the sideboard. 'Let's see what's for dinner,' said Charles after finishing his Martini. He walked into the dining room and shrieked. Fearing the worst, Camilla dashed in after him. 'What's this?' trembled her husband, pointing at the food.

'It's cling film, darling,' she replied.

However, there were limits to her common sense. In public she appeared as a benign, good-hearted, amusing woman, but in private her expectations continued to grow. Bowing to Buckingham Palace's complaints about his acceptance of free holidays from questionable hosts, Charles had chartered a private yacht for an eleven-day Caribbean cruise, at a cost of about £210,000. Camilla later grumbled that the boat was smaller than Yiannis Latsis's or Donald Gosling's. Thankfully for the royal family, the public were unaware of such complaints.

The success of Camilla's ambition to be queen depended upon her silence. She knew that the latest polls showed a decline in her popularity to just 17 per cent in her favour. Wisely, she realised that a single misplaced interview could torpedo her long-term plans. The contrast with the increasing popularity of William and his girlfriend Kate Middleton was all too obvious.

Prince Andrew's behaviour, too, was harming Charles's efforts to win support. To the public he represented the worst of hereditary privilege. Damned as 'useless' across Whitehall while undertaking so-called 'official trips' in the Far East and America, he was chasing women with a protection officer in tow at a cost of between £140,000 and £250,000 per trip, including private jets. Back in Britain, he attracted criticism for inviting John McEnroe and Bjorn Borg to use the tennis court at Buckingham Palace for a charity match sponsored by bankers. More troublesome was his relationship with Timur Kulibayev, the son-in-law of the president of Kazakhstan, who had bought Andrew's marital home, Sunninghill Park in Berkshire, for £15 million, a suspiciously inflated price suggesting an inappropriate relationship between the two men. But Andrew's worst mistake was his friendship with Jeffrey Epstein, an American businessman he invited to Balmoral, Windsor and Sandringham. Although Epstein was already notorious for seeking out underaged girls, Andrew refused to end the relationship. Without considering the consequences, he asked Epstein to help resolve his ex-wife Fergie's £2 million debts.

Andrew's conduct prompted a visit to Buckingham Palace by a Whitehall official to discuss with the queen whether the by-now middle-aged prince should continue as an official trade ambassador for Britain. Warned in advance about the coming encounter, Andrew asked a public relations consultant to visit him and discuss how his position might be improved. As the consultant was escorted down the palace corridor to Andrew's office, he could hear the prince screaming down a telephone. 'It was appalling behaviour. He was demanding respect for his entitlement,' reported the visitor.

Prince Edward was little better. As the new president of the Duke of Edinburgh Award he frequently flew 'on business' to the Caribbean, including the Cayman Islands and Barbados, where few local young people undertook the award's challenges. For Edward it was an opportunity to play golf in the sunshine, but his excuse quickly wore thin. Prince Michael of Kent was another misbehaving royal who was actually reprimanded for using his position to further his business dealings with unsuitable partners. A Buckingham Palace official told Kent that the British ambassador in Moscow would henceforth refuse to help him during his visits to Russia, or to arrange meetings with oligarchs and other unappealing Russians.

Repeated descriptions in the media of these and other royals exploiting their privileges bespattered Charles, and to his irritation magnified reports about his own extravagances and mismanagement. And just when he would have benefited from a calmer profile, he was embroiled in another dogfight – once again attracting attention to his hubris.

To Malcolm Ross's distress, 'Peat failed to seal a relationship between Buckingham Palace and Clarence House,' and in 2008 he was abruptly dismissed by Peat. This was followed soon after by the unexpected departure of Ross's deputy, Andrew Farquharson. Both had been recruited by Charles from Buckingham Palace, and both, colleagues agreed, were 'unceremoniously dumped after half a lifetime's work'. The two men were irate. The queen was also angry. 'If you take my staff,' she reportedly told Charles, 'you should look after them, not sack them.' But that was not the main disagreement at issue.

25

King Meddle

The opportunity must have seemed irresistible. Ever since Richard Rogers had been appointed Ken Livingstone's architectural adviser, the mayor had encouraged the construction of tower blocks across London. In response, at a conference at St James's Palace in early 2008, Charles had criticised the proliferation of skyscrapers – especially 'the Gherkin' and 'the Cheesegrater' – for having 'vandalised' the capital, overshadowing the Tower of London and Westminster. 'Not just one carbuncle on the face of a much-loved friend,' he said, repeating his signature insult, 'but a positive rash of them that will disfigure precious views and disinherit future generations of Londoners.'

In recent months, plans had been submitted for even taller buildings in or near central London, including 'the Wireless' and the Shard, five times higher than the proposed Mies van der Rohe tower at One Poultry that Charles had sabotaged. The prince's war of 1984 appeared lost. In consolation, some developers had been influenced by the idea pioneered at Poundbury that contented communities were created by building houses that would enhance their occupants' lives. The councils restoring the centres of Birmingham, Manchester and other cities were aware of the value of protecting Britain's heritage, and had taken note of Christopher Smallwood's recent report, commissioned by Charles to show how health and crime levels were influenced by the layout of urban areas. (Rashly, as he knew Charles's ways, Smallwood had asked for a £25,000 fee for the six-month study. Inevitably, he was not commissioned again.)

Charles's position of authority had persuaded developers to seek his opinion discreetly about ambitious schemes at King's Cross, the Battersea Power Station and the Thames Gateway. Consulting him in advance might avoid a potentially fatal later intervention. 'The prince has a big voice,' admitted Peter Freeman, the developer of King's Cross. That strategy had been ignored in 2006 by the developers of Smithfield Market, who intended to demolish the listed 150-year-old Victorian buildings and erect a seven-storey office block. After an appeal to Charles by opponents of the scheme, he denounced it, saying it would 'destroy yet another part of London's heritage'. The demolition was stopped, to await the developers' revised proposals.

Those were small but important victories. In Charles's opinion, the Poundbury philosophy was still the only route to happiness – even though his Dorset dream was still no more than a large village of 252 homes, lampooned by modernists as 'HRH's theme park'.

Despite his sporadic forays since 1984, Britain's modernist architects continued to be globally acclaimed. Few were rewarded with more prizes and prestigious commissions than Richard Rogers, now Lord Rogers, the proud recipient of a Companion of Honour from the queen in 2008. Besides his design of new airport terminals at Heathrow and Madrid, he had carried out luxury developments for the super-rich, most recently at One Hyde Park, a prominent building near Harrods owned by the property tycoon brothers Christian and Nick Candy. Each flat would cost its owner up to £100 million, despite the whole construction being criticised as an eyesore, a home for billionaire oligarchs and Arabs who avoided British taxes. In self-defence, Rogers pleaded that there was no perfect client, which was nearly equivalent to Charles's lament that he had no choice about his parents.

Politics and personality divided Rogers and his royal nemesis. For twenty-five years they had been jousting. Now they were destined for an outright confrontation. In 2009, Charles chose his ground: a Rogers-designed residential development on the site of the Old Chelsea Barracks, originally built in 1862, demolished and rebuilt in 1960–62, to be used for its original purpose by the army.

Charles had been alerted to Rogers's design by the classicist architect Quinlan Terry, one of Poundbury's leading designers. In 2007 the 12.8-acre site had been sold by the British government to the Candy brothers and the Emir of Qatar for £959 million. The Candys had been promised a fee of £81 million by the emir's representatives once Westminster council granted initial planning permission for the £3 billion scheme.

Rogers proposed 320 luxury flats and some social housing in high-tech blocks built of coloured steel and glass. Chelsea's conservative residents were outraged. To them, his 'monotonous glass buildings' jarred with the adjacent Royal Hospital, designed in the 1690s by Christopher Wren. Pertinently, a new extension to the hospital devised by Quinlan Terry perfectly matched Wren's style and showcased Charles's ideas. In the local residents' opinion, Wren's architecture of traditional brick was the ideal model for the Barracks. Terry shared Charles's opinion of Rogers. 'Modernism,' he said, 'is the work of the devil.' In reply, modernists dubbed Terry 'not a good architect'.

During 2008, as the emir's planning application was formally considered, opponents of the development, led by resident Georgina Thorburn, unsuccessfully sought support from local MPs and councillors. To attract attention, Thorburn chained herself to the Barracks' railings during that summer's Ascot week – dressed in Ascot clothes. That gesture, like other protests extending over nearly two years, was ignored by the council. Even her letter seeking Charles's help remained unanswered. In January 2009, Thorburn met Terry. 'What took you so long to get to me?' he asked. He sketched an alternative design and sent it to Charles, requesting that the prince intervene.

By arrangement, Charles and Terry met at the official opening of the hospital extension. Charles now opposed any design by Rogers – his disapproval had earlier prevented Rogers's name being included in a development scheme for the Royal Opera House. Not surprisingly, he and Terry agreed that Rogers's design was unsuitable. To stop the scheme, Charles decided to contact Sheikh Hamad bin Khalifa Al Thani, the Emir of Qatar.

He knew the emir personally, but he should have paused before making a direct approach: any interference before the democratic planning process was completed risked being seen as an abuse of privilege. Michael Peat had tried, at Downing Street's request, to modify Charles's criticisms of the government, but controlling his protests about architecture was particularly difficult, and Peat was powerless to curb his employer's scorn for 'greedy money-grabbing property tycoons' and their acolytes who employed modernist architects. With a high-minded sense of protecting the interests of the capital, Charles was determined to prevent what he saw as the desecration of Chelsea – especially because at that very moment he was seeking to justify his future role as a 'meddling king'.

A test of public opinion had been presented by Jonathan Dimbleby in the *Sunday Times* in November 2008. Under the headline 'Crown Me King Meddle', Dimbleby had written about 'discreet moves' to allow the future Charles III 'to speak out on matters of national and international importance in ways that at the moment would be unthinkable'. Clearly briefed by Charles or his friends to test the water, Dimbleby, who had maintained a good relationship with the prince since his 1994 biography, described 'murmuring' between the palaces, Whitehall and Westminster for 'tomorrow's monarchy' to become 'more "active" as we move into ever more testing times'. He suggested that in the 'vacuum of national leadership' Charles should not submit to the constitutional straitjacket worn by his mother. Instead, through Dimbleby, Charles's friends suggested that the new king could safely model himself as head of state on Germany's president, because 'It is inconceivable that he would misuse such responsibility to ride one of his hobbyhorses'. But that was precisely Charles's intention. He was determined to stop Rogers.

Rather than writing directly to the emir, he addressed his cousin, Sheikh Hamad bin Jassim bin Jabr Al Thani, Qatar's prime minister. Charles's letter of 1 March 2009 complained about 'the destruction of many parts of London with one more "brutalist" development after another', and continued, 'This gigantic experiment with the very soul of our capital city and with many others in the UK and elsewhere has reached the point where it is no longer sustainable. Quite frankly my heart sank when I saw the plans for the Old Chelsea Barracks site.' Urging the Qatari to reconsider his proposal, Charles wrote: 'Many would be eternally grateful to Your Excellency if [you] could bequeath a unique and enduring legacy to London.' He enclosed Terry's sketches for a classical scheme. The letter was sent to Qatar in the FO's diplomatic bag.

News of Charles's protest soon bounced back to London. The emir had asked his representatives to consider amending the design. Rogers was outraged. His work was threatened, he said, by Charles 'acting in an underhand and undemocratic manner'. The Candys were also furious. Their £81 million fee was jeopardised because Charles, as Christian Candy sniped, 'pissed in the emir's ear about how awful the scheme was'. Charles himself would tell *Vanity Fair*, 'I just wrote a letter – a confidential letter to somebody I happen to know … Frequently, I've written letters to people [who] pay no attention at all.'

At the beginning of April the Qataris' media spokesman, a former officer in the Life Guards, passed Charles's letter to a newspaper. Many believed that the leak was intended to help the Candys, and that the publicity-shy Qataris would prefer to pay their £81 million fee to avoid the embarrassment of their secret communication with Charles being publicised. But the ruse rebounded, and the Qataris chose to stick to the contract. As the Candys' hopes of payment faded, Charles became, Peat revealed, 'very unhappy that the matter had become public'. But instead of retreating, he renewed his attack.

On 8 April Peat met John Ward, the emir's manager responsible for the development. Ward told him that the ruler was 'unhappy that Charles was unhappy', and promised that the problem would be sorted out. Since the emir was 'not wedded to the Rogers design', he would consider modifications. The conversation, however, did not end well. Peat became angry at the Qataris' equivocation over the process to manage Charles's objections. In an echo of other misinterpretations, he failed to understand that the Qataris were seeking to placate Britain's heir, but also to avoid circumstances making them vulnerable to the Candy brothers' legitimate demand for their £81 million. By meddling in their commercial agreement, he was steering Charles towards an embarrassing cameo appearance in a nasty legal battle.

In mid-April, Rogers publicly complained that Charles's abuse of his privileged access and secret lobbying had usurped the 'established planning consultation process'. He would later add that 'most local groups were supportive' of his scheme, and that Westminster's planners 'were going to recommend approval'. 'What utter humbug,' Quinlan Terry fulminated, and accused Rogers of hypocrisy.

Seven years earlier, after Westminster council had approved Terry's design for the Royal Hospital extension, Rogers had, in a last-minute bid to avert the democratic process, emailed his political ally John Prescott, the deputy prime minister and environment minister, asking him to overturn the decision. Prescott, said Rogers, should insist on a modern building to replace Terry's 'architectural plagiarism'. That secret plea was rejected, but news of Rogers's use of privileged access leaked.

Delighted by Terry's riposte, Charles approached Simon Milton, Westminster's deputy mayor responsible for planning. They met at Poundbury, and after their conversation Milton declared his opposition to Rogers's scheme, although he knew the council's officials still supported Rogers. Accordingly, Charles asked Andrew Hamilton, an architectural adviser, to approach the planning officials employed by Boris Johnson, London's newly elected Conservative mayor. Since Johnson's attitude was unpredictable, Charles offered the emir the help of Manon Williams, his deputy private secretary, and Hank Dittmar, another architectural adviser, through the Prince's Foundation for the Built Environment. Both could provide support against the Candys.

Belatedly, Peat grasped the constitutional implications of what Charles was doing. In an internal message written in his elegant handwritten script he noted, 'This would suggest the personal involvement of the prince.' John Ward was also upset. Charles's opposition, he believed, would cause 'a huge embarrassment to Qatar', and would cost the emir money.

Not to be deterred, Charles met Sheikh Hamad at Clarence House on 11 May. Afterwards Peat noted, 'The Emir was surprised by the Rogers design[s] for Chelsea Barracks and said he would have them changed.' The accuracy of this memorandum would be disputed by the Qataris, and a judge would agree that Peat had recorded what he hoped the emir meant, rather than what was actually said.

By coincidence, two days later, as a gesture of reconciliation, Charles addressed RIBA, twenty-five years after his groundbreaking 'carbuncle' speech. 'I think RIBA are completely mad to invite such a terrible thinker about architecture,' wrote Piers Gough, a well-known London architect, in the *Guardian*, 'and to kow-tow to this noblesse oblige is absolutely appalling.' Poundbury, he added, 'is despicable and decadent'. He appealed to fellow RIBA members to boycott the speech.

In the event, the meeting was packed. 'I am sorry,' Charles told his audience, 'if I have somehow left the faintest impression that I wished to kick-start some kind of "style war" between classicists and modernists, or that I somehow wanted to drag the world back to the eighteenth century.' His speech in 1984, he said, was a protest about 'the brutal destruction of our towns and countryside ... [because] much of the urban realm was becoming depersonalised and defaced'. He was applauded, no longer a pariah.

Without restraint, he urged Peat to continue lobbying against Rogers. In a telephone conference call on 29 May, Peat discussed how to stop the scheme with Simon Milton, Westminster council officials and a representative of the emir. In another call, he explained to the Qataris' executives that Charles would press for them to use Terry. The prince, he added, was 'going to fight to the finish'. In a note written after the conversation, Peat boldly told Charles that the Qataris understood that using Rogers was 'a problem'.

Neither Peat nor the prince, it appears, realised the consequences of seeking to disrupt a commercial agreement. Collateral damage to a professional's income never troubled Charles. But, after receiving legal advice, Peat did finally understand that his intervention was unwise. To protect himself, he made it clear that he had not participated fully in the conference call of 29 May, saying that he had abruptly ended his involvement after grasping that it was not appropriate.

To distance Charles and himself from the accusation of commercial sabotage, Peat would later say that Charles's letter to the emir was 'not down to any personal opposition', but merely reflected the opinions of local residents: 'They asked him to do what he could to ensure that their views received exposure. It is part of the Prince of Wales's role and duty to make sure that the views of ordinary people that might not otherwise be heard receive some exposure ... For many developers, hearing the views of local residents is very unexpected and unwelcome. They are just wanting to make money.' But tellingly, in his letter to the emir Charles had not once mentioned local residents. He wrote only about his personal abhorrence for Rogers's design – precisely the 'personal opposition' that Peat would later deny had been his motivation. As the Candys would highlight, while Charles claimed to be supporting powerless local residents, he had not replied to any of the protesters against the building of two thousand houses on duchy land near Truro. Contradictions rarely stymied the prince.

By June, Charles scented victory. Boris Johnson declared that he 'strongly opposed' the scheme as 'repetitive', and Westminster councillors, led by Simon Milton, announced their opposition. Under pressure, the council's planning officers switched from support to a neutral stance. The following day, 11 June, the Qataris withdrew their application and asked Westminster council to 'look favourably' on a new scheme. 'It knocked the stuffing out of me,' admitted Rogers. 'Charles single-handedly destroyed the project.' Unelected power, he protested, broke 'the bond of trust' and was 'totally unconstitutional'. Clarence House replied tersely, 'The Prince of Wales, like everybody else, has the right to express his opinion.'

Angry about losing both his fees and the scheme, Rogers wrote in the *Guardian*: 'He sees this debate as a battle of the styles which is against the run of history because architecture evolves and moves, mirroring society.' Charles, he continued, 'knows little about architecture … I think he pursues these topics because he is looking for a job … He is actually an unemployed individual which says something about the state of the royal family … The idea that he is a man of the people fascinates me. He is a man of the rich people, that is for sure.'

Rogers's jibes did not compare to the embarrassment heaped upon Charles by the Candys. In their legal claim against the Qataris for breach of contract and the loss of their fees, they demanded the disclosure of the prince's administrative records. Charles resisted, seeking as usual to influence a sensitive decision without public scrutiny. A judge rejected his bid for secrecy, and the royal file, including Peat's revealing memos, was the highlight of a widely publicised trial. For a moment, Charles was also at risk of being sued by the Candys, and being compelled to testify, for inducing a breach of contract. But thanks to a loyal monarchist lawyer, the brothers were persuaded not to summon the prince. At the end of the trial, Mr Justice Vos was certain that Charles's intervention had persuaded the emir to abandon the Rogers design. In an obscure judgement, he ruled in the Candys' favour that there had been a breach of contract, but also ruled that it was not a 'bad faith breach'. He made no immediate award of damages, but said that a claim would be considered, and advised the Candys and the emir to negotiate a settlement. To recover their fees, the Candys would have to prove that their plans would have been approved by Westminster council had the emir not withdrawn them. The brothers did eventually receive compensation. Only Charles walked away financially unscathed. Described by *The Times* as 'a self-appointed vigilante wreaking revenge on any proposal to build a column of glass and steel', he accepted his supporters' praise.

'That's another reason why I battle so hard ... despite the unbelievable abuse that's heaped on me every time I open my mouth,' he told them at the next annual conference of the Prince's Foundation for the Built Environment. Richard Rogers and others may have trampled on his good name, but, posing as the traumatised hero, he hoped that after his death he would finally be appreciated. To reaffirm his values, he resigned as president of the patrons of the National Museums of Scotland to show his disapproval of the modernist extension to the National Gallery in Edinburgh.

The alliance between Boris Johnson and Britain's heir was short-lived. Not long afterwards, Charles heard from prime minister David Cameron that control of the royal parks had been transferred to the Greater London Authority.

'Boris is taking over the royal parks?' he screamed. 'Why have you given the royal parks to Boris?'

'The queen agreed,' replied Cameron.

'What? Mama down the road? What does she know about the royal parks?'

26

The Divine Prophet

'It's no fun having your head shot off all the time,' Charles said, musing about the ridicule heaped on his book *Harmony*, co-written with Tony Juniper and Ian Skelly. The subtitle, *A New Way of Looking at Our World*, described his preference for an absolute monarch ruling over a pre-industrial feudal society. Barely noticed by the public, Charles believed in a world guided by the spiritualism practised in medieval times. In giving voice to his incomprehension of an entire epoch, he appeared to judge people without seeking to understand them. 'Some of his book reads like the ravings of a Buddhist mystic,' wrote the historian Max Hastings, who in his previous jobs as editor of the *Daily Telegraph* and the *Evening Standard* had been a long-term critic of Charles. 'Anyone who reads the Prince of Wales's new book will have little doubt that the chief peril to our royal institution in the decades ahead lies within his well-meaning, muddled, woolly head.'

Charles's book contained multiple inconsistencies. No one could criticise his dislike of political oppression, but his passion made little sense when offset by his disdain for democracy. His condemnations were selective. He particularly sympathised with religious and cultural victims like the Buddhists in Tibet. Still under Laurens van der Post's influence, he attacked those who suppressed spiritual freedom. He had accordingly turned against Nicolae Ceaușescu, the former communist dictator of Romania, while ignoring other European communist tyrannies. In 1983 he had publicly opposed Ceaușescu's suppression of Christianity. The following year, after reading a letter in *The Times* describing a particular horror in Romania, he invited Jessica Douglas-Home, the wife of the newspaper's editor, to brief him at Sandringham. She and a group of friends had established the Mihai Eminescu Trust (MET) to help Romanian dissidents.

In 1984, to create the 'New Socialist Man' and impose 'rural systematisation', Ceaușescu had begun to demolish hundreds of historic buildings in Bucharest and to destroy the country's unique peasant culture. Thirteen thousand ancient villages, including their churches and graveyards, were targeted. Farming communities, many dating back to the twelfth century, were coerced into appalling urban tower blocks. Charles was shocked. For some years he had privately criticised the British government's friendly relations with Ceaușescu, whose state visit in 1978 had included a night in Buckingham Palace. On 27 April 1989 he publicly attacked Ceaușescu's vandalism in a speech to MET supporters in London. Later he confessed to Douglas-Home that he had doubts whether his rebuke was wise. As he was speaking, he wrote, he had 'a terrible knotted feeling in the pit of my tummy as [if] the courage is plucked up from somewhere deep inside … But there is something, somewhere, telling one that I wouldn't be true to myself if I did stay quiet instead of taking the risk and accepting the challenge.' Later that year, Ceaușescu was overthrown and summarily executed. His legacy was a devastated country.

Among the regions that suffered was Transylvania, north of the capital, the home of unique Saxon communities. Their secluded lives dated back to the twelfth century, when German mercenaries settled in the area to defend the Austro-Hungarian empire from invasion by the Ottoman Turks. Over the following nine hundred years these Saxons had intermarried and developed distinctive laws, systems of education, religious practices and crafts. Their customs had barely changed for centuries. After Ceaușescu's death, Douglas-Home and her group were horrified by an unexpected development.

Although the Transylvanian people had been saved from the worst of Ceaușescu's brutality, the villages were rapidly being abandoned after the German government offered financial help to Saxons if they returned to their Fatherland. Those who remained, mostly gypsies and native Romanians, lacked the Saxon skills to protect their fairytale-like idyll. Beautiful buildings, churches, bridges and cobbled streets were vandalised or left to fall into disrepair, and the last vestiges in Europe of authentic Saxon culture were threatened with extinction.

To rebuild the communities and their heritage, Douglas-Home and the MET raised money in Western Europe to hire German and

British craftsmen to teach the remaining villagers the Saxon skills of building, weaving and agriculture. The project started in 1999 with five villages around Viscri, 150 miles from Bucharest. MET's restoration of houses, churches and castles eventually spread to ninety-six villages and four towns.

To encourage interest and donations, Douglas-Home asked Charles to visit Viscri. After seeing the picturesque village and its fortified church, built in 1225, he was enraptured. Attracted by MET's devotion to the region's spiritual values, in 2000 he agreed to become the trust's patron and to support the return of the 'full architectural cohesion and harmony of mediaeval streetscapes'.

In that unspoiled wilderness, Charles had found a divine paradise. Walking through the countryside, he discovered an ancient landscape with flowers, fauna and insects that had disappeared from Britain since the Industrial Revolution. Over the next five years he returned regularly with British friends, especially John Hatt, a publisher and a favourite among the royal family, Charles's personal doctor, and a botanist who encouraged his enthusiasm for the unspoilt if impoverished countryside. Eventually, Charles asked whether he could buy a home in what he regarded as an idyllic world. In 2006 he was offered 'the Blue House', a formerly derelict building in the centre of Viscri that had been restored with the help of craftsmen brought from Ludlow in Shropshire. Over the following years Charles's staff gave the impression that the prince had paid for the house's repair (in fact, MET paid the bills) so that he could spend his time in a 'human' refuge surrounded by unspoilt countryside; or alternatively, since he was so often elsewhere, so he could rent out the house to tourists, thus supporting the local community.

Those fictions glossed over Charles's familiar way with his enthusiasms. Although he did organise the construction of an efficient sewerage system for the town, he only ever spent two nights in the Blue House. On subsequent visits to Romania he stayed with Count Tibor Kálnoky, the Hungarian owner of a comfortable hunting lodge about forty miles away. That relationship led to a breakdown between Charles and MET's staff. To their anger, after buying another house in the Saxon area, Charles sold it to Kálnoky, provoking protests fed by the Romanians' historic antagonism towards Hungarians. And then, with Kálnoky's help, Charles bought a series of houses in Valea Zalanului, in the Hungarian part of Transylvania.

For one week every year he enjoyed the region's countryside with British friends, showing increasing ambivalence towards the plight of the Saxon areas and Romanian culture. Some Romanians in the capital praised Charles for highlighting their country's advantages, but those living in the Saxon areas accused him of insensitivity, not least for forging a financial partnership with Kálnoky.

In 2013 he resigned from MET to establish a rival foundation, but kept the Blue House as a headquarters and a guest house. His new organisation duplicated MET's work. Its scale was small by comparison, yet in a speech in Bucharest in March 2017, after receiving the Order of the Star of Romania in recognition of his charity work in the country, he would claim to have trained 120 local people and architects. This embellishment of the facts irritated MET's directors. 'You can achieve anything in life if you do not mind who takes the credit,' commented Jessica Douglas-Home, who otherwise remained grateful to Charles for his sympathy to her dying husband and his concern for her afterwards.

Given Charles's mindset, one reason he alighted on Transylvania was to overcome embarrassments elsewhere. Putting his trust in the ancient Saxon way of life justified his objections to modern science. Unmentioned were the false pieties exposed by his sudden enthusiasm. To enjoy the beauty of a pre-industrial region, Charles flew to Romania in a private jet. After landing, he hastened to live in comfort rather than among the farming community. Like so many ideological rebels, he never explained these contradictions. He seemed instead to hope that the glowing local accolades would help offset the criticism about the controversies he ignited in Britain, including his promotion of complementary medicine.

In the wake of the Foundation of Integrated Medicine's collapse, Michael Dixon had helped to create a new entity, the College of Integrated Medicine. Charles was not formally involved, but he was present at meetings after the college was established. 'He accepted that he'd got to be patient,' said Dixon, appointed as director.

'Instead of banging tiny fists against steel walls,' Charles reminded him, 'we have to become part of the conventional health service involving doctors and nurses.'

Sensing continued opposition from the medical profession, Dixon soon dropped the danger word 'integrated', and renamed the organisation 'The College of Medicine'. Orthodox British doctors now agreed to become advisers. The college's first conference was followed by a dinner, sponsored by Nelsons Homoeopathic Remedies and hosted by Charles, at St James's Palace.

The gap between the prince and his critics remained wide. 'He was totally depressed by the opposition to what he was trying to achieve,' said Dixon, who also attacked Edzard Ernst as 'cruel' for personalising Charles as 'the enemy'. Ernst, he wrote, inhabited 'a grey and nihilistic desert that denies the role of the doctor as healer and condemns us to being slaves of population-based statistical totalitarianism'.

The deadlock with Ernst about the relevance of scientific evidence to assess the value of complementary therapies was irresolvable. But Charles refused to be deterred. In 2009 the duchy launched 'Detox Tincture', made up of liquid extracts of dandelion and artichoke, charging £10 for each fifty-millilitre bottle, with the promise of eliminating poisons from the body. Instantly Ernst condemned the prince as a 'snake-oil salesman' peddling an 'expensive hoax'. No such mixture, he said, could detoxify a body. Alerted, the Advertising Standards Authority demanded changes to the claims. In turn, Charles wrote a succession of letters to the Medicines and Healthcare Products Regulatory Agency (MHRA) asking for the rules governing the labelling of herbal products to be relaxed. After amendments to the label, the tincture remained on sale.

Charles's obstinacy was indefatigable. Whenever he was defeated, he tried again to tilt the balance in his favour. Unlike Ernst, he had access to powerbrokers. 'I cannot bear people suffering unnecessarily when a complementary approach could make a real difference,' he told the new health secretary Andy Burnham, in 2009. The proof of homeopathy, he argued, was the 'spectacularly good results' of Peter Hain's initiative in Northern Ireland. Charles urged Burnham to approve the NHS's use of homeopathic medicines in England as well. The pliant Burnham agreed. At this time, 20 per cent of Britons were spending a total of £1.6 billion every year on complementary medicines, part of a $100 billion annual global trade.

Charles fused homeopathy and other alternative therapies with his environmental campaign. The 'overuse and abuse of antibiotics', he told environmentalists, 'could lead to a potentially disastrous scenario.' In 2016 he would reveal his use of homeopathic remedies for the duchy's cattle. Even some ardent republicans were impressed: they might distrust the missionary, but they supported his mission. Charles's cause had won support in Whitehall despite the disapproval of some MPs.

In 2010 the House of Commons Scientific and Technology Committee dismissed homeopathy as an 'active deception', no more effective than sugar pills. Although the committee acknowledged that homeopathy scored a 70 per cent satisfaction rating among its users, it recommended that, to avoid bestowing an 'unjustified badge of authority', the NHS should not support such treatments. The committee's finding was rejected. No government, especially on the eve of a general election, could afford to alienate a large section of the public. Popular approval for Charles stretched across the political parties as he notched up another small victory.

Three years later he met Jeremy Hunt, the Tory health secretary, at Clarence House. The new minister was a supporter of homeopathy, and reassured the prince that the NHS would continue to consider the use of complementary therapies despite their use being condemned by the BMA as 'witchcraft'.

There was little that Edzard Ernst could do but accuse the Prince of Wales of using his position 'to hinder scientific research while actively promoting quackery'. Charles's 'pseudo-science', he continued, 'constitutes an attack on rationality and treason against progress in healthcare'. The prince's supporters in turn denounced Ernst for wielding 'sinister powers of indoctrination' over the medical profession. Ernst could not win. Sensitive to the trend, the sponsors of his university department withdrew their financial support, and in 2011 the unit was closed. Simon Mills, one of the original supporters of Charles's campaign, acknowledged a bittersweet victory: 'Ernst did expose a vacuum and he was not punctured. We didn't deliver a fully argued opinion against him, or incorporate the old skills as they've done in Europe.' The prince's beliefs excluded any concern for his opponents being cast into the wilderness. He had moved on.

At the very moment that Ernst's department was being wound up, Charles spoke about the West facing 'a crisis of the soul' and in particular a growing risk to the environment. One of its protectors, he thought, was Islam. In a speech to the Oxford Centre for Islamic Studies, he advocated the religion's 'spiritual principles', which

prescribed 'no separation between man and nature'. To convince the
doubters of Islam's 'sacred traditions' towards the environment, his
office told Downing Street that he wanted to use the G20 summit in
London in April 2009 to host a climate change conference. The
headline would repeat his warning to a group of businessmen in Rio
de Janeiro: 'We only have a hundred months to act to save the world.'
Clarence House sent out invitations to national leaders, including
several who were not invited to the summit. Among those who
accepted were eight national leaders, including Kevin Rudd from
Australia, Nicolas Sarkozy from France, Germany's Angela Merkel,
Italy's Silvio Berlusconi, and those from Guyana, Indonesia, Japan
and Norway, and Hillary Clinton, America's secretary of state.
Charles had cannily anticipated the politicians' interest in the
Copenhagen climate change conference scheduled for the end of the
year.

One instant success was an agreement by thirty-five countries to
invest $4 billion over three years to stop the destruction of rain-
forests. The conference also identified as an act of villainy the EU's
regulation that palm oil should be added to diesel for use as a bio
fuel, an incentive that had persuaded the Indonesian government to
increase the deforestation of ancient woodlands so it could plant
palm oil trees. Charles promptly set up a Rainforest Project to offer
to pay Indonesia to stop cutting down its trees. The only irritation
was his conduct. Once again, he borrowed the ideas and staff of a
well-established British organisation for his new charity, rather than
cooperating with the existing and effective charity.

Charles sought acclaim for his crusade. For twenty-two years, he
wrote in a film script, 'nobody wanted to know about the
environment except a few people who thought it was pretty crazy'.
He recalled, 'I was described as old-fashioned, out of touch and
anti-science, a dreamer in the modern world, too sophisticated for
"obsolete" ideas and techniques.' Up to that point his audience might
have been sympathetic, but some potential supporters became
sceptical after reading *Harmony*. Like his claim that 'We only have
a hundred months to act to save the world,' his new hyperbole also
cost him support.

Charles had correctly predicted that his opinions about imminent doom would 'induce howls of laughter from the usual suspects
and unleash the full throttle of their mockery'; but the future king

was certain that he was in the right. He was on a mission to abolish unquestioning trust in science, which he criticised as being 'entirely based upon the gathering of results that come from subjecting physical phenomena to scientific experiment', and to launch a revolution against the 'great juggernaut of industrialisation'. He was enraptured, he admitted, 'by the era before scientists, planners and socialists upset the old order'. In the pre-industrial world he so admired, people believed in God. Even better was the era before the agricultural revolution, because God's creation was not challenged. In the way of life ordained by the heart and soul of that era, everyone knew their place – and that had been ruined by globalisation. 'We seem to have lost that understanding of the whole of nature and the universe as a living entity,' he wrote. The Earth could no longer afford consumerism; the 'age of convenience' should be terminated. 'The destruction of Nature is ultimately the destruction of our own inner being,' Charles continued. 'We need to understand that we are born into a universe that has meaning and purpose.' He urged the world to abandon its current lifestyle and revert to the pre-industrial era, like the Saxons in Transylvania. In that spiritual wonderland, placed within the Divine Order, Charles presented himself as 'the defender of Nature. Full stop.' And he did not occupy that role by chance, but by destiny: 'I can only imagine that I find myself being born into this position for a purpose.'

Like all sages, Charles was inflexible, especially about his views on genetically modified foods. Despite twelve million farmers planting GM crops across the world, he reasserted that their use was leading to 'the biggest environmental disaster of all time'. In response to his apocalyptic predictions, Alison Smith, a professor of plant biochemistry, accused him of stoking fears based on his 'lack of scientific understanding'. Millions of people had eaten GM food since 1996, she said, without any evidence of it endangering health – although it was true that biodiversity would suffer. Steadfastly, Charles refused to debate the issue. He did not trust scientific research, and so would not respond to the challenge by Phil Woolas, the environment minister, to produce any evidence that GM crops were harmful. In his mind, his 'truth' was answer enough.

Charles appeared oblivious to the contrast between what he preached and what he practised. At the beginning of 2009 he chartered a jet for a ten-day environmental tour of Chile, Brazil and Ecuador. The cost was £700,000. Two months later he flew in a chartered Airbus A319 to Italy and Germany to promote the British government's climate change policies. The cost was £80,000, instead of £15,000 for scheduled flights. As usual, his justification was convenience and his inordinate amount of luggage – including his own organic beef and other special foods to be cooked in British embassies. On his return he used the royal train for a five-day 'green' tour to encourage young people to 'tread more lightly on our planet'. That journey cost £90,000.

Soon after, he travelled on the royal train to a Manchester conference, pulled by a steam engine that produced ninety times more carbon dioxide than a family car. To his credit, he did use the train for meetings: first, for a one-day summit aimed at preventing the demolition of old wool mills in Burnley, and on another day in an effort to preserve the potteries in Stoke-on-Trent. At key moments in those discussions, he made a carefully timed entrance after all the rival parties had gathered. 'Right, how far have you got?' he would ask, then contribute to a solution. Those invited to the carriage were impressed, but the vast majority of Britons, suffering in the wake of the financial crash, remained at best neutral about the prince's lifestyle and views.

'Life isn't easy,' said Michael Peat, repeating his employer's mantra, as he explained to journalists that although Charles's income for 2009 was £17.1 million, his staff had grown to 149 people. 'We are trying to be prudent. We are mindful of the current economic climate and are obviously always looking for economies.' When pushed to explain, he joked, 'To save more money, we could cut the prince and duchess down to fewer meals a day.'

Camilla's requirements were not helpful. To promote his campaign to protect the rainforests, Charles had insisted on a chartered plane for a Far East tour including a visit to Brunei. The total cost was £694,000. After a short spell on the tour, Camilla made her familiar complaint that she hated flying, suffered from jet lag, and felt ill in hot climates. She was too exhausted, she said, to continue to Brunei. 'I need to plan Charles's birthday,' she said on her return home, although Michael Fawcett as usual was undertaking the chores.

For future trips, Charles agreed that Camilla should leave in advance for 'acclimatisation'. The next official tour was to Mexico.

She stayed at Carlisle Bay in Antigua, a luxury hotel of which her former husband was a director of the holding company, but she did stay on for Charles's time in Mexico. He was delighted. And the new coalition government had become reconciled to the couple's idiosyncrasies. Charles's personal agenda, it decided, could be helpful, especially his sympathy for Islam.

Every year, Charles renewed his relationship with the rulers and their ministers along the Gulf. In 2010, after William Hague's appointment as foreign secretary, he sought Charles's help to restore relations, and later to promote the sale of seventy-two Euro-fighter Typhoon jets to the UAE. The sales pitch would fail, but Charles's new role was used to justify an annual increase of 3.6 per cent in his expenses. His personal income from the duchy also rose to £18.3 million. At the same time, the queen's expenses were reduced by 26 per cent in real terms over three years. His mother's strictly controlled finances did not interest him.

27

Scrabbling for Cash

Manuel Colonques knew that flattering Michael Fawcett would secure access to Charles, and with that the prince's invaluable promotion of Porcelanosa tiles. Accordingly, in 2010 the valet was invited to the wedding of Colonques's daughter, and was listed by the company as Charles's 'private secretary'. In the Spanish media, the British guest was called 'Sir Michael Fawcett'.

Through Fawcett, Charles had over the years accepted about £1.6 million from Colonques for the Architectural Foundation, more money for Dumfries House, and also a substantial donation for the Prince's Foundation for Children and the Arts. That last donation was the price for allowing Colonques to invite 250 guests to Buckingham Palace for a dinner captured by a ¡Hola! photographer. Under the headline 'Prince of Wales Hosts a Gala Dinner in Honour of Porcelanosa', ¡Hola!'s thirty-six pages of photographs illustrated Charles promoting the Spanish tiles. The company faithfully abided by the prince's stipulation that the photographs should not be available to the British media. 'Ask Manuel if I made him look good,' Charles said through an interpreter at the end of yet another dinner, this one for a hundred architects at St James's Palace. Colonques's inability to speak English meant he could not enjoy a natural conversation with his host, but he did provide tiles the following year for the kitchen and bathrooms at Birkhall, and thereafter for other royal homes, including Highgrove's garden.

In May 2001, at Charles's suggestion, Porcelanosa had exhibited an Islamic garden at the Chelsea Flower Show with cypresses, fruit trees, a marble fountain, terracotta pathways and seventy thousand handmade mosaic tiles. That same year, the prince flew to Spain to open a new wing of the company's factory and be its guest of honour at a dinner for 452 people. In return, the company agreed that an extended version of the Islamic garden would be installed at its expense at Highgrove. 'We gave the garden to him, and he repaid us with a dinner for our clients,' company director Pedro Pseudo admitted. As part of this arrangement, Colonques sought and received an invitation to Prince William's wedding to Kate Middleton on 29 April 2011, a watershed moment for the monarchy. In the run-up to the ceremony, Colonques boasted to Spanish journalists that he had provided the tiles for the young couple's personal bathrooms.

If Charles's relationship with his parents was set in a permanent frost, his connection with his sons was almost as uneasy. He painfully recalled a visit to Kensington Palace while Diana was still alive, and they were small children. Young Harry ran towards him, then pulled up. 'Mummy says I mustn't,' he cried, just as Charles was about to hug him. Diana had poisoned the boys' minds towards their father. After her death, the revelations about both parents' adultery and much worse haunted their youth. Grieving, William would say, was especially difficult because 'it was so raw', and with Diana's story so widely known, there was minimal privacy. Since leaving university, William had not shared his father's interests or offered to continue his charities. Specifically, he refused involvement in the Prince's Trust. Detached from politics and from Charles's cultural pursuits, he appeared a very different royal from his father. Charles's relationship with William and Harry was not helped by Camilla's presence, a constant reminder of their mother's torment.

Having failed to interest his sons in classical music, Charles invited Kate to her first opera, Bellini's *La Sonnambula* (The Sleepwalker) at Covent Garden. As usual, Fawcett organised for dinner to be sent from Clarence House and served in the Royal Box during the interval on Charles's personal china and using his silver cutlery. Sadly, the prince had ignored warnings about the production. 'It's awful,' he later told the Opera House's chief executive. His hope that Kate might be converted to classical music was lost. Like William, she preferred *Phantom of the Opera*.

Charles had a new fear: that the public's attention was switching to William and Kate. The Canadian government had told Buckingham Palace that a proposed tour by Charles and Camilla should be delayed, so that it would follow a visit by William and Kate after their wedding. The reaction in Clarence House was mixed. Charles was disappointed, while Camilla was unconcerned about Kate taking the limelight. 'She didn't give a damn,' noted Robert Higdon. 'She loved Charles and wanted him to be a success; Charles saw Kate and William as the new stars and feared he'd be in trouble.' Camilla also dismissed the presumption that Kate would be the first commoner queen. 'That'll be me,' she would say with a laugh.

Regardless of the opinion polls, that was certainly Charles's intention. In a public display of her status, Camilla had lunch with Kate at a Knightsbridge hotel just before the wedding ceremony, to give her advice about marriage. Many of Diana's old friends were not invited to the wedding – taken off the guest list, it was said, by Camilla. Neither Tony Blair nor Gordon Brown was invited, but Jon Zammett, the senior public relations director for Audi, was in the Abbey. Many royals drove Audis, and the company had agreed to sponsor a charitable tour of California in July for the newlyweds. Like his father, William was not one to let an opportunity go to waste, and also among the guests were Lily Safra, Don Gosling, Jürgen Pierburg (the nephew of a former Nazi SS officer and a generous donor to Dumfries House) and Joe Allbritton of Riggs Bank.

Two years earlier, at Charles's request, Higdon had persuaded Allbritton to invest about £500,000 in Duchy Originals, the prince's food brand that produced and sold organic oat biscuits, sausages and a growing number of other products in duchy shops. By way of thanks, in 2007 Allbritton and his wife rode in the fourth carriage behind the queen at Ascot. Now, on the eve of the wedding, Allbritton was asked for more money, this time to save Duchy Originals. Although in the past the brand had contributed about £7 million towards the Duchy of Cornwall's income, in 2009 bad management had caused £3.3 million losses. Temporarily, Duchy Originals managed to survive with a loan from the Prince's Charities Foundation, a sensitive arrangement because the financial demands of Dumfries House were depriving his other charities of funds. Not only were they financially stretched, but Charles's £2.5 million investment with three property tycoons in an environmental development project in Wales had ended badly. Once again, poor financial management was destabilising his philanthropic ambitions. The saviour was Allbritton, who at Higdon's request agreed to give

Duchy Originals $3.25 million in exchange for the rights to sell its products in America, and to spend $2.5 million on the American launch of the brand.

Then he was asked for another favour. Just before William and Kate's wedding, Charles agreed to meet President Barack Obama in Washington. The Foreign Office refused to provide a private jet, and insisted that he fly on British Airways. His foreign travel costs, a civil servant pointed out, had increased over the previous year by 18 per cent, to nearly £2 million. He would also spend £29,786 on a round trip with Camilla on a private jet to Balmoral for a four-day holiday, and £19,583 for a day trip from Aberdeen to London after the capital was blighted by riots. Furious that Peat had failed to persuade the RAF to provide a suitable plane, Charles asked Leslie Ferrar, his office's treasurer, appointed in 2006 to supervise the charities, to telephone Higdon.

'Can you find a private jet for Charles's trip?' she asked.

Higdon was not surprised. 'It was quite normal,' he said, 'for me to call and ask people like Joe Allbritton, "Can we borrow your G5?" People like the Allbrittons got a fascination of lending Charles their trophy plane. The gift of their plane gave legitimacy to folk from Texas and Colorado.'

Allbritton agreed that his Gulfstream would fly empty across the Atlantic to collect Charles, transport him to Washington, and then, after returning him to Wiltshire, fly back empty to Texas. When asked to justify the flights, a Clarence House spokesman replied, 'In the current economic climate, it was felt that it was right to accept the Allbrittons' offer.'

Joe and Barbara Allbritton duly took their place in Westminster Abbey for the royal wedding. 'Other patrons,' said Higdon bitterly, 'were not invited.' Among those off the list was Kip Forbes, an important donor to Charles's Foundation in America. Forbes turned his anger on Higdon. The fundraiser himself was also in some difficulty. American donors' interest in Charles and Camilla was still declining. The foundation's annual revenues had fallen to less than £1 million, and half of that income was spent on Higdon himself. 'When I wasn't invited to the wedding,' he admitted, 'I knew I was in trouble.'

Four months later he was shocked by what he interpreted as the high-handed treatment of Joe Allbritton by Leslie Ferrar. In

September 2011 Higdon discovered that during Ferrar's visit to Washington 'the auditors had gone into Duchy Originals'. To save Charles's reputation and the company from insolvency, the brand's licence rights had been sold to Waitrose.

'What about the American rights?' Higdon asked Ferrar. 'Have you secretly sold them?'

According to Higdon, Ferrar looked surprised. 'You know, Robert,' she replied, 'people are very uncomfortable about you and your relationship with Prince Charles.' She went on to say that Higdon's familiarity with the prince had crossed the line. He acted like a friend, while in reality he was a servant.

'Is my relationship with Charles unprofessional?' asked Higdon.

'Everyone believes it is,' said Ferrar.

'You're out of your mind,' exploded Higdon, and their argument escalated.

Higdon dug deeper, and discovered that Duchy Originals' global rights had indeed been sold; the Allbritton investment, which he had delivered, had been ignored. Ferrar subsequently insisted that she had told Allbritton the full details, albeit after the sale, and the two sides eventually agreed an amicable settlement.

In the aftermath, despite fourteen years' loyal service, Higdon was fired. The reason, he assumed, was his alcoholism. News of his departure was leaked to a newspaper, for which he blamed Michael Fawcett. 'He's one of the most horrible people I've met in my life,' Higdon complained. 'It was just such a nasty story. I didn't do anything to anyone. I just did my job. I put up with the corrupt, mean, vicious people Charles is surrounded by. The most horrible people I've ever worked with. They used my resources. I didn't like their Machiavellian behaviour, the dishonesty. They weren't straight.' He also criticised Ferrar: 'We were a team, and Leslie played the alcoholic card and it hit the wall at 100 mph. I had raised $40 million, and it baffles me that they wanted to fire me. They were ungrateful and stupid.'

As with Bolland and others, neither Charles nor Camilla called Higdon after his departure. 'I loved Charles and I loved Camilla. It hurts that I had a relationship with them and then no "Goodbye." Not even a Christmas card. It was hard. In their world it's all about them. Charles probably doesn't know about the casualties, but Camilla does.'

Bolland called Camilla to ask about Higdon. 'Yes,' she replied, 'there was a problem of too many cocktails.'

In New York, Joan Rivers was upset by the dismissal. Not only was Higdon a friend of long standing, but his contribution to both the prince's profile in America and his finances did not deserve to be passed over so carelessly. For a time she considered breaking with Charles, but was persuaded by calls from London to stay loyal.

Not without coincidence, Higdon's firing was followed by other changes at Clarence House – a total overhaul of the prince's top team. The clearing of the decks included the departures of Leslie Ferrar and Paddy Haverson, Charles's media spokesman. To some it appeared that the queen's private secretary Christopher Geidt was orchestrating the start of a new era, but others denied that Buckingham Palace had any influence. The departures, said Charles's spokesman, were coincidental rather than the outcome of a conspiracy. The resignation of Geoffrey Kent as chairman of the American Foundation after twenty-five successful years contradicted that bland explanation. Ominously, Fawcett was present when Charles personally told Kent that he would be replaced by an unknown American who lacked the same relationships and flair to lure rich donors. Fawcett's influence was always paramount. The truth was that employment by Charles invariably ended in tears, but the gloss was advantageous: to make Charles more acceptable as the future monarch, he was to be surrounded by new staff.

Above all, at the age of sixty-one and after nine years' service, Michael Peat announced that he too was to leave. He wanted to earn more money, and his wife complained about Charles's constant telephone calls – at night, at weekends and while they were on holiday. Among his future employers would be Roman Abramovich, the Russian oligarch and owner of Chelsea FC, who was closely associated with Vladimir Putin. At Peat's request, Abramovich had provided his helicopter to ferry Charles across Gloucestershire for social visits. In gratitude, and with an eye to securing Peat's future loyalty, Charles agreed to generous severance terms. After the deaths of Diana, the queen mother and Princess Margaret, their staff had been told to leave their apartments in Kensington Palace within twenty-eight days. Peat, however, was allowed to remain in his five-bedroom flat for a further eleven months, a reward for increasing the duchy's annual income from £10 million to £18.3 million, and its value to £712 million.

Peat was replaced by William Nye, a forty-six-year-old former Treasury official. Nye was not allocated an apartment in Kensington Palace, or anywhere else. Unlike Peat, he was prepared to forge the close relationship with Buckingham Palace that had never come to pass with Peat. Also unlike his predecessor, he did not welcome telephone calls after 6 p.m. – a restriction that Charles would not tolerate for long.

Peat did not bequeath a perfect legacy, especially for the charities. In spite of Tom Shebbeare's efforts, Charles had set up even more of them, the latest being the Countryside Fund, intended to highlight rural problems. Over twenty chairmen were still bidding for his time. Without coordination, the same problems that had been identified in 1997 and again in 2003 had re-emerged. The prince's charities were bureaucratic, expensive, overmanned and increasingly ineffective. Traditional Arts, meant to be a self-financing charity supporting artists, was losing £2 million a year. Business in the Community, under its new director Stephen Howard, was criticised as unimaginative and institutionalised, and lacking its former influence in the business community. The Prince's Foundation for the Built Environment had, despite serious debts, dispatched full-time officials to the Galápagos Islands, Mumbai and Sierra Leone. The Prince's Charities Foundation had a £4 million deficit without any reserves. The income of the Prince's Trust, the flagship, was declining, and relied on an annual £15.8 million from the government. To cover a recurring yearly deficit of £2.6 million, the duchy lent the trust about £9 million. In parallel, the trust's success was also declining. Civil servants discovered that despite its contractual commitments, the Prince's Trust could not provide enough people to join the government's new National Citizen Service. Even the more flourishing charities struggled to survive the endless management meetings: Arts & Business, which had been successfully managed since 1985 by Colin Tweedy, lost its autonomy in 2012. Many of these financial problems had become more acute since the purchase of Dumfries House in 2007.

An added complication in the prince's life was Camilla's demand for private dinners – jolly gatherings of friends. She wanted Charles to be rid of some responsibilities and people. Among her targets was

Sane, a thriving charity for the mentally ill that he had energetically supported. She appeared to have taken against Marjorie Wallace, the charity's resolute founder and director, who had been close to Charles during his troubles with Diana. Fawcett made onerous financial demands on Sane as a condition for Charles to continue fundraising. Then Tom Shebbeare intervened and told Wallace that Charles had decided to focus on complementary medicine rather than mental health. 'Camilla didn't give a damn,' recalled Higdon. The prince's association with Sane duly ended.

At that moment, Shebbeare hoped his principal task was about to be accomplished. Over the past six years he had forlornly attempted to merge the charities' administration under one roof. By 2010 he had found a perfect site in King's Cross, but Charles Dunstone, the chairman of the Prince's Trust, opposed the move, and won Charles's backing. That decision set the seal on Shebbeare's career with Charles's charities. He offered his resignation to Peat, only to be told that Peat had 'beaten you to it'.

Shebbeare's departure coincided with another challenge to the charities' finances, especially from Dumfries House. Besides repaying the original £43 million for the purchase, millions of pounds were needed for reconstruction and new outbuildings to accommodate the working community. A further £600,000 was required for annual maintenance. To bring in additional money, the house was let out for weddings and conferences, was put into use as a hotel, and also promoted as a tourist attraction.

Three months after Jonathan Bryant described his appointment as Dumfries's first manager as 'a dream come true' he was replaced by Fawcett. Just as he had done at Birkhall, by then rebuilt and open for weddings and conferences, Charles's indispensable aide provided Dumfries's guests with 'the Sandringham experience'. They would be greeted by a retinue of servants – maids for women and valets for men – who unpacked their suitcases, ironed their clothes and filled the well-furnished rooms with flowers. In the previous year Premier Mode, Fawcett's catering company, had made a profit of about £250,000. Over the following years it would perform even better.

Within his first six months at Dumfries, Fawcett arranged four fundraising events hosted by Charles. In cultivating his network of relationships, the valet-turned-consultant appeared indiscriminate, so long as the millionaires donated sufficient cash. Among those targeted were the Indian businessmen Lakshmi Mittal and the Hinduja brothers, and Mick Flick, the son of a convicted Nazi war criminal whose mines and factories killed thousands of European slave labourers during the Second World War. Others invited included Hans Kristian Rausing, the Tetra Pak billionaire and former drug addict, who gave £10 million, and Cyrus Vandrevala, another Indian businessman, who contributed £200,000 for an adventure playground. The hedge fund operator Michael Hintze gave £5 million. That relationship had started after Fawcett organised Hintze's fifty-fifth birthday party in 2008. Coincidentally, Charles was at that moment seeking money for Dumfries House, and he accepted Hintze's invitation to the party along with four hundred other guests. Soon after Hintze made his donation, he was appointed chairman of the Prince's Foundation for the Built Environment.

Within four years, Fawcett had helped Charles raise about £19 million to repay the loan from his charitable foundation. More money was raised from rich Sunni Muslims, especially Saudis and Qataris, including Dr Mahfouz Marei Mubarak bin Mahfouz, a forty-five-year-old Saudi businessman, and Sheikh Hamad bin Abdullah Al Thani, who had presumably forgiven Charles for the debacle over Chelsea Barracks. Like all donors, both Dr Mahfouz and Sheikh Hamad were promised that a bench, garden or fountain in the grounds of properties they had never visited would be named in their honour.

The seamless process of money-raising would even recruit the queen to travel to the Goring Hotel in London to meet Sheikh Hamad at a charity reception. None of the donors believed their money was wasted. Charles had hired unemployed local young people to train as plasterers and craftsmen to restore the house and garden, or as chefs to work in the kitchen. Those young people owed their enhanced lives to him. During a tour of the property, one group of visitors listened for more than an hour while Charles explained the importance of preserving traditional farmyard sheds. Fastidious about every tree, bench and compost heap, he soon created a garden at Dumfries that was as immaculate as Highgrove's.

Charles's eccentricities were often on show at events to raise money. At one dinner to honour the German industrialist Jürgen Pierburg for his donations, Charles sat between Pierburg's wife

Clarissa and Lily Safra. To Clarissa Pierburg's embarrassment, the prince sat with his back to her throughout the meal and spoke only to Safra. By Charles's reckoning, his behaviour was not a social sin, but his position in society affirming itself. At another dinner at Dumfries House to thank the Armenian businessman Bob Manoukian, an erstwhile partner of Prince Jefri of Brunei, Fawcett, wearing a dinner jacket and with a large diamond stud in his tie, placed himself next to Manoukian's wife. After Charles left the table at 10.30, Fawcett announced that dinner was over, and ordered the guests to leave.

28

Marking Time

In June 2012, the sixtieth anniversary of the queen's accession was seized on by Buckingham Palace as another opportunity to promote the monarchy. There were concerts, military parades, fly-pasts and a documentary tribute. The TV programme, narrated by Charles, showed the heir and the queen animatedly watching private film of him and his sister Princess Anne as children on the beach in Norfolk and on the royal yacht. Charles had good reason to involve himself in such a positive record of sentimental family moments. Bathing in the glow of his mother's popularity would ease his succession.

The following day, the oldest monarch in Britain's history stood with her husband for four hours in the rain on a boat proceeding along the Thames. Despite the BBC's poor production, the spectacle of two elderly people, devoted to duty and service, united the nation. Eighty per cent of Britons, according to the polls, trusted the monarchy. Twenty-four hours later, Philip fell sick as a result of his exposure to the weather. 'Ladies and gentlemen,' appealed Charles to a huge crowd in front of Buckingham Palace for a pop concert and fireworks, 'if we shout loud enough he might just hear us in hospital.' The queen was visibly moved by the roar of 'Philip, Philip, Philip.' Much more could have gone wrong, but the biggest celebration since the coronation appeared to have restored the monarchy to its previous high point, Charles and Diana's wedding thirty years before. One rare blip was an exchange overheard inside the palace between Charles and his mother. 'Have you tried my new strawberry jam?' he asked. 'Another time,' she replied.

One noticeable difference for the public was the entourage around the queen on the palace's balcony. With Philip in hospital, just five royals – Charles, Camilla, Harry, William and Kate – stood beside her. That reduction, so long orchestrated by Charles, had taken fifteen years to accomplish – which was, as Robin Janvrin told a colleague, 'a short time in the life of the monarchy'. All six of the family were on their best behaviour. Discreet Kate was utterly supportive of William, a paradigm of virtue; Harry, on the eve of his second deployment to Afghanistan, was Britain's popular 'lad'; while Charles and Camilla seemed to have overcome their worst moments.

Anne, Andrew and Edward and their families were not invited. Andrew was particularly angry at the snub. Denied even an invitation to the queen's lunch for the livery companies in Westminster Hall, he stayed at home in Windsor Great Park fuming about his elder brother. Charles, however, had general support. 'Andrew is a menace and a rudderless wreck,' growled one of the queen's confidants.

Andrew's rake's progress had started in 2010. The release by WikiLeaks of a stash of American diplomatic cables included a report by the US ambassador in Kyrgyzstan of the prince's 'rude' and 'cocky' remarks about the French and the Americans during brunch in 2008 with British businessmen in the capital, Bishkek. The ambassador's most damaging comment mentioned Andrew's tolerant attitude towards corruption.

The WikiLeaks release appeared at the same time as more revelations about Andrew's relationship with Jeffrey Epstein, by then jailed for sexual offences involving underage girls. Andrew's reputation sank further after he was accused of a relationship with a young girl he had met through Epstein. Although there was no actual evidence of guilt, Buckingham Palace urged newspaper and TV editors to ignore the allegations, pleading, 'This is about the monarchy.' Andrew would later admit, 'You don't get it right all the time. You just have to get on with it. It doesn't bother me really. It's just part of life's rich tapestry.'

Andrew was not only compelled to give up his post as trade ambassador, but also to resolve the latest scandals surrounding his former wife Sarah Ferguson. Plagued by debt, she had been recorded asking an undercover journalist employed by the *News of the World* for £500,000 for access to Andrew. In a separate incident, she accepted yet another free holiday, this time on Richard Branson's Caribbean island Necker, to celebrate the tycoon's sixtieth birthday. Such indulgence in unearned privileges, especially by 'freebie Fergie', always frayed the public's sympathy for the royals, and suggested some ulterior motive on the part of whoever the host might be. Despite Andrew's protests, at Charles's request his daughters Beatrice and Eugenie were removed from official duties and lost their police protection officers.

Andrew's enforced departure from public life was matched by Charles's increasing prominence. Every week he took another step to build support. He and Camilla travelled down The Mall with the queen in an open carriage during a state visit, and at the next opening of Parliament, the two would sit next to her. In a gradual shift of duties, Charles took investitures, met diplomats and chaired the Privy Council.

But just as everything seemed to be under control, a website showed a video of Harry, drunk and undressed, playing strip poker with naked young women in a Las Vegas hotel. Shortly afterwards, a French magazine published photos of Kate topless on holiday in France. The royal family was reeling. Then Prince Philip delivered another blow.

In a snub to his elder son, he assigned the shooting rights at Sandringham to Princess Anne and her husband Tim Laurence, and the shooting at Balmoral to Edward. For Charles, an excellent shot despite handicapping himself with a pair of less powerful twenty-eight-bore guns, to be shunted off the royal estates was an embarrassment. He resolved the insult by renting the challenging Invercauld estate grouse moor near Birkhall, and friends' estates, for pheasant shoots. The emotional warfare with his father never abated.

As he approached his sixty-fifth birthday – his £500,000 party at Buckingham Palace would be financed by the Indian businessman Cyrus Vandrevala – Charles despaired that while every royal mishap was given widespread coverage, there was little interest in his official activities. 'He bangs on about the same issues,' said a senior BBC editor who regularly rebuffed invitations to film the prince. 'He's repetitive, dull, tedious and worthy.'

To improve his image, Charles hired Kristina Kyriacou, formerly the spokeswoman for the singer Cheryl Cole. Kyriacou's task was to stifle the myths, in all their glorious variety: that he demanded seven boiled eggs lined up for breakfast, talked to his plants, did not like a single modern building, and relied on untested herbal potions rather than orthodox medicines. More importantly, his staff sought to tone down his public speeches about architecture, alternative medicine and the environment, and to reduce his public appearances in a black tie.

Their efforts were undermined by Charles himself. In a video broadcast in 2013, he again extolled the countryside's 'spiritual' dimension, waxing lyrical about 'the tractors in the fields, the skilled workers, the livestock, the growing crops and the landscape's biodiversity, now so much under threat from climate change, diseases and insensitive development'. Shortly afterwards, he allowed the Duchy of Cornwall to sell fifty-five acres of prime farming land in the Tregurra Valley, east of Truro, for a housing development, a Waitrose supermarket and a huge car park. 'Prince Charles must have the skin of a rhinoceros not to recognise the hypocrisy of it,' complained the farmers who grew winter feed and grazed their cattle on that land.

Readers of *Country Life* magazine were also puzzled. In the November issue, guest edited by Charles, he wrote about the 'folly' of losing agricultural land to developers, and condemned supermarket chains for squeezing the incomes of farmers. In Truro, Waitrose ranked among the accused; but ever since the company had saved Duchy Originals from bankruptcy, it had joined the prince's angelic choir. Self-interest appeared to overrule any sympathy he might have felt for the farmers.

In another video message, recorded for Earth Day (on 22 April) and delivered on behalf of the World Wildlife Fund, he urged people to turn off their lights for the sake of the environment. At the same time, he flew eighty miles from Highgrove to Ascot in a helicopter based at Farnborough, a round distance of 250 miles. In mitigation, to show his concern about social deprivation, he invited the three party leaders, David Cameron, Nick Clegg and Ed Miliband, to Buckingham Palace to help launch a programme to encourage volunteering and provide work and activities for two million young people characterised as the 'lost generation'; and in a second campaign, to help families whose children had been killed on the streets. 'I simply can't see what I see and do nothing about it,' he said. 'I could not live with myself.'

Few could disapprove of that sentiment, but there was a marked change in the public attitude to Charles after Jonathan Dimbleby predicted in November 2013 that, as king, 'he will not shy away from issues that are contentious or controversial'. Dimbleby's authoritative echo of Charles's own refusal to 'see purdah as a likely option' contradicted Michael Peat's statement to the High Court in 2005, when he challenged the *Mail on Sunday*'s publication of Charles's Chinese journal. The prince, Peat told the judge, 'does not campaign on contentious issues'. Eight years later, Charles was still casting himself as a politician. His lifestyle, trenchant campaigns, contradictions and absence of transparency made him a target for MPs who resented his outspokenness.

His latest refusal to be accountable attracted the attention of Margaret Hodge, the feisty Labour chairman of the House of Commons Public Accounts Committee. Like her predecessor, the Tory Edward Leigh, she wondered about the duchy's rise in value to £847 million, and the fact that while Charles's income was nearly £20 million a year, his voluntary tax bill was just £4.4 million. At the outset of the committee's public hearing, Hodge questioned William Nye, and called the duchy's tax payment 'shockingly wrong'. Austin Mitchell, another Labour MP, accused Charles of 'dodging around' to avoid paying capital gains and corporation tax. As the questioning progressed, Nye's dry performance convinced other Labour MPs on the fifteen-strong committee that the duchy was concealing transactions. 'It was a witch-hunt,' said the Treasury official responsible for supervising Charles's Cornish estate. 'They wanted blood on the carpet. They wanted to find us guilty of something.' But the MPs' suspicions about Charles's secrecy proved justified. Soon afterwards, he used the Human Rights Act to prevent access to his tax returns. For Labour MPs, that inconsistency devalued his leadership. His authority depended upon virtue and talent, and that, in their opinion, was lacking.

To mitigate this latest humiliation, Charles invited a group of opinion-formers for a weekend in Sandringham. As usual, each guest was assigned a servant. The principal worry for the visitors was that they should have the appropriate clothes for lunch, tea, breakfast, church on Sunday morning, and the afternoon outings. Dinner was naturally black tie.

During their Saturday walk, Charles spoke about a sustainable environment. As in all such conversations, his guests were careful to avoid debate: their host, they had been cautioned, was easily offended. 'People think I'm bonkers, crackers,' he suddenly groaned in the middle of a field. 'Do you think I'm mad?' he asked, in a manner that forbade a positive reply. The writers and journalists refrained from any challenge to his beliefs and inconsistencies. In the silence, some of his guests understood that the prospect of being an impartial rather than a meddling prince appalled him. 'I have no power, but I have influence,' he announced. The group then set off back towards the house.

Charles's old-fashioned courtesy convinced some of his guests that any final barriers to his smooth succession had been overcome. William and Kate's wedding, the birth of their son George, and Charles's own marriage seemed to have dried up the public appetite for scandal. The dynasty was stabilised. Finally, Charles could present the code of principles that he hoped would act as a compass to bind the nation. His misfortune, his guests knew, was time. As each day passed, the length of his future reign decreased, and his significance diminished. In the public's mind he was not a hero, and for too many he was defined by his flaws.

The two-hour walk ended back at the house for tea. 'Right, we're off,' Charles announced, striding out of the house after a quick cup. Jumping into his Aston Martin, he drove at breakneck speed down narrow, twisting lanes, reassured that police motorcyclists had cleared other traffic. His guests followed in a fleet of gleaming Land Rovers. They arrived at Charles's local church in time to hear a short concert. After that, instead of visiting a number of other churches, as Charles would normally do on such weekends, he headed for a village fête. Clearly enjoying himself, he shook endless hands before judging the biggest turnip and best bottled onions competitions.

The villagers' flattery was gratifying, but Charles's quirks undermined the public image. One guest, an occasional visitor to Balmoral for grouse-shooting, recounted Charles's irritation when one of the small metal peg numbers taken by each gun to show where he should stand was dropped in the heather. Instead of abandoning the worthless object, Charles ordered his aides to riffle through the thick vegetation, then demanded that a metal detector be brought from the castle. The search for a small disc costing a few pence inevitably drew comparison with the large group dinner that night, at a table covered with rose petals and lit by candelabras brought from Highgrove. The conversation was strained. Although the guests had been summoned to contribute their opinions about the arts and culture, Charles did not encourage debate.

Friday after dinner was listed as a cinema night. The chosen film was Robert Altman's *Gosford Park*, depicting upstairs/downstairs life to an audience who were surrounded by the reality of that social order. The film became a regular feature of Charles's culture weekends. By coincidence, that evening his neighbours at Holkham Hall, eighteen miles away, had invited the prince and his guests to watch Valery Gergiev, the artistic director of the Mariinsky Theatre of St Petersburg, conduct a private orchestral performance. 'We can't go,' said Charles, allowing nothing to interfere with the schedule he had organised (Gergiev would be invited to visit Sandringham another year). Michael Fawcett supervised the placing of chairs in front of a screen in the ballroom. In the front row were two throne-like armchairs for Charles and Camilla. Soon everyone was seated, and servants entered with silver platters of ice cream. The film started. Charles and Camilla instantly fell asleep, and the ice cream slowly melted away.

On Sunday, female guests had been instructed to wear appropriate hats and gloves for the local Anglican church, St Mary the Virgin and St Mary Magdalen. The two who chose to go to mass at a nearby Catholic church felt Charles's displeasure. By Sunday dinner, some of the guests had become puzzled about their host. His habit of commandeering a small bowl of olive oil just for himself provoked one visitor to recount a story of Charles during a recent trip to India. The prince had invited Jacob Rothschild, and asked that other billionaires be rounded up to accompany him. During the tour, a sumptuous lunch was held in a maharaja's palace. Unexpectedly, a loaf of Italian bread was placed on the table. As an American billionaire reached out to take a piece, Charles shouted, 'No, that's mine! Only for me!' In reply to that story, another visitor recalled that on a previous weekend at Sandringham, a guest had brought Charles a truffle as a gift. To everyone's envy, Charles did not share the delicacy at dinner but kept it to himself. Once those stories were completed, Charles's guests did not laugh; there was merely bewilderment.

At the end of the Sandringham weekend – the guests were asked not to leave until the Monday morning – some were told to leave £150 in cash for the staff, or to visit the estate's souvenir shop. Most would tell their friends that Charles seemed genuine, but that the weekend was surreal.

The benefit to Charles was unquantifiable but his campaign to win public affection could not stop. 'He wants it to be relaxed and normal,' his equerry briefed another set of guests before a private dinner in a restaurant in Cornwall. 'There's no need to say "Your Royal Highness". The occasional "sir" will suffice.'

The first course was a boiled egg, freshly laid that day. Charles explained its healthy properties. The next course was organic meat. The guests struggled for conversation, waiting for their host to speak. His thoughts, it dawned, were somewhere else. 'Did you notice the problems of Cornish nationalism on your way down here?' asked one guest. Charles looked puzzled. 'Many signposts have been daubed with Cornish names,' another guest explained.

'One travels by helicopter,' Charles replied.

Some guests reported that Charles needed protection from himself, but the barriers he erected seemed impenetrable. Seeking to cultivate his image as an ascetic man of principle, he lived in a world of his own. Unwilling to explain to the public how he balanced duty and pleasure, he appeared unable to consistently strike the right trade-off with employees, professional guests, friends or family. One sign of his awkwardness was his fraught relationship with William. He would regularly agonise about the young prince's lack of interest in culture, his reluctance to undertake public duties (including Ascot, which relied on royal patronage) or to take over the Prince's Trust. Instead, William and Kate chose to retreat to Norfolk, where they could preserve their privacy. Some interpreted the move as confirmation that William was somewhat lazy and spoilt.

The distance between Highgrove and Norfolk isolated Charles from his grandchildren, and allowed Kate's mother Carole Middleton to take charge. Charles was aware of the gossip that Carole had plotted Kate's marriage to William. When her daughter had joined the prince at St Andrews University, she had urged Kate to be patient when William saw other girls, and similarly to remain serene in London during a break in their relationship. Once they were reconciled, and after they were married, William preferred to spend Christmas with the Middletons rather than at Sandringham. Charles's fears about being usurped had persuaded several of the queen's courtiers to ignore Carole Middleton at social occasions. To counter such gossip, at William's request the queen made a point of inviting a TV cameraman to film her driving her fellow in-law around the Balmoral estate. Similarly, the TV presenters Ant and Dec were invited to interview Charles, William and Harry together, to help show them as a united family; but in private Charles and his sons struggled to overcome the barriers of the past: Diana, Camilla and their starkly different interests.

Few outsiders knew Charles better than Jonathan Dimbleby, whose latest description of the prince as a 'prophet in his own land' and a 'national treasure' seemed hyperbolic to many. A *Time* magazine writer depicted Charles as introspective, permanently unhappy, and joyless at the prospect of becoming king – not because he had waited so long, but because he no longer wanted the position. The magazine portrayed a man who feared 'prison shades' once he was crowned, meaning that he regretted how little time remained for him to fulfil his ambitions before he was crowned.

Clarence House, in a letter to *The Times*, dismissed the magazine's article with the assertion that King Charles would continue to champion his controversial causes. 'There has been ill-informed speculation recently in your columns and elsewhere,' wrote William Nye, 'about the attitude of the Prince of Wales to the role of sovereign.' Charles, he continued, was 'inspired by the examples of his mother and grandfather while drawing also on his own experience of a lifetime [sic] service'. He understood the 'necessary and proper limitations' on the constitutional monarch. Charles's staff were told to put an end to the controversy. Dismissing any hint of the future king as a dissenter had become a priority.

In November 2013, to Buckingham Palace's relief, Charles opened his first Commonwealth conference, in Sri Lanka. 'Nine years' work paid off,' said a relieved Simon Gimson of the Commonwealth Secretariat. 'McKinnon's stomping foot had worked. Charles was invited without anyone batting an eyelid.'

To celebrate, Michael Fawcett supervised a banquet, Charles wooed fifty-one Commonwealth leaders, and Camilla smiled beneath a sparkling tiara last worn by the queen mother. On official advice, Charles did not mention climate change – 'The prime ministers of Australia and Canada will either tell you to shut up or walk out if you do,' Gimson had warned. Even so, the Canadian and Indian prime ministers boycotted the conference in protest at Sri Lanka's abuse of human rights. At its end, the officials concluded that the conference had not been a success, and that Charles had little feel for this historic grouping of nations. Two years later, the Commonwealth Secretariat decided that only the queen could salvage Charles's bid for the organisation's leadership. Contrary to her original plan, she flew to the conference in Malta and urged the leaders to accept him. Charles's performance during the conference was an improvement, but Camilla, obviously bored during the opening speeches, talked animatedly to her neighbour. People noticed; Charles's succession to the leadership remained in doubt.

A more urgent problem was Charles's heartfelt sympathy for Islam. Ever since his opposition to the invasion of Iraq, he had not been critical of the global aggression of political Islam. Speaking at the World Islamic Forum in London in October 2013, he blamed Syria's civil war on President Bashar al-Assad's destruction of the nation's rural economy. Seven years of drought, he said, had driven farmers and their families from the land, and as they fled to the cities tensions had boiled over. Blaming Assad's brutality solely on the depletion of 'nature's capital reserves, like water and soils' was consistent with Charles's belief in 'harmony', but seemed to ignore the context of the Syrian conflict within the 1,350-year war between Shia and Sunni Muslims. A subsequent study debunked Charles's claim as 'exaggerated ... when the evidence is so thin'.

Two months after that speech, Muslims began to murder Christians in Syria, Iraq and Egypt. Churches were destroyed and their priests killed. Finally, Charles acknowledged the threat posed by fundamentalist Islamic militants throughout the Middle East to 'my own Christian faith'.

After reading briefs provided by British intelligence that Saudi and Qatari nationals were financing terrorism across Europe, Charles admitted that the world was 'descending into the Dark Ages of public executions'. Nevertheless, he still equivocated about Islam's ambitions. Unlike many politicians, he understood that only worse would follow if the House of Saud collapsed, or Qatar's rulers were removed.

Finally, in early 2015 his views changed. After a hurried flight to Riyadh to pay homage on the death of King Abdullah, Charles began to reassess the popular anger about Saudi Arabia's abuse of human rights and its challenge to Western liberal values. The 'alarming' radicalisation of Muslims, he admitted, was 'heartbreaking'. He had spent twenty years, he said, trying to build bridges between faiths, and now realised the danger that 'very, very few Christians could be left in the Middle East'. He expressed genuine hurt about the fractured relationship between Muslims and Christians in the region. 'What doesn't bear thinking about,' he lamented, 'is that people of one faith, you know, a believer, could kill another believer. That's the totally bewildering aspect.' Shocked by the mass murder of Yazidis and other Christians by Islamic State after the American withdrawal from Iraq in 2011, he told an Islamic audience, 'The tragedy is even greater because Christians have been in the Middle East for two thousand years, before Islam came in the eighth century. We were in the Middle East before you.'

The Church of England, he said, would protect all faiths, and he himself would particularly defend 'Christian values – the values we hold dear'. Echoing the widespread anti-immigration sentiments that would galvanise the British vote to leave the EU in June 2016, Charles told Muslims who had either been born in or migrated to Britain that they ought to 'abide by Christian values and outlook'. One more impediment to his smooth succession had been removed. That change of heart was followed by another belated epiphany. Twenty-one years after he had first articulated his desire to be the defender of 'faiths', and so jeopardised his future role as head of the Anglican Church, he finally accepted the full meaning of the coronation oath, acknowledging that he would be the defender of *the* faith, namely Anglicanism, which would protect the freedom of other religions in Britain.

And then the reconciliation programme was abruptly derailed. Since he had turned twenty-one, Charles had met eight British prime ministers and countless politicians. There was little respect from either side. The 2010 election of the coalition government led by David Cameron, an Old Etonian, might have improved relations between the prince and the incoming ministers, not least because Cameron appeared to be an enthusiastic protector of the environment. But Charles was suspicious.

In early 2014, floods engulfed Somerset. Long before any government ministers felt stirred to travel from London, the prince was standing in the waterlogged streets with irate locals. 'The tragedy,' he let journalists hear, 'is that nothing has happened for so long.' The government, he told the stranded families, had reduced spending on flood defences, including dredging rivers. He had trespassed on sensitive territory. Cameron's irritation increased after Charles headed north to more floods in Cumbria. Standing near the new but breached riverbanks, the prince told the latest victims, 'We have known for decades that we are heading towards catastrophic climate change and we're at the point of no return – yet still we procrastinate.' He damned critics of this for ignoring the imminent Armageddon – 'Sceptics rubbish climate science and ignore the accumulating disaster' – and refused to make any concessions to politicians. Once he had returned to London, he invited two hundred experts to a 'summit' at St James's Palace. 'I have said all this kind of thing before – endlessly,' he told his audience, 'and I sometimes feel I am just talking to myself. We have no time left in which to prevent dangerous climate change.' Soon after, a flood washed away much of his own garden at Birkhall.

Cameron fumed about the criticism and the heated language. Charles's opponents, particularly the climate change deniers, ridiculed his interpretation of the world's likely future. Once again he was causing the political mischief he had so often been asked to avoid.

And once again he was going solo. He refused to attend the queen's banquet at Buckingham Palace for Chinese president Xi Jinping, his third such Chinese boycott, agreeing only to meet him at his hotel in Knightsbridge, the same formula as with Hu Jintao in 2009. The public, he sensed, had swung behind him, and he looked around for other occasions on which he might advance his cause – not just his political or environmental agendas, but to reassert his independence from Buckingham Palace.

Seventeen years after Tony Blair negotiated the Good Friday Agreement to end the ongoing civil war in Northern Ireland, one gesture remained: the reconciliation between Charles and the murderers of Lord Mountbatten, his father's uncle and his own early mentor, killed with his nephew and two others by an IRA bomb while fishing in Mullaghmore Bay in County Sligo in 1979. At the time Sinn Féin's leader Gerry Adams had justified the murders.

Thirty-two years later, the queen made a historic visit to Dublin to cement the new agreement. Her visit included a meeting with Adams. The following year she shook hands with Martin McGuinness, the IRA's godfather and a brutal murderer. After that meeting, McGuinness wore a white tie at a state banquet in Windsor.

The symbolism of the royal family's reconciliation would seal the peace – but Charles refused to follow his mother. Those close to the queen complained that he was putting off meeting Sinn Féin's leaders unless it was on his terms. Officials condemned his behaviour as petulant. Eventually, in 2015, Charles met Adams in a university building in Galway, shook hands and spoke briefly about the lost lives.

The next day, he drove to the coast to meet the villagers who had lifted the dying Mountbatten out of the water. He was welcomed by Mountbatten's boatkeeper, local fishermen, the coroner, and the people who had greeted the admiral of the fleet every August when he stayed at Classiebawn Castle. 'Recent years have shown us,' Charles told a tearful audience, 'that healing is possible.' Two days later he shook hands with McGuinness in a Belfast church. In his own way, he had drawn a historic line. That, however, was the limit of his power. The extent of his influence was proven to be much less than the sum of the parts.

Among the legacy of contentious issues was a legal battle in the supreme court. In 2005 the *Guardian* had applied under the Freedom of Information Act to see twenty-seven letters between Charles, government ministers and their private secretaries that had been sent in the previous year. Ten of those letters were from the royal hand. Charles had lobbied David Blunkett, the first of Tony Blair's education ministers, to resurrect grammar schools; Michael Meacher, the environment minister, to ban GM crops; and Peter Hain, the new Welsh minister, to launch complementary medicine there after he had introduced it in Northern Ireland.

Regardless of any misgivings about his conservative prejudices, the Labour government was obliged to protect the heir to the throne, first by arguing against publication of the letters, and later by an amendment of the Information Act, to prevent future applications for their contents to be disclosed. In 2009 the information commissioner had blocked disclosure, but that was overturned in 2012. The upper tribunal ruled that Charles's letters, and the ministers' replies, qualified as 'advocacy correspondence', and there was thus 'a public interest strongly in favour of disclosure'. This was a marked shift from the decision against the *Mail on Sunday* six years earlier over his Chinese journal. Unlike in that case, the tribunal's judges rejected Charles's demand that his letters be classified as a state secret.

During the appeal to the upper tribunal, Dominic Grieve, the Conservative attorney general, had exaggerated Charles's vulnerability: 'The Prince of Wales is party-political neutral. Moreover, it is highly important that he is not considered by the public to favour one political party or another. This will arise if, through these letters, the Prince of Wales was viewed by others as disagreeing with government policy.' Describing the letters as 'particularly frank' and reflecting Charles's 'most deeply held personal views and beliefs', Grieve urged the court to ban publication, 'because if he forfeits his position of political neutrality as heir to the throne he cannot easily recover it when he is king'.

Grieve lost. The upper tribunal ordered that the letters should be released. 'I never discussed the issue with Charles,' said Grieve, and appealed once more to the Court of Appeal. This application was successful, and publication was blocked. After more trials the *Guardian* appealed to the final arbiter, the supreme court – just as another obstacle to normalising Charles's succession arose.

In March 2015 the supreme court declared that Charles was not acting as a private citizen, and ordered the publication of the correspondence. Charles's spokesman expressed his disappointment that 'the principle of privacy had not been upheld'. But after so many years of conflict, the letters were disappointing. Charles's opinions were expressed in a public-spirited but neutral manner, and gave scant ammunition to his enemies. His attempts at persuasion demonstrated only his lack of power. The only consolation for monarchists was that government lawyers had, presumably on Charles's behalf, acknowledged to the supreme court that his advocacy letters would need to cease once he became king. Overt lobbying, they recognised, would be incompatible with expectations of impartiality. The pledge was not entirely convincing.

The Prince's Coup

Eighteen years after Camilla's fraught visit to New York, Charles celebrated her seventieth birthday in July 2017. The work started by Mark Bolland was nearly complete.

The climax was a party at Highgrove on Saturday, 15 July. Over two hundred guests including Camilla's family, her closest friends and many young people invited by Tom and Laura Parker Bowles, and William and Harry, crowded into the Orchard Room to eat avocado salad followed by tarragon chicken. Charles sat between his friend Sarah Keswick and the Duchess of Wellington; Camilla was between the Duke of Wellington and Jacob Rothschild. Hovering on the side, as usual, was Michael Fawcett embarrassed by his wife's faux pas: in the printed invitations, Debbie Fawcett had stipulated the dress code as 'black suit'. A grovelling apology had been sent with the correct term, 'black tie'. The mistake had cheered Fawcett's critics.

'Mercifully the speeches were brief,' said one spirited guest. Charles thanked Camilla and his friends, after which Tom Parker Bowles made some tactful jokes about his mother. Once the birthday cake had been cut, the sound system exploded with rock music. The older guests held back as a hundred young people invaded the dance floor, partying until after 2 a.m. The gossip around Gloucestershire and beyond over the following days was electric. Thanks to the 'Parker Bowles's gang', everyone agreed, the party was a success. The only disappointment was felt by the uninvited 'oldies' – quietly muttering 'NFI' (Not Fucking Invited) – irritated by their unexpected exclusion from Highgrove and having to make do with a drinks party at Clarence House.

Charles had good reason to feel satisfied. Twenty years earlier, after Diana's death, his approval ratings had hit rock bottom. Since then, he had succeeded in overcoming successive crises and critics. Now his marriage to Camilla was accepted, and while there was still speculation about his likely performance as king, his succession to the throne was unopposed by a majority of Britons. All that remained was to remove the opposition to Camilla being crowned as queen. Although she herself suggested that the title was irrelevant, clues about her ambition and Charles's stubborn determination surfaced during the birthday celebrations.

Profiles and interviews portrayed Camilla as a woman of charm and hard work, and as the champion of charities caring for the disadvantaged. The resemblance to Diana was not coincidental. To support that image, the *Mail on Sunday*, featuring an inconsequential but rare interview with the duchess, prominently protested that Camilla had been 'fobbed off' as the mere princess consort. Now was the time, urged the paper, to 'lay the ghost of Diana to rest' and pave the way for Camilla to be eventually crowned queen by immediately giving her the 'rightful title of Princess of Wales', not least because William and Harry 'adored' Camilla – something of a confection to those who knew the truth. To sustain the campaign, Clarence House released a photograph of Charles and Camilla by Mario Testino, Diana's favourite photographer. Wrinkles and blemishes had been airbrushed from their glowing faces,which exuded the appearance of youth and enduring happiness. Winning public support for the couple as Britain's next monarchs was difficult, but Charles was, as ever, undeterred. Concealed behind his and Camilla's promotion were the final stages of a coup orchestrated by him to ease his succession.

Throughout his adult life, Charles had bridled against the efforts of Buckingham Palace, and particularly by the queen's private secretaries, to influence his activities. Under Christopher Geidt's steady guidance, some of the friction generated during Michael Peat's era had diminished, although one further attempt to merge the palaces' media operations had collapsed on Charles's insistence some years earlier. Despite that obstacle, Geidt's diplomacy had eased the negotiations between Charles and his mother to transfer some of her ceremonial duties to him. At the age of ninety-one, she could no longer undertake many official duties, not least walking up flights of stairs in the Palace of Westminster. Accordingly, they agreed that Charles's destiny as the king in waiting would be publicly sealed during the year leading up to his seventieth birthday in November 2018. He would lead the nation at Trooping the Colour, on Remembrance Sunday, and on all foreign trips. Based on that understanding, Geidt was expected to serve the queen until the end of her reign. But the continuing discussions had rattled Charles.

Geidt was negotiating the queen's role at the next Commonwealth summit, to be held in London in April 2018. Most of the fifty-two government leaders expected the queen to act as their host, but that was unacceptable to Charles. Despite the difficulties over the previous twenty years, he insisted that his supremacy should be asserted, although he still refused to commit himself, either as the heir or as the future king, to tour the Commonwealth countries he had steadfastly ignored. Once he was king he would be beyond any persuasion, and would continue to maintain his relations with the Arab world rather than develop new contacts in Africa and the Caribbean. Geidt was caught in the middle of an irreconcilable argument, not least because he must have been aware of Prince Philip's opinion of his son.

At a recent dinner with friends in Mayfair, Philip had joked about his determination to live beyond ninety-five. The reason for his and the queen's longevity, he explained amid his friends' laughter, was to keep Charles from the throne. At ninety-one, he said, the queen was in robust health and, he implied, could well live for another ten years. Charles would have little opportunity to damage the monarchy if he was king for only a brief period. Philip did not hide his scorn for his son's achievements and vision, and showed little confidence that Charles could impress himself upon history as an exceptional king. Many believed that Philip doubted whether his son, who had barely come to terms with the twentieth century, could unify the country in the twenty-first. His enduring image as a landowner hankering for a forgotten world threatened the institution of the monarchy. His reign would be about the past rather than the future. In a nutshell, some believed that Charles lacked the common touch. The rebel prince, Philip feared, would become a meddling monarch. The risk was the replacement of tact by wilfulness, causing a constitutional crisis which would jeopardise the monarchy's very existence. The scenario, depicted in the recent successful play *Charles III*, of King Charles abdicating rather than sign an Act of Parliament to limit media freedom, had not surprised the informed audience. Charles refused merely to mutely symbolise British values; he wanted to assert them too.

Philip's fears about his son's intentions reflected the opinions of many in Buckingham Palace. The queen's death could trigger repercussions among the public, most of whom had no experience of a change of monarch. Christopher Geidt's task was to mitigate that uncertainty. To manage continuity and prepare for change was a test of his wisdom. In Charles's opinion, Geidt had failed that test.

In early May 2017, without disclosing the reason, Geidt summoned the entire royal staff to travel from Scotland, Norfolk, Windsor and the other royal estates to Buckingham Palace. At 10 a.m on Thursday, 4 May, five hundred people gathered in the ballroom. The excuse for the unprecedented assembly was Geidt's announcement of Prince Philip's retirement from public duties. But Geidt's true reason for inviting that exceptional audience was to herald a turning point in the queen's reign, and obliquely to warn Charles about tampering with the long-established timetables and traditions once he became king.

The queen – and therefore Geidt – was disturbed by any threat to the monarchy's focus on continuity and stability. To Buckingham Palace, Charles and his sons appeared to be pursuing their own celebrity interests at the expense of quietly fulfilling the royal family's traditional duties. Influenced by Charles, neither of the young princes enthusiastically participated in ceremonial events, and all three performed half-heartedly, rather than as the natural focus, during moments of national celebration and crisis. If Charles failed to enhance the dignity of the crown, the queen feared, the end of her reign would become desultory, and his own reign would lack majesty and grandeur.

To resolve that problem, Geidt urged his audience – and members of the royal family – to intensify their support for the queen. Elizabeth, explained Geidt, wanted all members of the royal family to work as a team on official duties, rather than pursuing their individual interests. Philip's retirement, he said, was 'an opportunity to pause, reflect and refocus as a family'. The discordant relations among the royals, and their self-indulgence, he implied, had to end. The public criticism of Prince William's recent skiing holiday in Switzerland, when the rest of the royals were at a Commonwealth Day service in Westminster Abbey, could not go unheeded.

In the few hours after the announcement, the media's glowing headlines about Philip as a national treasure were a successful smokescreen for the queen's serious message. Unnoticed was Charles's irritation. First, he disliked the melodrama of summoning five hundred people to London. Second, he regarded Buckingham Palace's briefing that the queen would encourage Edward and Sophie Wessex to play a more prominent role as offensive. Third, Geidt's call for loyalty to the queen was a calculated snub to himself. Finally, he resented the criticism of his personal activities. If he allowed that challenge to pass, he might still be denied the prominent role he expected at the forthcoming Commonwealth conference and other state occasions in London. He refused to be relegated to the sidelines in the years before his coronation. Charles demanded from his mother that Geidt be reined in, while his office encouraged media speculation about a regency – a notion firmly rejected by Buckingham Palace. Their dispute had clearly not been settled by 20 June, when an obviously grumpy heir accompanied the queen for the truncated state opening of Parliament after the general election.

Shortly afterwards, the careful advancement of Charles and Camilla was unexpectedly derailed by the twentieth anniversary of Diana's death. Among the deluge of television programmes and newspaper features came the first broadcast in Britain of Peter Settelen's videos featuring Diana describing her adultery, her attempted suicide and her forlorn appeal to the queen about her wayward husband. The resurrection of Diana's misery – magnified by replays of her revelation on *Panorama* about Camilla's omnipresence throughout her marriage – reignited the public's antagonism towards Charles. All the careful rehabilitation since the mysterious end to Paul Burrell's trial fifteen years earlier evaporated.

Worse followed. The high point of the media's coverage was a TV documentary featuring William and Harry recalling their mother's universal fame. With self-indulgent emotion, Diana's sons praised the princess, described their happy memories and intimately recounted twenty years of grief – all without any mention of Charles. In a succession of other interviews, the brothers established their separate identities from Charles. For some, the suggestion of tension between Clarence House and Kensington Palace was reminiscent of the media war between Charles and Diana during the 1990s. Clearly,

Geidt's appeal just weeks earlier for self-discipline had been flouted by the princes' public soul-searching. Geidt's private criticism of the princes provoked William's fury. Harry was more measured. Already planning to announce his engagement to the American actress Meghan Markle, he felt greater affinity than William for his father. Nevertheless, the damage was done.

The blowback hurt Charles. Opinion polls showed that his popularity had plunged again. At most, only one third of Britons welcomed the prospect of Charles's succession, and at least half the population preferred that William should be the next king. Only 14 per cent supported Camilla becoming queen. The public's disapproval of Charles and Camilla was personal, because the polls also found that the vast majority of Britons continued to support the monarchy. By contrast, the republican movements in the Commonwealth were strengthening. However unjustly, Charles's legitimacy was still vulnerable to a single crisis. Both he and Camilla were distraught. In the future, even when he was king, the Diana anniversaries would continue to deflate his self-confidence and undermine his popularity. His succession once again faced hostility, and more than usually, his response would test how he would behave as king.

As the heir to the throne, Charles should have automatically consulted advisers to bridge the gap between his instinctive impulses and the benefit of reason. Over the previous thirty years, that serious counsel had often been missing. By relying on sycophants willing to tolerate his tirades and his rejection of any criticism, Charles had made damaging mistakes. His grudges and disloyalty had deprived him of wise advisers. Many feared the same situation would continue once he became king. One consolation was that the embarrassments had diminished. Many credited Camilla. She offered stability and a circle of loyal friends who did not carp to the media. With her support Charles's temper had mellowed, but the absence of a counsellor like Christopher Geidt in Clarence House aroused apprehension about the future king's court. What followed reinforced those anxieties.

Charles's answer to Geidt's challenge was to re-emphasise his own interests – which was just what Buckingham Palace opposed. He also demanded to take over even more of his mother's public duties. The obstacle, he assumed, would be Geidt, who he felt had become a hindrance rather than a help. Without a restraining adviser, Charles demanded Geidt's resignation from his mother. Faced with that implacable demand from a man accustomed to regularly dismissing his own staff, and despite Geidt being especially trusted, the queen reluctantly agreed.

On 31 July 2017, Geidt unexpectedly announced his retirement. Insiders soon realised that his departure after ten years as private secretary was a coup orchestrated by Charles. To combat one headline – 'Turmoil at Palace as Queen's Right Hand Man to Quit' – the palace forlornly tried to minimise the mayhem, but the attempt was abandoned after Samantha Cohen, an assistant private secretary, also announced her resignation, followed by Mark Leishman, Charles's private secretary, openly frustrated by the prince. Although Geidt was contractually expected to remain in place until October, he immediately headed for his farm in the Outer Hebrides. To show her personal affection, the queen later made him a Knight Grand Cross of the Royal Victorian Order, her highest honour. Later he was made a peer and a Knight Grand Cross of the Order of the Bath. Geidt's demise suggested that as king Charles would only tolerate sycophants in his court, and that spelled trouble.

Charles's victory was short-lived. Geidt's fate reopened the debate about whether Charles's forthright opinions threatened the constitution. The assurance from his staff that he understood the expectation of impartiality from the monarch did not reassure witnesses of his unwillingness to remain an enigma in the shadows. Few believed that he would resist continuing to promote his opinions about architecture, the environment, alternative medicine, education and other matters. There were grounds to fear that King Charles, an elderly monarch in a hurry, would spark a constitutional crisis. One possible cause was his attitude towards money.

Few doubted the outstanding value of Charles's charitable deeds, but to continue entertaining rich donors to sustain his organisations – especially the Prince's Trust, which William has refused to take over – would be inappropriate for a king. Fundraising would compromise his status. Persuading Charles to reduce his charitable work was not difficult. Ever since Higdon's dismissal, his income from America had declined, and the number of international donors had also fallen. In 2016 he had no alternative but to cut the grants to his charities – some by half – and, to save money, finally begin to merge his twenty-one organisations into a single entity. On other matters however, in the absence of an independently-minded private secretary, there were misgivings about whether in King Charles's court there would be anyone to persuade the new monarch to change his way of life.

The legacy of Charles's noble causes, good intentions and interest in individuals has been tarnished by his addiction to luxury, his financial mismanagement, his disloyalty to professional supporters, and the torrid relationships with his family. The release of Buckingham Palace's accounts in autumn 2017 showed that the plane used by Charles for his spring tour around Europe, including his annual visit to Romania, had cost £154,000. His summer break, sailing around the Greek islands on a yacht with Camilla as the guest of shipping magnate Theodore Angelopoulos, confirmed that Charles would not yield to any critic, especially his father. Even in their lifetime, his parents' influence had waned. In the future there would be no one to restrain his self-indulgence. Public approval of the queen's frugality would be replaced by disdain for her successor's extravagance. Charles appeared impervious to the absence of popular acceptance. The same resilience that had overcome so many humiliations during his life now powered his demands of Buckingham Palace. With Geidt replaced by his amenable deputy Edward Young, Charles continued to discuss the transition of his mother's duties and to plan his response during the six months between his mother's death and his own coronation.

The monarchy's success, Charles knew, depended on appealing to emotion and mythology. Sensitive to any public resistance, he had agreed with Downing Street that as king he would 'hit the ground running'. Like a political campaign, he would first address the nation and then barnstorm through the country, with appearances in London followed by flights to Cardiff, Belfast and Edinburgh. His message would reflect the king's in Giuseppe di Lampedusa's celebrated historical novel *The Leopard*: 'If we want things to stay as they are, things will have to change.' Charles was a mortal prepared to bend to the changing reality, but nevertheless certain that his values – spiritual and moral – would unite the nation. At least there would be no further opposition in Buckingham Palace.

On his return to London after the tour, his own staff from Clarence House will have quietly replaced the queen's officials. The handover, he stipulated, would demonstrate the nation's trust of himself and the monarchy, although, according to one senior official, 'there are doubts whether Charles trusts his own staff'. A parallel doubt is whether he loves his own fate. As king, he will be expected to symbolise the best of British values, and to unify the nation in crisis and celebration. The question is whether he can meet that necessity. If he chooses, as rumoured, to remain in Clarence House and not move into Buckingham Palace, he would weaken one enduring symbol and confirm his self-interest.

In anticipation of his coronation, the Royal Mint has finalised the plans to replace his mother's portrait on coins with that of Charles. That task was complicated by Charles's requests. Like the Duke of Windsor, the former King Edward VIII, Charles prefers his left profile rather than the conventional right-hand side. The Mint agreed to prepare drawings of both profiles for Charles's approval, but he was dissatisfied with the result. Both portraits showed his thinning hair and reflected his age. He demanded that he should be shown with a full head of hair, and considerably younger. The revised version was more satisfactory. He was less pleased when the Mint suggested that it should also prepare portraits for King William. That, Charles ordained, was pushing fate too far. As king, there seems little likelihood that Charles will be generous towards his two brothers, or will bond more closely with his sons. As in all his personal relationships, it seems likely that he will act alone, without any restraining adviser. For committed monarchists, that independence is alarming. They can only hope for the best.

Finally, there was the detail of the coronation. Tampering with the ritual ceremony, Charles has been persuaded, would be folly. The monarch's strength depends upon tradition. Despite the decline of Christianity, the supremacy of the Anglican Church, Charles agreed, will be reaffirmed by the Archbishop of Canterbury's unchallenged authority to crown the prince as defender of the faith. The alternative would be unacceptable to most Britons. Nevertheless, agreement about the final details, the participants and the words remains undecided, except for the finale. At the end of the ceremony the congregation will shout, 'God Save the King!' Charles profoundly hopes that the country will echo that plea.

Acknowledgements

This book was born out of an explosion of anger from a friend about Prince Charles's enthusiasm for complementary medicine. 'You should write a proper book about Charles,' she urged. The result is not what she imagined, but then it is also not what I anticipated. At the outset I assumed that since there were so many biographies of the prince, there was little new to write. I was encouraged to ignore the existing library by Tony Holden, a superb journalist and early biographer of Charles. 'There's an untold story,' he said. Still uncertain, I contacted Richard Kay, the doyen of royal journalists and, as I knew, among the most kind and generous of our trade. Kay added to Tony Holden's enthusiasm. Thereafter, I encountered help from many people – former employees of the royal family, public servants, employees of Charles's charities, politicians, lawyers and Charles's friends – who generously gave me remarkable help over many months. For obvious reasons, many spoke off the record, and would not want to be individually mentioned. Others, it will be clear from the text, spoke on the record but do not want to be individually thanked.

In writing the book, I was particularly helped by Claudia Wordsworth, an outstanding researcher upon whom I have come to rely.

Rupert Earle and David Hirst were the assiduous libel lawyers.

I am hugely indebted to Richard Cohen, a proven friend, for his inspired editing over an intensive period, and then to Robert Lacey at HarperCollins for his meticulous completion of the manuscript. Also at HarperCollins, I am grateful to Arabella Pike, my editor, to my publicist Katherine Patrick, and to Lottie Fyfe for the photo research. Throughout, I was supported as always by Jonathan Lloyd, my agent at Curtis Brown.

Finally, nothing is possible without the support of my wife, Veronica, the best and most generous friend.

Sources

This book relied on interviews with about 120 people directly involved with the royal family – former employees of the family, public servants, politicians, lawyers and journalists. For the usual reasons, few of the people who I interviewed wanted to speak on the record. The vast majority did not want their contribution quoted. Providing sources in books that rely on those off-the-record conversations is always unsatisfactory. Rather than endlessly list 'private conversation' as the source, I have decided to eschew any references to all the interviews which contributed to the narrative. Assiduous readers seeking the source of a quotation will be understandably irritated by that omission. I can only ask for forbearance and the assurance that most of the contentious quotations were sourced for the two libel lawyers who read the book, and that many others came from the public record.

Chapter 2: Plots and Counterplots
 7 'very few people' *Mail on Sunday* 4.6.17; Reagan Library
10 The obvious suspect' Woodrow Wyatt diary 29.10.00, quoting John Major
12 'willingly cooperated' *Mail on Sunday* 20.11.94
16 'Others accused' Penny Junor, *Charles: Victim or Villain?* (HarperCollins, 1998), p.133
21 'Charles, they said' *Mail on Sunday* 24.8.03
21 'The surge of' Jonathan Dimbleby, *The Prince of Wales: An Intimate Portrait* (Little, Brown, 1994), p.190
21 'Twenty-three years' Junor, op. cit., p.13
22 'Parker Bowles avoided' Anne de Courcy, *Daily Mail* 26.11.93
22 'made no protest' Gyles Brandreth, *Charles and Camilla: Portrait of a Love Affair* (Century, 2005), p.93
22 'the perfect escort' Junor, op. cit., p.89
23 'her affair was' Robert Lacey, *Monarch: The Life and Reign of Elizabeth II* (Free Press, 2003), p.270

Chapter 3: The Masters of Spin

30 'retreat into isolation' *Sunday Times* 4.12.94
30 'I don't see' Dimbleby, op. cit., p.427
30 'I pointed out' Ibid., p.149
31 'Perhaps the most' Ibid., p.153
31 'I have always' Letter to Shebbeare 21.1.93, quoted ibid., p.493
31 'wanted to promote' *Financial Times* interview 22.11.93
31 'He judged' Tony Blair, *A Journey* (Hutchinson, 2010), p.150
31 'which he complained' Ibid., p.137
33 'a fairly decent' Alastair Campbell, *Diaries Vol. 2: Power and the People 1997–99* (Hutchinson, 2011), p.218
36 'You will need' Peter Mandelson, *The Third Man: Life at the Heart of New Labour* (HarperPress, 2010), pp.233–4

Chapter 4: Uneasy Lies the Head

38 'They're all going' Lacey, op. cit., p.352
38 'In the hours' Ibid., p.385
38 'Would you rather' Junor, op. cit., p.20
39 'she had a' Blair, op. cit., p.133
39 'good cause to' Ibid., p.134
40 'Blair did not' Ibid., p.143
40 'I talked less' Ibid., p.150
40 'His idea that' Jonathan Powell, *The New Machiavelli: How to Wield Power in the Twentieth Century* (Bodley Head, 2010), p.40
41 'want a monarchy' Roy Strong, *Scenes and Apparitions: Diaries 1988–2003* (Weidenfeld & Nicolson, 2017), p.235
44 'It only goes' Mandelson, op. cit., p.236
45 'All he wanted' Mark Bolland, *Sunday Times* 10.4.05
49 'Janvrin immediately hired' Campbell, *Diaries Vol. 2*, op. cit., p.154

Chapter 5: Mutiny and Machiavellism

58 'We're going to' Campbell, *Diaries Vol. 2*, op. cit., p.154
58 'a journey back' Alastair Campbell, *The Blair Years: Extracts from the Alastair Campbell Diaries* (Random House, 2007), p.324
58 'the problems and' Dimbleby, op. cit., pp.421–36
59 'tone down his' Mandelson, op. cit., p.236
60 'an opinion poll' Brandreth, op. cit., p.291
61 'as a priority' *Sunday Times* 12.7.98
66 'a Christmas card' Campbell, *The Blair Years*, op. cit, p.351
67 'remained in love' Junor, op. cit., p.292
67 'some suspected that' *Daily Mirror* 18.1.99
71 'Hanoverian' Strong, op. cit., pp.275, 284

Chapter 6: Body and Soul

72 'Charles had decided' Anthony Holden, *Diana: Her Life and Legacy* (Random House, 1997), p.339
72 'financing his charities' Dimbleby, op. cit., p.361
73 'Charles's pay-off' Ibid.
73 'What really worries' Holden, op. cit., p.193

73 'I have no' Charles letter to Shebbeare 21.1.93, quoted Dimbleby, op. cit., p.493
74 'an excessive amount' Dimbleby, op. cit., p.379
76 'practised by folk' Ibid., p.306
77 'would later admit' Ibid., p.313
77 'Sir James Watt' Ibid., p.306
78 'Charles continued to' Catherine Mayer, *Charles: The Heart of a King* (W.H. Allen, 2015), p.300
80 'unwilling to distinguish' Edzard Ernst, *A Scientist in Wonderland: A Memoir of Searching for Truth and Finding Trouble* (Imprint Academic, 2015), p.137
80 'a course in' Ibid., pp.83–4
81 'incompetent' House of Lords Science and Technology Committee, Sixth Report, 2000
81 'The information' Ernst, op. cit., pp.157ff

Chapter 7: The Masterbuilder
84 'class war' Gavin Stamp, 'Charlie Come Lately', *Spectator* 13.1.89
85 'hideous little boxes' Dimbleby, op. cit., p.367
85 'to roll back' Ibid., p.277
86 'utter nonsense' *Daily Mail* 28.6.06
86 'At his happiest' Mayer, op. cit., p.293
90 'she rejected' Holden, op. cit., p.208; John Campbell, *The Iron Lady: Margaret Thatcher – From Grocer's Daughter to Iron Lady* (Jonathan Cape, 2009), p.467
90 'They want to' Dimbleby, op. cit., p.277
91 'a clever way' Prince Charles, *A Vision of Britain* (Doubleday, 1989), pp.44–5
91 'based on ridicule' Sally Bedell-Smith, *Prince Charles: The Passions and Paradoxes of a Misunderstood Life* (Michael Joseph, 2017), p.237; *New York Times* 4.11.89
92 'the hovering hordes' Charles, *A Vision*, op. cit., p.59
92 'But why does' Strong, op. cit., p.6
92 'I want the' Dimbleby, op. cit., p.470
93 'human feeling' Junor, op. cit., p.194
93 'Charles was criticised' Holden, op. cit., p.222
94 'he doubted that' *Guardian* 27.10.16
95 'compromised and' Junor, op. cit., p.194

Chapter 8: Teasing the Government
99 'Blair ordered' Alastair Campbell, *Diaries Vol. 3: Power and Responsibility 1999–2001* (Hutchinson, 2011), p.38
100 'walking through' *Sun* 2.6.99; *Daily Mail* 3.6.99
100 'unknown to him' Blair, op. cit., pp.139ff
101 'political act' Campbell, *The Blair Years*, op. cit., p.426
101 'He had people' Campbell, *Diaries Vol. 3*, op. cit., p.151
102 'he now understood' Blair, op. cit., p.143
102 'Britain's future king' Campbell, *The Blair Years*, op. cit., p.437
103 'a misjudgement' *Guardian* 12.3.99
103 'hapless' *Independent* 14.3.99
105 'The prince's complaint' Campbell, *The Blair Years*, op. cit., p.510; *Guardian* 25.4.05
105 'It's amazing' Campbell, *The Blair Years*, op. cit., p.512
106 'He's well-meaning' Campbell, *Diaries Vol. 3*, op. cit., p.677
107 'immensely helpful' *Guardian* 5.7.11

Chapter 9: Diana's 'Rock'

112 'Do you have' Peat Report, p.47
113 'Her perfume' 'Police List of Items Allegedly Stolen by Princess Diana's Butler', ABC News 6.1.06
114 'had transferred them' Paul Burrell, *A Royal Duty* (Michael Joseph, 2003), p.344
114 'They are very' Court report, *Daily Mail* 29.10.02
114 'write to Charles' Burrell, op. cit., p.344
114 'Most sensitively' Ibid.
115 'But Lamport was' Peat Report, p.55
119 'There is no' Ibid., p.54
120 'He told his' Ibid.

Chapter 10: A Family at War

121 'Andrew's brother' Junor, op. cit., p.344
122 'Charles paid off' Mark Bolland, *Sunday Times* 10.4.05
122 'She has never' Junor, op. cit., p.103
123 'had been exposed' *News of the World* 16.5.99
124 'he was persuaded' *Sunday Times* 13.2.05
125 'He Came' *Sunday Times* 10.4.05
130 'did not believe' Mary Francis, Channel 4 documentary 30.11.09

Chapter 11: A Butler's Warnings

142 'To him, it' Don McKinnon, *In the Ring: A Commonwealth Memoir* (Elliott & Thompson, 2013), p.32
142 'very determined' Peat Report, p.55
143 'She, like the' Sarah McCorquodale testimony 29.1.07
143 'The rape was' Note made by O'Kane's paralegal, Peat Report, p.36
144 'I was totally' Peat Report, pp.26–7
145 'At 3 a.m.' *Mail on Sunday* 10.11.02
145 'not to listen' Burrell, op. cit., p.379
146 'Smith told Aylard' Peat Report, p.18
146 'Smith's accusations' Ibid., pp.43–4
147 'there may be' Ibid., p.21
147 'very serious claims' Ibid., p.18
147 'without explosion' Ibid., p.28
148 'Others thought' Ibid., p.37
148 'Two years later' Ibid., para 2.25, p.57
149 'He had told' Boyce statement on Brown, 'Review of Operation Plymouth', para 10, p.39
152 'Charles had already' Peat Report, para 2.48, p.61
153 'There was no' Ibid., para 2.55, p.63
154 'his lawyers did' Ibid., para 2.30, p.57; pp.59–60
154 'strongly influenced' Ibid., para 2.41, p.60
155 'to say later' *Sun* 23.10.02
155 'he also patted' Peat Report, para 2.37, p.59
156 'Bolland mentioned' Ibid., para 2.55, p.63
158 'but they offered' Ibid., para 2.68, p.67
158 'Burrell described' Burrell, op. cit., p.365
159 'The threat was' Peat Report, para 2.63(e), p.65

159 'If Burrell described' Ibid.
159 'O'Kane ordered' Ibid., p.61
159 'extreme delicacy' Ibid., pp.65-6
160 'They could not' Ibid., paras 1.140-1, p.35; Burrell, op. cit., pp.160ff
160 'Unknown to the' Burrell at Diana inquest 17.1.08
161 'Yates, he submitted' Peat Report, pp.65-6; *Evening Standard* 1.11.02

Chapter 12: A Struggle for Power

165 'Today we commend' *News of the World* 13.1.02
167 'Who knows what' *Daily Mail* 7.7.01
168 'simultaneously receiving' Peat Report, paras 4.18-34

Chapter 13: A New Era Begins

170 'What we really' Strong, op. cit., p.388
170 'an embarrassing' *Sun* 4.4.02
170 'Her immediate response' Mary Francis, Channel 4 documentary 30.11.09
171 'a friend of' Ibid.
171 'The latest opinion' YouGov poll, *Daily Telegraph* 4.2.02
176 'dead wood' McKinnon, op. cit., p.37
178 'destroying the' Campbell, *The Blair Years*, op. cit., p.639
178 'Charles had mentioned' Alastair Campbell, *The Burden of Power: Countdown to Iraq* (Hutchinson, 2012), p.241
179 'he had also' Mayer, op. cit., p.211
179 'had little choice' Campbell, *Burden of Power*, op. cit., p.309
179 'environmentally friendly' *The Times* 9.10.17
180 'the potential to' Campbell, *Burden of Power*, op. cit., p.309

Chapter 14: Shuttlecocks and Skirmishes

184 'I told my' Peat Report, para 2.69, p.67
185 'The waters were' Ibid., para 2.75, p.68
185 'In the Burrell' Ibid., para 2.78, p.68
187 'His advice to' Ibid., pp.69-70
188 'deceived by' Ibid., para 2.63(b), p.65; pp.70-2
188 'huge assumption' Ibid., paras 2.88-9, p.71

Chapter 15: The Queen's Recollection

189 'he had planned' Court report, *The Times* 26.10.02
190 'forced and broken' Burrell, op. cit., p.379
194 'subsequently described' Peat Report, paras 2.103ff, p.74
194 'Janvrin wanted' Ibid.
197 'three hours' Burrell, op. cit., p.389
197 'safekeeping or acting' Peat Report, para 2.74, p.68
197 'You're overreacting' Ibid., para 2.112, p.76
199 'then consulted' Campbell, *Burden of Power*, op. cit., p.349
200 'Led by Goldsmith' Ibid.
200 'He will have' *Evening Standard* 4.11.02
201 'no crime and' Ibid.
203 'In graphic detail' Burrell, op. cit., p.365
204 'The paper splashed' *News of the World* 3.11.02

Chapter 16: A Private Secretary Goes Public

205 'unreliable alcoholic' *News of the World* 10.11.02; *Evening Standard* 11.11.02
205 'That explanation' Peat Report, para 1.163, p.42
206 'Telling my story' *News of the World* 10.11.02
207 'Yes, I suppose' *Sun* 14.11.02
207 'Peat announced' Michael Peat TV interview 12.11.02
207 'I, and more' *Daily Telegraph* 25.2.05
207 'I can give' *Sun* 17.11.02
208 'The police well' *Evening Standard* 4.12.02
209 'Inevitably, under' *News of the World* 15.12.02; *The Times* 16.12.02
211 'Blair was also' Campbell, *Diaries Vol. 3*, op. cit., p.390

Chapter 17: Money Matters

213 'Hammer had no' *Daily Mail* 8.3.03
214 'He had also' *Financial Times* 4.11.04
216 'Working for Charity' *Observer* 16.3.03; *Daily Telegraph* 18.6.03
217 'bad-mouthed Peat' *Daily Mail* 16.10.03
219 'The newspaper report' *Sun* 25.9.03
221 'In a quaint' PAC report 2004

Chapter 18: Whitewash

223 'express any view' Peat Report, p.7
223 'but the report' Ibid., p.21
223 'I'll tell' Ibid., p.24
223 'an improper' Ibid., p.3
223 'Peat and Lawson' Ibid., pp.35–40, 46
224 'puzzled' Ibid., pp.46–7
224 'remains something of' Ibid.
224 'There is no' Ibid., p.54
225 'inappropriate' Ibid., para 2.34, p.58
225 'consistent' Ibid., paras 2.80ff, p.69
225 'The suggestion that' Ibid., para 2.97, p.73
225 'Philip had allegedly' Ibid., p.74
226 'Lawson did not' Ibid., para 2.104, p.74
226 'He wrote that' Ibid., para 2.105, p.74
226 'Yet William Boyce' Ibid., para 2.107, p.75
226 'finds no support' Ibid., para 2.122, p.77
226 'were criticised by' Ibid. para 2.41, p.60
227 'The officers concerned' Press Association 11.04.03; *Daily Mail* 12.04.03
227 'scandalous' *Daily Mirror* 12.4.03
227 'without receiving' *Guardian* 9.3.03
227 'received improper' Peat Report, p.5
228 'to be financed' *Daily Telegraph* 16.3.03
228 'allegations of' Ibid.

Chapter 19: Revenge and Dirty Linen

229 'Burrell would deny' Burrell at Diana inquest 20.12.07
230 'I do not have' Burrell, op. cit., p.411
230 'safekeeping' Burrell at Diana inquest 17.1.08

230 'I warned Charles' *News of the World* 2.11.03
230 'gifts were an' Burrell, op. cit., p.341
230 'twenty telephone lines' Ibid., p.342
231 'They did nothing' *Daily Mirror* 23.10.03
232 'One week earlier' *Daily Telegraph* 11.11.03
232 'I was astonished' *News of the World* 9.11.03
233 'Fawcett was not' *Sun* 7.11.03
234 'Quite frankly' *Sun* 18.10.08

Chapter 20: Drowning Not Waving
240 'Rowan Williams' *Daily Telegraph* 13.2.03

Chapter 21: New Enemies
243 'Wisdom' Mayer, op. cit., p.342
244 'My twenty-five' *American Journal of Medicine* 122 (11): 973–4
244 'a deleterious' *Guardian* 14.5.15
245 'I know of' *Guardian* 27.6.04
245 'Charles is a' Ernst, op. cit., p.138
248 'He added that' *British Journal of General Practice* 1.1.06
248 'The solution' https://www.ncbi.nlm.nih.gov/pmc/articles/PMC1821425/
248 'These are outrageous' *The Times* 24.8.05
249 'complementary medicine is' *The Times* 29.8.05
249 'He would subsequently' *Guardian* 8.10.05
249 'the King's Fund' https://www.kingsfund.org.uk/press/press-releases/some-good-
    evidence-complementary-therapies-more-research-needed-says-kings-fund,
    23.5.06
253 'Under the banner' *Guardian* 11.3.09

Chapter 22: For Better or Worse
256 'The majority' *Sunday Times* 10.4.05
256 'government lawyers' House of Commons written answer 22.3.05
256 'The shambles' *Sunday Times* 10.4.05
258 'When he becomes' *Guardian* 11.2.05; *Daily Mail* 25.3.05
258 'Honesty about' *Sunday Times* 10.4.05

Chapter 23: Resolute Rebel
263 'only £1 million' *Mail on Sunday* 11.4.04
265 'a journalist could' *News of the World* 6.11.05
272 'This tour has' *Mail on Sunday* 12.11.17
272 'unthinking prejudices' Holden, op. cit., p.303
273 'a capital offence' Christopher de Bellaigue, *The Islamic Enlightenment* (Liveright,
    2017)

Chapter 24: Rules of Conduct
282 'fourteen staff' *News of the World* 14.1.07

Chapter 25: King Meddle
290 'The emir had' Mr Justice Vos's judgement 18.6.10, paras 75–7, 81, 86
291 'At the beginning' Ibid., paras 58, 69, 112
291 'very unhappy' Ibid., para 262

291 'unhappy that' Ibid., para 265
291 'not wedded to' Ibid., paras 73, 74
291 'he was steering' Ibid., para 260
291 'established planning' Richard Rogers, letter to *Guardian* 16.5.15
292 'a huge embarrassment' Vos judgement, para 42
292 'The Emir was' Ibid., para 74
292 'a judge would agree' Ibid., para 264
293 'going to fight' For details see note in ibid.: *Daily Mail* 6.2.10; *Sunday Times*
    16.5.10; *Guardian* 18.6.10 and 30.6.10; *The Times* 30.6.10
293 'Westminster councillors' Vos judgement, paras 268, 79, 89
293 'Under pressure' Ibid., paras 92, 122, 221
294 'It knocked' *Guardian* 16.6.09
294 'He sees this' Ibid.

Chapter 26: The Divine Prophet

296 'Anyone who' *Daily Mail* 18.12.10
301 'active deception' House of Commons Science and Technology Committee report,
    22–23.2.10; *Guardian* 2.8.10
301 'sinister powers' *Daily Mail* 3.3.10
302 'One instant success' Mayer, op. cit., p.69
303 'the biggest' *Daily Telegraph* 13.8.08

Chapter 27: Scrabbling for Cash

307 'We gave the' *Guardian* 23.8.01
307 'it was so raw' *GQ* magazine June 2017
310 'eventually agreed' *Sunday Times* 25.9.11

Chapter 28: Marking Time

317 'This is about' *Sunday Times* 3.12.17
317 'another free holiday' *Daily Mail* 12.7.10
319 'Prince Charles must' http://www.cornwalllive.com/prince-charles-branded-8216-
    hypocrite-8217-save/story-17790447-detail/story.html#hkBXyKp7R32jGfjc.99
325 'exaggerated' *The Times* 8.9.17, citing *Political Geography*

Chapter 29: The Prince's Coup

331 'fobbed off' *Mail on Sunday* 16.7.17
335 '14 per cent' *The Times* 21.8.17 and 16.9.17; *Prospect* September 2017
336 'To show her' *The Times* 7.10.17

Index

Abercrombie & Kent (travel agent), 3
Aberdeen University, 104
Abramovich, Roman, 311
acupuncture, 76, 79, 80, 244, 246, 248
Adams, Gerry, 327, 328
Adeane, Edward, 13, 85
Advertising Standards Authority, 300
Ahrends, Peter, 87–9
Airlie, David Ogilvy, Earl of, 2–3, 26, 56, 64, 129, 162, 222
Airy, Major General Christopher, 13, 14
Aitken, Jonathan, 187
Alderton, Clive, 272
Alefza, Knanysher, 281
Alexandra, Princess, 71
Allan, Alex, 61
Allbritton, Joe, 132, 174, 264, 308–10
Althorp estate, 41, 204
American Young Presidents' Organization, 259
Amory, Colin, 34
Andrew, Prince, 17, 57, 210, 338; behaviour of, 135, 139, 175–6, 181, 219, 285–6, 317; as British trade ambassador, 135, 175, 285, 317; WikiLeaks leak about, 317
Angelopoulos, Theodore, 4, 337
Anglican Church, 8–9, 11–12, 42, 240–1, 255, 258, 326, 338
Anne, Princess, 10, 17, 57, 63, 130, 258, 318
Annenberg, Leonore, 282–3
Anson, Charles, 8, 27, 39
Ant and Dec, 324
Anyaoku, Emeka, 141
Archer, Jeffrey, 187

architecture and urban planning: and American fundraising, 34, 35; Rogers' conflict with Charles, 83–5, 87–92, 288–95; Victorian buildings, 84, 85, 288; modernists, 84–92, 94, 270, 287–9, 292; traditionalists, 84–9, 93, 94, 96, 131, 288, 289; Poundbury principles, 85–6, 94, 95, 97–8, 287, 288; Cambridge history faculty, 86; Hampton Court speech, 86–8; National Gallery extension, 87–9; One Poultry, 87–9, 287; Paternoster Square, 90–1; Mansion House speech, 90–2; Urban Villages Group, 94; One Hyde Park, 288; Old Chelsea Barracks development, 288–95; houses on duchy land, 293, 319; see also Prince's Foundation for the Built Environment
Argentina, 102–3
art, music and literature, 24, 30, 31, 62, 83, 216, 268, 307; art colleges, 131–2; Traditional Arts, 312
Arts & Business, 312
Arup Associates, 90–1
al-Assad, President Bashar, 325
Astor, Brooke, 2, 4
Australia, 62, 67, 102, 141, 239, 283, 324
Aylard, Richard, 13, 15, 19, 20, 24, 56, 267; and Dimbleby project, 7, 10, 11, 14; as scapegoat, 7, 14, 18, 26; and Charles–Diana separation, 8–9; 'no intention of remarrying' announcement, 16, 17; on Diana, 18–19; Bolland on, 26; dismissal of, 26–7, 146; and Smith allegations, 146, 147

Bach Barcapel (charity), 79
Bagehot, Walter, 7
Bagshot Park, 136
Bain management consultants, 212
Ball, Peter, 13–14
Balmoral, 10, 47, 122, 219, 323–4; Diana
    at, 15, 67; prime minister's annual visit,
    25, 31; and Diana's death, 38–40;
    shooting rights at, 318
Banks, Tony, 179
Bannerman, Julian and Isabel, 51
Barry, Stephen, 24
Barrymore, Michael, 206
Bass, Perry and Nancy, 174
Bassey, Shirley, 166
Baum, Michael, 244
BBC, 52, 63, 83, 92, 103, 211, 316, 318;
    Panorama interview (1995), 14–16,
    23–4, 146, 334; *You Decide*, 27, 37; Reith
    Lectures, 104; and death of queen
    mother, 133, 170; Charles's dislike of
    Witchell, 257; *The Passionate Prince*, 284
Beatrice, Princess, 57, 318
Beaufort, Miranda, 235
Bell, Tim, 52, 132, 214
Berlusconi, Silvio, 302
Berry, Wendy, 14
Bessent, Scott, 3
Betts, Stephen, 113–14
Biddlecombe, Julia, 263
biofuels, 302
Birkhall (house on Balmoral estate), 35,
    122, 171, 175, 231, 254, 261, 306, 313,
    327
Black, Conrad, 168
Black, Guy, 6
Blackburne, Mr Justice, 266, 267, 269
Blair, Cherie, 31, 136, 137, 211
Blair, Tony: tensions with Charles, xi,
    57–9, 83, 99–107, 177–9, 265, 266,
    270–2; 1997 election victory (1997), 30;
    views on royal family, 31–2, 102, 138,
    271; and death of Diana, 39, 40; 'change
    and modernise' announcement, 41–2;
    and Charles's reinvention campaign, 42;
    at Charles's fiftieth birthday party, 66;
    and Charles–Camilla marriage, 71,
    255–6, 308; and Charles's charities, 76,
    100, 215; on 'forces of conservatism',
    100–1; Sophie Wessex on, 136, 137; and

the Commonwealth, 142, 240; and royal
    tax affairs, 163; and Golden Jubilee
    (2002), 174; and fox-hunting ban,
    177–9; and Burrell trial, 199; lunch with
    Charles at Clarence House, 211; and
    complementary medicine, 244; dislike of
    autocratic monarchs, 273; Good Friday
    Agreement, 327
Bloomingdale, Betsy, 129, 166, 174
Blunkett, David, 328
Bolland, Mark, xii; and Camilla's trip to
    New York (1999), 1–3, 70; media
    contacts, 2, 6, 19, 21, 24, 60–1, 66–7,
    69–70, 99, 156–7, 181; relationship with
    Charles, 2, 19–20, 157, 209; and
    Camilla's image, 2–3, 20–1, 24–5, 27,
    60–70, 124–5, 128–31, 136, 158, 164–7;
    and Lamport, 4–5, 29, 64, 158, 162;
    background and private life, 6, 27, 157;
    Charles tempted to appoint, 6, 14, 19;
    friendship with Camilla, 19, 20, 60,
    64–5; appointed by Charles, 19–20; and
    Aylard's dismissal, 26–7; Buckingham
    Palace's distrust of, 27, 49, 50, 63, 64, 70,
    128–30, 134, 137–8, 164, 181–2; and
    Diana, 27, 147; and Shackleton, 27, 157,
    158, 201, 204; advice to Charles, 34, 44;
    and Junor's book, 37, 61, 63; and death
    of Diana, 38, 42; and departure of
    Fellowes, 46; and Fawcett crisis, 53–5;
    on Charles's political meddling, 59, 80,
    267, 269; aim to demythologise Diana,
    61–4; and Ritz hotel photograph (1999),
    68–9; and Charles's Institute of
    Architecture, 94, 96, 130–1; on
    Mandelson, 106; and Burrell case, 114,
    120, 142–3, 150–8, 201, 204, 225, 226,
    230, 231, 233–4; on Camilla, 122, 259,
    263; dispute with van Cutsem, 133–4;
    and Sophie Wessex press stings, 137–8;
    and Smith allegations, 143–6, 232; on
    Charles's character, 154; and Peat, 164,
    165, 169, 181–2, 186, 209–10, 228,
    232–4, 256; leaves St James's Palace, 182;
    ends part-time consultancy, 210, 228,
    230; 'Blackadder' column, 210–11, 230,
    231; and Elaine Day complaint, 241, 242;
    on Camilla–Charles relationship, 258–9;
    and Higdon, 264, 311
Booker, Christopher, 86

Borg, Bjorn, 285

Boswell, James, 90

Bowyer, Timothy, 155

Boyce, William, 160–1, 187, 189–94, 196–200, 208–9

Brandreth, Gyles, 262

Branson, Richard, 72, 317

Bristol Centre, 78

British Library, London, 91

British Medical Association (BMA), 76–7, 301

Brooks, David, 215

Brown, Gordon, 163, 222, 271

Brown, Harold, 108–9, 111, 118, 120, 149, 154, 186, 208–9, 224–5

Brown, John, 34

Brown, Peter, 3, 4

Brown, Tina, *The Diana Chronicles*, 276

Browne-Wilkinson, Hilary, 6–7, 18, 19, 94, 96, 131

Browne-Wilkinson, Nico, 6, 18

Brownlow, David, 252

Brunei, 304, 315

Bryan, Johnny, 135

Bryant, Jonathan, 313

Buchanan, Elizabeth, 52, 106, 132, 214, 216, 218

Buckingham Palace (building): Burrell's employment at, 20, 109, 234; royal family on balcony of, 57, 171, 316–17; Charles's fiftieth birthday party at, 65, 66; fundraising dinners at, 124, 129–30, 166, 174–5, 212, 213, 217, 306; Jubilee concerts at, 173; in need of renovation, 261; banquets for Chinese presidents, 265, 267, 327; Charles's sixtieth birthday party at, 284; tennis court, 285; sixtieth anniversary concert at, 316; Charles's sixty-fifth birthday party at, 318; and Charles's living arrangements as king, 338

Buckingham Palace (royal court/ household): opposes Camilla, 1, 7, 26–8, 36–7, 69; ineptitude of queen's advisers, 8, 128; and War of the Waleses, 8, 13, 27, 28, 181; and Dimbleby project, 10; Way Ahead Group, 25–6, 56–7, 61, 102, 129, 135; distrust of Bolland, 27, 49, 50, 63, 64, 70, 128–30, 134, 137–8, 164, 181–2; and death of Diana, 38–40; Janvrin

replaces Fellowes, 46–7; and Charles's court, 46–50, 57, 63–5, 128–31, 162–3, 168–9, 240–1, 277, 286, 311–12, 331; Camoys as lord chamberlain, 48, 50, 128; layers of hierarchy, 48, 49; and Blairite tactics, 49–50, 57; and Sophie Wessex press stings, 136–8; homosexuality among servants, 145; Peat's role at, 162–3; plans for queen's funeral ('London Bridge'), 240; coup to remove Geidt, 334–6; *see also* Elizabeth II, Queen; Philip, Prince

Burnham, Andy, 300

Burns, Terry, 177–8

Burrell, Graham, 113, 148, 200

Burrell, Paul: prosecution for theft, xi, 120, 151, 154–61, 183–200, 208, 224–6; as Diana's confidential accomplice, 20, 109–10, 145–6, 158–60; employed at Buckingham Palace, 20, 109, 234; and Spencer family, 41, 110–11, 116–19, 143, 157, 159, 187–8, 190, 204, 230, 231; as celebrity, 109, 117, 148, 191–2; and mahogany box, 110–12, 143–5, 148, 160, 190–1, 230; knowledge of royal secrets, 111, 115, 120, 143, 145–6, 148–51, 158–61, 185, 187–8, 190–1, 202–4; and Smith allegations, 111, 143, 145, 148–50, 160–1, 187, 191; 'Burrell photograph', 112, 155, 161, 191, 201; arrest and questioning of, 112–16, 190, 207–8; contacts in America, 113–14, 117–18, 149, 160, 184; letter to Charles, 114–15, 118–19, 189–90; use and misuse of information, 116–17, 146; St James's Palace briefing on, 116–19; meeting with queen, 119, 150, 183–4, 192–202, 225–6; letter to Prince William, 142–3, 189–90; sexuality, 145, 150, 206; *Entertaining with Style*, 148; meeting with Bolland, 151, 157, 233–4; 'victims' consultation meeting', 151–6, 161, 188, 191–2, 227; cancelled meeting with Charles, 151–3, 156, 157; thirty-nine-page statement, 158–9, 161; charged with theft, 159, 208; and car-crash plot predictions, 160, 229, 276; St James's Palace meeting about (11 September 2002), 186–7, 202, 225, 226; trial of, 189–200, 225–6; cashes in after trial, 200, 203–4, 206, 230–1; collapse of

Burrell, Paul (*cont ...*)
  trial, 200–2, 224; Peat report on trial,
  223–8; Taylor report on case, 227; *A
  Royal Duty*, 229–31; admits lying at
  crash inquest, 234; threatens further
  revelations, 234
Bush, George W., 262, 264–5
Bush, Laura, 264
Business in the Community, 73, 282, 312
Bute, Marquess of, 280
Butler, Robin, 8, 9

Caernarvon, 12, 16
Calvert-Smith, David, 144, 147, 186, 198,
  199
Cameron, David, 295, 319, 326–7
Camilla, Duchess of Cornwall and
  Rothesay: queen opposes marriage to
  Charles, xi–xii, 2, 16, 27, 28, 46, 59–60,
  63–4, 68–71, 257; and Bolland, 1–3, 6–7,
  19, 20, 60, 63–5, 69–70, 128–9, 164–7;
  visit to New York (1999), 1–5, 70, 330;
  popular dislike of, 2, 15, 27–8, 37, 235,
  256, 285; dislike of flying, 3, 282, 304–5;
  travel requirements, 3, 282, 304–5; and
  Higdon, 3–5, 129, 167, 262, 264, 283;
  310–11, 313; laziness, 3–4, 22, 122, 235,
  259, 282; and van Cutsems, 4, 65, 133–4,
  236–7; luxurious lifestyle, 5, 122–3,
  125–6, 132–3, 237, 261, 275, 282, 284–5,
  305, 337; Camillagate tape, 9–10, 25, 54,
  60, 146, 181, 262; Diana's *Panorama*
  allegations, 15, 23–4; confronted by
  Diana (1989), 15–16; views on Diana,
  15–16, 18, 121, 185; constitutional status
  of, 16, 256–8, 331; divorce (1994), 17,
  18; relationship with Parker Bowles,
  21–4, 62–3; affair with Charles (from
  late 70s), 22–4, 63, 254; friendship with
  Diana, 23; and Mandelson, 36; fiftieth
  birthday party, 36–7, 276; impact of
  Diana's death, 42, 45–6, 60; financial
  position, 54; at Charles's fiftieth birthday
  parties, 65–6; Ritz photograph with
  Charles (1999), 68–9; increased public
  popularity, 70–1, 121, 171; and Burrell's
  knowledge of secrets, 120, 160; public
  opposes becoming queen, 121, 256, 262,
  274, 285, 331, 335; domestic life with
  Charles, 121–2; at Charles's table in

Buckingham Palace, 129–30; at
  Constantine's birthday party, 130; and
  Charles's charities, 131, 174, 312–13; car
  accident, 164–5; and Peat, 165, 169, 217,
  228, 237, 254–6, 275; Samaritans dinner
  at Buckingham Palace, 166; and queen
  mother's funeral, 170–1; increased
  acceptance after queen mother's death,
  171, 173; meets the queen, 171; and
  Golden Jubilee (2002), 173; and
  Bolland's departure, 182, 210; and
  Shackleton, 185; personal upkeep as
  tax-deductible, 222; and Burrell's book,
  229–31, 235–7, 256; whispering
  campaign against, 235, 237; George
  Carey on, 236; Charles's proposal to,
  254–5; shambolic lead-up to wedding,
  254–7; 'unwilling bride' disinformation,
  257, 258; marries Charles, 258–60;
  married life with Charles, 261–2, 275,
  284, 335; and state visit to USA, 262–5;
  and the Commonwealth, 272, 283, 324,
  325; gifts from Saudi royals, 274, 283; in
  USA with Charles, 282–3; and Kate
  Middleton, 308; increasing prominence,
  318; seventieth birthday party at
  Highgrove, 330; 2017 media campaign,
  331
Camoys, Lord, 48, 50, 56, 122, 128
Campbell, Alastair, 32–3, 49, 58, 66, 83,
  99, 101, 102, 105, 106
Canada, 141, 239, 281, 307–8, 324
Canary Wharf, London, 92
cancer care: orthodox medicine, 77, 104,
  244, 245; complementary treatments, 78,
  244, 245, 250
Candy brothers, 288, 290–4
Caplin, Carole, 211
Carey, George, Archbishop of Canterbury,
  14, 16, 129, 236
Carlile, Alex, Lord, 115, 150, 183, 187–92,
  225
Carnarvon, Earl of, 59, 71
Carroll, Lewis, *Alice in Wonderland*, 127
Castell, William, 214–16
Castle of Mey, Thurso, 175, 261
Ceauşescu, Nicolae, 296–7
charities, Charles's: for disadvantaged
  youth, 66, 73–6, 89–90, 93, 214–16, 319;
  financial problems, 72, 93–5, 214–19,

243, 252–3, 281–2, 308–10, 312–13; as platform, 72, 76; proliferation of, 73, 94, 216, 218, 219, 302, 312; management/governance of, 73–6, 93–8, 214–19, 243, 250–3, 279–82, 308–10, 312–13, 336–7; duplication, 74, 215, 216, 252, 302; running costs, 74, 259, 263, 312; impact of Charles's reputation, 74, 93, 212; absence of dissenting views, 74–5, 95–6; sycophancy, 74–5, 95–6, 216, 218; infighting, 75–6, 93, 94, 96–7, 219, 309–10; and Blair, 76, 100, 215; taxpayer support for, 76, 100, 215, 244–5, 278; and complementary medicine, 79–80, 243–53, 299–300; Saudi donations, 92, 131, 274, 281, 314; Urban Villages Group, 94; need for rationalisation of, 218–19, 252, 279–80, 312, 313, 336–7; and Commonwealth, 272; Peat on Charles's benevolence, 279; Dumfries House, 280–1, 313–15; Camilla's demand for private dinners, 312–13; *see also* fundraising for charities; Prince's Trust

Charity Commission, 74

CHARLES, PRINCE OF WALES

causes and beliefs: xii, 49, 57–9, 72, 243–53, 267–71, 284, 324; and political impartiality, xi, xiv, 25, 59, 72, 90, 99–105, 177–81, 265–71, 289–95, 319–21, 326–9, 336; fox-hunting, xii, 36, 49, 54, 100, 101, 177–9; refusal to engage in debate, xiv, 83, 104, 106, 303, 320, 321; as divinely ordained, 9, 77, 92–3, 303; spiritualism and mysticism, 11, 42–3, 76–82, 86, 92–3, 95–6, 104, 243, 269, 272–3, 296–303, 319; religious views, 11–12, 47, 77, 92–3, 104, 240–1, 303; and modern world, 16–17, 31, 77, 83–6, 131, 243, 296, 302–3; mad cow disease, 25; views on politicians, 30–2, 57, 58, 102, 178, 326; dislike of Chinese leaders, 32, 100, 265–7, 327; political speeches, 76–8, 86–9, 103, 178, 180–1, 268–9, 272–3, 292–3, 301–2, 325–6; idolises pre-modern world, 77, 86, 243, 273, 299, 303, 332; rejection of science, 77, 78, 104, 106, 303; *Harmony*, 86, 296, 302; pro-Islamic sentiments, 95–6, 177, 238, 239, 272–4, 301–2, 305, 306, 325–6;

foot-and-mouth disease, 104–6, 179; letters to ministers, 179–81, 267, 328–9; visits to Transylvania, 298–9, 337; on Syria's civil war, 325; on radicalisation of Muslims, 325–6; and 2016 floods, 326–7; *see also* architecture and urban planning; charities, Charles's; complementary medicine; education; environmental issues

character: refusal to accept blame, xii, 7, 11, 25, 43, 270, 335; self-doubt, xii, 11, 16, 90, 153–4; disloyalty, xiii–xiv, 4–5, 13, 14, 26–7, 51, 96–7, 162, 210, 310, 335, 337; victims of, xiii–xiv, 50–1, 93–4, 96–7, 210, 264, 310–11; dislike of criticism/dissenting views, xiv, 9, 11, 46, 52, 55, 74–5, 92; scapegoats, 7, 14, 18, 129, 162; self-pity, 7–8, 12–14, 16, 36, 38, 41, 43, 67–8, 243, 257; intolerance/bad temper, 9, 11, 13, 14, 29, 49, 52, 125, 335; sense of superiority, 11, 43, 57, 58, 76; grudges, 13, 14, 49, 335; selfishness, 14, 27, 62, 177, 210, 230, 319, 322; resentment of Diana, 18–19, 62; derogatory comments about Diana, 24, 42, 61; on himself, 44–5, 67–8; discourteousness, 52, 88, 126, 138, 314–15, 322

financial matters: 212–22, 277–81, 305, 336; extravagance, xi, 32–3, 35, 126–7, 172, 175, 214, 220, 278, 285, 286, 304; luxurious lifestyle, xi, 5, 26, 32–3, 35, 124–8, 219, 337; 'rent-a-royal' accusations, xi, 123, 168, 217; advisers expected to work without payment, 17–18, 51–2, 93, 247, 287; problems with charities, 72, 93–5, 214–19, 243, 250–3, 281–2, 308–10, 312–13; mismanagement, 93–5, 215–19, 243, 250–3, 280–2, 308–10, 312–13, 337; travel costs, 122, 127, 138, 177, 278, 282, 303–5, 309, 319, 337; household costs, 127, 175, 221, 228, 261, 278, 304; tax affairs, 163, 219–22, 278, 320; and Peat, 163–4, 214, 216–19, 220–2, 277–82, 304, 311–12; parliamentary investigation, 220–2, 320; *see also* Duchy of Cornwall; fundraising for charities

private life: adultery with Camilla, xi–xii, 7, 9–10, 12–15, 120; and queen's hostility

Charles, Prince of Wales (*cont ...*)
  to Camilla, xi–xii, 2, 59–60, 63–4,
  68–71, 129–31; War of the Waleses,
  7–10, 12–16, 18–19, 26–8, 36–7, 40,
  145–6, 181; separation from Diana, 8–9;
  Camillagate tape, 9–10, 25, 54, 60, 146,
  181, 262; relations with parents, 10–11,
  28, 47–8, 60, 63–4, 123, 135, 138–9, 204,
  284, 318, 332; education, 11, 127;
  misjudged friendships, 13–14, 123, 132,
  166, 213, 264, 285; suspicions about his
  siblings, 17, 57, 135; divorce from Diana
  (1996), 19, 24; early love for Camilla,
  21–2, 63, 254; affair with Camilla (from
  late 70s), 22–4, 63, 254; engagement to
  Diana, 23; resumes relationship with
  Camilla (mid-80s), 24, 254; and Spencer
  family, 39–41, 60, 117, 133, 156, 231;
  Charles Spencer's enmity towards, 40–1,
  60, 117, 231; and gardening, 51–2;
  letters to 'close relative', 67–8; domestic
  life with Camilla, 121–2; Aegean cruise,
  122–3; travelling lifestyle of, 125–6;
  Jephson book, 134–5; alleged
  homosexual act, 145, 146, 232–3; at
  Mount Athos, 171–2; moves into
  Clarence House, 175; Burrell's post-trial
  revelations, 203–4; portrayal of in
  Burrell's book, 229–31; and Settelen
  tapes, 236; relationship with sons,
  237–8, 307, 323–4, 334–5, 338; proposes
  to Camilla, 254–5; shambolic lead-up to
  wedding, 254–7; marries Camilla,
  258–60; married life with Camilla,
  261–2, 275, 284, 335; TV dramas based
  on his infidelity, 262; thaw in relations
  with queen, 274–5, 284; sixty-fifth
  birthday party, 318
  public life: campaign for Camilla's
  acceptance, xi–xiii, 1–7, 17–21, 24–9;
  and the Commonwealth, xi, 141–2,
  176–7, 238–40, 271–2, 283, 324–5, 332;
  relationship with Blair, xi, 30, 57–9, 83,
  99–107, 177–9, 211, 265, 266, 270–2;
  low approval ratings, xi, xiv, 6, 10, 27–8,
  37, 41, 173, 211, 234, 335; encounters
  with public, xii, 16, 43–4, 66, 70, 97, 125,
  283, 321; public opposes Camilla
  marriage, xii, 7, 37, 46, 60, 70, 256; view
  of duty, xii, 8, 14, 24–5, 41, 42, 59; on

  role as king, xiii–xv, 30–1, 290, 319–22,
  332–3, 336, 338; and media
  manipulation, xiii, xiv, 57, 66–71, 267;
  Dimbleby project, 7–8, 10–14, 21, 30–1,
  146, 240; stops talking to media (1993),
  10; Major's irritation at, 25; and
  privileges of minor royals, 26, 47, 57,
  135–6, 138–40, 171, 285–6, 317–18; at
  Hong Kong handover (1997), 31–5,
  265–7; and Mandelson, 36, 42–5, 49, 59,
  65, 66, 106; and Junor's book, 37, 61–3,
  67; and death of Diana, 38–41; seeks
  reinvention after Diana's death, 41–6;
  suspension of Camilla campaign, 42;
  trip to South Africa, 44–5; rising
  approval ratings, 45–6, 121, 330–1;
  disdain for old guard at Palace, 48; and
  Golden Jubilee (2002), 57, 173–4;
  resumed Camilla campaign, 59–71,
  122–5, 128–31, 136, 165–7; aim to
  demythologise Diana, 61–4, 67; trips to
  Australia with Diana, 62, 67; queen's
  abdication issue, 63–4; fiftieth birthday
  parties, 63–7; Ritz photograph with
  Camilla (1999), 68–9; increased support
  for Camilla marriage, 70–1, 121, 171,
  173; visits Argentina, 102–3; and Burrell
  case, 114–20, 142–4, 148, 151–61,
  184–8, 191–2, 224–7; lord high
  commissioner of Church of Scotland,
  124–5; and Smith allegations, 143–8,
  160–1, 187, 191, 205–7, 223–4, 231–3;
  police briefing at Highgrove, 151–6, 161,
  188, 191–2, 227; and death of queen
  mother, 170–1; and queen's recollection,
  193, 195–6, 201, 204, 225–6; blames
  police for Burrell fiasco, 201; ends
  Bolland's consultancy, 209–10, 228, 230;
  and Peat inquiry/report, 223–8; courts
  Sun journalists, 234; disdain for
  symbolic customs, 241; continued public
  scepticism about, 256, 274, 283–4,
  334–5; absence of public excitement
  about wedding, 257, 259; state visit to
  USA, 262–4; borrowing of planes from
  donors, 264, 309; and *Mail on Sunday*
  China case, 265–7, 269, 320, 328; visits
  Pakistan, 272; invites terror victims to
  Highgrove, 275; visit to Tottenham after
  riots, 275; fear of William and Kate's

appeal, 307–8, 323–4; increasing prominence of, 318, 331–2; campaign to improve image, 318–23; and reconciliation in Ireland, 328; and Geidt's message (May 2017), 333–4; coup to remove Geidt, 335–6; drawings for portrait on coins, 338; *see also* court/household of Charles

Charles III (play), 332–3

Chartres, Richard, Bishop of London, 110, 258

Chatsworth House, 54, 125–6

Chelsea Flower Show, 173, 306

China, 32, 100, 101, 179, 265–7, 320, 327

Chipperfield, David, 88, 92

Church of Scotland, 124–5, 129

civil list, 26, 47, 135, 162, 163

civil marriages, laws on, 255, 256

Clarence House, 9, 175, 219, 228, 237, 259; *see also* court/household of Charles

Clarke, Charles, 268

Clegg, Nick, 319

Cleverdon, Julia, 74–5, 172, 218, 282

Clifford, Max, 136, 203

Clinton, Hillary, 302

Clooney, George, 72

Cobra (government's crisis committee), 105

Cohen, Ronnie, 279

Cohen, Samantha, 336

Colonques, Manuel, 72–3, 156, 306–7

Commonwealth, xi, 141–2, 176–7, 238–40, 257–8, 271–2, 283, 324–5, 332, 335

complementary medicine, xii, 11, 73, 76–82, 243–6, 250–1, 328; and Charles's charities, 79–80, 243–53, 299–300; Smallwood's report on, 246, 247–9; 'The College of Medicine', 299–300; duchy's 'Detox Tincture', 300

Conservative Party, 52, 90

Constantine, King (of Greece), 127, 130, 174

constitutional issues: political impartiality, xi, xiv, 25, 59, 72, 90, 99–105, 177–81, 265–71, 289–95, 319–21, 326–9, 336; status of Camilla, 7, 16, 26, 256–8, 331; Charles's divorce, 9, 26, 42; Accession Oath, 12, 47, 240–1, 326, 338; Protestant settlement (1701),

12, 47; female succession, 26, 47; leadership of Commonwealth, 238–40, 271–2, 283, 324–5, 332

Cook, Robin, 36

Copenhagen conference (2009), 302

Corus Steel, 105–6

Costner, Kevin, 72

Country Life magazine, 319

Countryside Alliance, 178, 180

Countryside Fund, 312

court/household of Charles: feudal exercise of power in, xiii–xiv, 50–2, 55–6; absence of dissenting views, xiii–xiv, 8–9, 14, 20, 28–9, 48–9, 52, 55, 164; treatment of staff, xiii–xiv, 4–5, 13, 14, 26–7, 29, 50–6, 125, 210, 241–2, 310–13; sycophants, xiv, 20, 29, 46, 52, 66, 106, 164, 218, 335–6; rivalries and plots, 4–5, 14, 18, 20, 26, 34–6, 162, 164–5, 181–2, 209–10; scapegoats in, 7, 14, 129, 162; and War of the Waleses, 13, 14, 26, 145–6, 181; Higdon's criticism of, 35; campaign against Fellowes, 46; and Buckingham Palace, 46–50, 57, 63–5, 128–31, 162–3, 168–9, 240–1, 277, 286, 311–12, 331; layers of hierarchy, 49–51; 'vipers' nest', 49, 63, 234, 310; reversed dismissal of Fawcett, 53–6; staff mutiny at Highgrove, 53–6; height of courtiers, 71; sales of unwanted gifts/pilfering, 114, 118, 153, 207–9, 227; travelling staff, 125–6; gay staff, 145, 147; Peat replaces Lamport, 162; atmosphere of fear, 169; vulgarity and tawdriness, 212–13; overhaul of top team, 311; absence of wise counsellor, 335, 337; plans for Charles's succession, 337–8; *see also* Fawcett, Michael; Smith, George; rape allegations

Crichton, Andy, 54

Crisp, Nigel, 243–4

Cumbria floods (2016), 327

Cunningham, John, 99

Cutsem, Emilie van, 4, 65, 133, 237

Cutsem, Hugh van, 4, 65, 79, 122, 133–4, 236–7, 258

Daily Mail, 21, 68, 157, 217, 219, 233, 234; Kay as Diana's confidant, 15, 24, 110; supports Charles over GM crops,

Daily Mail (cont ...)
99–100, 267; reports on Prince Andrew, 135; interviews with Charles, 167, 211; on Burrell trial, 200–1; and Higdon's background, 264

Daily Mirror, 9–10, 67–9, 113, 117–18, 200, 203, 204, 229–30, 234

Daily Telegraph, 10, 21, 57, 99, 165, 181–2, 210, 233–4

Dalai Lama, 265, 267

Davis, Peter, 75

Davy, Chelsy, 238

Day, Elaine, 241–2

de Brunner, Det. Chief Insp. Maxine: and Howard Brown case, 108–9, 112, 118, 120, 149; and Ward's report on Burrell, 109, 110; and McCorquodale, 110–11, 187, 201–2, 226; at Burrell's home (18 January 2001), 112–13, 191, 207–8; and Shaw, 115, 159; briefing at St James's Palace, 116–18; and Shackleton, 142, 148, 204; trip to America, 149; phone call from Wharfe, 150; at Highgrove briefing, 152–3, 156, 191, 227; meeting with Peat, 186; and Burrell's trial, 189, 191–3, 196–202; and queen's recollection, 193, 196–9, 202–4; threat from terrorist, 200, 202; media attacks on, 200–2; phone call from Stuart Osborne, 202–3; Yard supports, 208; cleared by Taylor report, 227

de Gaulle, Charles, 31

Devonshire, Debo, Duchess of, 54–5, 125–6, 258

Diana, Princess of Wales: trip to America with Charles (1985), 2, 262; and Morton book, 7–8, 15, 146, 232; War of the Waleses, 7–10, 12–16, 18–19, 26–8, 36–7, 40, 145–6, 181; ancestry, 8; health issues, 8, 61, 62; separation from Charles, 8–9; affairs, 10, 14–15, 61, 148, 158–9, 185, 203–4, 236; *Panorama* interview (1995), 14–16, 23–4, 146, 334; denunciations of Camilla, 15, 19, 23–4; portrayed as manipulative, 15, 61–2, 276; confronts Camilla (1989), 15–16; divorce from Charles (1996), 19, 24; Burrell as confidential accomplice, 20, 109–10, 145–6, 158–60; engagement to Charles, 23; friendship with Camilla, 23;

Charles's derogatory comments about, 24, 42; and Bolland, 27, 147; and Blair, 31; death of (1997), 37–40; funeral of, 40–1, 117; aim to demythologise, 61–4, 67; trips to Australia with Charles, 62, 67; letter to Charles's 'close relative', 67; Brown's apparent theft from, 108–9, 111, 118, 120, 149, 154, 186, 208–9, 224–5; possessions of after her death, 108–20, 148–58, 184, 186–8, 207–9; executors' destruction of documents, 110, 159; Philip's letters to, 110–11, 150, 160, 191, 229–30; mahogany box, 110–2, 143–5, 148, 160, 190–1, 205, 230; 'Her Royal Highness' title, 117; Jephson's book on, 134–5; and Smith allegations, 144–7, 223; Squidgygate, 146, 181; Settelen tapes, 148–9, 235–6, 334; reported drug abuse, 151; predicts car-crash plot, 160, 229, 276; Wharfe's book on, 185; Burrell's post-trial revelations, 203–4, 206; Taj Mahal photograph, 233; tenth anniversary memorial service, 275; inquest into death of, 276; twentieth anniversary of death, 334

Diana Memorial Fund, 111, 117

Dimbleby, Jonathan, xii, 18, 42, 258, 324; biography and TV documentary, 7–8, 10–14, 21, 31, 146, 240; on Charles as meddling king, 290, 319–20

Dittmar, Hank, 292

Dixon, Michael, 81–2, 244, 251, 253, 299–300

Dobbie, Peter, 46

Douglas, Michael, 2

Douglas-Home, Jessica, 296–9

Douro, Marquess of, 258

Drummond, John, 83

Duchy of Cornwall, 14, 127–8, 172, 175, 279, 300–1; farms, 78, 126–7, 163–4, 220, 281, 319; Poundbury, 85–6, 97–8, 288; income from, 126–7, 138, 163–4, 220–1, 228, 277–81, 305, 311–12, 320; tax issues, 220–2, 278, 320; finances of, 220–2, 320; rise in value of, 221, 312, 320; housing developments, 273, 293, 319

Duchy Originals, 308–10, 319

Duke of Edinburgh Award, 215, 286

Dumfries House, Ayrshire, 280–1, 306, 308, 312–15

Dunstone, Charles, 313

Earth Day, 319
Eaton Hall, Cheshire, 126
Ecclestone, Bernie, 83
education, 73, 78, 216; Charles's views, 30–1, 241–2, 268–9, 328; and New Labour, 83, 268, 328; and spiritualism, 92, 269; art colleges, 131–2; summer school in Devon, 268–9; standards of school food, 270; *see also* Prince's Foundation for the Built Environment
Edward III, King, 220
Edward VII, King, 131, 283
Edward VIII, King, 157, 338
Edward, Prince, 17, 136–7, 139–40, 181, 286, 318, 334, 338
Edwards, Arthur, 68, 234
Egypt, 271
Elizabeth, Queen, the Queen Mother, 9, 41, 59, 69, 128, 162, 260; advice to queen, 47; hundredth birthday celebrations, 130, 133; death of, 170–1, 175; funeral, 171, 178; inheritance tax avoidance, 219
Elizabeth II, Queen: opposes marriage to Camilla, xi–xii, 2, 16, 27–8, 46, 59–60, 63–4, 68–71, 130, 257; ability to unite nation, xiv, 48, 173–4, 316; and Charles–Diana warfare, 8, 13, 16, 28; relations with Charles, 10–11, 28, 48, 60, 63–4, 204, 284; frugality, 26, 118, 138, 337; Golden Jubilee (2002), 26, 46–7, 57, 119, 172–4; and Way Ahead Group, 26, 56–7, 129, 135; 'annus horribilis' speech, 28; and Blair, 31, 40, 102; dislike of Fawcett, 35, 65, 257, 260; and death of Diana, 38–9; conservatism of, 45, 47; Whitehall speech (November 1997), 48; at Charles's fiftieth birthday party, 66; meeting with Burrell, 119, 150, 183–4, 192–202, 225–6; and millennium celebrations, 128; at Constantine's birthday party, 130; hosts 'Dance of the Decades', 130; and follies of Andrew/Edward, 139–40; tax affairs, 163, 219, 222; and death of queen mother, 170–1; Jubilee speech, 172–3; Burrell recollection, 192–202, 204, 225–6; plans for funeral of ('London Bridge'), 240;

and Charles–Camilla marriage, 255–7, 259–60; eightieth birthday party, 274; Charles's television tribute to, 274–5; and Charles's fundraising, 314; sixtieth anniversary of accession, 316; at Malta Commonwealth conference, 325; visit to Dublin, 327–8; reduction in ceremonial duties, 331–2; and Geidt's message (May 2017), 333–4
Elliot, Annabel (Camilla's sister), 18, 66, 68
Elliot, Simon, 18
Emin, Tracey, 131
English, David, 19
environmental issues, 73, 83, 101–2, 179, 270–1, 302–3; van der Post's influence, 11; and Charles's travel arrangements, 14, 282, 303–5, 319; genetically modified crops, 57–9, 99–101, 104, 106–7, 179, 267, 270, 303, 328; climate change, 58, 262, 302, 304, 319, 324, 327; rainforest protection, 58, 302, 304; royal cattle, 78, 278, 300–1; Charles's Reith Lecture, 104; badger culling, 270; Charles wins Harvard award, 282–3; sale of duchy farmland for housing development, 293, 319; and Islam, 301–2; 2014 floods, 326–7
Epstein, Jeffrey, 285, 317
Ernst, Dr Edzard, 78–82, 245–9, 252, 253, 300, 301
Eugenie, Princess, 57, 318
European Union (EU), 105, 176, 244, 270–1, 302, 326
Evening Standard, 201, 208, 254
Exeter University, 78–82, 246, 249, 253, 301

Falconer, Charles, 255
Falkland Islands, 103
Farquharson, Andrew, 286
'Fashion Rocks', 216–17
Fawcett, Michael: importance of to Charles, 1, 20, 33–6, 53–6, 65, 143–6, 206–7, 212–13, 242, 307, 311; and Camilla, 5, 122, 275; Aylard plots removal of, 20; character of, 25, 33, 35, 53; and Hong Kong dinner party, 33–5; conflict with Higdon, 36, 146, 167–8, 310; and fundraising, 35, 132, 166–8,

Fawcett, Michael (*cont ...*)
212–13, 217, 275, 306, 313–15; as
organiser of parties, 35, 37, 65, 166–8,
174–5, 274, 304, 314, 322, 324, 330;
queen's dislike of, 35, 65, 257, 260; and
Buchanan, 52; reversed dismissal of,
53–6; and Colonques, 73, 156, 306; and
Smith allegations, 143–7, 205–6, 223,
228, 232–3; Diana seeks dismissal of,
145, 147; gifts to from donors, 168, 227;
and Burrell revelations, 203; injunctions
against Smith allegations, 205–6, 232–3;
'Fawcett the Fence' allegations, 206–7,
227; given 'indefinite leave', 206, 212;
continues working for Charles, 207,
212–13; on Charles's 'modest' lifestyle,
220; and Peat report, 223, 227–8;
generous exit package, 228; Premier
Mode commissions from Charles, 228,
313; and Dumfries House, 281, 313–15
Fayed, Mohamed, 41, 229, 276
Federation of Spiritual Healers, 80
Fellowes, Robert, 10, 19, 27, 49, 56, 134;
and War of the Waleses, 8, 15, 26, 28, 37,
40; queen's working relationship with, 9;
Charles's bitterness towards, 27, 39–40,
46, 48, 117, 133; and death of Diana,
39–40, 42, 46; ousted by Charles's
campaign, 46
Ferrar, Leslie, 264, 309–11
Flatley, Michael, 212
Flecha de Lima, Lucia, 229
Flick, Mike, 314
foot-and-mouth disease, 104–6, 179
Forbes, Kip, 34, 309
Foster, Norman, 88, 91, 92
Foundation for Integrated Health:
creation of, 79–80; Charles's loss of
confidence in, 81, 243; financial
problems, 243, 250–3; management
issues, 243, 246–7, 250–3; Peat as
chairman, 243, 246–51; relaunch, 243–4;
government finance for, 244–5;
*Complementary Healthcare: A Guide for
Patients*, 245–6; collapse of, 252–3, 299;
Gray's theft from, 252–3
Fox, Michael, 79–80, 243–7
fox-hunting, xii, 36, 49, 54, 100–1, 177–9
Freedom of Information Act, 328
Freeman, Peter, 287–8

Fresh Minds, 246–7
Freud, Lucian, 51–2
Fry, Stephen, 45
fundraising for charities: selling of access
to Charles, xi, 72–3, 123, 132–3, 166–8,
174–5, 212–13, 216–17, 259, 264, 281,
306–9; in America, 3, 34–5, 124, 167,
259, 263–4, 309–11; entertaining of rich
donors, 34–5, 44, 95, 123–4, 129–32,
166–8, 174–5, 313–15, 336; and Fawcett,
35, 132, 166–8, 212–13, 217, 275, 306,
313–15; during official trips, 35, 44,
263–4; and Charles's bureaucracy, 74,
312; from complementary medicines
manufacturers, 79, 245, 247, 252; in Gulf
region, 92, 131–2, 314; dinners at
Buckingham Palace, 124, 129–30, 166,
174–5, 212–13, 217, 306; high-profile
events, 216–17; *see also* Higdon, Robert

G20 summit (London, 2009), 302
Gale, Adrian, 93–6, 131
Gates, Bill, 279
Gavron, Nicky, 135
GCHQ, 10
Geidt, Christopher, 311, 331–6
genetically modified crops, 57–9, 99–101,
106–7, 179, 267, 270, 303, 328
George IV, King, 30
George VI, King, 47
Gergiev, Valery, 168, 322
Gerson Therapy, 245, 250–2
Gibbins, Michael, 116, 145–6, 149, 186–7,
195, 202, 225–6
Gimson, Simon, 283, 324
Global Foundation, 35, 44
Goldsmith, Lady Annabel, 15
Goldsmith, Peter, 194, 198–200
Goodall, Sarah, 242, 265
Goodman, Clive, 274
Goodwin, Fred, 162, 214, 217–18, 279–80
Gordonstoun school, 11, 127
Gore, Al, 283
Gosford Park (film), 322
Gosling, Sir Donald, 275, 285, 308
Gough, Piers, 292
Gray, George, 247, 252–3
Green, Hugh, 263
Greene, Graham, *The Quiet American*, xii
Grieve, Dominic, 329

Grimes, George, 111, 113
Grosvenor, Gerald, Duke of Westminster, 126
Grosvenor, Lady Tamara, 236–7
Guardian, 227, 232, 234, 244, 253, 258, 292, 294, 328–9
Guggenheim, Eileen, 124
Gulf region, 238–9, 272, 305, 314, 325–6, 332
Gwilliam, Steve, 148, 206

Hackney, Rod, 74, 89–90
Hague, William, 136, 305
Hain, Peter, 249, 300, 328
Halifax, Lord, 121, 126, 258
Halliwell, Geri, 165
Hamad, Sheikh (of Qatar), 281, 314
Hambro, Charlotte, 22
Hamilton, Andrew, 292
Hammer, Armand, 213
Hammond, Anthony 'Wally', 241
Hampton Court, 66, 86–8
Harris, Colleen, 186, 231
Harry, Prince, 27, 65, 123, 149, 174, 181, 194, 324, 330; birth of, 24; safari in Botswana, 44; press speculation on paternity of, 111, 209; press speculation over drug-taking, 133–4; smokes cannabis at Highgrove, 165, 237–8; coolness towards Camilla, 237, 265, 307, 331; grieves for Diana, 238, 307, 334; wears Nazi uniform, 238; military service, 265, 317; strip poker story, 318; pursuit of individual interest, 333–5; TV documentary about Diana, 334–5; and Meghan Markle, 335
Harvard Aids Institute, 174
Haskins, Christopher, 106
Hastings, Max, 296
Hatt, John, 298
Haverson, Paddy, 269, 311
Havlik, Jan, 108, 149
Heale, Jonathan, 51
Hearst, Patty, 129, 166
Heath, Edward, 31
Heinz, Drue, 45, 131–2
Henney, Sandy, 16, 20, 165
Henriques, Mr Justice, 232
Heseltine, Bill, 170
Hewitt, Gavin, 63

Hewitt, James, 14–15, 61, 110–11, 190, 209
Heywood, Jeremy, 147
Higdon, Robert, 44, 124, 132, 156, 174, 212, 231, 282–3, 308–10; relationship with Charles, 3, 34–5, 123–4, 166–7, 264, 310; and Camilla, 3–4, 5, 129, 167, 262, 264, 283, 310–11, 313; recruited by Charles, 34–5; conflict with Fawcett, 36, 146, 167–8, 310; and death of Diana, 37–8; alcoholism, 123–4, 310–11; and friends–donors distinction, 166, 174; expenses/salary, 166, 259, 263–4, 309; and Peat, 182, 217; and state visit to USA, 262–5; background of, 264; sacking of, 310–11, 336
Higgins, Stuart, 60–1, 64
Highgrove, 1, 14, 121, 174–5, 223, 275, 330; as sanctuary, 17, 41; Burrell works at, 20, 145, 203; purchase of, 23, 221; garden, 51–2, 126–7, 278, 306–7; staff mutiny at, 53–6; Charles's lavatory at, 58, 121; meeting with Blair at, 58–9; Philharmonia concert, 72–3; police visit to, 151–6, 161, 188, 191–2, 227; Harry smokes cannabis at, 165, 237–8; Islamic garden at, 307
Hinduja brothers, 314
Hinton, Les, 70
Hintze, Michael, 281, 314
Hoare, Oliver, 61
Hodge, Margaret, 320
Hodges, Mark, 148
Hodges, Richard, 94
Holden, Anthony, xii
Holkham Hall, Norfolk, 281, 322
homeopathy, 76, 79–81, 244, 247–8, 250–1, 300
Hong Kong handover ceremony (1997), 31–5, 265–7
Hornby, Amanda, 151–2
Horton, Richard, 249
House of Lords, 80–1, 89, 101
Howard, Stephen, 312
Hu Jintao, President, 265, 327
human rights legislation, 180–1, 256, 269, 320
Hungary, 298–9
Hunt, Jeremy, 301
Hunter, Anji, 42, 71

Hussey, Susan, 65
Huth, Angela, 45

India, 233, 271, 314, 322, 324
Indonesia, 302
Inner City Aid, 74, 89–90
Invercauld estate grouse moor, 318
Invermark, Sutherland, 126
Iran, 238
Iraq war (from 2003), 177–9, 199, 223,
  240, 262, 270–1, 325–6
Irvine, Derry, 180–1
Islamist terrorism, 172, 272, 274–5, 325–6
Israel, 272–3
Italy, 89, 92, 131
It's a Royal Knockout, 181

Jagger, Mick, 165
Janvrin, Robin, 27, 28, 240, 271, 317; and
  Bolland's tactics, 2, 63, 64, 70, 128–30,
  134, 164, 181–2; and Way Ahead Group,
  26, 56–7; and death of Diana, 38–9; and
  Golden Jubilee (2002), 46–7, 57, 119,
  172–3; and Charles's court, 48–50, 63–5,
  128–9, 168; and Blairite tactics, 49–50,
  57; and Burrell case, 116, 119, 193–4,
  199–200; and Sophie Wessex scandal,
  136–8; and Prince Edward's behaviour,
  139; replaces Lamport with Peat, 162;
  and 'rent-a-royal' phrase, 168; and
  Prince Andrew's behaviour, 176
Jay, Michael, 177
Jefri, Prince (of Brunei), 315
Jephson, Patrick, 10, 19, 29, 145–6, 163;
  Shadows of a Princess, 134–5
Jiang Zemin, President, 32, 265
Jobson, Robert, 254
John, Elton, 128, 165
John Paul II, Pope, death of, 259
Johnson, Alan, 244–5
Johnson, Boris, 292, 293, 295
Johnson, Samuel, 30, 90
Jordan, 238
Jung, Carl, 76
Juniper, Tony, 296
Junor, Penny, 37; Charles: Victim or
  Villain?, 61–3, 67, 134; The Duchess, 62

Kálnoky, Count Tibor, 298–9
Kaufmann, Julia, 175

Kavanagh, Trevor, 206–7
Kay, Richard, 21, 182, 231; as Diana's
  confidant, 15, 24, 110; and Burrell, 114,
  151–2, 156, 195, 200, 234
Kelly, Angela, 34
Kennedy, John and Caroline, 123
Kensington Palace, 9, 13, 145–6, 155, 163,
  223, 229; Burrell works at, 20, 146,
  158–9, 203–4; Brown's flat at, 108–9;
  Burrell removes Diana's possessions
  from, 109–10, 112–14, 150, 189–91, 231;
  apartments in, 163, 311–12; the Kents at,
  163, 171
Kent, Geoffrey, 3, 4, 34–5, 44, 123–4, 311
Kent, Prince Michael of, 286
Kent, Princess Michael of, 163, 171
Keppel, Alice, 131
Kerr, Jane, 149
Kerr, John, 103
Keswick, 'Chips', 126
Keswick, Sarah, 126, 330
Khaled Al-Faisal, Prince, 273–4
Khan, Hasnet, 203–4
Kilkenny, Alan, 17–19
Kime, Robert, 55
King's Cross development, 287–8
King's Fund, 249
Kirdar, Neimar, 132–3
Knatchbull, Amanda, 22
Knatchbull, Nicholas, 133
Knott, Kevin, 255
Krier, Léon, 85–6, 97–8
Kulibayev, Timur, 285
Kyriacou, Kristina, 318–19

La Leopolda (estate in South of France), 5
Lake, Mike, 218, 281
Lampedusa, Giuseppe di, The Leopard, 337
Lamport, Stephen, 31, 35, 48–9, 101, 106,
  134, 164, 267; and Bolland, 4–5, 29, 64,
  158, 162; replaces Aylard, 26–7, 146;
  background and private life, 28–9; and
  fundraising, 34–5, 131, 168; and death
  of Diana, 39, 42; and Fawcett crisis,
  53–6; and Mori opinion poll (1998), 57;
  and Brown's apparent theft, 109, 118,
  224–5; and Burrell case, 114–16,
  118–20, 157–8, 224–6; tension with
  Shackleton, 117; as scapegoat, 129, 162;
  and Sun 'Marry Her' headline, 130; and

the Commonwealth, 141–2; and Smith allegations, 146–7; replaced by Peat, 162
Lancet, 249
Lansdale, David, 163–4
Lansdowne, Charles, 65
Latsis, Yiannis, 5, 65, 122–3, 213, 285
Laurence, Tim, 318
Lavely, Kim, 250–2
Lawson, Edmund, 159, 188, 194, 202n, 223–7
Legge-Bourke, Tiggy, 160
Leicester, Earl of, 281
Leigh, Edward, 320
Leishman, Mark, 252, 336
Lemos, Chrysanthi, 72–3
Lendrum, Rupert, 242
Lewis, Simon, 49–50, 56–7, 137
Linley, Lord, 174
Livingstone, Ken, 84, 268, 287
Lloyd's insurance building, 84
Lord, Shirley, 166
Lowther-Pinkerton, James, 238
Lubbock, Jules, 86, 93
Luce, Richard, 136, 138, 139, 172
Lumley, Joanna, 165
Lunts, David, 94, 96–8
Lynch, Tom, 251
Lyndon, Neil, 213
Lynx helicopters, 270

McCartney, Paul, 173
McCorquodale, Sarah, 40, 120, 151, 188, 201; and de Brunner, 110–11, 187, 201–2, 226; and Diana's possessions, 110–11, 117–19, 156–7, 187, 230, 236; at St James's Palace briefing, 116–18; dislike of Shackleton, 117; at meeting in Shackleton's office, 142–4, 223–4; and 'rape tapes', 143–4, 223–4; Burrell's shredding accusation, 149, 159, 196; at St James's Palace meeting (11 September 2002), 186–7, 202, 225–6; and Burrell's trial, 190–1, 225–6
McEnroe, John, 285
McGrady, Darren, 150
McGuinness, Martin, 327–8
McKinnon, Don, 141–2, 176–7, 238–40, 271–2, 283, 324
McKinsey management consultants, 212
McManus, Amanda, 3, 55

mad cow disease, 25
Mahfouz, Dr Mahfouz, 314
Mahmood, Mazher, 136, 137
Mail on Sunday, 46, 134, 137, 155, 210, 232, 265–7, 269, 320, 328, 331
Major, John, 8, 9, 25
Mallalieu, Ann, 45
Malta, 271, 325
Manchester, 43–4
Mandela, Nelson, 44
Mandelson, Peter, 36, 42–5, 49, 59, 65–6, 106
Manley, Charlotte, 176
Mannakee, Barry, 61, 148, 236
Manoukian, Bob, 315
Manser, Michael, 86, 87
Margaret, Princess, 59, 60, 65, 109, 128, 130, 172, 262
Mariinsky Theatre, St Petersburg, 168
Markle, Meghan, 335
Marks, Ian, 79
Marriage Acts (1836/1949/1953), 255–6
Marsden, William, 103
Mary Rose (Tudor warship), 213
Maurice Laing Foundation, 78
Maxwell, Ghislaine, 135
May, Brian, 173
Meacher, Michael, 328
The Meddling Prince (Channel 4 documentary), 269
medical profession, 76–82, 243–4, 300–1
Medicines and Healthcare Products Regulatory Agency (MHRA), 300
Mendham, Victoria, 144
Menem, Carlos, 103
Merkel, Angela, 302
Mexico, 304–5
Middleton, Carole, 323
Middleton, Kate, 257, 316–17, 323–4; public popularity of, 285, 307–8; marries William, 307–9; topless photographs, 318
Mies van der Rohe, Ludwig, 87–8, 94, 287
Mihai Eminescu Trust (MET), 296–9
Milburn, Roger, 110, 112, 115, 142, 150, 154, 159, 192, 203; trips to America, 149, 184; meets Bolland at St James's Palace, 156–7; meeting with Peat, 186; and Burrell's trial, 189–91, 196–9; meets McCorquodale after trial, 202

Miliband, Ed, 319
Millennium Dome, 83–4, 91, 102, 128
Mills, Simon, 79–81, 251–2, 301
Milton, Simon, 292–3
Mimpriss, Peter, 237
Mishcon, Lord, 276
Mitchell, Austin, 320
Mitchell, Sandy, 274
Mittal, Lakshmi, 314
Monckton, Walter, 157
Monsanto, 270
Moore, Charles, 99, 165, 181–2
Morgan, Chris, 123, 133–4
Morton, Andrew, *Diana, Her True Story* (1992), 7–8, 15, 146, 232
Mountbatten, Lord Louis, murder of, 327, 328
Mowlam, Mo, 135
Mugabe, Robert, 179
Munday, Louis, 111–12, 155

nanotechnology, 244
The Nation Decides (BBC TV programme), 27–8
National Audit Office, 219–21
National Citizen Service, 312
National Farmers' Union, 105
National Museums of Scotland, 295
National Osteoporosis Society, 37, 167
National Theatre, London, 91
Nazir-Ali, Dr Michael, Bishop of Rochester, 273
New Labour, 30–2, 36, 39, 49–50, 57–9, 83, 238–9, 244–5; 'Urban Vision' scheme, 84; and Charles's GM campaign, 99–100, 106–7; tensions with Charles, 99–107, 177–80, 268–9, 328; 'Cool Britannia', 100
New York Academy of Art, 174, 259
New York Post, 263
New Zealand, 141, 239, 257, 283
News of the World, 24, 69–70, 134, 157, 203–6, 210, 265; Tom Parker Bowles story, 123; Sophie Wessex sting, 136–8; 'Harry's Drug Shame' headline, 165; and Prince Harry's paternity, 209; Bolland's 'Blackadder' column, 210–11, 230, 231; phone-hacking scandal, 274; Sarah Ferguson sting, 317
Nixon, Richard, 31

Noor, Queen (of Jordan), 174
Norfolk, Duke of, 240
Northern Ireland peace process, 327
Nutting, John, 187
Nye, William, 312, 320, 324

Obama, Barack, 309
O'Brien, Stephen, 73
Office of Fair Trading, 270–1
Ogilvy, Angus, 71, 215
O'Kane, Michael, 114, 119, 147, 149, 153, 158–9, 183; briefing at St James's Palace, 116–18; meeting in Shackleton's office, 142–4, 148, 224
O'Neill, Eva, 21, 235
Oppenheimer, Mary, 44
Osborne, Stuart, 202–3
osteopathy, 79, 245–6
Oxford Centre for Islamic Studies, 273, 301–2

Pakistan, 272
Palmer-Tomkinson, Charlie, 18, 21, 65, 77, 258
Palmer-Tomkinson, Patty, 18, 19, 21, 54, 65–6, 123, 258
Palmer-Tomkinson, Tara, 123
Palumbo, Peter, 87–9
Papamarkou, Alecko, 34
Parker Bowles, Andrew, 4, 6, 17–18, 21–4, 59, 62–3, 130, 260, 262
Parker Bowles, Laura, 330
Parker Bowles, Richard, 121
Parker Bowles, Tom, 123, 133, 237, 330
The Passionate Prince (BBC TV documentary), 284
Pavarotti, Luciano, 72
Pead, Gregory, 150
Peat, Michael: and Buckingham Palace's finances, 26, 129, 162–3; and Way Ahead Group, 26, 56; Burrell inquiry/report, 143n, 188, 194, 202n, 207, 223–8, 231–2; and Smith allegations, 143n, 187, 223–4, 231–3; becomes Charles's private secretary, 162–5; apartment in Kensington Palace, 163, 311–12; and Charles's finances, 163–4, 214, 218–22, 277–82, 304, 311–12; and Bolland, 164–5, 169, 181–2, 186, 209–10, 228, 232–4, 256; and Camilla, 165, 169, 217,

228, 237, 254–6, 275; insistence on total control, 165, 168–9, 177; and Fawcett's fundraising, 168; loyalty to Charles, 169; and the Commonwealth, 176–7, 238–40, 272; and impartiality issue, 179, 181, 266, 269–70, 289, 292; and Burrell case, 185–8, 192–5, 197–8, 200, 202, 207–8, 225–6, 230; St James's Palace meeting (11 September 2002), 186–7, 202, 225–6; and queen's recollection, 192–4, 197–8, 226; and Charles's charities, 216–20, 243, 246–51, 278–81, 312–13; relations with Buckingham Palace, 241–2, 277, 286, 312, 331; chairs Foundation for Integrated Health, 243, 246–51; shambolic lead-up to royal wedding, 254–6; and *Mail on Sunday* China case, 265–6, 320; sacks Ross, 286; and Charles's architectural views, 289, 291–4; leaves Charles's employment, 311–12

Pelli, Cesar, 92

Perry, David, 198, 199

Perspectives magazine, 94–5

Petrie, Carol, 124

Philharmonia Orchestra, 72–3

Philip, Prince: 'rent-a-royal' comment, xi; scorn for Charles, xi, 123, 138–9, 332–3; and Charles's childhood, 10–11, 48, 127, 138–9; relations with Charles, 10–11, 47–8, 123, 135, 138–9, 284, 318, 332; advises break with Camilla, 16; opposes marriage to Camilla, 20–1, 28, 138; and Way Ahead Group, 26, 56–7, 129, 135; and death of Diana, 40; letters to Diana, 110–11, 150, 160, 191, 229–30; and minor royals, 135–6, 138; and Sophie Wessex press stings, 138; childhood of, 139; Turner biography, 139; and follies of Andrew/Edward, 139–40, 176; and queen's recollection, 193, 225–6; and sixtieth anniversary of accession, 316; snubs Charles over shooting rights, 318; retirement from public duties, 333–4

Phillips, Hayden, 218–19

Phoenix Trust, 124, 174

phone-hacking scandal, 274

Physic Garden, Chelsea, 251

Pierburg, Clarissa, 315

Pierburg, Jürgen, 308, 314–15

Piper Alpha oil rig disaster, 213

Pitman, Rosemary, 24

Pollard, Stephen, 201

polo, 3, 4, 88, 153, 156, 174, 203, 278

Pompidou Centre, Paris, 89

Porcelanosa (Spanish company), 72–3, 156, 306–7

Porritt, Jonathon, 106

Porter, Adrian, 94–7

Porter, David, 93

Porter, Dame Shirley, 247

Poundbury, Dorset, 85–6, 97–8, 288

Powell, Carla, 36

Powell, Jonathan, 102

Premier Mode (Fawcett's catering company), 228, 313

Prescott, John, 84, 85, 291–2

Press Complaints Commission, 6, 27, 130, 136, 138

Prime (charity), 218

Prince of Wales's Foundation in America, 3, 34–5, 124, 259, 263–4, 309–11

Prince's Charities Foundation, 245, 308, 312

Prince's Drawing School, 131–2, 216

Prince's Foundation for Children and the Arts, 306

Prince's Foundation for the Built Environment, 92–8, 292, 295, 306, 312; move to Shoreditch, 95, 130–1; Islamic art course, 95–6; Hintze made chairman, 314

Prince's Teaching Institute, 216

Prince's Trust, 16–17, 89, 100, 228, 279–80, 313; creation of, 72–3; administrative costs, 74; twenty-fifth anniversary dinner, 165–6; financial problems, 214–16, 312–13; achievements of, 214–15, 268, 284; 'Skilled City' exhibition, 215; William refuses involvement in, 307, 323, 336

Prince's Trust Volunteers, 216

Prince's Youth and Business Trust, 74–6, 89–90, 123

Priory Hospital, south London, 144–5

Pseudo, Pedro, 72, 307

Pusztai, Arpad, 104

Qatar, Emir of, 288–94

Rafferty, Anne, 190, 191

Raine, Kathleen, 42–3, 243
Rainforest Project, 302, 304
Rausing, Eva, 167
Rausing, Hans Kristian, 314
Ray Mill, Wiltshire, 65, 121, 275, 282
Reagan, Nancy, 7–8, 34, 264
Reid, John, 244
Rhodesia, 22–3
Richard, Cliff, 173
Riddell, John, 13, 54
Rippon, Geoffrey, 87
Rivers, Joan, 124, 166, 259, 311
Roberts, Sir Hugh, 148
Robinson, Geoffrey, 66
Rockefeller family, 34, 174
Rogers, Richard, 83–9, 91–2, 287–95
Romania, 296–9, 337
Ross, Malcolm, 168–9, 242, 277, 286
Rostropovich, Mstislav, 171
Rothschild, Jacob, 65, 127–8, 217–19, 279,
    322, 330
Rothschild, Leo, 45
Rothschild, Miriam, 51
Royal Army Veterinary Corps, 59
Royal Collection, 118, 148
Royal Horticultural Society, 51
Royal Institute of British Architects
    (RIBA), 86–7, 93, 292–3
Royal London Homeopathic Hospital, 81
Royal Opera House, 289, 307
royal parks, 295
royal protection officers, 25, 47, 54, 61,
    109, 148, 202–3, 236; leaks by, 10, 152–3,
    156–7; breaking of confidentiality by, 185
Royal Society of Medicine, 77–8
royal train, 47, 219, 278, 304
Rudd, Kevin, 302
Ruff, Ron, 113–14, 184
rural affairs, 25, 73, 100–2, 106–7, 179,
    270–1; foot-and-mouth disease, 104–6,
    179; see also environmental issues
Rushdie, Salman, The Satanic Verses,
    273–4

Safra, Edmond, 2, 5
Safra, Lily, 5, 166, 174, 217, 308, 315
St Andrews University, 139
St James's Palace, 121–2, 127, 169, 197;
    Charles assigned to after separation, 9;
    briefing at (3 April 2001), 116–19;

meeting (11 September 2002), 186–7,
    202, 225–6; see also court/household of
    Charles
St John Wilson, Sir Colin, 91
Salisbury, Molly, 51, 52
Salisbury Cathedral, 92
Sandringham, 10, 20, 65, 122; 'culture
    weekends' at, 45, 320–2; shooting rights
    at, 318
Sane (mental illness charity), 312–13
Sarah, Duchess of York, 17, 135, 285,
    317–18; toe-sucking incident, 135, 181
Sarkozy, Nicolas, 302
Saudi Arabia, 92, 131, 238, 272–4, 283,
    314, 325–6
Savile, Jimmy, 13
Schiffer, Claudia, 156
Scotland, 56–7, 124–6
Scott Baker, Lord Justice, 276
Seabrook, Robert, 116, 150, 152, 160–1,
    187–8, 191, 194, 197–8, 225–6
Serota, Nicholas, 45
Settelen, Peter, 148–9, 235–6, 334
Shackleton, Fiona, 53, 117, 150, 160, 186,
    192, 200, 224–6; importance of to
    Charles, 6, 16, 18, 116, 146–7; and
    Bolland's appointment, 6–7, 19; and
    Bolland, 27, 157–8, 201, 204; at St
    James's Palace briefing, 116–19; and de
    Brunner, 142, 148, 204; meeting in office
    of (30 April 2001), 142–4, 148, 223–4;
    and Smith allegations, 143–8, 223–4;
    police briefing at Highgrove, 152–3, 161;
    deterioration in relationship with
    Charles, 184–5; at St James's Palace
    meeting (11 September 2002), 186–7,
    225; and queen's recollection, 197–8,
    204, 226
Shand, Bruce (Camilla's father), 17
Shand Kydd, Frances, 110, 116–17, 159,
    190
Shaw, Andrew, 113, 115, 150, 157–60,
    183, 185, 197, 225
Shebbeare, Tom, 42, 73, 75–6, 246, 249,
    264; deference of, 74–5, 218; critics of,
    214–16, 281; promoted, 216–17; and
    creation of new charities, 218–19;
    rationalisation attempts, 252, 279–80,
    312–13; departure, 313
Sheffield, 66

Sherrington, Amanda, 281
Short, Clare, 268
Sierra Leone, 239, 272
Skelly, Ian, 296
Smallwood, Christopher, 246–9, 287
Smith, Alison, 303
Smith, George: 'rape tapes', 111, 143–5, 148–50, 160–1, 187, 191, 205; and Shackleton's outburst, 143–4, 148, 223–4; background, 144; redundancy payment, 144, 147, 205, 223; allegation involving Charles, 145, 232–3; views on veracity, 145–7, 150, 223; police investigation, 147–8, 205–6; Fawcett's injunctions, 205–6, 232–3; sells story to *News of the World*, 205; Peat's investigation, 207, 223, 228, 231–2; extends accusations, 231–3
Smith, Steve, 249
Smithfield Market development, 288
Snow, Jon, 42, 73
Soames, Nicholas, 1, 2, 21, 65–6, 133
Somerset, David, Duke of Beaufort, 235
Somerset floods (2016), 326
South Africa, 44–5
Southwell, Clair, 114
Spencer, Charles, 9th Earl, 40–1, 60, 117, 204, 231, 276
Spencer, Jane, 40, 133
Spice Girls, 44
Spitting Image (ITV programme), 77
Sri Lanka, 324–5
Stanley, Ted, 129–30
Stanley Mills, Perthshire, 124
Stevens, Sir John, 207, 227, 276
Stevens, Patrick, 183, 196, 197, 198
Stewart, Colonel Bob, 238
Stewart, Rod, 173
Still, Andrew Taylor, 244
Sting, 165
Stirling, James, 86, 89, 91
Straw, Jack, 238–40
Stronach, Ken, 14
Strong, Roy, 41, 51–2, 55, 70–1, 92, 172
Studzinski, John, 212
Sun, 2, 33, 68–70, 130, 138, 171, 206–7, 234
Sunday Times, 12, 57, 60–1, 69, 123, 125, 133–4, 256, 290
Sunninghill Park, Berkshire, 285

Swift, Dr Will, 118, 149, 154
Syria, 325

Tallon, Billy, 260
Taylor, Sue, 196
Taylor, William, 227
Temenos Academy, 43
Terry, Quinlan, 288–92
Testino, Mario, 64, 331
Thatcher, Margaret, 34, 36, 66, 75, 90, 264
Thorburn, Georgina, 289
Tibet, 100, 265, 296
Time magazine, 324
The Times, 248–9, 294–5
Tooke, Professor John, 81
Transylvania, 297–9
Travolta, John, 262
Trinity College, Cambridge, 11, 88
Trump, Blaine, 166, 174
Trump, Donald, 166
Trump, Robert, 174
Tryon, Dale 'Kanga', 21, 60, 235
Tugendhat, Mr Justice, 232
Turnbull, Andrew, 173
Turner, Graham, 138–9
Tweedy, Colin, 312

Uzan, Cem, 132, 166, 174, 213

Valea Zalanului, Hungary, 298
van der Post, Laurens, 11, 43, 76–7, 86, 176, 272, 296
Vandrevala, Cyrus, 314, 318
Vanity Fair, 166, 217, 291
Veness, David, 152, 184, 198, 202
Verey, Rosemary, 51
Versace, Donatella, 72, 131
Victoria, Queen, 34, 47
Victoria and Albert Museum, 111
Villa Lante, Italy, 92
Viscri, Romania, 298, 299
Vogue, 217
Vos, Mr Justice, 294

Waddesdon Manor, Buckinghamshire, 127–8
Wade, Rebekah (later Brooks), 70, 137, 157, 209–10, 234
Waitrose, 310, 319
Wakeham, Lord, 138

Walker, Simon, 137–8, 140
Wallace, Marjorie, 313
Walters, Barbara, 2
Ward, Gerald, 21
Ward, John, 291–2
Ward, Kevin, 109–10
Watson, James, 104
Watt, Sir James, 77–8, 80
Way Ahead Group, 25–6, 56–7, 61, 102, 129, 135
Webb, Chuck, 113–14, 184
Wellesley, Antonia, 235, 330
Wellington, Duke and Duchess of, 235, 330
Wessex, Sophie, 135–8, 258, 334
Westenholz, Piers von, 65
Westmacott, Peter, 103
Weston, Galen, 4
Wharfe, Ken, 115, 148, 150; *Diana: Closely Guarded Secret*, 185
Whitaker, James, 68
White, Jeremy, 75–6
Whittam, Richard, 198–9
Wilcocks, Sir Michael, 178
William, Prince, 27, 65, 116, 119, 130, 156, 330; support for direct succession of, xiv, 17, 256, 274; Camilla introduced to, 60; Charles takes hunting, 101; and Diana's possessions, 112, 114, 118, 149, 159, 189–90, 196, 202, 208, 230; and Tom Parker Bowles, 123, 133; unfounded drug allegations, 133–4; Prince Edward's documentary, 139; letter from Burrell, 142–3, 189–90, 231; police briefing at Highgrove, 151, 153, 155–6, 161, 227; trip to South America, 165; twenty-first birthday party, 228; on Burrell's betrayal, 231; coolness towards Camilla, 237, 307, 331; relationship with Kate Middleton, 257, 285; grieves for Diana, 307, 334; marries Kate Middleton, 307–9; public popularity of, 307–8, 323–4; and sixtieth anniversary of accession, 316–17; married life with Kate, 323–4; pursuit of individual interests, 333–5; TV documentary about Diana, 334–5
Williams, Lord (of Mostyn), 147
Williams, Manon, 292
Williams, Rowan, Archbishop of Canterbury, 240, 259

Wilson, Christopher, 235
Wilson, Richard, 102–3
Wilson, Robert, 245, 247, 252
Wimpey, 97
Windsor, House of: name change from Saxe-Coburg (1917), 8, 50; fiction of infallibility, 9; exploiting of privileges by, 26, 47, 57, 135–40, 171, 285–6, 317–18; approval ratings, 28, 316, 335; traditionalism, 31–2, 39, 41, 45, 47, 57–8, 241, 333, 338; continuity and stability of, 39, 41, 48, 172–3, 333–4, 338; attempts to modernise, 49–50, 56–7, 102; and aristocracy, 50; line-up on Buckingham Palace balcony, 57, 171, 316–17; seating protocols, 129–30, 236–7, 258; decline of deference towards, 133; commercial connections, 135–40; Sophie Wessex press stings, 136–8; tax affairs, 163, 219–22, 278, 320; official investigation of accounts, 219–22
Windsor, Lord Frederick, 133
Windsor Castle, 118, 171, 173, 206, 241, 261; fire (1992), 28; Charles–Camilla wedding, 254–6, 259–60
Winston, Lord, 80
Wintour, Anna, 217
Witchell, Nicholas, 257
Wolpert, Lewis, 81
Woolas, Phil, 303
World Health Organization, 246, 248
World Wildlife Fund, 319
Worsley, Giles, 94–5
Wren, Christopher, 289
Wright, Peter, 265–6
Wyatt, Lynn, 166

Xi Jinping, President, 327

Yates, Commander John, 147–8, 183–4, 187, 208; at Highgrove briefing, 152–6, 161, 188, 191–2; and 'Burrell photograph', 155, 161, 191; and queen's recollection, 192–4, 198–9, 202, 226
You Decide (BBC TV show), 37
Young, David, 75
Young, Edward, 337

Zammett, Jon, 308